1968: Culture and Counterculture

1968

Culture and Counterculture

A CATHOLIC CRITIQUE

Edited by

Thomas V. Gourlay
and Daniel Matthys

◦PICKWICK *Publications* · Eugene, Oregon

1968—CULTURE AND COUNTERCULTURE
A Catholic Critique

Copyright © 2020 Wipf and Stock Publishers. All rights reserved. Except for brief quotations in critical publications or reviews, no part of this book may be reproduced in any manner without prior written permission from the publisher. Write: Permissions, Wipf and Stock Publishers, 199 W. 8th Ave., Suite 3, Eugene, OR 97401.

Pickwick Publications
An Imprint of Wipf and Stock Publishers
199 W. 8th Ave., Suite 3
Eugene, OR 97401

www.wipfandstock.com

PAPERBACK ISBN: 978-1-7252-7679-6
HARDCOVER ISBN: 978-1-7252-7680-2
EBOOK ISBN: 978-1-7252-7681-9

Cataloguing-in-Publication data:

Names: Gourlay, Thomas V., editor. | Matthys, Daniel, editor.

Title: 1968—culture and counterculture : a Catholic critique / edited by Thomas V. Gourlay and Daniel Matthys.

Description: Eugene, OR: Pickwick Publications, 2020. | Includes bibliographical references.

Identifiers: ISBN 978-1-7252-7679-6 (paperback). | ISBN 978-1-7252-7680-2 (hardcover). | ISBN 978-1-7252-7681-9 (ebook).

Subjects: LCSH: Christianity and culture. | Theology, doctrinal. | Catholic Church—Doctrines. | Nineteen sixty-eight, A.D. | Social change.

Classification: BX1795 A17 2020 (print). | BX1795 (ebook).

Manufactured in the U.S.A.　　　　　　　　　　　　　　NOVEMBER 5, 2020

In chapter 2 Scripture quotations are taken from the Jerusalem Bible (London: Eyre & Spottiswoode, 1968).

In chapter 6 some Scripture quotations are taken from the Holy Bible, NEW INTERNATIONAL VERSION®, NIV® Copyright © 1973, 1978, 1984, 2011 by Biblica, Inc.® Used by permission. All rights reserved worldwide. Other Scripture quotations are taken from the Douay-Rheims Bible, which is in the public domain.

In chapters 9, 16, and 17 Scripture quotations are taken from New Revised Standard Version Bible, copyright © 1989 National Council of the Churches of Christ in the United States of America. Used by permission. All rights reserved worldwide.

Contents

Acknowledgments vii
List of Contributors ix

Introduction xiii
THOMAS V. GOURLAY AND DANIEL MATTHYS

1 What Happened in the Church and the World in 1968? 1
   TRACEY ROWLAND

2 The Importance of a Comma in *Humanae vitae* 22
   WOJCIECH GIERTYCH OP

3 '*De la présence, seulement de la présence*':
   1968 in the Experience of Luigi Giussani 49
   JOHN KINDER

4 1968 and the Internationalisation of Terrorism 64
   MATTHEW OGILVIE

5 Narratives of Nonviolence: Catholic Responses to the Political
   Violence of the Late 1960s and the Italian Red Brigade
   Terror of the 1970s 87
   MARCO CECCARELLI

6 Christ in Hyperreality:
   Cultural Marxism, *Kulturkritik*, and Fake News 103
   MATTHEW JOHN PAUL TAN

7 Stonewalling?
   The Catholic Church and the Gay Liberation Movement 116
   PHILIPPA MARTYR

8 1960s Psychologists:
   Beguiling Ideologues and Smiling Assassins 142
   WANDA SKOWRONSKA

9 Moral Maximalism: Seeds for the Renewal of Moral Theology 158
   HELENKA MANNERING

10 Two Freedoms: Herbert Marcuse and Romano Guardini 183
   LAWRENCE QUMMOU

11 Rahner's Last Gambit:
   The Idea of Christianity in a World of Pure Ideas 200
   MADDISON REDDIE-CLIFFORD

12 A Curran Affair: The Triumph of the Liberal Model
   of the Academy in Catholic Higher Education 220
   THOMAS V. GOURLAY

13 Del Noce and Ratzinger on 1968 and Beyond 236
   MICHAEL LICCIONE

14 Walter Kaufmann and Modern Manichaeism 253
   GARY FURNELL

15 Germain Grisez, Ultimate Ends, and the Magisterium:
   Revising Revisionist Narratives 269
   REGINALD MARY CHUA OP

16 The Law of Adam and Eve:
   Judith Butler Matters, and so Does the Fall and Jesus 292
   DANIEL R. PATTERSON

Acknowledgments

THE PAPERS COLLECTED HERE were first delivered at the conference *1968: Five Decades On* held by the Christopher Dawson Society for Philosophy and Culture at the Fremantle campus of The University of Notre Dame Australia in 2018. The editors would like to thank both The University of Notre Dame Australia and the Knights of the Southern Cross for their sponsorship of that event. We would also like to thank Helen Renwick for her expertise and editorial assistance in the compilation of these papers. Finally, the editors wish to express their particular thanks and gratitude to those who contributed papers to the conference, and later to this volume. The conference in 2018 was truly a rare example of interdisciplinary exchange and friendship. The editors are proud that some of the fruits of that exchange should be contained in this volume.

Contributors

Marco Ceccarelli MA PhD (The University of Western Australia) is an Adjunct Lecturer in Church History and Theology at The University of Notre Dame Australia and Director of the Centre for Faith Enrichment, the adult faith formation agency of the Archdiocese of Perth. Marco has published in the areas of interfaith dialogue, soft-counterterrorism and non-violence, violent extremism and the persecution of Christian minorities in the world. Marco has taught European history, literature, and culture at The University of Western Australia, Perth where he received his PhD on Catholic Responses to Islamic Terrorism.

Reginald Mary Chua, OP is a Dominican brother in solemn vows, and a chaplaincy team member at the University of Notre Dame Australia (Sydney Campus). He is a clerical candidate for the Province of the Assumption, and an MTheol candidate at Catholic Theological College, University of Divinity, Australia.

Gary Furnell is secretary of the Australian Chesterton Society. A librarian by profession, a flâneur by inclination, he has in recent years been working as an undertaker's assistant, hoping to gain some of the proverbial wisdom associated with "the house of mourning." He writes short fiction, book reviews, and essays. He lives in the mid-north coast region of NSW.

Fr. Wojciech Giertych, OP is a Polish Roman Catholic priest in the Dominican Order. He has served in the Prefecture of the Pontifical Household as Theologian of the Pontifical Household during the pontificates of Pope Benedict XVI and Pope Francis.

CONTRIBUTORS

Thomas V. Gourlay is a lecturer and doctoral candidate in the School of Philosophy and Theology at The University of Notre Dame Australia, where he is also the manager of Campus Ministry. He holds bachelors and masters degrees in education from the University of Notre Dame Australia and a Masters of Theological Studies from the John Paul II Institute for Marriage and Family Studies in Melbourne, Australia. Tom is the president and co-founder of the Christopher Dawson Society for Philosophy and Culture.

John Kinder is professor of Italian at the University of Western Australia, and has published widely on the history of the Italian language in Australia and in Italy. On his first trip to Italy, as a young graduate student, he had the very good fortune to meet certain individuals who showed him a new way to approach the old questions, taking everything very seriously and enjoying everything more than before. He is the Australian responsible for the Communion and Liberation movement.

Michael Liccione earned his doctorate in philosophy from the University of Pennsylvania and has taught at both secular and Catholic institutions. He has published in *The Thomist* and *First Things*, and has also done occasional freelance work for *Intellectual Takeout* and *The Stream*. He is currently writing a book about why the world exists.

Helenka Mannering is an associate lecturer at the University of Notre Dame, Sydney. Her areas of interest are moral theology, theological anthropology, and theology and culture. She completed postgraduate studies at the John Paul II Institute for Marriage and Family in Melbourne.

Daniel Matthys is a teacher and gardener. He is the co-founder of the Christopher Dawson Society of Philosophy and Culture and long-time aficionado of the works of G. K. Chesterton. He resides on a small farm on the outskirts of Toodyay, Western Australia.

Philippa Martyr, PhD, is a lecturer in the School of Biomedical Sciences, University of Western Australia. She taught at the University of Tasmania for six years before moving to the UK to become a Visiting Scholar at Oxford Brookes University, and a Visiting Research Fellow at the Wellcome Unit for the History of Medicine, Norwich, UK. Martyr is the author of *Paradise of Quacks: An Alternative History of Medicine in*

Australia (Macleay Press, 2002). Her current research interests include women's health, spirituality and mental health, epidemiology, and service evaluation.

Matthew C. Ogilvie, PhD (Syd), is professor of theology at the University of Notre Dame Australia. He previously served in academic and leadership positions at the University of Dallas, Boston College, and various Australian institutions. He is a specialist in the work of Bernard Lonergan SJ and has research interests in science and theology, religious extremism, and theological methodology. In his "spare time," Prof. Ogilvie is a licenced venomous snake catcher and certified self-defence instructor.

Daniel R. Patterson lectures in theology and hermeneutics at St. Trivelius Institute in Sofia, Bulgaria, and is an adjunct researcher at Sheridan College in Perth, Australia. He completed his PhD in theological ethics at the University of Aberdeen under the supervision of Brian Brock and Stanley Hauerwas.

Lawrence Qummou is a sessional lecturer in theology at Campion College and the University of Notre Dame Australia. His current PhD research focuses on theological epistemology in the Catholic and Russian Orthodox traditions. He has a background in secondary education and also holds an MA in Education.

Maddison Reddie-Clifford is a Research Assistant and PhD student in Religious Studies and Theology at the University of Durham. He holds Bachelor of Arts and Honours degrees in History from Murdoch University. He also holds bachelor and masters degrees in Philosophy from the University of Notre Dame Australia. He is a recipient of the Louis Lafosse Memorial Scholarship provided by the Centre for Catholic Studies at the University of Durham and the Institution of Christian Education.

Tracey Rowland holds the St John Paul II Chair of Theology at the University of Notre Dame Australia. Her civil doctorate (PhD) is from the Divinity School of the University of Cambridge and her pontifical doctorate (STD) is from the Lateran University in Rome. She was a member of the 9th International Theological Commission and her more recent works are: *Catholic Theology* (2017), *The Culture of the Incarnation:*

Essays in Catholic Theology (2017), and *Portraits of Spiritual Nobility* (2019).

Wanda Skowronska is a Catholic psychologist and author living and working in Sydney. She completed a Ph.D. at the John Paul II Institute in Melbourne in 2011 where she did sessional lecturing. Her most recent book is *Angels, Incense, and Revolution: Catholic Schooldays of the 1960s* (2019). She has written for several periodicals, including the Australian Catholic journal *Annals Australasia* for over 15 years.

Matthew John Paul Tan is a senior lecturer in Theology at the University of Notre Dame Australia, and works in chaplaincy formation and outreach in the Archdiocese of Sydney. He is the author of two books, the most recent being *Redeeming Flesh: The Way of the Cross with Zombie Jesus* (Cascast, 2016). He blogs at *Awkward Asian Theologian*.

Introduction

There has seldom been a time in which men were more dissatisfied with life and more conscious of the need for deliverance. If they turn away from Christianity it is because they feel that Christianity is a servant of the established order and that it has no real power or will to change the world and to rescue man from his present difficulties.

THE GREAT ENGLISH CULTURAL historian Christopher Dawson was referring to an earlier time when he wrote this, but he could have just as easily written this about the 1960s, and the year 1968 in particular.

The unprecedented cultural upheaval of 1968 makes it something of a watershed in Western culture. For many cultural critics, the 1960s gave birth to wholly positive forms of civil engagement and cultural discourse in the civil rights movement and in anti-war protests, for example. Others see the legacy of 1968 solely as a disastrous sexual revolution accompanied by the harmful deterioration of moral values. They look at 1968 as the year in which the Catholic Church's dialogue with the modern world came to a disastrous head, with the promulgation of, and widespread dissent from, Pope Paul VI's encyclical *Humanae vitae*, which he addressed to "all men and women of good will."

In their assessment of 1968, delivered fifty years on in 2018, *Time* magazine ranked the year alongside 1776, 1861, and 1941 as watershed moments in American history. In some sense this grouping must seem surprising. For while 1776, 1861, and 1941 are associated with the start of great events in American history, 1968 is associated less with a singular event and more with a broad swathe of events that considered together the sense of the 1960s as a revolutionary epoch both in the United States and across the world.

It is of course difficult to measure the significance of a year or even of a decade. It would be impossible and undesirable to cleanly separate 1968 from the years and decades that led to it or to pretend that the events of that year appeared from a historical vacuum disconnected from underlying economic, social, and spiritual forces. Rather the papers contained in this book take 1968 as starting point, as a year when underlying trends and movements suddenly became manifest and it became apparent that the order that had governed the world since the Second World War no longer held currency. Indeed, this is perhaps the best understanding of a watershed moment—a moment in which worldviews are radically shifted so that understandings of the world before that moment are alien to the understandings of the world after it.

The twenty-first century has been replete with years in which worldviews had to be abandoned to accommodate new realities. 2001 was such a year, when the order and progress that many imagine governed the post-Cold War world disappeared with the collapse of the Twin Towers. 2016 was another such year, when the Brexit and US presidential elections exposed a wide disconnect between voters and those pundits employed to explain a world they clearly did not understand. And already in March, all signs point to 2020 being another such year. But the legacy of these years is still in question. Even as this introduction is being written, Joe Biden has become the presumptive nominee of the Democratic Party, with the promise that 2016 may be written off as a historical accident. This is clearly not the case for 1968. The reactionary attempts to erase the legacy of 1968 have clearly failed.

The fifty years since 1968 have only confirmed the year as a watershed moment in twentieth-century history. But unlike years that are associated with events such as the American Revolution, the Civil War, and the Second World War, the events of 1968 have seen no natural terminus. The movements associated with 1968 have yet to declare "mission accomplished," and the revolutionary fervor of the decade still bubbles below the surface of contemporary society. In a very real sense the 1960s are still a part of contemporary society in a manner in which the era of the Second World War, for instance, is not.

This collection contains papers first presented at a conference held by the Christopher Dawson Society for Philosophy and Culture at the University of Notre Dame Australia in July of 2018, and as such it makes no attempt at comprehensiveness. Instead it offers something of an opening to a broader conversation. Indeed, in examining the papers collected in this volume, one cannot help but recognize the movements and events of 1968 that deserve the kind of critical examination offered in this collection. While it would be unnecessary—and indeed almost impossible—to offer a comprehensive list of topics for future study and evaluation, some of the more significant omissions deserve recognition. These include the Civil Rights Movement and the assasination of Martin Luther King Jr.; the Cold War and its associated conflict in Vietnam; the rise of second-wave feminism. In the realm of pop culture, too, one witnesses evidence of a new self-awareness with the release of The Beatles' *White Album*.

The choice of topics for publication in this volume in no way reflects a priority of importance. Rather it is hoped that any omissions are received as an invitation for future study and reflection.

As a Catholic critique, these papers see a number of themes coming to the fore with particular prominence. Perhaps most noteworthy is that of the developments in the realm of moral theology that occurred during that year with the promulgation of the controversial encyclical of Pope Paul VI, *Humanae vitae*. A number of papers in this volume directly address this document, the strengths and weaknesses of its argumentation, and its reception amongst Catholics and others.

Appropriately for a decade marked by violence and sexual revolution, sex and violence are prominent themes running through a number of the papers. The 1960s were a time of new forms of violence from both state and non-state actors. Meanwhile, the widening availability of the oral contraceptive pill throughout the 1960s prepared the foundations for a sexual revolution, the legacy of which is still unfolding today. Sex and violence often appeared in tandem, with the Stonewall Riots and the May student protests in Paris both erupting into violence from which were met in turn with violence from defenders of the status quo.

The legacy of 1968 is particularly fraught in matters of sex and sexuality, with its players and movements automatically cast into the roles of heroes or villains by contemporary ideologues. As the sexual revolution is still undeniably a fraught topic in contemporary society, there can be a temptation to read history backward through either a triumphant or a calamitous lens. However it would also be meaningless to ignore the fifty years of consequences that have followed these movements. Recent revelations of historical sexual abuse manifest in the #metoo movement as well as in the reports of governmental inquiries into institutional child sexual abuse the world over make examination of this facet of the 1960s particularly pertinent. Where possible, it is hoped that the present volume will occasion discussion rather than celebration or condemnation and a measured assessment of the successes and failures of the decade.

While many of the papers examine discrete events occurring at the time, others look to examine particular responses that developed within the context of 1968 itself. While the revolutionary movements were manifestations of a growing discontent with the previous order, those revolutionary impulses too prompted a range of responses. The reactionary response attempted to shore up previous modes of societal and ecclesial organization. This is exemplified in the reaction of the Catholic bishops of the United States to the public dissent of moral theologian Fr. Charles Curran.

Various postmodern thinkers active at this time attempted their own revolution in their efforts to deconstruct those structures that they deemed to be oppressive. This is found in the work of those associated with the Frankfurt School—such as Herbert Marcuse, Theodore Adorno, and Max Horkeimer—and others such as Roland Barthes and, later, Judith Butler. The Italian Catholic priest and educator Fr. Luigi Giussani took a different approach. His example took the unfolding crises of the year 1968 as an opportunity to reassess what it was that truly motivated his own life and the lives of those who surrounded him.

The collection of papers presented here demonstrates an attempt to get beyond simplistic ideological narratives that would merely commend or condemn the movements of this era. These papers seek to verify the realities that they investigate, measuring each on its own merits, and, following Pope St. John XXIII's exhortation to the Catholic Church at the beginning of the Second Vatican Ecumenical Council, to discern "the signs of the times" (Matt 16:4), and in so doing, to "make out, in the midst of so much darkness, more than a few indications that enable us to have hope for the fate of the Church and of humanity."

Thomas V. Gourlay and Daniel Matthys
March 25, 2020
The Solemnity of the Annunciation of Our Lord

1

What Happened in the Church and the World in 1968?

Tracey Rowland

This paper will be divided into two sections: The first will offer a panoramic retrospective snapshot of the events of 1968; the second will focus on how these events were mere epiphenomena of underlying seismic movements in the fields of philosophy and theology. Particular attention will be given to the influence of Frankfurt School philosophy on Catholic theology, changes in the field of Catholic eschatology, the secularization of Catholic social teaching, and the rise of the New Age "nun."

JUAN ARANZADI, A SPANISH Maoist, said of 1968 that its principal characteristic "was a kind of spectacle that embodied all the goals of the French Revolution until then."[1] He also described it as a "surrealist utopia" which not only he lived, but his entire generation. Historians now refer to the generation of 1968 as the first global generation, and French sociologists have coined the expression the *soixante huitards* to refer to its members.[2] The year 1968 is like the years 1789, 1848, or 1914. It was one of those years in which history dramatically changed its course.

---

1. Interview with Juan Aranzadi Martinez conducted by NT, Madrid (April 21, 2010), cited in *Europe's 1968*, 338.

2. Fietze, "1968 als Symbol der ersten globalen Generation," 365–86.

So, how did this "surrealist utopia" unfold? The year began quietly on January 1, the only significant event of international significance on that day being the death of the Irish judge and playwright Donagh MacDonagh. However, two weeks later, on January 15, the campus of the Catholic University of Leuven erupted in student protests after the administration announced that classes would continue to be offered in French, in addition to the Flemish language. This was notwithstanding the fact that the Francophone Walloons were a minority group on the campus. This decision led to rolling protest events across Flanders which brought down the Belgian government. The crisis was only resolved by splitting the university into two institutions, one French-speaking and one Flemish-speaking, located twenty-one miles apart.

Such student protest movements were to become a significant element in the surrealist utopia. March 1968 began with the Battle of Valle Giulia (*Battaglia di Valle Giulia*). As the name suggests, this battle was not in Vietnam but in Rome. It took the form of violent clashes between some four thousand students and the Italian police. Some of the students were of the Left, others of the Right, occupying different buildings. In the clash, there were 148 injuries to police recorded and 478 to students; 228 students were arrested; eight police cars were destroyed; and five police guns were stolen by students.[3]

A week later protests broke out in Poland after students were expelled from the University of Warsaw for their criticisms of Soviet-style Marxism. Among those expelled was the philosopher Leszek Kołakowski, author of the magisterial *Main Currents of Marxism*, who was later to become a friend of St. John Paul II. While students in Italy were embracing Marxism, some five thousand students in Warsaw and others in Kraków, Poznan, Lublin, and Wrocław were protesting against Marxism, or at least the version of it that had been imposed upon their country by the Soviet leaders.

A month later in the United States, Columbia University students protesting against the Vietnam War took over administration buildings and effectively shut down the university during a six-day siege—the time it took for the New York Police Department to take control of the situation.

However, by far the most dramatic of the student protest movements began on March 22. Daniel Cohn-Bendit, who became known as

---

3. Iacona, *1968. Le origini della contestazione globale*, 86–87.

"Danny the Red," led 150 students to occupy the administration building of the University of Nanterre. They had a number of demands, but the highest on their list was the right to sleep together. In December of 1967 the French government had passed the Neuwirth Law lifting the restrictions on the sale of contraceptives, so it is not so surprising that three months later students were demanding the freedom to sleep together on university property. This protest led to the temporary closure of the university, and this act set off further protests at other institutions including the Sorbonne, beginning on May 3. On May 6 twenty thousand student protesters marched towards the Sorbonne and clashed with police wielding batons and tear gas. On May 10 student protesters set up barricades to seal off the streets around the Sorbonne and keep police from entering the area. Jesuit and Dominican priests who were chaplains to various student groups sided with the students against the police and handed out Communion to the protesters regardless of their religious/baptismal status. On May 11 police stormed the barricades around the Sorbonne and on May 13 a one-day general strike was called, with labor groups walking off their jobs to show support for the students. By May 21 eight million French workers were on strike and both the stock market and Orly international airport had been closed. On May 24 President Charles de Gaulle publicly pleaded for an end to the strike and announced an election, which his party won with a large majority.

The French political philosopher Émile Perreau-Saussine once joked that the events of May 1968 were not serious because no one died. There were, he noted, no student martyrs, at least not in Paris.[4] Nonetheless, notwithstanding the fact that the protests fizzled out in Paris as the summer ended and the weather turned cold, the culture of university life had undergone a revolution. The university, one of the great institutions of Western civilization, had been a product of medieval Christendom. All the great universities of Europe has been founded by either Christian monarchs or clerics.[5] While the Reformation and the rise of atheistic philosophies in the eighteenth and nineteenth centuries had begun the

---

4. The comment was made by Émile Perreau-Saussine at Fisher House in Cambridge in 1996. While Perreau-Saussine was correct about there being no deaths caused by the student protests in Paris in 1968, there was one student killed by a policeman during a demonstration in West Berlin in 1967.

5. For example, the universities of Oxford, Cambridge, St. Andrew's, Edinburgh, Glasgow, Granada, Coimbra, Wrocław, Heidelberg, Leipzig, Bologna, Salamanca, Complutense de Madrid, the Sorbonne, the Charles, and the Jagiellonian were all founded by Christian monarchs or clerics.

process of their secularization, after 1968 the campuses of universities across the world, not merely in Europe, turned into incubators for varieties of anti-Christian ideologies. Universities changed from merely offering a social sanctuary to skeptics and atheists to being the primary agencies of criticism of Western culture in general and Christianity in particular.

In Marxist philosophy, the concept "cultural hegemony" refers to the beliefs, explanations, perceptions, values, and moral norms of a ruling class whose worldview is accepted as the cultural norm or universally valid dominant ideology. According to the student radicals of 1968, the ruling classes of Western societies had for centuries promoted Christianity as their dominant ideology, not because it was true, but because it served their political and economic interests. Thus, in order to destroy the power of the nefarious bourgeois social leaders, it followed that one had to undermine the so-called cultural hegemony of Christianity itself.[6]

Different Marxist factions had different ideas about how best to go about this. The Italian Communist Antonio Gramsci drew a distinction between what he called a "war of maneuver" and a "war of position." The war of maneuver was the Stalinist model. One simply used political violence to achieve one's ends. Gramsci thought this would not work in the more highly developed Western countries. For these countries, he recommended a war of position. In a war of position, one first identifies "switch-points of social power" and then seeks to peacefully take control of those switch-points. The switch-points all relate to the field of cultural values. The most important are positions like school principal, university professor, government policymaker, education department bureaucrat, and journalist.

In 1967 Rudi Dutschke, the leader of the West German leftist political movement APO, reformulated Antonio Gramsci's philosophy of cultural hegemony with the phrase "the long march through the institutions." Instead of a long military march such as the one undertaken by the Chinese Marxist Mao Tse-Tung, in the highly developed Western countries the long march would be through the most culturally significant of our social institutions—that is, through schools, universities, courts, and parliaments, and through the media, via newspapers and television.

6. Material in these three paragraphs on the cultural hegemony topic has been used by the author in a previous on-line publication entitled "Comunione e Liberazione: Christ and culture in the contest between Giussani and Gramsci," ABC Religion and Ethics website (Monday March 25, 2013).

A second significant element in the surrealist utopian vision of 1968 was the pacifist movement, with its focus on opposition to the Vietnam War. The war in Vietnam began in the mid-1950s and ended in 1975, while the greatest loss of life occurred in 1968. On one side were the anti-Communist forces of South Vietnam, who were supported by some 2.7 million American troops, 320,000 South Korean troops, 61,000 Australian troops, 10,000 troops from the Philippines, 3,800 troops from New Zealand, a small battalion from Thailand, special forces and transport aircraft from Taiwan, and some 30,000 Canadian volunteers. The North Vietnamese Communist team had the support of 3,000 troops, 2,000 tanks, 7,000 artillery pieces, 5,000 anti-aircraft guns, 200 surface-to-air missile batteries, and daily financial aid of US$2 million from the Soviet Union, plus 90,000 rifles and millions of dollars-worth of rice from China, two squadrons of MiG fighter-jets from North Korea, and an assortment of brutal interrogation experts provided by Cuba.[7] What is known as the battle of Khe Sanh began in the third week of January, 1968. Over the course of the next seventy-seven days the North Vietnamese Army destroyed the Americans' main ammunition dump and claimed the lives of 274 American soldiers. This was followed by the Tet Offensive on January 30, which claimed the lives of 245 Americans in one day. A week later, on February 7, American forces shelled the South Vietnamese city of Ben Tre, which had been infiltrated by North Vietnamese agents. Some 1,000 civilians died and 45 percent of the town's buildings were destroyed in a great propaganda victory for those opposed to the US presence in Vietnam. This was followed in March by the My Lai massacre, when Company C of the First Battalion of the US Army's 20th Infantry Regiment killed 504 women, children, and elderly men in a Vietnamese village. The following day a demonstration in London's Grosvenor Square turned violent, with 91 people injured and 200 demonstrators arrested. In Australia, where young men were conscripted to fight in the Vietnam War, the number of student demonstrators was small in 1968. However, by May 1970 the anti-Vietnam War movement had swelled to such a level that there were demonstrations of 100,000 people on the streets of Melbourne. Across Australia the combined protest numbers were around two hundred thousand. Spin-off political activist groups which owed their origins to the Vietnam Protest movements were later funded by the

---

7. These statistics may be found in the article "America Wasn't the Only Foreign Power in the Vietnam War," posted on the website of *Military History Now* (October 2, 2013).

World Peace Council (WPC) which was set up by the Soviet Communist Party between 1948 and 1950 as a means of undermining the military strength of the Western powers.

While Americans and Australians were reeling from the loss of so many lives and asking questions about the manner in which the war was being conducted, British people were informed that their pop music heroes the Beatles, who were all "brought up in Irish Catholic pre-Warlockian Liverpool," were travelling to India to visit the Maharishi Mahesh Yogi, the teacher of transcendental meditation known to his followers as Your Holiness.[8] Although his status as guru to the Beatles was short-lived, his association with the Beatles brought the Yogi rather a large amount of public interest and business. Though not the most important event of 1968, it was symbolic of another element of the surrealist utopia, which was the abandonment of all forms of Christianity for experimentation with Eastern religions and the mushrooming of gurus claiming to be legitimate purveyors of some Eastern religious tradition.

In March 1968 the Australian government lifted its ban on the sale of the *Kama Sutra*, the Indian Hindu text on the arts of courtship and lovemaking. In 1968 things Eastern were "in" and things Western were "out." In February 1968 the number one song on *Billboard Hot 100* was "Green Tambourine" by the group the Lemon Pipers, published under the record label Buddah. The song's instrumentation included both a tambourine and an electric sitar, the sitar being a plucked, stringed instrument used in Hindustani music. Modes of dress relating to both India the country and indigenous North American Indians also became fashionable. Later in 1968 the Lemon Pipers also released a song called "Love Beads and Meditation." Love beads, or multiple strings of multicoloured beads worn by both men and women, have an origin in Hindu and also native American cultures.

The love-bead fashion had begun at least a year earlier during the so-called "Summer of Love" when some hundred thousand young people converged on the suburb of Haight-Ashbury in San Francisco wearing hippie-style clothing. Their slogan was "turn on, tune in, and drop out." The hallmarks of their subculture were communal living, multiple sexual partners, experimentation with drugs, rock and protest folk music, hippie

---

8. The fact that the Beatles were from the social milieu of pre-Worlockian Liverpool was an observation made by the British journalist William Oddie. Worlockian Liverpool is a reference to Archbishop Derek Worlock.

styles of dress, and dropping out from mainstream society. A similar but smaller movement arose in London.

On April 27, 1968 the UK's *Abortion Act 1967* came into effect, legalizing abortion on a number of grounds, with the abortions provided by the National Health Service. One might summarize these elements of the surrealist utopia with the statement that the sexual revolution was a significant component of the cultural upheaval of 1968. In her book *Autobiography of a Generation,* Luisa Passerini wrote, "The idea was to destroy. Abolish the connection between sexuality and love, reject the family, violate fidelity."[9]

In the United States 1968 was also a presidential election year. On June 5, after thanking supporters for his win in the California primary, Senator Robert F. Kennedy was assassinated in Los Angeles. His assassination followed that of the American civil rights leader Martin Luther King Jnr. on April 4. In West Berlin, on April 11, Rudi Dutschke was seriously wounded in an assassination attempt and was to die from these injuries eleven years later.

In the United States the civil rights movement was also an element of the civil unrest of the time, though unlike other elements identified above, the civil rights movement was not entangled in a war against Christianity. In many cases leaders of the movement actually appealed to the Christian belief that men and women of all races have been created by God with a common humanity. Martin Luther King Jnr. even appealed to the idea of a natural moral law, which is a key element in Christian ethical theory.

Later in 1968, on August 20, the Soviet government led a Warsaw Pact invasion of what was then called Czechoslovakia to put an end to anti-Soviet-style Marxist political developments in these former provinces of the Hapsburg Empire. In opposition to the so-called "Prague Spring"—a movement within the ruling Czech and Slovak Communist party to allow Czech and Slovak citizens greater freedom of expression and greater freedom to travel as well as some economic reforms—the Soviets deployed some 500,000 troops, 6,300 tanks, 550 combat aircraft, and 250 transport planes to regain control of this particular Soviet satellite.

Amidst all this political violence and social turmoil and experimentation with Eastern forms of religion, music, food, and dress, the Catholic Church was the only institution with any hope of offering an alternative

---

9. Passerini, *Autobiography of a Generation,* 44.

voice and social vision. So let's now turn to look at what was happening in Catholic circles in 1968.

The Second Vatican Council had ended in December 1965. In 1966 the Dutch bishops issued what became known as the "Dutch Catechism"—*De Nieuwe Katechismus, geloofsverkondiging voor volwassenen*. Its key authors were Edward Schillebeeckx OP and Piet Schoonenberg SJ. It was translated into many languages and became an international best seller. However, it was widely regarded as doctrinally unsound, to such a degree that Paul VI set up a Commission of Cardinals to make a report on the document. The Cardinals' report included some fifty pages of criticism which was then published by the Dutch bishops as an appendix to their Catechism. Paul VI, however, went one step further and on June 30, 1968 he issued the Apostolic Letter, *Solemni Hac Liturgia*, in the form of a Motu Proprio, known in English as the *Credo of the People of God*, which was a more expansive creed, affirming such doctrines as the Virgin Birth, the notion of the Mass as a sacrifice, not a mere memorial meal, the real presence of Christ in the Eucharist, and the primacy of the Petrine Office. The *Credo* was initially drafted by the French philosopher Jacques Maritain, who in the same year published the book *The Peasant of the Garonne: An Old Layman Questions Himself about the Present Time* in which he criticized the Church for kneeling before the world.

While the publication of the *Credo* was an attempt to deal with the doctrinal chaos created by the *Dutch Catechism* and some theological interpretations of the Second Vatican Council and thus was something of a countercultural move for the era, a couple of months earlier, on March 29, Paul VI had lost the goodwill of significant members of the Italian aristocracy by permitting something of a mini cultural revolution in the papal palace in Rome. Specifically, Paul VI announced a reorganization of the papal court that included the abolition of the centuries-old hereditary papal nobility. This decision was not well received among the members of the Italian aristocracy who had served the papal court for centuries. Many concluded that Paul VI was a middle-class philistine with no understanding of the role of cultural traditions, the social importance of ceremony, and the political importance of keeping Italy's leading families on the side of the papacy.

Of greater significance, however, was Paul VI's encyclical, *Humanae vitae*, released on July 29, 1968, which upheld the Church's centuries-long teaching against the practice of contraception. One of the encyclical's opponents, the German theologian Bernhard Häring, wrote that "No papal teaching document has ever caused such an earthquake in the church as the encyclical *Humanae vitae*."¹⁰ He may well have been correct about this. Cardinal Francis Stafford, who supported the document, described 1968 as Year of the *Peirasmós (spiritual trial)*. The magnitude of the seismic pressures placed on the papacy and the priesthood after the July 29 release of the encyclical is evident in the following memoir of Cardinal Stafford:

> The summer of 1968 is a record of God's hottest hour. The memories are not forgotten; they are painful. They remain vivid like a tornado on the plains of Colorado. They inhabit the whirlwind where God's wrath dwells. In 1968 something terrible happened in the Church. Within the ministerial priesthood ruptures developed everywhere among friends which never healed. And the wounds continue to affect the whole Church. The dissent, together with the leaders' manipulation of the anger they fomented, became a supreme test. It changed fundamental relationships within the Church. It was a Πειρασμός for many.¹¹

Opposition to *Humanae vitae* fostered a widespread culture of dissent. If one magisterial teaching could be rejected or read-down or declared to be a mere moral ideal then the teaching authority of the magisterium was in crisis. The unity of the Church was stretched to breaking point, with different priests, bishops, and even bishops' conferences offering the laity a variety of interpretations and tax-lawyer-style loopholes. The possibility for the Church to offer an alternative vision of the meaning of human sexuality to the generation of 1968 was lost. It was not for another decade, with the election of Karol Wojtyła in 1978, that an alternative vision was finally offered in the form of John Paul II's *Catechesis on Human Love*.

One significant Catholic intellectual contribution in 1968 was Joseph Ratzinger's book *Introduction to Christianity*. It did not address all the issues of the time, but it did at least plead the case for the reasonableness of Christianity, and it was an international bestseller that was translated into some fourteen languages. It was even described by one reviewer as an alternative to the *Dutch Catechism*.¹² In this work, Ratzinger begins by

---

10. Häring, "The Encyclical Crisis."

11. Stafford, "Year of the *Peirasmòs*."

12. Burns, in "Review of *Introduction to Christianity*," 748–49, concluded that Ratzinger "does his best to explain the Creed's classic categories to a contemporary audience beyond the post-Tridentine catechisms of their childhood and yet bewildered

addressing the myopia of those within the Church who thought that the solution to the social marginalization of Christianity was to dress up the Christian message in more contemporary garb. Rhetorically, he asked:

> Need we only call on the *aggiornamento*, take off our make-up and don the mufti of a secular vocabulary or a demythologised Christianity in order to make everything all right? Is a change of intellectual costume sufficient to make people run cheerfully up and help to put out the fire which according to theology exists and is a danger to all of us?[13]

This was the project that came to be known by the concept "correlationism": the idea was to find elements of contemporary culture that were popular and then to tie or correlate the Catholic faith to them. The project was particularly popular with theologians from Belgium and Holland, especially Edward Schillebeeckx OP. These countries were precisely the places that experienced the most dramatic drop in ecclesial participation and religious vocations in the 1960s and 70s. As a general sociological principle one can say that the more money an archdiocese spent on correlationist pastoral programs the fewer people it had in its pews.

Ratzinger summed up the feeling of many a faithful Catholic in 1968 by quoting from the monologue at the beginning of Paul Claudel's play *Le Soulier de Satin*:

> Fastened to the cross—with the cross fastened to nothing, drifting over the abyss. The situation of the contemporary believer could hardly be more accurately and impressively described. Only a loose plank bobbing over the void seems to hold him up, and it looks as if he must eventually sink. Only a loose plank connects him to God, though certainly it connects him inescapably and in the last analysis he knows that this wood is stronger than the void which seethes beneath him and which remains nevertheless the really threatening force in his day-to-day life.[14]

Fifty years later, it could be said that the situation has not really improved, though we do now have some significant intellectual antidotes. If we combine the publications of St. John Paul II and Joseph Ratzinger/Benedict XVI we have quite an arsenal. There are also many lesser names who have undertaken excellent academic work on various aspects of

by the *Dutch Catechism*."
13. Ratzinger, *Introduction to Christianity*, 16.
14. Ratzinger, *Introduction to Christianity*, 19.

the surrealist utopia. Some of the best material has come from scholars in formerly Communist countries who have been able to identify the strands of the intellectual DNA shared by cultural Marxists and Liberal social engineers. Poland's Ryszard Legutko is an example of someone who has undertaken this kind of analysis. The British philosopher Roger Scruton also stands out as an Anglophone academic whose works offer a sustained critique of the *zeitgeist* of 1968. It is also the case that St. John Paul II defeated the Old Left—the Stalinist types—and through his leadership and with help from leaders in countries such as the United States and the United Kingdom, the Soviet Union collapsed and with it the countries of central and eastern Europe were free to make their own political and economic policies. The new problem is that the European Union now tries to control these countries, including promoting anti-Christian social engineering programs within them, with much more political sophistication than the Soviets. That said, the fact is that one heroic pope did manage to destroy one whole evil system. No less a person than Mikhail Gorbachev said that the destruction of the Soviet Union and its external influence would have been impossible without John Paul II.[15]

Having recalled the seismic events of 1968, the argument to be made now is threefold: first, the attack on Christianity arose not from outside the Church, but from inside the Church. In other words, 1968 would not have been possible without certain defects and crises within the Church herself. Secondly, if we are to turn the ship of Western civilization around to face Christ again we need to fix these problems within the Church herself. Thirdly, we need to rebuild tertiary education institutions where the intellectual patrimony of the West can be taught again to a new generation of students who are growing up amidst the debris of a trashed, and in some ways mutated, Christian culture.

One work which helps to explain the Church's own complicity in the events of 1968 is *The Spirit of Vatican II: Western European Progressive Catholicism in the Long Sixties* by Gerd-Rainer Horn. This work is an historical overview of western European leftist Catholicism in the long sixties (1956 to 1976). It helps to explain how some of the strongest Catholic communities in the world (for example the Dutch Church of the 1950s) could within a decade become penetrated by Marxist ideology. In 1962 there were 388 seminarians in Holland; by 1968 there were only

---

15. Gorbachev, quoted in *La Stampa* (March 3, 1992).

sixty-eight. Between 1968 and 1970, four hundred Dutch priests abandoned the priesthood in order to marry.

In the first chapter Horn examines elements of Catholic theology in the 1960s which led lay and clerical leaders to see elements of the surrealist utopia as something positive. There is not space in this paper to give a detailed account of these elements, but simply to flag them. First there are the liberal readings of the Conciliar document *Gaudium et spes*, or what may be called the "Schillebeeckxian reading" rather than the "Wojtyłian reading." This includes the "signs of the times" theme. The liberal reading of Christ's exhortation to his apostles to "read the signs of the times" is that the Holy Spirit speaks through social movements. The way that Joseph Ratzinger interprets the same exhortation is to say that Christ was making an eschatological point. He was telling his apostles that they must understand that he, Christ, was the sign of their time. They must understand that they are now living in the Christian era, the era after the Incarnation and the era before the return of Christ in glory. According to Ratzinger, Christ was not telling his apostles that the Holy Spirit makes his intentions known through the claims of leaders of social movements. A second flag can be placed over liberal readings of the Conciliar document *Lumen Gentium*, especially its "people of God" theme, which has been latched upon by people wanting to foster a more Congregationalist-style ecclesiology. A further flag can be hoisted over the contributions of theologians associated with the *Concilium* journal, above all by the contributions of Edward Schillebeeckx and Johann Baptist Metz.[16]

The second of Horn's chapters is titled "Red Priests in Working-Class Blue." It examines the influence of the worker-priest movement in France, Belgium, Holland, and Switzerland. Horn draws attention to the activities of radical priest associations that sprang out of the experience of the worker-priest movement and the episcopal attempts to close them down. He makes the point that the priests who had been members of the worker-priest movement were often radicalized to such a degree that they found it easy to embrace Marxism.

The fourth chapter, however, is perhaps the most sociologically interesting insofar as it examines the strongly Christian backgrounds of the leading student radicals of the mid to late 1960s. As Horn moves from

---

16 This is not to say that Horn shares the author's negative judgments on the theological movements associated with each of these "flags." The author regards Horn's research as historically valuable, even though the author and Horn may have different value judgments about the movements and ideas whose history is unfolded.

country to country citing the national student leaders who in their time were household names, their biographies reveal one after another that not only did they have strong Christian formations, but in many cases they were former seminarians.

Horn's macro-level thesis is that a utopian, messianic dimension of Catholicism overlapped with the secular ideals of the generation of the 1960s. Messianic Catholicism and Marxism captured the imagination of a generation and these twin forces reinforced one another. The ground for this was prepared by the idea of "reading the signs of the times" and being "open to the world," and especially by theologians like Johann-Baptist Metz who linked the concepts of salvation and liberation. In the 1960s the idea of building the kingdom of God morphed into the project of working for various types of minority liberation. From this perspective the liberation movements of the 1960s can be construed, at least in part, as secular mutations of the earlier pre-war Catholic Action projects.[17]

Another most interesting academic analysis is by Julie Pagis.[18] In her research on the social backgrounds and belief systems of student leaders of 1968, Pagis notes that as many as 40 percent of those she interviewed reported having experienced a primary religious socialization, and many began their activist careers by joining a religious youth association. One of the key concepts used in Pagis's research was the distinction between "mass religiosity," understood in a Weberian sense as the need for ritual and institutionally dispensed supernatural aid (what in Catholic theological parlance is called a strong participation in the sacramental life of the Church), and what Pagis calls the "religiosity of the virtuous," which is less about sacramentality and more about ethics. Those whose formation fell into the type of the "religiosity of the virtuous" were the more easily politicized. They had been brought up to understand that Christianity was about being "good people" interested in the welfare of others.

Pagis also develops the theme of religious activism as a vehicle for social mobility. Some young students who were the first generation of their family to attend university found themselves disconnected from the values of their families because of their upward social mobility. For these students the more radical Catholic Church Action organizations, which had already distanced themselves from the hierarchy of the Catholic

---

17. For an enlarged review of Horn's work by the author see *Reviews in Religion and Theology* vol. 23(4) (October 2016), 513–14.

18. Pagis, "The Politicization of Religious Commitments," 61–89.

Church, provided them with an opportunity to reconcile political activism with religious practice. Pagis writes:

> The cause of the Third World was an essential gateway facilitating the contextual redefinition and transfer of hitherto "religious" activities into "political" activities. The sensitivity to otherness, the imperative "to place oneself in the place of the other, far away," to take up the defense of the "poorest," the importance of engagement as a Christian necessity for coming to an understanding of the self, are all dispositions that the respondents acquired in religious youth organizations, which predisposed them to take part in the anti-colonial movement . . .[19] Thus, it was through contact (physical and intellectual) with young political activists from very different social and political milieus that these young first-generation intellectuals were progressively radicalized. The humanist critique of capitalism in which they were raised via Emmanuel Mounier's personalist philosophy then gave way to a Marxist critique of capitalism.[20]

Speaking of one particular French couple in her survey, Pagis wrote:

> The political translation of indignation, conceived at first in a religious key, led [the couple] to a veritable conversion that was associated with a total break with their earlier belief system. Through a knock-on effect and their involvement in networks where they would encounter far-left activists, they ended up totally detaching themselves from the religious sphere and became Trotskyist militants.[21]

Pagis also notes that in some cases the attraction to Marxism was fuelled by Catholic guilt. In the French context many of the children from Catholic families had parents or grandparents who had supported the Vichy regime or otherwise collaborated with the Nazi officials during World War II. An involvement in Leftist political causes was thus a way of assuaging the shame and guilt of having such parents or grandparents.[22]

A third academic work of value in this context of analyzing the Church's own contribution to the social phenomena of 1968 is Mark S. Massa's *Catholics and American Culture: Fulton Sheen, Dorothy Day and the Notre Dame Football Team*. In particular, Chapter 8 of this work provides

---

19. Pagis, "The Politicization of Religious Commitments," 69.
20. Pagis, "The Politicization of Religious Commitments," 70.
21. Pagis, "The Politicization of Religious Commitments," 70.
22. Pagis, "The Politicization of Religious Commitments," 79.

an account of the history of the Congregation of the Immaculate Heart of Mary, a Californian order of nuns which in 1968 boasted some 560 religious women renowned for the academic excellence of the schools they administered. At their flagship school Immaculate Heart College, the art department in the 1960s was run by Sr. Corita Kent. Massa writes:

> "Corita" (as she became known to millions of fans in the mid-1960s) was known nationwide for her whimsical and often provocative art work—creative pastiches of biblical quotes, boldly juxtaposed colours, and commercial images. In 1964 she had transformed Immaculate Heart College's annual religious festival, "Mary Day," into what was arguably the first college-based "happening" in the US, grabbing national headlines: with black-robed nuns parading in flowered necklaces, poets declaiming from raised platforms all over the campus, and painted students parading in the grass, Mary's Day became a prototype for the hippies' 1967 "be-in" in San Francisco.... At a 1966 convention of broadcasters in Philadelphia, she had cajoled hundreds of usually sober media journalists to put on paper hats, float balloons, and recite poetry to the person sitting in the next seat.[23]

Corita left her Congregation in 1968. In 1971, she designed the Boston Gas Company's gas storage tank and in 1985 she designed the US Postal Service's 22-cent "Love" stamp, which was launched on the set of the romantic comedy show *The Love Boat*. Cardinal Francis McIntyre, the Archbishop of Los Angeles from 1948 to 1970, described Corita's art as "blasphemous" and warned parents that Communists were being invited to her College as guest speakers. Today Immaculate Heart High is famous as the alma mater of Meghan Markle, the first American divorcee and self-proclaimed feminist activist to marry into the British royal family. It is also the alma mater of the actor and transgender advocate Elliot Fletcher.

Massa goes on to detail the decline of Corita's Congregation and observes that while in 1966 there were 7,257 novices in orders of female religious across the United States, by 1981 this figure had dropped to 780.[24] Massa's macrolevel point is that in California at least, the epicentre of the hippie movement, it was a Congregation of female religious, infected with some

---

23. Massa, *Catholics and American Culture*, 175.
24. Massa, *Catholics and American Culture*, 190.

peculiar interpretations of the documents of the Second Vatican Council on the renewal of religious life, which anticipated elements of the hippie culture.

A further factor in the Church's failure to offer an alternative to the surrealist utopian visions of the generation of 1968 is the influence of Frankfurt School social theory, commonly called "critical theory," upon Catholic theology. Pope John XXIII's buzzword *aggiornamento* (renewal), coupled with the "reading the signs of the times" mantra, fostered the idea that Catholic theology needed to engage with the fashionable philosophies and social theories of the era, and the most fashionable was the Frankfurt School's Critical Theory.

Critical Theory is all about enlightenment and emancipation.[25] Raymond Geuss, one of the leading scholars of critical theory, says: "The assumption upon which the whole critical enterprise rests is that the agents to whom the critical theory is addressed are ideologically deluded, ie they are suffering from false consciousness."[26] Through a process of self-reflection the deluded individual can (a) dissolve pseudo-objectivity and "objective illusion," (b) become aware of his or her own origins, and (c) uncover unconscious determinants of consciousness and behaviour.[27] Geuss writes:

> A critical theory brings to the agent's awareness unconscious determinants of their consciousness and behaviour in that it points out to them that their own coercive social institutions are "determining" them (by distorting the communication structure in the society) to cling to their ideological world-picture. In the initial state the agents falsely think that they are acting freely in accepting the world-picture and acting on it; the critical theory shows them that this is not the case by pointing out social determinants of their consciousness and action of which they were not aware.[28]

Since Critical Theory could be described as the dominant ideology of the generation of 1968 it was certainly desirable that Catholic intellectuals engage with it. However instead of offering a critique of Critical Theory, Catholic theologians, especially those who published in the *Concilium* journal, embraced many of its presuppositions and applied them to a

---

25. Geuss, *The Idea of a Critical Theory*, 2.
26. Geuss, *The Idea of a Critical Theory*, 64.
27. Geuss, *The Idea of a Critical Theory*, 64.
28. Geuss, *The Idea of a Critical Theory*, 70.

deconstruction of Catholic ecclesiology and ancillary elements within the architecture of Catholic theology.[29]

In his article "Theology and Praxis" published in 1973, Charles Davis, one of the big British Catholic names of the 1960s, and by 1973 a laicized Jesuit, described the attraction of the Frankfurt School's Critical Theory to contemporary Belgian and Dutch theologians in the following terms:

> Fundamental for them as a consequence of their acceptance of the Marxist unity of theory and *praxis* is a conviction that the permanent self-identity of the Christian faith cannot be presupposed . . . Truth does not yet exist; it cannot be reached by interpretation, but it has to be produced by change. For these theologians therefore, faith is in a strong sense mediated in history through *praxis*. *Praxis* is not the application of already known truth or the carrying out of a transhistorical ideal; it is that process in and through which one comes to know present reality and future possibilities. If faith is mediated in *praxis*, it must renounce an a priori claim to self-identity and universality.
>
> However, if the mediation of faith through *praxis* is consistently accepted, that means the destruction of theology in the current sense of the articulation of the immanent self-understanding of faith. Theology loses its boundaries as an independent discipline, because the only appropriate context for the conscious articulation of *praxis* is a theory of the development of society in its total reality. Included within such a comprehensive theory would be a critique of theological consciousness, replacing theology as a separate science.[30]

In the final paragraph of his article Davis pointed to the significance of this appropriation of Critical Theory with the rhetorical question: "Is theology, as Schillebeeckx says, the critical self-consciousness of Christian *praxis*, or is [Leszek] Kołakowski right when he says: "For theology begins with the belief that truth has already been given to us, and its intellectual effort consists not of attrition against reality but of assimilation of something which is ready in its entirety."[31]

This rhetorical question could be described as the billion-dollar issue of post-Conciliar Catholicism. The pontificates of St. John Paul II and Benedict XVI and the scholars who supported these pontificates were

29. For a more extensive account of this see the author's *Catholic Theology*.
30. Davis, "Theology and Praxis," 167.
31. Davis, "Theology and Praxis," 167.

based on the principle that the truth has already been given to us. The alternative—the idea that theology should be the critical self-consciousness of Christian praxis—undergirds the work of those Catholic scholars and ecclesial leaders who reject scripture and tradition as the foundation stones for Catholic belief and practice and seek to replace them with their own personal judgments based upon social theories. For some of these theologians who have been heavily influenced by the cultural Marxism of the Frankfurt School, an intense anti-intellectualism drives their projects. Some even go so far as to argue that the Holy Spirit chooses to speak through the uneducated: that is, people who have not been corrupted by a bourgeois education. Typically, these are people who themselves received a bourgeois education, though this irony does not seem to enter their critical consciousness. For example, it is an historical fact that all the big name proponents of liberation theology in Latin America were educated at elite European universities, mostly in Belgium and Germany, where they encountered Marxism and later brought it back to Latin America as a souvenir of their studies abroad. Today we have the surreal situation of the Cardinal Archbishop of the great Bavarian Catholic city of Munich not only having the surname Marx but also making all kinds of positive noises about Marxism. In an interview with the *Frankfurter Allgemeine Sonntagszeitung*, Cardinal Marx made the claim that "Without him [Karl Marx], there would not be any Catholic social doctrine."[32] No doubt contemporary Catholic social teaching does owe something to its engagement with Marxism, but the claim that there would be no Catholic social teaching without this engagement is breathtaking in its ignorance of intellectual history. Whole books have been written on the social teachings of Augustine and Aquinas and scores of other patristic, medieval, and post-Reformation-era authors.

We thus find ourselves in the situation where we have to ask Vladimir Lenin's question, "What is to be done?"

For those of us who believe that the truth has already been given to us, that we find this in the scriptures and the tradition of the Church, and that while our understanding of this tradition may deepen, what cannot happen is that the tradition should go into reverse, where something that is morally wrong today is a virtue tomorrow, we have to begin the slow and arduous work of salvaging the intellectual and other cultural treasures of the Christian centuries, including the music, the poetry, and the

---

32. Von Rainer, "Kardinal Marx im Gespräch."

liturgical practices, and building new communities and new academic institutions where this patrimony can be shared. We also need to continue to engage with the ideas of the cultural elites at the great universities. We should not withdraw our best and brightest students from these institutions. While they may not be desirable institutions for the student of average intellectual ability, the more talented Christian students will benefit from the experience of having to seriously engage with ideas of cultural Marxists and a rich assortment of postmodern scholars, just as special-forces soldiers—SAS types—can be sent in behind enemy lines for special operations.

We also need a generation of Catholic scholars who will take on the task of a serious intellectual engagement with Frankfurt School ideas and other contemporary social theories. Like all fashionable ideas they usually have a grain of truth in them somewhere, and this grain has to be affirmed but then separated from the problematic elements.

To return to the observation of Juan Aranzadi about the surrealist utopian vision of the *soixante-huitards*, one can say that here was a generation in rebellion against an imperfect world. It was also, for the most part, in rebellion against Christianity. Almost twenty centuries of Christianity had failed to deliver the perfect society, so this generation sought an explanation for this and an alternative way forward. The French revolutionary recipe of liberty, equality, and fraternity was more appealing than the Christian idea of socially embodied truth, goodness, and beauty. The French revolutionary recipe requires a change in social structures. The Christian idea requires a change within the person. The Christian worldview also includes the concepts original sin and grace, for which there is no analogue in Marxism or Liberalism. Without these concepts it is difficult to explain why social perfection is an impossible ideal and how a wounded human nature can be healed. The surrealist element in the utopian vision of the *soixante-huitards* is related to their naivety. They believed that original sin could be denied and social problems could be resolved by bureaucratic means—a change in political structures, policies, and procedures. They also underestimated the complexity of the nature of freedom and the problems which would arise if truth were to be replaced by political correctness. The *soixante-huitards* were also utopian in their belief that social differences and even the differences between the sexes could be eradicated. Their success in separating love from sexuality and then separating sexuality from reproduction has not diminished the numbers of those seeking counselling for all manner of sexual experience-related psychological problems.

Half a century after the Year of the *Peirasmós* new generations are beginning to opt out of the social experiment. A feminist has designed a fertility app which operates like a Fit-Bit, monitoring changes in body temperature so that fertility can be judged by the flick of a wrist, eliminating the need for environmentally unfriendly chemical contraceptives. Young Catholics often show a greater interest in Latin Masses than forms of worship using a more mundane vernacular idiom. Thousands of parents across the Western world prefer to home school their children than subject them to the ideologies of education department bureaucrats, including Catholic education bureaucrats who can often be found fawning over secular authorities, often for the low-minded purpose of siphoning more money out of the government for salaries for more bureaucrats. Catholic education department bureaucrats could be accused of putting financial interests ahead of faith-formation interests. Some of them perhaps think that the Catholic identity of a school can be satisfied by having a few policy documents on the subject which are annually given a tick by the principal. Like the *soixante-huitards*, they have a bureaucratic "solution" to a spiritual issue. It may well be the case that in some countries there would be higher participation rates in the sacramental life of the Church if there were fewer nominally Catholic schools teaching children ideas which actually have more in common with the philosophies of the French revolutionaries and the critical theorists than they do with creedal Christianity. The rather lopsided emphasis on social justice in many Catholic school curricula is a recipe for producing the kind of leftist political activists identified by Pagis as people who were brought up on a version of Christianity which is all about caring for minority groups. Even an atheist can do this, as the intellectual leaders of the generation of 1968 concluded. The fact that many faithful Catholic parents understand this and keep their children away from such nominally Catholic institutions is a sign of hope for the future. Finally, in some pockets of the world, new Catholic tertiary education institutions have been established to carry on the liberal arts tradition and especially the Greco–Christian *Paideia*.

The intellectual fashion of a decade is rarely the truth of a century.

Bibliography

Burns, S. J. "Review of *Introduction to Christianity*." *Theological Studies* 30 (1969).
Davis, Charles. "Theology and Praxis." *Cross Currents* 2 (1973) 154–68.
Fietze, Beata. "1968 als Symbol der ersten globalen Generation." *Berliner Journal für Soziologie* 3 (1997) 365–86.
Geuss, Raymond. *The Idea of a Critical Theory: Habermas and the Frankfurt School*. Cambridge: Cambridge University Press, 1981.
Gildea, Robert, James Mark, and Annette Warring, eds. *Europe's 1968: Voices of Revolt*. Oxford: Oxford University Press, 2013.
Häring, Bernhard. "The Encyclical Crisis." *Commonweal*, September 6, 1968; reprinted June 15, 2018.
Horn, Gert-Rainer. *The Spirit of '68: Rebellion in Western Europe and North America, 1956–1976*. Oxford: Oxford University Press, 2008.
———. *The Spirit of Vatican II: Western European Progressive Catholicism in the Long Sixties*. Oxford: Oxford University Press, 2015.
Iacona, Marco. *1968: Le origini della contestazione globale*. Chieti Scalo: Solfanelli, 2008.
Massa, Mark. S. *Catholics and American Culture: Fulton Sheen, Dorothy Day and the Notre Dame Football Team*. New York: Crossroad, 1999.
Pagis, Julie. "The Politicization of Religious Commitments: Reassuring the Determinants of Participation in May '68." *Revue Française de Science Politique* 60.1 (2010) 61–89.
Passerini, Luisa. *Autobiography of a Generation: Italy 1968*. Middletown: Wesleyan University Press, 1996.
Rainer, Hank von. "Kardinal Marx im Gespräch: 'Ohne Karl Marx gäbe es auch die katholische Soziallehre nicht'." *Frankfurter Allgemeine Sonntagszeitung*, May 1, 2018.
Ratzinger, Joseph. *Introduction to Christianity*. Translated by J. R. Foster. London: Search, 1969.
Rowland, Tracey. *Catholic Theology*. Doing Theology. London: Bloomsbury, 2017.
Stafford, Cardinal J. Francis. "Year of the *Peirasmòs—1968*." *Catholic News Agency*, online post. https://www.catholicnewsagency.com/resources/life-and-family/humanae-vitae/the-year-of-the-peirasms-1968.

2

The Importance of a Comma in *Humanae vitae*

Wojciech Giertych OP

The 1968 Cultural Revolution

As a result of a faulty translation, the message of *Humanae vitae* was weakened. Both the unitive and procreative dimensions of marriage are necessary for growth in charity. The failure to teach the full force of St. Paul VI's 1968 encyclical has brought about the crash of paternity and male egoism. The Church has been furnished with supernatural tools that can heal these dire consequences, but they have to be received in faith and their meaning has to be articulated.

THIS YEAR WE ARE recording the fiftieth anniversary of a symbolic year. Those of us who were around and conscious then or had observing parents who shared with us their impressions know that in 1968 the Western world saw a cultural revolution. In Paris there was the May revolt that almost toppled the government of de Gaulle; people carried posters of Karl Marx, Mao TseTung, and Herbert Marcuse; and it was announced that "It is forbidden to forbid." There were strikes in many American and European universities. There was the hippy movement, with the promotion of the use of drugs, free sex, and loud intoxicating music. All this added up in a fundamental social and moral upheaval. One interpretation of these events describes it as a Freudian revolution engineered in a Marxist—that is, an organized, political—way.[1] Even if this interpretation is not fully adequate it captures the general atmosphere, which resembled a Freudian decapitation of a father in the name of an adolescent, nihilist revolt against traditional values.

Central Europe at the time was suffering from Soviet oppression, which denied peoples their national identity, human rights, and religious values. The most dramatic events happened in Czechoslovakia, when hope for liberty was shattered by invading Soviet tanks in August 1968. Ripples of the Western atmosphere reached the communist parties of central Europe, leading to internal conflicts. Many of those who then broke with the regimes in the name of liberty retained the leftist mentality and avidly inhaled the post-1968 Western spirit.

The events of 1968 coincided with a period of renewal in the Catholic Church. The Second Vatican Council that had just ended initiated internal ecclesial reforms. Many changes, however, were introduced in an almost revolutionary, grassroots way, to be subsequently accepted by the Holy See. Few people really perceived the true sense of the Church's renewal. In April 1962, the bishop of Vittorio Veneto, Albino Luciani (the future John Paul I) told the priests of his diocese that the Council was not to be a constituent body called to change the nature of the Church. The teaching of the Council would have to be interpreted in continuity with the Church's Christ-given identity. Its fruits maybe would appear only centuries later, after times of turmoil, but the ultimate result would be the flowering of sanctity.[2] Another young bishop coming from an oppressed country, Karol Wojtyła, took part in the writing of *Gaudium et spes*. He insisted that the Church was present in the world primarily through the conscience and gift of self of individual Christians and not through political and social clout.[3] In a book entitled *Le visage du Ressuscité (The Face of the Risen One)*, French Dominican Fr. Marie-Joseph Le Guillou explained that the true intent of the Council was such an internal

---

1. Cf. Slezkine, *The Jewish Century*.
2. Luciani, "Note sul concilio," 440–62.
3. Cf. d'Ornellas, *Liberté, que dis-tu de toi-même?*

transformation of Christians that they would shine with divine charity resplendent through their personal generosity.[4]

The Council did not formulate a precise program of renewal of moral theology, but it did focus on some essential points. The crisis that immediately erupted and is still with us concerns moral theology. The issue is not how the moral qualification of some particular act is to be assessed. The major question is how the impact of the saving, redemptive work of Christ on human existence and therefore also morality is to be articulated.

St. Paul VI was elected Pope on the crest of the joy and hope of the Council, but he soon suffered grief and anxiety when he saw that expectations were high but often misguided. Therefore, on June 30, 1968 he published the *Credo of the People of God*, an expanded version of the Nicene Creed that reiterated basic dogmatic truths. And on July 25, 1968 he published *Humanae vitae* on the transmission of life, confirming the age-old teaching of the Church on Christian marriage and the rejection of contraception. Immediately, this encyclical met with worldwide protests coming from Catholic theologians, universities, bishops, and the media. As a result, its teaching was practically ignored in the pastoral leading of souls, although the rejection was not universal.

Now that half a century has passed since these events, we are slowly seeing a reaction. In many countries there is a growing distrust of the ideologies that have been thrust on the world in the past decades. The attack on the family in preference for the solitude of the single status, the reduction of sexuality to the source of immediate pleasure, the dismissal of the nation as a social moral unit in the name of globalization, the rejection of the principle of subsidiarity replaced by the socialist omnipotence of states, all this is slowly being questioned. People are now having second thoughts. At the moment it seems that there is a move against the heritage of 1968, but there is little clarity about what to put in its place. Thus there is a need for a host of thinkers who will articulate this trend in many fields of the humanities and direct it, showing how perennial values can be restored in all walks of life.

---

4. Le Guillou, *Le visage du Ressuscité* (*The Face of the Risen One*). In another book, *Le mystère du Père: Foi des apôtres, Gnoses actuelles*, Le Guillou showed that the 1968 ecclesial crisis was a Gnostic attempt to refashion the Church according to human ideas, hoping thereby to make her "relevant." In fact, it distorted the relationship towards the heavenly Father.

The Decisive Comma

In this paper, I want to focus on what appears to be a detail: a comma in the text of *Humanae vitae*. Reading a central passage of the encyclical, I noticed an error in the translations that has weakened the message. In all the official versions of the encyclical, in languages that I know (and I know quite a few), this error is constantly repeated. I went therefore to the Latinists who work in the Secretariate of State of the Holy See and showed them the text. A few of them came together and they all said that the translation is correct. I insisted that it is wrong. So they looked again at the Latin text, and they repeated that the translation is correct, but they said there is a comma here that is unnecessary and could be deleted. Well, I answered, if the comma is there, and St. Paul VI knew his Latin and was very insistent on details, then the comma cannot be ignored. My Latinist friends finally agreed. Yes, if we take the comma into account, then a different reading of the text is possible.

So, let me explain.

In numbers 11 and 12 of *Humanae vitae*, in the official English version, we read:

> The Church ... teaches that each and every marital act must of necessity retain its intrinsic relationship to the procreation of human life. This particular doctrine ... is based on the inseparable connection, established by God, which man on his own initiative may not break, between the unitive significance and the procreative significance which are both inherent to the marriage act.

Then we have a sentence which has been separated by the introduction of a paragraph indent. This was probably done by the editors of the *Acta Apostolicae Sedis*, and not necessarily by St. Paul VI himself. This sentence, in Latin, says the following:

> *Etenim propter intimam suam rationem,* [comma] *coniugii actus, dum maritum et uxorem artissimo sociat vincula, eos idoneos etiam facit ad novam vitam gignendam, secundum leges in ipsa viri et mulieris natura inscriptas.*

This is translated into English as:

> *The reason is that* the fundamental nature of the marriage act, while uniting husband and wife in the closest intimacy, also

> renders them capable of generating new life—and this as a result of laws written into the actual nature of man and of woman.

And then the text follows:

> And if each of these essential qualities, the unitive and the procreative, is preserved, the use of marriage fully retains its sense of true mutual love and its ordination to the supreme responsibility of parenthood to which man is called.

St. Paul VI then ends the paragraph with a line that does not articulate a moral principle but only expresses a papal opinion (in Latin *putamus*) or maybe even hope, which the translation has presented as belief, rendering it thus:

> We believe that our contemporaries are particularly capable of seeing that this teaching is in harmony with human reason.[5]

So the text ends optimistically with the Pope's confidence that what has been said will be immediately grasped by the post-1968 generation as being sensible, in accord with the intrinsic rationality of marriage.

The phrase *Etenim propter intimam suam rationem* in the central sentence is separated by the perplexing comma from the following *coniugii actus*. This means that the line is not to be read in one go, because the initial phrase does not refer to the conjugal act. It refers to what had been said in the previous sentence. And there the Pope wrote about "the inseparable connection, established by God, which man on his own initiative may not break, between the unitive significance and the procreative significance which are both inherent to the marriage act." The phrase therefore speaks of the inherent connection between the two significances, the unitive and procreative, of the marriage act. And this is again stressed in the subsequent sentence, where the Pope repeatedly insists that when both the unitive and procreative essential qualities are

---

5. *Humanae vitae*, n. 11-2: *Verumtamen Ecclesia . . . docet necessarium esse, ut quilibet matrimonii usus ad vitam humanam procreandam per se destinatus permaneat. Huiusmodi doctrina, . . . in nexu indissolubili nititur, a Deo statuto, quem homini sua sponte infringere non licet, inter significationem unitatis et significationem procreationis, quae ambae in actu coniugali insunt. Etenim propter intimam suam rationem, coniugii actus, dum maritum et uxorem artissimo sociat vinculo, eos idoneos etiam facit ad novam vitam gignendam, secundum leges in ipsa viri et mulieris natura inscriptas. Quodsi utraque eiusmodi essentialis ratio, unitatis videlicet et procreationis, servatur, usus matrimonii sensum mutui verique amoris suumque ordinem ad celsissimum paternitatis munus omnino retinet, ad quod homo vocatur.*

preserved, "the use of marriage fully retains its sense of true mutual love and its ordination to the supreme responsibility of parenthood."

The entire n. 12 of the encyclical speaks therefore of the necessity of maintaining both significances—the unitive and the procreative—of the marital act in the mental focus. The translators unfortunately have changed this message, substituting the intrinsic, intimate union of the two moral meanings with the physiological and psychological intimacy of the couple engaging in sexual intercourse, attributing supreme value to it. We find this faulty translation in many versions: in Italian, "Infatti, per la sua intima struttura, l'atto coniugale . . ."; in French, "En effet, par sa structure intime, l'acte conjugal . . ."; in Spanish, "Efectivamente, el acto conyugal, por su intima estructura . . ." (I skip the Polish version, which does the same.)

Thus the translations all claim that the intimate warm psychic experiential moment of the sexual act makes the spouses capable, fit (the Latin says *idoneos*) to generate new life in accord with the nature of men and women. This is evidently false. If the couple is healthy and the woman is in her fertile period, the physiological union does permit the biological conception of new life. But it does not follow that the psychic intimacy of the sexual union makes the couple morally capable of receiving the child and being responsible for it. Marital abuse, separation, divorce, the abandonment of children, and abortion all prove that spouses engaging in intimate sexual activity very often are not capable or willing, *idoneos* to receive new life. In fact, frequently they opt for the exact opposite. The entire thrust of St. Paul VI's message is that both significances—the unitive and the procreative—have to be upheld in the minds of the couple for the maintenance and development of parental responsibility, and when the inseparable connection—*nexus indissolubilis*—of these two significances is broken, this distorts the morale of the couple, tainting their approach with egoism and aggressiveness towards the future child.

St. Paul VI did not use the term "finality," which speaks of an inherent natural purpose. He specifically chose the word "significance," applied to both the unitive and the procreative dimensions of the marital act. The "significance" refers therefore to the "moral meaning" attributed by the spouses to their action, but this attribution is not to be arbitrary, because these significances have their objective foundation in the *essentialis ratio*, the objective nature of things that justifies the *intimam suam rationem*, the intrinsic reason for the indissoluble nexus of the two significances. That is why "each and every marital act must of necessity retain its intrinsic relationship to the procreation of human life." It is *ad vitam humanam procreandam per se destinatus*.

The Two Significances

What does all this mean? What is implied and to be maintained in the minds and hearts of the spouses as both of them approve the inseparably joint two significances—the unitive and the procreative—of sexual intercourse? Let us first of all look into the procreative significance. It means that husband and wife both have the capacity to become parents and this is cherished by them and approved. As the husband views his wife, he sees that she can be a mother, and he is glad of it, because she is the type of woman that he would like to be the mother of his children. Maybe, even, he would like to have a daughter who would be just like his wife. And as the wife views the husband, she sees that he can be a father, that he has the human, moral capacities to be a father. She appreciates his responsibility, his value system, his qualities that she would like to see transmitted to their children. Maybe, even, she would like to have a son who would be just like her husband. She may note that there are some aspects of childrearing that her husband does not yet understand, that he is inclined to forget about ensuring that the child has a cap and scarf when it is out in the cold, and so she is willing to remind him of this, or she notes that he exaggerates in imposing a moral order on a child who is too small to understand and so the husband has to learn how to be gentle, but in spite of all this, she perceives in her husband—at least in embryonic form—those paternal virtues that are necessary for the wellbeing of the family, and she hopes that he will grow in them.

The appreciation of the procreative significance is also possible when sexual intercourse takes place during the woman's infertile period. Parenthood may be loved and cherished even when, for various justified reasons, the conception of children is planned to be appropriately spaced. And couples who have passed the age when conception is possible, and when their children are already adults, they too can mentally maintain an approval of parenthood and they can be mutually grateful for their capacities and talents as mother, father, grandmother, and grandfather as they engage in sexual intercourse in their later years.

Openness towards procreation fundamentally is more an issue of the soul than of the body. It entails an inner moral stance that may continue even when biologically the transmission of life is no longer possible.

And what is the meaning of the unitive significance of the marital act? Almost instinctively, many think that it refers to the emotional involvement of the couple in sexual activity. This is probably not what St. Paul VI had in mind. With a slight shift of terminology, the current *Code of Canon Law* and the *Catechism of the Catholic Church* specify that marriage is ordered towards the good of the spouses and towards procreation coupled with the education of offspring.[6] What is this "good of the spouses" to which marriage is ordered? Should it not be identified as that specific object that is decisive within the unitive significance of the marital act?

What is this good? It cannot be understood as some private good of the spouses that rivals with the good of the children, nor is it some subjective experience of the personal union, because this could suggest that whenever there is a marital conflict and this union is not experienced, this could question the validity of the marriage. The Roman Rota does not follow this logic.[7] The critical annotated edition of the *Code*, which gives the sources of the canonical formula,[8] refers here to the teaching of Vatican II on the universal call to holiness and on marriage as a specific vocation on the way to sanctity.[9] It also quotes a fragment of the encyclical *Casti connubii*, published in 1930. There Pius XI had declared that married love:

> demands not only mutual help but must go further; [it] must have as its primary purpose that man and wife help each other day by day *in forming and perfecting themselves in the interior life*, so that through their partnership in life they may advance ever more and more in virtue, and above all that they may grow in true love toward God and their neighbour.[10]

---

6. *The Code of Canon Law* 1055.1 and *Catechism of the Catholic Church*, 2184.

7. Bertolini, *La simulazione del "bonum coniugum" alla luce della giurisprudenza rotale*.

8. Pontificia Commissio per Interpretationem Codicis Iuris Canonici. Cf. May, *Marriage, the Rock on Which the Family is Built*, 24–27.

9. Second Vatican Council, *Lumen gentium*, 39–42; Second Vatican Council, *Gaudium et spes*, 48; Second Vatican Council, *Apostolicam actuositatem*, 11.

10. Pius XI, *Casti connubii*, n. 23.

And in the following paragraph, which is not given as a source reference to the *Code*, Pius XI was even more explicit:

> This mutual interior conformation of husband and wife, this persevering endeavour to bring each other to perfection, may in a true sense be called, as the *Roman* [Tridentine] *Catechism* calls it, the primary cause and reason of matrimony, so long as marriage is considered, not in its stricter sense as the institution destined for the procreation and education of children, but in the wider sense as a complete and intimate life-partnership and association.[11]

These Magisterial references insist that in marriage, objectively even if not always subjectively, the couple is united on a common life project that goes beyond the merely temporal perspective and is focused on sanctity. The couple are on a pilgrimage to heaven together, and through common life, through the daily living out of family virtues, through the growing out of conflicts and through reconciliation, they help one another in their growth in sanctity. Since openness towards this ultimate good of the spouses is placed on an equal par with procreation as a basic purpose of Christian marriage, it follows that the unitive significance of the marital act stressed by St. Paul VI in *Humanae vitae* is to be understood precisely as referring to this united endeavor working through a common life towards sanctity. Thus, the spouses may ask themselves whether their relationship is mutually spiritually beneficial. The wife may ponder whether she has become a better woman as a result of her husband's love, and whether her husband has become a better, holier man as a result of her love. And the husband may reflect whether the qualities of his wife that he has noticed and taken into himself (Mt 1, 24; Jn 19, 27) have made him better, and whether as a result of his responsible, generous love his wife has become a better, more charitable woman.

Thus, it is only when the married couple maintain both significances in their hearts and minds, both the mutually enriching awareness of their common pilgrimage through life towards heaven and their reciprocated appreciation of their procreative and educative capacities, that the inseparable nexus of both meanings expressed supremely but not only through the marital act conditions them spiritually and makes them capable, fit, *idoneos* to generate new life. Their true love then expands their hearts and

---

11. Pius XI, *Casti connubii*, n. 24. Here the English version is from Neuner and Dupuis, *The Christian Faith in the Doctrinal Documents of the Catholic Church*, n. 1829. The Latin text is found in *AAS*, 22 (1930), 548–49.

makes them open not only to their mutual needs, but also to the needs of the prospective child and in some sense also to the needs of the wider human community that likewise is loved with charity. Is it not precisely for this reason that Christian marriage is an image of the generous, free, truly healing and uplifting, redemptive love of Christ for His Church (Ep 5: 32)? And, even more, it is the prime locus in the Church, where the incarnated love of Christ is made manifest?

This understanding of marriage should not be viewed as strange and surprising, because basically it boils down to the general principle that everything that is done in life should be done out of charity. Charity is the supernatural love that has been infused in our souls at baptism. God in His grace has endowed us with supernatural tools, among which are the theological virtues. Charity enables us to befriend God and to bring people, who are loved in view of God, into that specific fellowship of divine friends that is made possible by grace. That is why fraternal correction is a central act of charity, because it expresses concern for the spiritual wellbeing and advance of the other. Is it surprising that Christians strive to ensure that the unique moment that is the marital act will be an expression of the supreme, supernatural love enabled by grace? Whoever believes God and repeats acts of faith directed towards Him opens up to the divine charity flowing from the open heart of Jesus, and then tries to live out that charity both towards God and towards the neighbour. What better moment for this can we imagine than the marital union of husband and wife?

The infused virtues of faith, hope, and charity as they are actively lived out trigger all the moral virtues that are also infused by grace but need to be consciously cultivated. Amongst these moral virtues, there is the virtue of chastity which enables the management of the sexual desire in such a way that it can serve charity and not derail it. Chastity is not the denial of sexual passion but its healthy integration in the ethos and life project of the person.

Both significances—the focus on the true good of the other that goes as far as concern for his or her eternal sanctity and the appreciation of potential parenthood—are not necessarily actively, consciously, and constantly kept alive in the mind and heart. These two finalities may be accepted in a general, habitual way, whereas the immediate focus may be different. Emotional involvement and sexual fascination naturally have a strong and vivid impact on the psyche and body, and this is completely normal, while the appreciation of partnership in life's pilgrimage and of procreative capacities, if they are present, are on a deeper level. Psychologically, therefore, they may recede to the background, without however being excluded or rejected.

St. Paul VI, as he stressed the indissoluble nexus of the two significances, insisted that neither of them should be consciously excluded. The unitive significance maintains the personalist character of the union. The marital act engages specific individuals and not just bodies, as is the case in pornography, and so a unique person united in the marital bond and common life is loved. Love of course is expressed in many ways, including work, mutual support, concern, and practical generosity, and this is then confirmed both by the marital act and by abstaining from it when a need requires it. But if these other ways of expressing love are missing, the marital act will lack the unitive significance and thus will be a lie. When it suddenly dawns upon a person that the experienced sexual intercourse does not express true and deepest unity, this is very painful.

Openness towards procreation expands the heart towards another and thus it preserves it from egoism. The contraceptive mentality taints the quality of love—contraceptive action even more so. It introduces an instinctive "safe-sex" reservation.[12] When, even subconsciously, it is held that sex has to be always safe, the question arises, safe from what? It has to be safe from the danger of conception. Thus the child that does not yet exist, and may not ever come into existence, is already branded as an enemy. The mental rejection of a potential child therefore locks the psyche in an egoist frame of mind. As the prospect of procreation is rejected, the main focus then falls exclusively on the experiential dimension of the sexual act. Divorced from its procreative finality, this then becomes a value of its own. But the elevation of sexual experience to a unique, self-explanatory, and self-sufficient status is contrary to truth, because the natural procreative finality of sexuality has thereby been excised. Such isolation of sexual experience itself makes it into an idol, and idols always enslave. Sexual experience that is void of the procreative significance is deficient. It can never be truly satisfactory and thus it generates a longing for more. Like a drug it draws, demands, subjugates, and deforms.

12. The term "safe-sex" has now been extended to mean not just "safe" from the unwanted child, but also "safe" from the risk of contracting sexually transmitted diseases. Thérèse Hargot, a youth counsellor with experience from Brussels, Paris, and New York, describes how teenagers thirsting for emotional contact want to trust the other and so they do not want to protect themselves from their partners, even though they have been schooled in the use of contraceptives in the name of public hygiene. Cf. Hargot, *Une jeunesse sexuellement libérée (ou presque)*.

Spiritual Deformation of Men

Chemical contraceptives attack the bodies of women. I do not have the medical competence to speak about this. Due to my ignorance in this field, I cannot therefore refer to any scientific empirical proof, but I suspect that the increased number of people with a dubious sexual identity may result from contraception. If the mother has taken hormonal contraceptives for years before finally changing her mind and conceiving, is it not possible that the child is contaminated from the start?

But a more evident immediate result of contraception is the spiritual and moral deformation of men. Contraceptives are primarily for men. They excise the procreative significance from the minds of men, making them egoists. The man who demands that his woman swallows contraceptive pills every day may say that he loves her, but simultaneously he conveys that there is something in her that he hates. That something is her capacity to be a mother, and he demands that that natural capacity be poisoned in her. The woman who desires contraceptive sex may tell her man that she loves him, but simultaneously she tells him that she does not want him to be a father, she does not want him to grow in responsibility and paternal virtues. She accepts his masculinity, but on the condition that it is deficient, void of that which is his vocation. As a man becomes habituated to nonprocreative, irresponsible sex, his urge for it, which is never fully satisfied, increases, until finally the woman can no longer stand his demands and his egoism.

One of the most evident results of the sexual revolution that has rocked the Western world with increased force since 1968 is the crash of paternity among men. Many do not want to marry, and they prefer to remain single without taking on the duties of a husband and father. The percentage of broken marriages and divorces has soared. The vast majority of single mothers are not widows but abandoned women. Often fathers refuse to pay alimonies for their children born within marriage, out of wedlock, or in previous marriages. There are multiple cases of direct aggression against children, with babies being battered by their fathers or by their mothers' current partners, who are not their biological fathers. Abortion, which nearly always results from male irresponsibility and the abandonment of the mother, is of course aggression against the child. On top of this there are increasing cases of direct sexual abuse of women, both within marriage and without. When sexual services are refused, the abuse becomes not just verbal but also physical. There are men who are convinced that they have a right to the body of a given woman and when she refuses, they persecute her by stalking, bombarding her with text messages and phone calls, and finally with physical attacks. In Italy, in the years 2009–2011, a woman was murdered every four days. In only 1.9 per cent of cases was the murder related to some criminal group. In only 11.5 per cent of cases was the murderer from outside the family circle, and then most of the victims were prostitutes. In the vast majority of cases, the murderer was the boyfriend, partner, fiancé, husband, or former boyfriend, former partner, former fiancé, or former husband of the victim. In 84 per cent of the murders, the murderer—who had probably previously had sexual encounters with the victim—was an ethnic Italian, presumably a Catholic, not an immigrant.[13] In April 2017 the *L'Osservatore Romano* informed about even more staggering figures from Mexico, where six women are killed every day.[14] In January 2018 Pope Francis spoke about this scourge in Peru.[15] If so many women are murdered, how many are abused, menaced, and beaten by their sexual partners? We need to add to this tragic picture the numbers of men who are living completely alone because their marriages have broken down. Some of these men are reduced to abject poverty and homelessness, living on the streets after their wives have changed the locks in their apartments and expelled them from home.

What is happening to men? Why are they becoming so violent towards the women with whom they have had sexual encounters? What is missing in sexual experiences which cease to be a means for furthering mutual caring love and responsibility? Why do they end in aggressive demanding egoism?

In this context, it may be good to recall the warnings found in the *Memorandum* prepared by Cardinal Karol Wojtyła and a group of Kraków theologians that was sent to St. Paul VI in February 1968 as

---

13. Salvini, SI, "Il 'Femminicidio.' Tragico finale delle violenze sulle donne," 466.

14. "Denuncia dell'archidiocesi di México. Femminicidio fallimento della società," 6.

15. Speaking at the Plaza de Armas in Trujillo, Peru on January 20, 2018 Pope Francis said: "But in thinking of our mothers and grandmothers, I want to invite you to combat a scourge that affects our American continent: the numerous cases where women are killed. And the many situations of violence that are kept quiet behind so many walls. I ask you to fight against this source of suffering by calling for legislation and a culture that repudiates every form of violence." Cf. *L'Osservatore Romano* (January 23–24, 2018), 8.

supportive material for the preparation of *Humanae vitae*. There, Karol Wojtyła observed that contraception generates egoism:

> Self-mastery, self-gift, and disinterestedness are eliminated for the sake of pleasurable experience, satisfaction of the senses, or emotion. Such acts not only do not constitute true love, but, when repeated, necessarily lead to the destruction of love . . . . Parents who cannot master themselves, who cannot sacrifice their egoism to the good of their spouse, will likewise lack generosity, patience, serenity, and calm assurance in their relations with their children. They will love their children to the degree to which their children bring them joy, i.e., selfishly and not for their own sakes. . . . Unrest will reign in the family, because the state of tension created by a truncated sexual act surrounded by precautions, an act that is not an unreserved gift of self, must in the long term be communicated to the children. It seems that the increasing prevalence of anxiety and even certain neuroses results in large part from contraceptive practices.[16]

Furthermore, Wojtyła stressed that biological differences place a greater moral duty on the male, but:

> When the man eschews this responsibility, the woman's equality in human dignity is no longer being respected. Her elementary human rights will not be protected. Contraception makes no contribution to the woman's personal rights. Since it is a process that makes it possible to satisfy the "needs of the sexual instinct" without taking on any responsibility for the consequences of sexual activity, it primarily benefits the man . . . . He ceases to regard the woman in the context of transmitting life. She becomes for him simply the occasion for enjoying pleasure . . . . Therefore, when contraception is used, the woman faces not only inequality, but also sexual slavery.[17]

St. John Paul II prophetically saw the dangers of male degeneration resulting from contraception. However, we need to supplement this picture with other obvious consequences of the sexual revolution which before 1968 seemed almost unimaginable: the disappearance of public shame about marital infidelity, the open promotion of homosexuality, the dissemination of easily accessible pornography generating totally

---

16. Wojtyła et al., "The Foundations of the Church's Doctrine Concerning the Principles of Conjugal Life," 331–32.

17. Wojtyła et al., 334–35. Cf. Gałuszka, *Karol Wojtyła e Humanae vitae*.

impersonal, crude sexual expectations, and also more dramatic abuses such as pedophilia and similar aberrations.

St. Paul VI hoped that the Catholic doctrine on marriage which he expounded would be immediately grasped and appreciated by his contemporaries. Did we have to wait half a century to see the tragic fruits of the distortion of sexual intercourse about which the Pope had warned?

Social Consequences of the Crash of Paternity

Changes in the understanding of the nature of sexuality and its finality coupled with growing male egoism have vast social consequences. In Europe the dramatic fall in the birth rate is catastrophic. Ettore Gotti Tedeschi, the former director of the Vatican Bank, sees in this the deepest cause of worldwide economic woes.[18] The tipping of the demographic balance increases consumers' means. The childless spend more, but this works for one generation. Then the aging population expects to continue to enjoy a high standard of living and throws the debts on the future generation that is limited in numbers. For millennia, certainly in the European tradition, societies have followed the economic rule, articulated by St. Paul (cf. 2 Co 12: 14), which requires that parents work so that their children will grow up in better economic conditions than the parents had experienced. Now, we see the reverse: expectations and a sense of entitlement have grown, and states have accumulated massive debts which they hope will be covered by future generations. This is also an example of aggressiveness towards offspring, less violent than abortion, but also dangerous. One way of resolving the socioeconomic drama is by increasing immigration. This then fills in the demographic lacuna. But when people come from a civilization that follows different social ethics, new problems arise.

Where there is economic and social incertitude those heroic people who have had a large family and have been generous and caring towards their children can look to the future with hope. If there are wars and economic crises, children will take care of elderly parents.

The practical consequences of the crash of paternity are becoming evident. However, what is most important and needs to be addressed is the immediate distortion of the quality of love, as sexual pleasure is elevated to the rank of an idol. More than about social and economic

---

18. Tedeschi and Cammilleri, *Denaro e Paradiso*, 144–45.

realities, the Church is concerned about divine redemptive love, which needs to be transmitted untarnished and in all its fruitfulness.

Adultery within Marriage

In his treatment of the theology of the body, St. John Paul II said that it "happens that a man commits adultery 'in the heart' even in respect to his own wife, if he treats her as an object that is to satisfy his sexual urge."[19] These words provoked a severe media critique, although it is clear that the Pope was speaking out in defence of the dignity of abused women and against sexual marital violence. We find a similar comment in St. Thomas Aquinas, who noted that the term "adulterer" may be applied with greater pertinence to a husband who is dishonest in the use of his own wife, even though he does not sin against marital fidelity.[20] The virtue of chastity handles the power of sexuality and it is needed both within and outside marriage, not only to maintain fidelity, but also to assure the quality of marital sexual encounters. A life project ultimately based upon charity—the supernatural love infused in the soul—requires such an integration of sexuality that respects human dignity and the corporal and spiritual finality of the self and of the other.

But when a husband is not particularly focused on the person of his wife and treats her like any random woman that he has seen in pornography and wants the same, this, according to Aquinas, is a mortal sin.[21] Following the early Church father St. Jerome, Aquinas insisted upon the personalist dimension of sexual contacts. The husband is not to demand from his wife the sort of pleasure that could be expected from a prostitute.[22] The conscious appreciation of parenthood lived out with the particular person that is the spouse raises the quality of encounters. A

19. Paweł II, *Mężczyzną i niewiastą stworzył ich*, 136.

20. S. Th., IIa–IIae, q. 154, a. 8, ad 2: "And since the man who is too ardent a lover of his wife acts counter to the good of marriage if he use her indecently, although he be not unfaithful, he may in a sense be called an adulterer; and even more so than he that is too ardent a lover of another woman."

21. S. Th., Suppl. q. 49, a. 6: "if pleasure be sought in such a way as to exclude the honesty of marriage, so that, to wit, it is not as a wife but as a woman that a man treats his wife, and that he is ready to use her in the same way if she were not his wife, it is a mortal sin.... If, however, he seek pleasure within the bounds of marriage, so that it would not be sought in another than his wife, it is a venial sin."

22. S. Th. Suppl, q. 49, a. 6, ad 1: "A man seeks wanton pleasure in his wife when he sees no more in her than he would in a wanton."

truly humane approach to marital sexual intercourse is necessary if it is to express charity that results from being in the state of grace. All lowering of these standards with a unique focus on gratification was deemed by Aquinas to be sinful, even though this may be only a venial sin, since it takes place within marriage.

In the mature thought of Aquinas, chastity is presented as a remedy against disorder in concupiscence. Being inherited from original sin, this disorder makes the integration of sexuality difficult. But the sexual urge itself is not intrinsically evil, being one of the natural passions. It is created and therefore good. All the passions are needed and play an important role in moral life. They supply the stuff out of which virtuous action is made. Moral virtues integrate the emotions, but do not deny their force. It is not required that the passions be constantly controlled by reason, because at times, for example during sleep, reason has a moment of repose.[23] Also in artistic activity, like in virtue, the mind allows the passions to go forward and express themselves.[24] Only a rigid neurotic individual, whom for some strange reason Aquinas calls a peasant, denies all pleasures.[25] Reason may therefore allow the emotions to exert their full force, when this is justified. This applies of course also to the sexual passion, which then is not sinful.[26]

The well-known adage *in medio virtus* does not mean that there is not to be too much or too little of passion. The strength of the emotions results from the individual's bodily disposition and temperament, whereas virtue controls not the pleasure itself, but only the adherence to the pleasure, which has to be appropriate, following the rational mean.[27]

23. S. Th., IIa–IIae, q. 153, a. 2, ad 2: "For it is not contrary to virtue, if the act of reason be sometimes interrupted for something that is done in accordance with reason, else it would be against virtue for a person to set himself to sleep."

24. S. Th., IIa–IIae, q. 158, a. 1, ad 2: "Nor is it incompatible with virtue that the deliberation of reason be interrupted in the execution of what reason has deliberated: since art also would be hindered in its act, if it were to deliberate about what has to be done, while having to act."

25. S. Th., IIa–IIae, q. 152, a. 2, ad 2: "The person who, beside the dictate of right reason, abstains from all pleasures through aversion, as it were, for pleasure as such, is insensible as a country lout."

26. S. Th., IIa–IIae, q. 153, a. 2: "Wherefore it is no sin if one, by the dictate of reason, makes use of certain things in a fitting manner and order for the end to which they are adapted, provided this end be something truly good . . . the use of venereal acts can be without sin, provided they be performed in due manner and order, in keeping with the end of human procreation."

27. S. Th., IIa–IIae, q. 153, a. 2, ad 2: "the mean of virtue depends not on quantity

The meaning of this precision can be clearly seen in the case of sobriety. The virtue controls the attachment to drink, and not the pleasure enjoyed in drinking. Thus, a man may virtuously refrain from alcohol because he is planning to drive a car, and yet he may still appreciate the taste of that specific brand of Scottish whisky! Thus contrition for all sins committed against temperance, including those against chastity, involves a rejection of an attachment that was excessive and inappropriate, but it does not require a repression of the experience of pleasure, which in itself is natural.

The Handling of Sexuality

Aquinas individuated three different ways in which the handling of the passions may be attempted. The first is through the infused moral virtue that requires the preceding exercise of the theological virtues, in particular charity, enabling the love of God and of neighbor in view of God. Chastity is located within the sexual passion itself, and that passion has an inherent need for cooperation with reason and the will[28] and with grace.[29] In chastity sexual dynamism finds its appropriate expression, respecting the true good of the other and of the self. The second way in which the management of the sexual urge may be attempted is through what Aquinas calls continence. This is not a true moral virtue, because it is not located in the passion itself but in the will, which puts a brake on the passion. As an emergency reaction, continence defends against the force of the sexual desire by sheer willpower, but it does not produce the psychic peace of true virtue. The sexuality of the continent functions identically as that of the incontinent and so it is still rebellious, even though for a moment it obeys the will. This is because the sexual passion is not yet

---

but on conformity with right reason: and consequently the exceeding pleasure attaching to a venereal act directed according to reason, is not opposed to the mean of virtue. Moreover, virtue is not concerned with the amount of pleasure experienced by the external sense, as this depends on the disposition of the body; what matters is how much the interior appetite is affected by that pleasure."

28 *S. Th., IIa–IIae*, q. 151, a. 1, ad 1: "For it belongs to chastity that a man make moderate use of bodily members in accordance with the judgment of his reason and the choice of his will." *Ia–IIae*, q. 74, a. 3, ad 1: "our sensitive appetite surpasses that of other animals by reason of a certain excellence consisting in its natural aptitude to obey the reason."

29 *S. Th., Ia–IIae*, q. 68, a. 4: "just as it is natural for the appetitive powers to be moved by the command of reason, so it is natural for all the forces in man to be moved by the instinct of God, as by a superior power."

habituated from within to the true good in authentic virtue,[30] whereas in chastity, the sexual desire is truly domesticated by the virtue.[31] The third way in which the handling of the sexual desire may be attempted is through neurotic repression, in which one emotion—for example that of fear or psychic energy—tries to stamp out an undesired emotion, before the reason or will have access to it. Aquinas did not explain this psychic process in detail and did not apply it to sexuality, but he did mention the repression of pain and anger, leading not to internal peace but to a greater flame and occasional explosions of the repressed feeling.[32]

It is generally said that virtue grants facility, speed, and pleasure in good action. Why is it that even when faith and love of God are expressed, instead of peacefully handling the sexual desire through chastity, the psyche sometimes opts for the willed force of continence or unconsciously reacts with neurotic sexual repression, when neither of these grant internal peace? To answer this query, the full psychic mechanism of the moral virtue has to be explained.

For virtue to exist, the truth of the matter has to be grasped by the practical reason. It is the same reason that at times functions on a speculative level and issues a general statement, and at times functions directly on a practical level without any extensive preceding reflection. The truth of the speculative reason is measured against objective existing

---

30. *S. Th., IIa-IIae*, q. 155, a. 1: "In this way continence has something of the nature of a virtue, in so far, to wit, as the reason stands firm in opposition to the passions, lest it be led astray by them: yet it does not attain to the perfect nature of a moral virtue, by which even the sensitive appetite is subject to reason so that vehement passions contrary to reason do not arise in the sensitive appetite . . . it has something of virtue, and somewhat falls short of virtue." A. 3: "Now the concupiscible has the same disposition in one who is continent and in one who is incontinent, since in both of them it breaks out in vehement evil desires. Wherefore it is manifest that continence is not in the concupiscible as its subject . . . . Hence continence must needs reside in that power of the soul, whose act it is to choose; and that is the will."

31. *S. Th., IIa-IIae*, q. 155, a. 4: "Now the good of reason flourishes more in the temperate man than in the continent man, because in the former even the sensitive appetite is obedient to reason, being tamed by reason so to speak, whereas in the continent man the sensitive appetite strongly resists reason by its evil desires."

32. *Ad Romanos*, c. 5, l. 6 (454): "The second reason is that internal affections, when they are kept within and permitted no outlet, burn the more strongly within. This is clear in sorrow and anger which, when they are kept within, continually increase; but if they are given any kind of release outwardly, their vigor is dissipated. But a prohibition, since it threatens a penalty, compels man not to give outward expression to his desire, so that being kept within, it burns more vigorously." Cf. Terruwe and Baars, *Psychic Wholeness and Healing*.

reality. But the practical reason is focused on a future act that as yet does not exist and will be located within some given circumstances. Its truth, however, has to be grasped spontaneously within action. How can this be done? Aquinas explains that what is decisive here is the rectified appetite. Within the subjectivity of the acting agent there is an immediate internal approval of the connatural practical truth.[33]

This explanation seems to suggest a vicious circle. The cognition of the practical truth depends upon the rectified appetite, but the appetite is rectified when it is directed to the practical truth. The moral virtues need a well-functioning prudence that focuses on the practical truth, whereas prudence needs the moral virtues so as to function well.[34] In reality there is no vicious circle here, because the movement of the passion is appropriate, when it is in accord with the natural finality of the emotion and of the object towards which it moves. Emotions and their objects—like all other things—have their intrinsic significances and natural ends and these have to be immediately grasped and appreciated, and this truth about the object of an inclination is the criterion for the practical reason. The spontaneous perception of this truth by the practical reason then attributes rectitude to the passions,[35] and this is necessary for the moral virtue to exist. The emotions and the will experience a connatural resonance resulting from the innate finality of the psychic

---

33. *S. Th.*, Ia–IIae, q. 57, a. 5 ad 3: "the truth of the speculative intellect depends on conformity between the intellect and the thing.... On the other hand, the truth of the practical intellect depends on conformity with right appetite. This conformity has no place in necessary matters... but only in contingent matters which can be effected by us, whether they be matters of interior action, or the products of external work." Q. 56, a. 3, ad 1: "Virtue... depends in some way on love, in so far as it depends on the will, whose first movement consists in love." Cf. Mezzalira, "Amore, virtù e 'conoscenza per connaturalità' sfumature della conoscenza affettiva in San Tommaso d'Aquino," 347–54.

34. *S. Th.*, Ia–IIae, q. 58, a. 5: "the right reason about things to be done, viz., prudence, requires man to have moral virtue." Ad 3: "Prudence not only helps us to be of good counsel, but also to judge and command well. This is not possible unless the impediment of the passions, destroying the judgment and command of prudence, be removed; and this is done by moral virtue."

35. *In decem libros ethicorum Aristotelis ad Nicomachum expositio*, l. 6, lect. 2, 1131: "the end and the means pertain to the appetitive faculty, but the end is determined for man by nature.... On the contrary, the means are not determined for us by nature but are to be investigated by reason. So it is obvious that rectitude of the appetitive faculty in regard to the end is the measure of truth for the practical reason. According to this the truth of the practical reason itself is the rule for the rectitude of the appetitive faculty in regard to the means."

faculties and their objects, when these are appropriate. The grasping by the practical reason of this instinctive connatural resonance in the face of an appropriate object is essential for the moral virtue. When it is grasped directly and persistently, the moral virtue is strengthened and its exercise is easy. Virtuous action is then spontaneous. The meaning or—to use St. Paul VI's terminology—the basic significance of the object of the sexual desire has therefore to be grasped correctly, for the virtue of chastity to function.

The decisive moment for the existence of the moral virtue is therefore the spontaneous grasping of the practical truth of moral action that has to be in accord with reality and the inherent finality of the engaged faculty. The perception of this practical truth is not, however, uniquely rational. It also has a physiological backing coming from the sensitive usefulness judgment. This sensitive, nonrational judgment is called the *vis aestimativa* as it appears in animals. Animals directly and sensitively grasp what is appropriate for them as food or as building material for a nest. They also immediately recognize what represents a danger. In humans, this sensitive cognitive faculty is called the *vis cogitativa*, because it is related to the judgment of the practical reason. Nevertheless, this faculty is always sensitive, conditioned by the body. It is not spiritual. The immediate perception and sensitive judgment of that which is appropriate is necessary in art, in sport, in speaking in a given language, and also in moral action. The pianist may reflect theoretically about music, but in playing he has to hit the appropriate key directly, without preceding reflection. Similarly, virtuous moral action must immediately grasp the inner truth of appropriate action.[36] Thus the just or chaste person immediately finds an appropriate move without necessarily naming the moral truths and going through a speculative syllogism about them.

The judgment of the *vis cogitativa* is sometimes mistaken for the practical reason, because it functions as if it were a spiritual faculty of the mind, when it instinctively sets inclinations together and with the memory and experience directly grasps the meaning and utility of the perceived reality. The sensitive connatural practical judgment then elicits an emotional reaction.[37] This judgment, however, is not spiritual but sensitive. It

36. Caldera, *Le jugement par inclination chez Saint Thomas d'Aquin*, 70–71.

37. *S. Th.*, Ia, q. 78, a. 4: "Therefore the power which in other animals is called the natural estimative, in man is called the *cogitative*, which by some sort of collation discovers these intentions. Wherefore it is also called the *particular* reason, to which medical men assign a certain particular organ, namely, the middle part of the head:

depends upon the functioning of the brain. Aquinas was perfectly aware that moral judgments are made through the central part of the brain, and that for various reasons they may be physiologically distorted. Today, it is known that neurological connections are made in the brain and they condition the perception of the *vis cogitativa*. The brain has great plasticity. These connections are in flux and so they can change, although with age this becomes difficult. The brain is *embodied* in the skull, but it is also *embedded* in a network of human social influences that have an impact on immediate perceptions.[38] Just as the knowledge of a language learned through social influence becomes immediate, so also some sensitive moral judgments become immediate—that is connatural—even though they may not necessarily be in accord with the true meaning of nature. Animals may be trained to react in a way that is contrary to their pristine nature, and also humans sometimes experience connatural inclinations deriving from the body that are unnatural, contrary to the natural law.[39] When this is the case, the execution of virtuous acts is not immediately easy.

There is a kernel of truth in protests against the natural law made by some people who claim that their nature is different. Of course, their nature is not different, because nature does not change, and the natural law

---

for it compares individual intentions, just as the intellectual reason compares universal intentions." Q. 81, a. 3: "In man the estimative power ... is replaced by the cogitative power, which is called by some *the particular* reason, because it compares individual intentions. Wherefore in man the sensitive appetite is naturally moved by this particular reason." *De veritate*, q. 14, a. 1 ad 9: "The cogitative power is that which is highest in the sensitive part of man, and, thus, sense in some way comes in contact with the intellective part so that it participates in something of that which is lowest in the intellective part, namely, discursive reason.... For this reason, also, the cogitative power is called the particular reason." Q. 15, a. 1: "But, sometimes, the cogitative power, which is a power of the sensitive soul, is called reason, since it makes comparisons between individual forms, just as reason, properly so called, does between universal forms .... This has a definite organ, the middle cell of the brain." *Sententia Ethic.*, lib. 6, l. 9 1255: "so in particulars unconditioned judgment about singulars belongs to the sensory power of judgment called understanding." [Author's translation: "Thus in dealing with singulars the cogitative power of man is called the intellect in so far as it has an absolute judgment about singulars."]

38. Glannon, *Brain, Body, and Mind*, 11–40. Cf. Rhonheimer, "Ragione morale, persona è virtù."

39. *De veritate*, q. 1, a. 11: "the spontaneous action of a thing always takes place in one way, unless by accident it is impeded intrinsically by some defect or extrinsically by some impediment. Consequently, the judgment of sense about proper sensibles is always true unless there is an impediment in the organ or in the medium."

can always be deduced from the fundamental metaphysical inclinations of being, but as a result of acquired distortions some people do experience a connatural inclination towards that which essentially is unnatural. Aquinas was aware of this and gave the example of sick people treating what is sweet as sour and the opposite and of those who find pleasure in eating coal or the soil, in engaging in sexual activity with animals or individuals of the same sex, or finding pleasure in cannibalism.[40]

With this clarification, it is understandable why the exercise of infused moral virtues can sometimes be extremely difficult. External influences and internal psychic factors may block facility and pleasure in the execution of acts of the infused moral virtues.[41] Due to the accumulation of sins and external cultural factors, a sort of quasi-habitus may appear within the *vis cogitativa*, which will impede the exercise of the infused moral virtue. Aquinas had doubts about how to name this contrary disposition. He knew that the sensitive apprehensive judgment ministers to the practical reason and also that it may be permanently distorted, and thus analogously such a disposition may be termed a sort of *habitus*.[42]

40. S. *Th.*, Ia–IIae, q. 31, a. 7: "Consequently it happens that something which is not natural to man, either in regard to reason, or in regard to the preservation of the body, becomes connatural to this individual man, on account of there being some corruption of nature in him. And this corruption may be either on the part of the body, from some ailment; thus to a man suffering from fever, sweet things seem bitter, and vice versa, or from an evil temperament; thus some take pleasure in eating earth and coals and the like; or on the part of the soul; thus from custom some take pleasure in cannibalism or in the unnatural intercourse of man and beast, or other such things, which are not in accord with human nature."

41. S. *Th.*, Ia–IIae, q. 65, a. 3, ad 2: "It happens sometimes that man who has a habit, finds it difficult to act in accordance with the habit, and consequently feels no pleasure and complacency in the act, on account of some impediment supervening from without . . . . In like manner sometimes the habits of moral virtue experience difficulty in their works, by reason of certain contrary dispositions remaining from previous acts."

42. Aquinas was not consistent here. Cf. *Scriptum super Sententiis*, lib. 3, d. 23, q. 1, a. 1: "Natural potencies, since of themselves they are determined to one, do not need habits. It is similar also with the sensitive apprehensive powers, because they have a determined mode of operation from which they do not defect, unless there is a deficiency of the potency." D. 33, q. 2, a. 4, qc. 2, ad 6: "The sensitive apprehensive power ministers to the intellect serving it its object; and thus it is more a case of the intellect participating in something coming from the sense than the opposite . . . and for this reason the sensitive apprehensive power cannot be the subject of virtue, just as the sensitive appetitive power can." S. *Th.*, Ia–IIae, q. 50, a. 3, ad 3: "And yet even in the interior powers of sensitive apprehension, we may admit of certain habits whereby man has a facility of memory, thought or imagination . . . these powers are moved to act at the command of the reason." Q. 56, a. 5: "Yet, in man, that which he acquires by

It is obvious therefore that also those who are living a life of celibacy and consecrated chastity need to ensure that their instinctive perception of sexuality includes within it an appreciation of its basic procreative finality and is accompanied by charity that is open toward the sanctity of the other. If this appreciation is missing, even as a result of an unconscious psychic slip that glues celibacy with the prevailing anti-procreative contraceptive mentality, the exercise of the infused virtue of chastity and of the vow will turn out to be extremely difficult.

Marital Chastity

When the instinctive sensitive grasping of the meaning of sexuality is distorted, the exercise of chastity becomes difficult. Such deformation results from accumulated sinful experiences and external influences. Perseverance and growth in chastity may therefore require a correction of the perception of the meaning of sexuality, not only on the speculative level, which is not so difficult, but also on the instinctive level of the *vis cogitativa*, and thus a longer period may be required before the truth will become immediately obvious. St. Paul VI insisted that both significances, the unitive and the procreative—that is, the joint engaging in a life project that ultimately leads to heaven and the simultaneous appreciation of parenthood—have to be maintained in the spiritual and moral focus of the spouses. Then their use of sexuality will not be tainted by egoism and their marital sexual intercourse may be an expression of charity, of love that is received from God and is in view of God.

But if the experience of sexuality has been tainted by contraceptive practices, by the "safe-sex" mentality aggressively disposed towards some future child, or by pornography, the immediate sensitive perception that conditions the practical reason will instinctively exclude both the procreative and the true unitive significance of the sexual act. When this happens the practice of chastity becomes difficult. The undoing of such acquired, sensitive hindering perceptions will not come about speedily or with ease.

---

use, in his memory and other sensitive powers of apprehension, is not a habit properly so called, but something annexed to the habits of the intellective faculty . . . . Nevertheless even if there be habits in such powers, they cannot be called virtues . . . such powers prepare the way to the intellective knowledge." *De virtutibus*, q. 1, a. 4 ad 6: "The sensory cognitive powers are naturally prior to reason, since reason receives objects from them."

Hope in Christ

This being said, I should not end here on a pessimistic note. The healing of a sick psyche and a depraved morale will not come about by natural therapies. We cannot save the world and the People of God who are the Church by human power. The world and the Church can only be saved by Christ, who is the Head of His Body, the Church. The power of grace, supremely manifested in the Paschal Mystery and made available through the sacraments infuses charity into wounded human souls and bodies and vivifies divine love wherever it has been shunned, forgotten, or dormant. We need to believe in the power of Christ's aid and invite Him into life through an active faith.

The cultural upheaval of 1968 and its concomitant sexual revolution seem to have won. But this is not the case. When Christ hung on the Cross, it seemed that the devil had won. In the preface for the feast of the Exaltation of the Holy Cross we pray:

> For You placed salvation of the human race on the wood of Cross, so that, where death arose, life might spring forth and the evil one, who conquered on a tree, might likewise on a tree be conquered, through Christ our Lord.

We may rephrase this line and say that just as it seems that the devil has won by promoting selfcentred, manipulative sexual gratification in bed, so he shall be conquered by those who trusting in the power of Christ's Cross, offer to one another generous fruitful love of the highest quality in their pure and chaste marital bed. Such marital love is pro-creative, extending in the name of God, His creative power, and it is supremely beatifying.

Bibliography

Aquinas, Thomas. *Commentary on the Letter of Saint Paul to the Romans*. Translated by F. R. Larcher OP. Lander, WY: Aquinas Institute for the Study of Sacred Doctrine, 2012.

———. *Commentary on the Nicomachean Ethics*. Translated by C. I. Litzinger OP. Chicago: Regnery, 1964.

———. *Disputed Questions on Virtue*. Translated by Jeffrey Hause and Claudia Eisen Murphy. In *Basic Works*, edited by Jeffrey Hause and Robert Pasnau. Indianapolis: Hackett, 2014.

———. *Questiones disputatae de veritate: Truth: Questions 1–9*. Translated by Robert W. Mulligan SJ. Chicago: Regnery, 1952.

———. *Questiones disputatae de veritate: Truth: Questions 10–20*. Translated by James V. McGlynn SJ. Chicago: Regnery, 1953.

———. *Scriptum super sententiis*. (The text is from the *Corpus thomisticum* available on the Internet.)

———. *Summa theologica*. Translated by the Fathers of the English Dominican Province. New York: Benziger, 1911–1925.

Bertolini, Giacomo. *La simulazione del "bonum coniugum" alla luce della giurisprudenza rotale*. Padova: Cedam, 2012.

Caldera, Rafael-Tomas. *Le jugement par inclination chez Saint Thomas d'Aquin*. Paris: Vrin, 1980.

Catechism of the Catholic Church. 2nd ed. Vatican City: Vatican Press, 1997.

The Code of Canon Law: in English Translation. London: Collins, 1983.

"Denuncia dell'archidiocesi di México. Femminicidio fallimento della società." *L'Osservatore Romano*, April 26, 2017.

d'Ornellas, Pierre. *Liberté, que dis-tu de toi-même? Vatican II 1959–1965*. Saint-Maur: École Cathédrale, Parole et Silence, 1999.

Francis. "Address at the Plaza de Armas in Trujillo, Peru on January 20, 2018." *L'Osservatore Romano*, January 23–24, 2018.

Gałuszka, Paweł Stanisław. *Karol Wojtyła e Humanae vitae. Il contributo dell'Arcivescovo di Cracovia e del gruppo di teologi polacchi all'enciclica di Paolo VI*. Siena: Cantagalli, 2017.

Glannon, Walter. *Brain, Body, and Mind: Neuroethics with a Human Face*. Oxford: Oxford University Press, 2011.

Hargot, Thérèse. *Une jeunesse sexuellement libérée (ou presque)*. Paris: Michel, 2016.

Jan Paweł II, *Mężczyzną i niewiastą stworzył ich*. Lublin: Wydawnictwo, 2008.

Le Guillou, Marie-Joseph. *Le mystère du Père—Foi des apôtres, Gnoses actuelles*. Paris: Fayard, 1973.

———. *Le visage du Ressuscité*. Paris: Ouvrières, 1968.

Luciani, Albino. "Note sul concilio." *Opera omnia*, vol. II. Padova: Messaggero, 1988.

May, William. *Marriage, the Rock on Which the Family Is Built*. San Francisco: Ignatius, 2009.

Mezzalira, João Baptista, "Amore, virtù e 'conoscenza per connaturalità' sfumature della conoscenza affettiva in San Tommaso d'Aquino." In *Persona e natura nell'agire morale. Memoriale di Cracovia—Studi—Contributi*, edited by Juan José Pérez-Soba e Paweł Gałuszka, 347–54. Siena: Cantagalli, 2013.

Neuner, J., and J. Dupuis. *The Christian Faith in the Doctrinal Documents of the Catholic Church*. New York: Alba House, reprinted in Bangalore: Theological Publications of India, 2001.

Paul VI. *Humanae vitae*. Vatican website, July 25, 1968. http://w2.vatican.va/content/paul-vi/en/encyclicals/documents/hf_p-vi_enc_25071968_humanae-vitae.html.

Pius XI. *Casti connubii*. Encyclical Letter. Vatican website, December 31, 1930. https://w2.vatican.va/content/pius-xi/en/encyclicals/documents/hf_p-xi_enc_19301231_casti-connubii.html.

Pontificia Commissio per Interpretationem Codicis Iuris Canonici. *Codex iuris canonici*. Vatican City: Libreria Editrice Vaticana, 1989.

Rhonheimer, Martin. "Ragione morale, persona è virtù: la prospettiva aristotelico-tomista di fronte alle sfide attuali." *Persona e natura nell'agire morale. Memoriale* di Cracovia—Studi—Contributi a cura di Juan José Pérez-Soba e Paweł Gałuszka. Siena: Cantagalli, 2013.

Salvini, GianPaolo, SI. "Il 'Femminicidio.' Tragico finale delle violenze sulle donne." *La Civiltà Cattolica* 3911 (June 1, 2013) 462–63.

Second Vatican Council. *Apostolicam actuositatem*. Vatican website, November 18, 1965. http://www.vatican.va/archive/hist_councils/ii_vatican_council/documents/vat-ii_decree_19651118_apostolicam-actuositatem_en.html.

———. *Gaudium et spes*. Vatican website, December 7, 1965. http://www.vatican.va/archive/hist_councils/ii_vatican_council/documents/vat-ii_const_19651207_gaudium-et-spes_en.html.

———. *Lumen gentium*. Vatican website, November 21, 1964. http://www.vatican.va/archive/hist_councils/ii_vatican_council/documents/vat-ii_const_19641121_lumen-gentium_en.html.

Slezkine, Yuri. *The Jewish Century*. Princeton: Princeton University Press, 2004.

Tedeschi, Ettore Gotti, and Rino Cammilleri. *Denaro e paradiso: I cattolici e l'economia globale*. Torino: Lindau, 2010.

Terruwe, Anna A., and Conrad W. Baars, *Psychic Wholeness and Healing: Using All the Powers of the Human Psyche*. New York: Alba, 1981.

Wojtyła, Karol, et al. "The Foundations of the Church's Doctrine Concerning the Principles of Conjugal life: A Memorandum Composed by a Group of Moral Theologians from Kraków." *Nova et vetera* (English ed.) 10.2 (2012) 331–32.

3

De la Présence, Seulement de la Présence
1968 in the Experience of Luigi Giussa

John J. Kinder

"Has the Church failed mankind," asked T. S. Eliot, "or has mankind failed the Church?" Italian priest Luigi Giussani (1922–2005) answered "Yes" to both questions. During the twentieth century, modernity sapped mankind of the thirst for ultimate meaning, and Christianity itself risked becoming an ideology—a system of beliefs, values, and practices cut off from the experience that generated them and thus unable to speak to the human heart. By 1968 Giussani was leading a Catholic movement of thousands of students and young workers, only to see his numbers decimated by the promise of social justice and political liberation. After 1968 he began again, with the rather 68-ish name "Communion and Liberation," based on the conviction that the only antidote to the seduction of utopia is a presence. In the words of one of the early 1968 slogans scrawled on the walls of the Sorbonne, "De la présence, seulement de la présence."

THE YEAR 1968 WAS the end of an age and a beginning of an age. Some things it closed, others it ushered in, enabled, created. Then there is a third category: those events, processes, initiatives that went through the 1968 period and came out the other side changed. In some cases that change was a correction, in others a deformation, and in others again the fires of the protest were a purifying force that refined, clarified, melted things down to their essence.

This essay will examine the experience of one individual, for whom 1968 brought the work of the previous fifteen years to a crashing end. The collapse of the certainties he had worked to build with others led him back to the origin of that earlier experience and to a new clarity that bore fruit in abundance. At the same time as we look back at events of half a century ago, we will also look forward to see how that experience contains lessons for us in Australia today as we face new challenges that are not going to go away but will only become more relentless in demanding that we too learn to see things clearly for what they truly are.

At the beginning of the 1950s, the Catholic Church in Italy was heading for a deep crisis. Churches were full, seminaries were full, youth ministries were full. Italian parents had the satisfaction of seeing their children receive all the sacraments, attend Mass regularly and spend their leisure time in organized church activities. So where was the crisis? To find out, we must go on a brief train journey.

It is summer 1953 or 1954 as we follow a young priest from Milan who leaves the hot, humid industrial city on a six-hour train ride to Rimini, the beachside city on Italy's long Adriatic coast. The priest found himself in a compartment with a few high-school students and they struck up a conversation about religion. He recalled, "I was immediately surprised by their enormous, colossal and tremendous ignorance." Although they were baptized and were familiar with church doctrine and practice, most of them knew nothing about what Christianity actually was or what it claimed to be, and those who did know something were not really convinced and in any case did not see how faith in Jesus Christ was relevant to their everyday lives.[1]

The young people's lives ran on parallel tracks, like the train they were travelling on. One track was their faith—public, active, social; the other was their life. And like parallel lines, in this universe anyway, the

---

1. Giussani recounted this episode in 1960, in a talk since translated as "Open Christianity." See Savorana, *Life*, 152. See also Rondoni, *Communion and Liberation*, 35, and Camisasca, *Don Giussani*, 10.

twain were never going to meet. The young priest would later describe this dualism as a new form of gnosticism among modern Christians that separated God and His creation and would ultimately relegate religion to a little corner of subjective feeling that could not be communicated to anyone.[2]

The priest's name was Luigi Giussani, and a number of conversations like the one just recounted prompted him to abandon a promising academic career as a professor of theology in the seminary in order to teach religion in the state high schools of Milan, a decision that would lead to the growth of a church movement now present in eighty countries. The year 1968 was an absolutely decisive moment in this story. Structurally it was a disaster for Giussani, because the majority of young people following him in his youth chaplaincy work abandoned him for left-wing politics. Substantially, however, the experience was one of clarification and purification.

Who was Father Luigi Giussani? He was born in 1922, in a small town outside Milan. At his funeral Mass in Milan Cathedral in 2005, Cardinal Joseph Ratzinger preached the homily. Giussani's childhood home was, Ratzinger recalled, "poor in bread but rich in music."[3] His father was a carpenter and a socialist, his mother a textile worker and a devout Catholic. One morning as he walked to morning Mass hand in hand with his mother, the morning star shining before them, Giussani remembers her exclaiming, "How beautiful is the world and how great is God!"[4] He received his first instruction in the faith from his mother, but learned the appreciation of beauty from both parents. He was educated in the large seminary at Venegono, where a Christocentric syllabus taught him to see the person of Christ as the centre and substance of all things, a presence invoked in literature, art, and music. From a young age, as Cardinal Ratzinger said in his funeral homily, Giussani was "wounded by beauty."[5] Upon ordination to the priesthood at age twenty-two, he was headed for a secure and prestigious career as a professor in the principal seminary of the largest diocese in Italy. Until that train ride.

---

2. See Busani, *Gioventù Studentesca*, 483, and nn. 6 and 7.

3. Ratzinger, "Funeral Homily." Zucchi, in "Luigi Giussani," footnote 1 recalls how the international press identified this homily as a central element in events leading to the papal election later that year.

4. Rondoni, *Communion and Liberation*, 30.

5. Ratzinger, "Funeral Homily."

In early 1953, Giussani was appointed "assistant," or chaplain, to the female section of Catholic Action in Milan. Catholic Action was essentially the lay apostolate of the Church at that time. Since the nineteenth century it had gone through many transformations, and in the 1950s had over three million members in Italy alone. The Vatican Council's Decree on the Apostolate of the Laity specifically named Catholic Action as the best example of structured lay participation in the life of the Church.

When Giussani was appointed as chaplain to the male section as well, he brought the two together into a new entity which he called Student Youth, *Gioventù Studentesca*.[6] I will refer to it as GS.

The world was changing fast. Italy in the 1950s was pulling itself out of a nightmare that had lasted a quarter of a century: two decades of Fascism then five long years of war—the last two a civil war.[7] By the end of the 1950s, Italy had the fastest growth in GDP in the world, second only to Japan. Millions emigrated, the Marshall Plan brought political stability and dollars to fund the rush to industrialisation, and in two short decades the country went from an archaic agricultural economy to the seventh largest economy in the world.

Many years later, Giussani would look back over the twentieth century and the position of the Church in Italian society. He took up the question T.S. Eliot posed in his *Choruses from the Rock*: "Has the Church failed mankind, or has mankind failed the Church?"[8] Giussani answered both questions in the affirmative.[9]

Certainly, on the one hand the consumer society was arriving with secular values of individualism and all that pointed away from the Church and Christian tradition, and towards 1968. However, the Church had also fallen short of its mission. The response of the hierarchy and of Catholic Action to the momentous social changes was to maintain the status quo and defend Christian values through official structures. As a youth chaplain under the Catholic Action umbrella, Giussani saw that the aims and method of the organization were inadequate in a rapidly changing social context. Its aims were all focused on the individual: each person was taught to develop their skills and talents. The method of Catholic Action

---

6. A succinct account of the origins and development of GS can be found in Horn, *The Spirit of Vatican II*, 200–5. A comprehensive archival-based history is now available in Busani, *Gioventù Studentesca*.

7. Cf. Ginsborg, *A History of Contemporary Italy*.

8. Giussani, "Religious Awareness in Modern Man," 104–40.

9. Savorana, *Life*, 658–64.

was, Giussani said, "moralistic and sentimental."[10] Participation in the life of the Church—using the talents you developed through prayer, study and work—was presented as a duty, and your ability to carry out your duty would be sustained by building up strong feelings towards the faith.

Giussani criticized this approach for two reasons. First, it didn't work. Worse still, it betrayed the nature of Christianity. It separated Christianity from the full experience of being human. A hard-hitting speech he gave in 1960 was a criticism of the way spiritual directors and clergy, starting with himself, were presenting Christianity to young people: "The Christian proposal today does not deny the structural needs of the human and Christian conscience, but it dodges or ignores them."[11]

At the same time as he became a youth chaplain in Milan, Giussani left his position as professor in the seminary and became a religious education teacher in a state high school in Milan. Turning up for his first day, he knew this was a significant decision and started on this road with deep awareness: "As I climbed for the first time the three steps at the entrance to the school where I had been sent to teach religion, it was clear to me, although I was aware of my limitations, that this was a matter of re-launching the announcement of Christianity as a present event."[12] However, he told his students in their first lesson, "I am not here so that you can take my ideas as your own. I am here to teach you a true method that you can use to judge the things I will tell you." The students were instantly engaged, their freedom respected and called into action.

Giussani was stunned to see that in the schools where he taught, most students were baptized, crucifixes hung in every classroom, priests were teaching religious education, but Christianity was effectively absent in the lives of the students. He did see groups of students who would spend time together in real friendship, sharing their lives and working on projects that interested them. They were the young communists or the young monarchist-fascists. There were no signs of Christian life.

Giussani's response was to begin with what he had in front of him. He began meeting after school with four of his students. They invited others, and soon Giussani found himself with large groups of young people who had not chosen to "join GS" but simply wanted to spend time

---

10. Camisasca, *Comunione e liberazione*, 96.

11. Giussani, "Open Christianity," 156.

12. *The Journey to Truth is an Experience*, 4–5. See also Zucchi, "Luigi Giussani," 131–50.

with him and with each other. They understood that this experience was something good for their lives.

Giussani developed an approach that awoke in these young people their desire for meaning, for fulfillment, for beauty, and for a full and rich way of being themselves and being in the world. This was very close to the catechesis of the new Archbishop of Milan, Giovanni Battista Montini, the future Pope Paul VI. In 1957, Montini launched a Mission to Milan and wrote a Pastoral Letter called "On the Religious Sense."[13] What did he mean by the phrase "religious sense"? Montini defined it as "the human openness to God, the inclination of the human person towards its beginning and towards its ultimate destiny" (p. 51). This, for Montini, was the key to the growing drama in Western societies. At the heart of that drama was a crisis in the sense of what it is to be human, more than any loss of "faith" or "piety" or "spirituality." This loss of the sense of our own humanity makes it increasingly difficult for the modern mentality, as Montini put it, to "think God" (*pensare Dio*, p. 63). For the future Pope, the religious sense is the essential foundation and context for re-imagining and re-experiencing religion in the modern world: "The issue of religion today must be studied and resolved principally at the level of the religious sense" (p. 54). A few months after this Pastoral Letter, Giussani published a short book, based on his talks with his students. He called it *The Religious Sense*.[14]

As part of the implementation of Archbishop Montini's Mission to Milan, Giussani was assigned responsiblity for work with students. He had great success, but a little later Montini called him in for a conversation. He had received complaints from officials of Catholic Action, from parents, and from priests in the diocese. First, that Giussani was holding meetings of boys and girls together, an unheard-of and dangerous practice at the time, and one that Catholic Action did not allow. Second, that he was, essentially, too successful and was taking children from the parishes. Giussani respectfully pointed out that before his students started attending his meetings, 97 percent of them did not attend church regularly. The

---

13. Montini, *Discorsi e scritti milanesi*, 1212–35. The English translation is *Man's Religious Sense*. Montini's letter has been republished together with Giussani's booklet *Il senso religioso*, published a few months after the letter, in Montini and Giussani, *Sul senso religioso*, from which quotations are taken (translated by this author).

14. Giussani's first volume of that title was a slim pamphlet of barely thirty-two pages published for Catholic Action in 1957. Rewritten several times, its definitive Italian edition appeared in 1997, the same year as its English translation. See Giussani, *Il senso religioso* and *The Religious Sense*.

archbishop listened carefully to his idiosyncratic but obedient priest and sent him on his way with a phrase Giussani recalled many times: "I do not understand your ideas and your methods, but I see the fruits, and so I say, keep doing what you are doing."[15]

Giussani kept doing what he was doing, and the fifties turned into the sixties. As the social and political climate warmed up, Giussani defined and deepened his way of proposing the Christian fact to young people. I will list three aspects here, because these are what ultimately led to the mass exodus of his students in 1968.

First, he argued that every attempt to establish a Christian presence had to use an adequate method.[16] The method was the systematic comparison of the Christian message with one's own lived experience. The place where you learned this method was the weekly meetings of GS. These were a free dialogue among all those present, under the guidance of a leader. Giussani developed an original and clear understanding of what this "dialogue" was: not a clash of ideas and not an attempt to reach the "truth" through rational argument. No, for Giussani dialogue was the communication of experience, "communicating one's own personal life to other lives," encountering the diversity of the other and sharing your own diversity with the other.

This insistence on experience was something that Archbishop Montini had reservations about, and he reminded Giussani that the young needed a guide, an authority, in order to learn to judge their experience. The friendship between the young priest and his bishop continued, even when Montini was elected pope in 1963, and Giussani was struck when he read this passage in the new pope's first encyclical *Ecclesiam suam*: "The mystery of the Church is not a truth to be confined to the realms of speculative theology. It must be lived, so that the faithful may have a kind of intuitive experience of it, even before they come to understand it clearly."[17]

The second aspect of GS that Giussani developed during the years leading up to 1968 was the community dimension of the faith. Whereas Catholic Action focused on developing individual talents, for Giussani the Christian personality is realized in the community. The community is not extrinsic but is a constitutive dimension of the person.

15. Savorana, *Life*, 222–23; Busani, *Gioventù Studentesca*, Chapter IV "Un movimento nazionale? GS tra Chiesa ambrosiana e GIAC Italiana."

16. Savorana, *Life*, Chapter 9 "A Movement, Not an Association."

17. *Ecclesiam suam*, 37. See the discussion in Busani, *Gioventù Studentesca*, 247–48.

The communitarian nature of Christian experience has three dimensions: culture, charity and mission. Young people needed concrete activities to teach them these essentials.[18] Giussani's approach, however, did not seem to fit any predetermined category and aroused strong antagonism from both sides of debates during the Second Vatican Council and then leading up to 1968. He engaged in charitable work with the poor, but the ultimate aim was to learn to live like Christ. He encouraged his students to engage with all forms of contemporary culture but, always and above all, to do all things in unity with each other. He sent young graduates as missionaries to Brazil and other places where they encountered severe social injustice, but strictly on condition that they obeyed the authority of the local bishop.

The moves Giussani made in the growth of the GS movement were nothing to do with steering a middle path between left and right, progressive and conservative. His was never a reactive position. Every step of his journey moved from an original position. He never had any intention of "founding" anything and was surprised to see a movement developing around him. He understood that this was happening simply because he had "felt the urgency to proclaim the need to return to the elementary aspects of Christianity, that is to say the passion of the Christian fact as such in its original elements, and nothing more."[19] He worked to indicate "the road toward the solution of man's existential drama. The road is Christ."[20]

The third important insight that grew through Giussani's work with GS was that all Christian initiatives had unity and obedience as their fundamental conditions. They were the foundations of an authentic Christian community; the place where the individual could reach their true human fulfillment.

This was the spirit with which Giussani enthusiastically welcomed the documents of the Second Vatican Council. He asked GS students to study the documents, to work on them together, in a spirit of "unity, collaboration, dialogue and help."[21]

---

18. Savorana, *Life*, 246–47.

19. This is how Giussani described his experience half a century later, in a letter he wrote to Pope John Paul II in 2004, on the fiftieth anniversary of the beginning of the GS movement. See *Life*, 1118–20.

20. This phrase occurs in an earlier letter John Paul II wrote to Fr. Giussani in 2002. Giussani quotes it in his 2004 letter to the Pope, cf. *Life*, 1119.

21. Savorana, *Life*, 326.

By 1965, Giussani was compelled to leave his position as leader and chaplain to GS. There were three reasons. For one thing, Catholic Action was increasingly hostile to the success of GS and its "difference," as Giussani insisted on following the experience of what he had before him rather than the objectives of an organization. Giussani would not, could not, walk away from the experience he was living with his young students. Second, at the suggestion of Archbishop Colombo, Giussani left high-school teaching to build an academic career in the Catholic University of the Sacred Heart in Milan. This involved a study trip to the United States. Finally, Giussani's own health was always uncertain, and he suffered a number of major health issues around this time. For all these reasons, Giussani left GS in 1965 and had no further official role in the movement from that time.

The sixties rolled on. In Italy the spark that ignited the protests came from Giussani's own university. In November 1967, six months before Paris exploded, the management of the Catholic University of Milan raised tuition fees. Students protested and occupied the university. They had to be removed by police. Giussani's clear negative judgment of these protests was a line in the sand and began the final stages of the process of the dissolution of GS.[22]

Members of GS in Italy, and many of their friends in Brazil, began defining their reason for being together and indeed for being Christian in terms of changing the social and economic structures that brought injustice and evil to so many parts of the world. For Giussani it was clear what happens when the Christian message is reduced in this way and when unity is not accepted as the cornerstone: "Jesus Christ becomes the tool for putting things in their place, and the community becomes a sociological cluster, the kingdom of God becomes some project of ours."[23]

Three-quarters of the members of GS left the movement during 1968. They mostly joined student movements and political parties of the left, sometimes even the extreme left, determined to make a difference, in the here and now. Giussani recognized their generosity of spirit in wanting to help build a better world, but he denounced the error of believing that it is we who can save the world and save ourselves.

Giussani kept meeting with the few friends who remained attracted by his proposal. As the year wore on, the full meaning of the 1968 crisis

---

22. Savorana, *Life*, chapter 14, "A Revolution of Yourself. Sixty-Eight."
23. Savorana, *Life*, 389.

dawned on him. This was the end of an era. Something seismic had shifted and the world would not be the same. Evangelization could not be the same.

In the summer of 1968, as Paris, Milan and other cities mopped up the debris of the riots, three important figures in the Catholic world all, independently, came to the same conclusion. If the Church had to find new ways to propose Christianity to the world, there was only one place to start from: the person of Jesus the Christ.

On June 30, Pope Paul closed the Year of Faith by proclaiming his *Credo of the People of God*. In a general audience a fortnight before, he asked, in the face of widespread religious apathy, "How can we succeed in having a faith that is alive?" First, he said, "faith must be a personal fact for us" and second, "faith has its focal point in Jesus Christ; it is, we might say, a personal encounter with Him."[24]

In Germany, Joseph Ratzinger, then a professor of theology, was completing a book for publication: *Introduction to Christianity*. In the preface, which he wrote in the summer of 1968, he came to the conclusion that faith is "more than the option in favour of a spiritual ground to the world . . . It is the encounter with the man Jesus; it is finding a 'you' that upholds me, the countenance of the man Jesus of Nazareth."[25]

That same summer, Giussani met with the young people who remained fascinated by his proposal of the Christian fact. A priest friend of his who was present as those meetings summed it all up: "From there we started up again; we started over on the word Jesus and on the word communion, and that's it."[26]

We might pause here and appreciate the very striking correspondence in the way these three Catholic figures saw that the only point of departure is the person of Jesus and how, in this present time of grace, we are continually being challenged by this original position. After Paul VI, we remember John Paul II and the opening sentence of his first encyclical: "The redeemer of man, Jesus Christ, is the centre of the universe and of history." Then we remember the opening paragraph of his successor's first encyclical, a paragraph that has been gifted to us again recently by Francis, in *Evangelii gaudium*: "I never tire of repeating those words of Benedict XVI which take us to the very heart of the Gospel: 'Being a

---

24. Savorana, *Life*, 407.
25. Ratzinger, *Introduction to Christianity*. See Savorana, *Life*, 404.
26. Savorana, *Life*, 407.

Christian is not the result of an ethical choice or a lofty idea, but the encounter with an event, a person, which gives life a new horizon and a decisive direction.'"[27]

The problem, however, remains: how to communicate this to the world? Giussani turned to the Gospels. The method Jesus used to communicate himself to others was through a direct, personal encounter. In this Giussani saw a confirmation of the basic human dynamic of knowledge. We know through experience, and we experience when we encounter.[28]

As the year 1968 wore on, Giussani returned again and again, with groups of students and of priests, to a new articulation of his understanding of what kind of thing Christianity was. Christianity is "what makes tradition—the past—a living reality. It's what makes thought, idea and value come alive. But alive means present! Methodologically, if we don't want to disorient ourselves, we cannot do other than go back to the origin, to how it rose up, how it started. It as an event. Christianity is an event."[29] He worked and reworked a form of words that could grasp the essence of his experience of Christianity and at the same time open up the possibilities of its inexhaustible mystery.

Christianity was born as an announcement. An announcement means an encounter with a presence. Here was the great lesson of the events of 1968. "It seems to me that the only thing that can be a reason for adhering is the encounter with an announcement, is Christianity as an announcement and not as a theory. An announcement, that is, a certain kind of presence, a certain presence charged with message."[30] Giussani recalled one of the earliest slogans painted on the walls of the Sorbonne in Paris: *"De la présence, seulement de la présence."*[31]

The few members of GS who continued to meet with Giussani did not withdraw from social engagement and political debate. They continued

---

27. Paul VI, General Audience (June 19, 1968); Paul VI, *Credo of the People of God*; John Paul II, *Redemptor hominis*, 1; Benedict XVI, *Deus caritas est*, 1; Francis, *Evangelii gaudium*, 7.

28. The implications of this intuition for education are explored in Giussani, *The Risk of Education*.

29. Savorana, *Life*, 411.

30. Savorana, *Life*, 408. See also Giussani's text from November 1968, "Alive means Present!" https://it.clonline.org/cm-files/2018/10/12/gia-assago-2018-ing.pdf/.

31. Giussani, *Il senso seligioso*, 39.

to struggle to find their own voice and their identity.³² They did not even have a name until November 1969, when a flier bearing a strange header began to circulate at the State University of Milan. "Communion and Liberation," it read, with an equally unusual subtitle: "To build the Church is to free mankind." Giussani approved: "We are the name the university students have given themselves. Because communion *is* liberation." Thus was born Communion and Liberation, known as "CL."

During the next few years, Giussani continued to explore the implications of understanding Christianity as an encounter with a presence. He worked with many of the leading Catholic personalities of the time as they all searched for new ways to communicate the truth of Christian experience in a world that seemed to going in the opposite direction. In 1971 a group of CL students in Switzerland invited two speakers to preach their annual Spiritual Exercises. One was Fr. Giussani, the other Hans Urs von Balthasar. Giussani concurred warmly as he heard the great theologian challenge the students: "So long as Christianity is seen to be principally a matter of traditions and institutions, other contemporary movements towards freedom will have no difficulties."³³ The following year, Balthasar and Ratzinger joined with Henri de Lubac in founding a new journal, *Communio*. Ratzinger recalled that the name *Communio* came from his friendship with Giussani and the CL community.³⁴

The years after 1968 were difficult for Giussani and for CL. Italy slid into terrible years of terrorism, from left and right. Giussani's new movement was attacked by political forces on the left and on the right. Offices occupied by CL were attacked and individuals received beatings. The stakes were high.

In 1976 Giussani took stock of what had happened since 1968. The choice facing the Christian individual and the Christian community was between "presence" and "utopia." The experience of 1968 showed how placing ultimate faith in human initiative, even with the best of intentions, led to "no place," οὐ–τόπος, utopia. The only antidote to the seduction of utopia is a presence, a "present presence."

Christianity was of a different, and unique, order. Christianity was, before anything else, the event of an encounter. Giussani returned to the

32. Savorana, *Life*, chapter 15, "Why communion is liberation."

33. von Balthasar, *Engagement With God*, 21. Balthasar's and Giussani's talks from those Spiritual Exercises have been collected in a recent Italian volume, von Balthasar and Giussani, *L'impegno del cristiano*.

34. Ratzinger, "Communio," cit. in Savorana, *Life*, 432–33.

beginning of Christianity, as recounted in the first chapter of the Gospel of John, that day, when at 4 o'clock in the afternoon, "about the tenth hour," we might say that Christianity began. The first two, Andrew and John, were attracted by a human presence, the presence of the man Jesus. Their attraction to Him then spread to others through the witness of their lives and the attractiveness of the change that occurred in them. Giussani would return to this page of the Gospel many times during his life.

So, in 1976, Giussani declared "the time of the person has come." The presence of the Church in the world could no longer be a reactive presence, defying the world and defending itself against threats, real or imagined. Christianity was always, by its nature, an original presence, born ever new in the encounter with the other world present in this world. Faith must always be a "new beginning."

Giussani would propose this experience of faith with unwavering commitment and ever deeper clarity for the rest of his life. In December 2004, when he was gravely ill, he selected the phrase for the "Christmas Poster," an annual initiative of the CL movement. The author he chose was one of his favorites: Cesare Pavese, an atheist Italian writer of the mid-twentieth century who died by suicide in 1950. Like many of his favorite writers and artists, Giussani loved Pavese not because he reached the right answers, but because he knew how to ask the right questions, the authentic questions of the universal human heart. Now, as he approached the end of his own earthly journey, the sentence Giussani selected was "The only joy in the world is to begin. It is good to be alive because living is beginning, always, every moment."[35]

We are all, always, open to the temptation to avoid a new beginning and instead to take the truth we have encountered and transform it into something we already know as we pursue the comfortable security of our own path. How many movements in the history of the Church have faced difficult challenges in the years after the death of their founder, in the struggle to live out the initial charism in circumstances that require discernment, fidelity and courage![36]

For this reason, Fr. Giussani's successor in the leadership of CL, Fr. Julián Carrón, requested a general audience with Pope Francis ten years after Giussani's death. On March 7, 2015, 80,000 people filled St. Peter's Square to hear Fr. Carrón tell the Pope they had come "like beggars, with

35. Savorana, *Life*, 1145.
36. See, for example, Fernández, "Charisms and Movements" and *I movimenti*.

the desire to learn, to be helped to live with ever greater faithfulness and passion the charism we have received." The clarity that Fr. Giussani had reached through the crucible of 1968 and all that followed needs to be regained and recovered, just as the Christian event itself needs to reoccur, always new.

The response of the Holy Father to Fr. Carrón is worth citing at some length, for it is ultimately the key to understanding the lessons that any great historical episode, such as 1968, can continue to have for us in our own present. Pope Francis said:[37]

> After 60 years, the original charism has not lost its youthfulness and vitality. However, remember that the centre is not the charism, the centre is one alone, it is Jesus, Jesus Christ! When I place at the centre my spiritual method, my spiritual journey, my way of fulfilling it, I go off the itinerary. All spirituality, all charisms in the Church must be "decentered": at the centre there is only the Lord! . . .
>
> Thus the charism is not preserved in a bottle of distilled water! Faithfulness to the charism does not mean "to petrify it"—the devil is the one who "petrifies," do not forget! Faithfulness to the charism does not mean to write it on a parchment and frame it . . . . It certainly entails faithfulness to tradition, but faithfulness to tradition, Mahler said, "is not to worship the ashes but to pass on the flame." Don Giussani would never forgive you if you lost your freedom and transformed yourselves into museum guides or worshippers of ashes. Pass on the flame of the memory of that first encounter and be free!

Bibliography

Balthasar, Hans Urs von. *Engagement with God: The Drama of Christian Discleship*. Translated by R. John Halliburton. 1975. Reprinted, San Francisco: Ignatius, 2008.
Balthasar, Hans Urs von, and Luigi Giussani. *L'impegno del cristiano nel mondo*. Milan: Jaca, 2017.
Busani, Marta. *Gioventù Studentesca: Storia di un movimento cattolico dalla ricostruzione alla contestazione*. Studium: Roma, 2016.
Camisasca, Massimo. *Comunione e liberazione: Le origini (1954–1968)*. Milan: San Paolo, 2001.

---

37. The text of the address by Pope Francis, and the opening remarks by Fr. Julián Carrón, are in the March 2015 issue of *Traces*: https://english.clonline.org/traces/traces-archive. See also http://w2.vatican.va/content/francesco/en/speeches/2015/march/documents/papa-francesco_20150307_comunione-liberazione.html/.

———. *Don Giussani: La sua esperienza dell'uomo e di Dio*. Milan: San Paolo, 2009.
Fernández, Fidel González. "Charisms and Movements in the History of the Church. The Ecclesial Movements in the Pastoral Concern of the Bishops." *Laity Today* (2000) 71–103.
Fernández, Fidel González et al. *I movimenti: Dalla Chiesa degli apostoli a oggi*. Milan: Rizzoli, 2000.
Ginsborg, Paul. *A History of Contemporary Italy: Society and Politics (1943–1988)*. London: Penguin, 1990.
Giussani, Luigi. *The Journey to Truth Is an Experience*. Translated by John Zucchi. Montreal: McGill-Queen's University Press, 2006.
———. "Open Christianity." *Logos* 10.4 (2007) 151–66.
———. "Religious Awareness in Modern Man." *Communio* 25 (1998) 104–40.
———. *The Religious Sense*. Translated by John Zucchi. Montreal: McGill-Queen's University Press, 1997.
———. *The Risk of Education: Discovering Our Ultimate Destiny*. Translated by Rosanna M. Giammanco Frongia New York: Crossroads, 2001.
———. *Il senso religios*. Milan: Rizzoli, 1997.
Horn, Gerd-Rainer. *The Spirit of Vatican II: Western European Progressive Catholicism in the Long Sixties*. Oxford: Oxford University Press, 2015.
Montini, Giovanni Battista. *Discorsi e scritti Milanesi (1964–1963)*. Brescia: Istituto Paolo VI, 1997.
———. *Man's Religious Sense*. London: Darton Longman & Todd, 1961.
———, and Luigi Giussani. *Sul senso religioso*. Milan: Rizzoli, 2009.
Ratzinger, Joseph. "Communio: A Program." *Communio* 19.3 (1992) 436–49.
———. "Funeral Homily for Msgr. Luigi Giussani." *Communio* 31 (2004) 685–87.
———. *Introduction to Christianity*. Translated by J. R. Foster. London: Burns & Oates, 1968.
Rondoni, Davide, ed. *Communion and Liberation: A Movement in the Church*. Montreal: McGill-Queens University Press, 2000.
Savorana, Alberto. *The Life of Luigi Giussani*. Montreal: McGill-Queens University Press, 2018.
Zucchi, John. "Luigi Giussani, the Church and Youth in the 1950s." *Logos* 10.4 (2007) 131–50.

4

1968 and the Internationalization of Terrorism

Matthew C. Ogilvie

In his seminal work *Inside Terrorism*, Bruce Hoffman observes that "The advent of what is considered modern, international terrorism occurred on July 22, 1968."[1] While terrorism has existed in different forms for many centuries, its internationalization changed terrorism in four crucial ways: (1) It turned terrorism from a tactic of achieving small-scale concrete objectives to a strategy of making notorious political statements; (2) There was a change in the "rules" about which citizens of non-involved nations could be attacked; (3) It forced *de facto* recognition and concessions from governments; (4) Terrorists found that they could gain recognition through major events transmitted by mass media. This paper will explore the changes to terrorism that were fermented in the pivotal events of 1968. It will examine the tactics and strategies used by terrorists, the changing "ethics" of terrorism, and the way that 1968's internationalization of terrorism fostered the radicalization of religion that we see in groups such as Al Qaeda, Hamas, Hezbollah, and Islamic State. The paper will also reflect on how these developments

1. Hoffman, *Inside Terrorism*, 63–64.

have promoted changed tactics in fighting terrorism, along with the ethical questions prompted by the "war on terrorism."

Introduction

WHILE DIFFERENT FORMS OF terrorism have been part of the world's history for millennia, the events of 1968 were pivotal in changing terrorism from a mostly localized form of guerilla activity to the radical form of asymmetric warfare that we know today. In 1968 terrorism was internationalized, its tactics and strategies changed, terrorist targets changed from practical targets to symbolic ones, terrorist organizations gained some form of international legitimacy, and publicity for terrorists became even more important through what can be called "performance violence." As I will outline later in this paper, the pivotal acts of 1968 also led to fundamental changes in the way that terrorism is fought, particularly with regard to such things as torture, human rights abuses, and technological warfare. I shall conclude the paper with some interpretative comments and questions for further consideration.

What Is Terrorism?

Before addressing the events of 1968, it may be necessary to clarify what I mean by "terrorism." Very often the word is misused casually when discussing guerrilla groups or rebel organizations. One example of such misuse is Syrian dictator, Bashir al Assad, who labeled Syrian rebels "terrorists"[2] at the same time that he was dropping barrel bombs[3] and using chemical weapons[4] on innocent civilians. From the other side, different states—most notably Israel—have been labeled "terrorist states" by leaders or organizations that use the term for propaganda purposes without any conceptual definition or evidence-based justification for the term.[5]

---

2. BBC News, "Syrian President Bashar al-Assad."
3. McKernan, "Assad 'Dropped 13,000 barrel bombs on Syria in 2016."
4. Gladstone, "US Says Syria Has Used Chemical Weapons."
5. Al Jazeera News, "Erdogan Calls Netanyahu 'Terrorist,' Israel 'Terrorist State.'"

Michael Jenkins notes that what is labeled "terrorism" very often depends upon where one's point of view falls.[6] To label someone or some group as "terrorist" makes a moral judgment about them and prompts hostility towards them. Simultaneously, whether one labels mass violence "terrorism" depends very much on whether one's sympathies are with the perpetrator or the victim. If we identify with the victims, we are more likely to identify a violent act as terrorism. If we identify with the aggressor, we may come up with excuses to justify their actions as those of desperate or oppressed freedom fighters. Because terrorists almost invariably identify themselves as victims, they do not see themselves as terrorists, and their victim status allows them the freedom to self-authorize their actions and turn to acts that most people would find abhorrent.

The definition of terrorism according to one's own priorities goes some way to explaining why the term seems to have attracted myriad definitions. Even US government departments and agencies have different definitions of terrorism, with the Departments of Defense, State and Homeland Security, and the FBI all having distinct definitions that reflect their particular concerns and responsibilities.[7] For the rest of this paper, however, I will not employ subjective definitions of terrorism. Instead, I shall employ a more objective definition of terrorism that draws mostly on the seminal work of Bruce Hoffman.

Most people agree that terrorism violates the rules of war and the ethics of civilized human conduct. However, Hoffman clarifies that terrorism also involves several crucial elements that distinguish it from guerrilla warfare, criminal activity, or harsh state action.[8] First, terrorism is inherently violent. It involves violence to persons or harm to property, or threatens such violence to people or property. Secondly, the motivations of terrorism matter with regard to distinguishing it from common criminal activity. Terrorism is not motivated by direct personal gain to a perpetrator, but by an ideological, political, or religious agenda. That is, a criminal and a terrorist may use the same tactics, such as kidnapping and torture. However, a criminal will use such tactics for their own benefit, while a terrorist will use those tactics for the benefit of others, be it a political cause, a religion, or a social agenda.

---

6. Jenkins, "The Study of Terrorism," 1–2.
7. Hoffman, *Inside Terrorism*, 1–41.
8. Hoffman, *Inside Terrorism*, 1–41.

Thirdly, terrorism differs from conventional warfare in terms of its targets. Conventional warfare will harm specific targets that are valuable to the outcome of a conflict. Terrorism, however, is intended to have a psychological impact, to cause fear, and to intimidate people beyond the immediate victims or target. To put the point concretely, the intended targets of the 9/11 attacks were not the thousands who died in New York, Washington, or Pennsylvania. The real targets were the millions who witnessed those events through mass media and who were thus traumatized, fear-struck, and anxious at the thought of what may come next.

Understanding this point is helped by noting that the psychological impact of terrorism is more like anxiety than fear. The distinction between anxiety and fear is explained very well by theologian Paul Tillich.[9] First, fear has an identifiable object; we are afraid of an enemy, the dark, or an accident. Anxiety, however, has no object; we are anxious at the unknown or the unknowable. So, while we may have a fear of a defined, known object, anxiety is the response to the prospect of what we cannot know. In the case of religious experience, Tillich says that we are afraid of death, which we can know; but we are anxious at what comes after death, which we do not humanly know. In the case of terrorism, I would say that we experience fear and perhaps shock at acts of violence. However, what makes something terrorizing is the anxiety at what may come next: it is the unknown future attack that prompts terror. Thus, I would add to Hoffman's point that the targets and effects of terrorism are not the immediate victims who are harmed, but instead they are the witnesses who experience traumatic anxiety as a result of terror attacks.

The concept of asymmetric warfare is also beneficial for considering terrorism. However, the asymmetry of terrorism goes beyond the mere numbers of fighters on each side. The asymmetry of terrorism firstly involves law. That is, that terrorists are not bound by either international or domestic law with regard to the conduct of warfare. Secondly, it involves morality. Terrorists conduct themselves and their operations as if they are beyond the normal range of standards of moral behavior. The terrorist mentality is such that almost anything can be justified by the ideological goals of a terrorist organization. As will be seen below, this mentality ties in with what Cardinal Ratzinger called the terrorists' ideology of "self-authorization." Thirdly, terrorism is an attack on democracy. The conduct

---

9. Wildman, "Review of *The Courage to Be* by Paul Tillich."

of terrorism works as an attempt by a self-authorized few to impose their will on the many.

Shift to Internationalized Terrorism

Prior to 1968 there was terrorist violence, or asymmetric violence that resembled terrorism, which was undertaken by various ethno-nationalists who found it to be a very effective tactic in places such as the Holy Land, Algeria, and Cyprus.[10] However, the nature of terrorism was changed in the pivotal events of 1968. As Bruce Hoffman writes, "The advent of what is considered modern, international terrorism occurred on July 22, 1968."[11] On that day, members of the PLO-affiliated Popular Front for the Liberation of Palestine (PFLP) hijacked an El Al flight from Rome to Tel Aviv. Prior to that hijack, Palestinians had attacked targets within Israel, and other commercial jetliners had been hijacked. There had been eleven previous hijackings in 1968 alone. However, those planes were mostly hijacked as a diversion or as a means of transporting terrorists from one location to another. However, this attack was pivotally different. It was the first of a new wave of hijackings that had international targets rather than local ones.

This particular hijacking in 1968 was pivotally different for four main reasons. First, it was intended to make a direct and immediate political statement. That is, instead of using the hijacked planes as transport for terrorists, the passengers were held as hostages to be traded for terrorists held prisoner in Israel. Secondly, the plane's national origin became important. No longer was the plane a means of getting from point A to point B: the plane acted as a symbol of the enemy state. Thirdly, the hijack and those that followed it were effective at engineering a crisis in which a government faced the prospect of bearing the blame for the deaths of passengers. In that way, the PLO forced the Israeli government to deal directly with its representatives. Thus, even though the PLO lacked legitimacy, it gained some measure of recognition, which meant that the terrorists could not be ignored. Fourthly, the combination of a dramatic political statement, the symbolic targeting, and the de facto recognition gained, revealed to the PLO that they had the capacity to create major

---

10. Hoffman, *Inside Terrorism*, 61.
11. Hoffman, *Inside Terrorism*, 63.

international media events and to engineer such events for their political gain.¹²

I want to highlight the second of Hoffman's reasons, namely the symbolism inherent in the 1968 attack and in the other attacks that followed. Part of the logic of terror is the performance of symbolic acts of violence. Such symbolic violence is intended to affect an audience that lies way beyond the physical target. This is one reason why terrorists attack targets such as embassies, business centers such as the World Trade Center, and, most notoriously, international airliners. Mark Juergensmeyer makes a clarifying comment about the symbolism of terrorist violence and the way that terrorists think. Very soon after the first attack on the World Trade Center in 1993, a Cairo coffeehouse was attacked with greater loss of life than the World Trade Center attack. However, most media attention was on the World Trade Center bombing because of the symbolism of the target,¹³ a symbolism that was not lost on Al Qaeda when they attacked the same target in 2001.

The 1968 hijacking highlights the logic of internationalized terrorism, which is that attacks on symbolic targets elevate terrorists to celebrity status. A key example of this is that after the Black September attack at Munich, the PLO gained observer status at the United Nations and within a decade had established diplomatic ties with many nations. Another way of putting this point is that through attacking symbolic targets, terrorists are able to elevate their apparent importance. A more recent example was the attack on a French church and killing of a Catholic priest by Islamic State/Daesh-affiliated terrorists.¹⁴ The attention given to this attack on a symbolic target was much more significant than attacks in less symbolic locations in which there was a much greater loss of life.

Thus the 1968 hijacking illustrates something characteristic of terrorism. It seeks to have an influence greater than the substantial body it represents. One cannot do this, of course, through conventional warfare, so the logic of terrorism as a form of asymmetric warfare dictates the targets be chosen for their symbolic value or with the potential for terrifying spectacle.

If we consider the 1968 hijacking and the attacks that followed it, we see that the attack not only internationalized terrorism, but also showed

---

12. Hoffman, *Inside Terrorism*, 63.
13. Juergensmeyer, *Terror in the Mind of God*, 127.
14. BBC News, "France Church Attack."

that terrorism could be most fruitful for its perpetrators. It certainly proved more effective than diplomacy and perhaps much more effective than conventional guerrilla warfare. One PLO leader claimed that "The first several hijackings aroused the consciousness of the world and awakened the media and world opinion much more—and more effectively—than 20 years of pleading at the United Nations."[15] Thus, the 1968 hijacking was pivotal in changing the quality and tactics of terrorism in several ways. First, the new strategy internationalized terrorism, with terrorists traveling from one country to another to carry out attacks. Secondly, it removed the protections traditionally given to non-combatants. One may contrast a previous mass-killing event like the bombing of the King David Hotel in Jerusalem. While civilians were killed, the perpetrators tried to justify the bombing as an attack on military forces present in the hotel, with the civilians being what would today be called "collateral damage."[16] After the 1968 hijacking, however, terrorists showed no compunction about involving civilians, even those from third-party countries. Without discrimination between combatants and noncombatants, or discrimination between citizens of involved or non-involved nations, all persons became legitimate targets in order to gain attention for the terrorists' cause. Thirdly, the aim of terrorism was focused firmly not on the immediate victims, but on the shocking, terrorizing, and alarming of people beyond the range of the immediate attack. Fourthly, and perhaps most importantly, the internationalization of terrorism was not just in the physical location of attacks or the people targeted, but through the international audiences who witnessed the attacks.

Through the 1968 attack and those that followed, the PLO showed that neglected or even unpopular causes could be thrust into the world's spotlight by well-publicized attacks. This success has been a pattern ever since, as we see with the rise to notoriety of Al Qaeda and Islamic State/Daesh. One can say that few people take these causes seriously, but they take their actions very seriously.

If we turn to attacks that followed the tactics and strategy set by the 1968 hijacking, the event that most symbolizes this internationalization and ability to manipulate the media was the Black September attack at the 1972 Munich Olympics. The media attention, especially on television,

---

15. Hoffman, *Inside Terrorism*, 64.
16. Hoffman, *Inside Terrorism*, 48–52.

meant that one-quarter of the world's population witnessed the attack.[17] Even if most people were revolted by the attack, it gained attention for the PLO that could never be generated by conventional warfare. Importantly, none of the substantial demands of the Black September terrorists were met; and in conventional military terms, the Munich operation was a failure. However, in terms of turning the attention of people to the Palestinians through what has been called "performance violence," the Black September attack was a victory beyond reckoning.[18]

The publicity during and immediately the Munich attack was overwhelmingly negative. Yet the saying that "any publicity is good publicity" certainly seems to apply to the Palestinian terrorists in this case. As mentioned above, the aftermath of the Munich attack saw Yasir Arafat given special observer status at the United Nations, and the PLO established diplomatic relations with many countries. So, even if the Palestinian terrorists were despised, in the light of attacks like Black September, they could no longer be ignored by the world.[19]

In that light, while I am arguing that the PLO was responsible for the internationalization of terrorism, it is clear that it would not have been possible without television news programs and the constant availability of news images. One should ask, then, what was the role of the media in the internalization of terrorism and, in today's context, what ethical responsibilities does the media have in reporting terrorism?

It is worth mentioning the "publicity violence" associated with the Tet Offensive of 1968 in Vietnam. That offensive serves as an analogate for the internationalized "performance terrorism" that emerged in the same year. How did the Tet Offensive work for the North Vietnamese? The reality is that the offensive was, in military terms, a staggering loss for the North Vietnamese and the Viet Cong. However, the offensive was not won on the battlefield, but in the living rooms of the American public. It became clear that the graphic broadcast images of fighting and death in Hue and Saigon had an effect on households in America and other places. Those images were crucial in harnessing opposition to the war, even among those who had previously supported American intervention in Vietnam.[20]

17. Reeve, "Olympics Massacre: Munich."
18. Juergensmeyer, *Terror in the Mind of God*, 122–26.
19. Hoffman, *Inside Terrorism*, 69.
20. Australian Government, Department of Veteran Affairs, "The Tet Offensive."

As with the Tet Offensive, internationalized terrorism worked and continues to work despite the loss of combatants "in the battlefield" because its real victories occur through the media, in the court of public opinion.

One cannot thus dismiss the importance of publicity to terrorists nor ignore the role that the media play, however unwittingly, in achieving the terrorists' objectives. Accordingly, publicity is just as essential to terrorism now as it was to the Irgun of the 1940s, the Black Septemberists of the 1970s, and the Zealots of two thousand years ago. Newspaper headlines and television stories are the standards by which terrorists judge the success of their acts. It is revealing to note how terrorists such as Carlos the Jackal, Hans Joachim Klein, and Razmi Ahmed Yousef collected the newspaper stories detailing their terrorist acts.[21] It may be easy to dismiss this as an act of narcissism or megalomania. However, at a deeper level, it shows the terrorist obsession with publicity and the fact that no amount of violence is sufficient unless it is accompanied by the publicity and shock of terrorism's psychological victims, whom one would argue are the primary targets of terrorism.

Terrorism since 1968 has thus played to a "theater of terror," which is why terrorist violence, especially that carried out by religiously motivated groups, is deliberately intense and graphic.[22] The reality is that terrorist violence is not aimed specifically at destroying buildings or infrastructure; nor is it aimed at killing combatants who presented a direct threat to the terrorist cause. Rather, it is aimed at harming people in spectacular fashion. This is one reason why Juergensmeyer refers to terrorism specifically as "performance violence."[23] While it is a term that causes moral discomfort, it does convey some central truths, chief among which is that terrorist violence is not strategic in the sense of contributing directly to a military objective. Instead, terrorist violence is demonstrative, rather than effective, and it is aimed at generating angst and feelings of revulsion in those who witness the terrorist acts.

So what net effect was there from the 1968 hijacking and the attacks that followed? As mentioned above, the PLO gained diplomatic recognition of which it could only dream before 1968. In the light of the success of internationalized terrorism, they more explicitly targeted civilians and

---

21. Hoffman, *Inside Terrorism*, 247–48.
22. Juergensmeyer, *Terror in the Mind of God*, 120.
23. Juergensmeyer, *Terror in the Mind of God*, 122–26.

third parties and created the sort of terrorism we have today, which is designed for prime-time television.

The PLO then trained forty different groups. They became the go-to training organization for aspiring terrorists. Ironically, while being generously funded by the Soviets, the PLO charged capitalist rates for their training camps and the organization became very wealthy. The PLO turned into a multinational business worth billions of dollars. Indeed, internationalized terrorism is a most profitable enterprise. For example, Arafat, a so-called "freedom fighter," was a multimillionaire in his own right. However, he was a rank amateur compared to Hamas's Khaled Mashal, who lives the high life in Doha and, along with several other Hamas leaders, is reportedly a multibillionaire.[24]

The Soviets

If we are to talk about the PLO and the internationalization of terrorism in the late 1960s, we should mention the Soviet involvement in these developments. Gen. Ion Pacepa, the author of *Disinformation,* is a valuable source on this issue.[25] A three-star general in Communist Romania who defected to the West in 1978, he remains the highest-ranking defector from the former Soviet Bloc. At the time of his defection, he served as an adviser to Nicolae Ceaușescu and the acting head of Romania's foreign intelligence service.

General Pacepa claims that the PLO was formed at the behest of the KGB. This allegedly happened in the mid-1960s, when the KGB leadership reasoned that anti-Zionism combined with a liberation ideology would be "rich source of anti-Americanism."[26] Pacepa also claims that KGB chairman Yury Andropov told him that greater damage could be done to America through the Palestinians. His strategy was to "instill a Nazi-style hatred for the Jews throughout the Islamic world, and to turn this weapon of the emotions into a terrorist bloodbath against Israel and its main supporter, the United States."[27]

---

24. Levi-Weinrib, "The Hamas Tycoons"; Danan, "Gaza's Millionaires and Billionaires."
25. Pacepa, with Rychlak, *Disinformation.*
26. Pacepa, with Rychlak, *Disinformation,* 286.
27. Pacepa, "Russian Footprints."

Accordingly, the ideology of the PLO was Soviet-influenced, especially through the personal work of Romanian dictator Nicolae Ceaușescu.[28] One must always be critical of anything emanating from the intelligence world, but Pacepa's claims fit the known realities of the PLO, its structure, governance, and methods. It would also seem that the brutality and amorality of PLO tactics certainly also bore the hallmarks of KGB training and indoctrination, being tactics that looked to functional outcomes and victories, with little to no care for human rights or values.[29]

Another Soviet contribution to internationalized terrorism was an ideology of victimhood. That is, if sources like Pacepa are to be believed, it seems that the corruption of Holy Land Arabs and other Muslims was achieved by the Soviets grafting the victimhood or grievance mentality, which characterizes Marxism, onto the Palestinian cause. Thus, neo-Marxist victimhood and class struggle added to Arab aspirations, which resulted in the self-authorization that enabled Black September, suicide bombings, and a range of other outrages. Of course, the Palestinians and other terrorists were not alone in this regard. In reflecting on the ideology of victimhood and grievance, one might draw a parallel with many grievance movements today in which civilized values are abandoned in pursuit of a cause. The recent "Grievance Studies" hoaxes have uncovered corruption in the university community in which the pursuit of truth has given way to the unprincipled pursuit of revolutionary causes.[30] Also, the relentless and unethical pursuit of untenable accusations against Justice Brett Kavanaugh shows a similar abandonment of principle and core values in the pursuit of a subversive or party political cause.[31] These recent events and their parallels with terrorism prompt a question: Is the internationalization of terrorism isolated, or is it part of a more widespread social phenomenon?

On the Soviet influence, it is worth mentioning credible allegations that the current Palestinian Authority dictator, Mahmood Abbas, was

---

28. Pacepa, *Disinformation*, 286.

29. Bergman, *The Secret War with Iran*, 98–100. One ironically sees the brutality of KGB tactics in their method of dealing with Hezbollah. As will be noted below, Bergman explains that KGB agents dealt with Hezbollah by using what we could call terrorist tactics against the terrorists themselves.

30. Pluckrose et al., "Academic Grievance Studies and the Corruption of Scholarship."

31. National Review Editors, "Justice Prevailed."

a KGB spy.[32] The evidence is somewhat ambiguous, though it tends to support the allegations. What is indisputable, though, is that Abbas's doctoral thesis, which was written at a Soviet university, shows some of the Soviet and KGB influence over the PLO. In his doctorate, Abbas claimed that the Nazi holocaust was a manufactured myth and that any Jews who may have been killed (in this non-holocaust) were actually killed by Jews who collaborated with the Nazis.[33]

With regard to the PLO and its influence, I would like to make one more point, and that is the brutality that the PLO introduced to religious terrorism. The context of this point is the allegation that the PLO corrupted religious movements that were allied with its objectives, even if they did not initially share its methods. To understand this point, we should recall that the PLO is a fundamentally secular organization, even if most of its members are Muslim. That is why they have been despised by Hamas (Sunni)[34] and Hezbollah (Shiite). The son of a Hamas founder, Mosab Yousef, argues credibly that Hamas began as a renewal of the "beautiful side of Islam" but that it was violently corrupted by PLO influence.[35] His argument has some merit. For example, suicide is a sin against mainstream Islam, but suicide terrorism was adopted by different Islamist groups, all through PLO influence.

In fact, suicide bombing serves as an example of the influence of KGB-driven ideology that led to the 1968 hijacking and the internationalized terrorism that followed it. We would be familiar with the typical comment that terrorism has nothing to do with mainstream Islam. Yet there are small but dangerous sects that have inverted the clear teaching of Islam to endorse the so-called virtue of suicide terrorism. Thus, while the Quran clearly teaches against suicide terrorism,[36] sects like Hamas have come to invert that teaching to encourage such suicide terrorism as a virtue that rewards such combatants with the promised bliss of Paradise.[37]

---

32. Eglash, "Palestinian President Mahmoud Abbas was once a KGB spy."

33. Middle East Media Research Institute, "Palestinian Authority TV Lauds President Abbas' Holocaust Denial." PhD diss.).

34. Hamas, "The Covenant of The Islamic Resistance Movement—Hamas."

35. Yousef, *Son of Hamas*.

36. Khan, "Sahih Bukhari," vol. 2, bk. 23, no. 446.

37. Bukay, "The Religious Foundations of Suicide Bombings"; Radwan, "Reward and honor bestowed on Muslim Martyrs."

So how was it that Hamas, an organization so dedicated to Quranic teaching, became so devoted to a tactic of suicide bombing that is contrary to Muslim principles? The Quran (Sura 4) is very clear that suicide for any reason is wrong. This prohibition against suicide is also reinforced in the Hadiths. For example, "The Prophet said, 'He who commits suicide by throttling shall keep on throttling himself in the Hell Fire (forever) and he who commits suicide by stabbing himself shall keep on stabbing himself in the Hell-Fire.'"[38]

Despite such clear prohibition, Hamas now indoctrinates its followers to accept the polar opposite of Quranic teaching: Hamas indoctrinates its recruits to believe that suicide is the vehicle through which they may gain a heavenly reward beyond that which would be possible for ordinary Muslims.[39] One may be familiar with the proverbial seventy-two virgins promised to suicide terrorists, but there are also promises made assuring them that they can intercede and gain divine favors for their relatives, and the promise that they will not feel pain in undertaking the act of suicide terrorism. In other words, to achieve the inversion of normal Islamic values to justify suicide, terrorism requires the use of pervasive and influential theology. So while the Quran teaches that suicide is one of the greatest sins, through theological sophistry the greatest of sins becomes the greatest of virtues. Thus suicide attacks are theologically reclassified from a selfish taking of one's own life to a selfless sacrifice of one's life, making oneself a martyr for the greater cause. As one Islamic scholar said on Fatah (PLO) Television:

> When the Shahid (Martyr for Allah) meets the Lord, all his sins are forgiven from the first gush of blood, and he is exempted from the torments of the grave. He sees his place in Paradise. He is shielded from the Great Shock and marries 72 Dark-Eyed (Virgins). He is a heavenly advocate for 70 members of his family. On his head is placed a crown of honor, one stone of which is worth more than all there is in this world.[40]

This sort of manipulation of religion to support, rather than condemn, suicide attacks has fostered and promoted suicide terrorism, encouraging many recruits to undertake suicide bombings.

---

38. Khan, "Sahih Bukhari," vol. 2, bk. 23, no. 446.
39. Bukay, "The Religious Foundations of Suicide Bombings."
40. Radwan, "Reward and Honor Bestowed on Muslim Martyrs."

I have dwelt on this issue because it is worthwhile to consider the clear and radical inversion of normal religious values that we see in PLO-influenced Islamic groups. From sources such as Yousef, Pacepa, and others cited above, we start to see a line that goes back to the pivotal events of the 1960s. The 1968 hijacking introduced us to terrorism that was internationalized and focused on publicity and performance violence. However, as we have seen above, it was also a form of terrorism that utterly abandoned any ethical, legal, or religious restraints. Accordingly, in current times when we witness the horrors of the Islamic State, the mass murders of Hamas and Hezbollah and the terrors of Al Qaeda, we may ask how Islam, which has its own clear rules about combat, could have reached this point? The answer would seem to be in the clear line that we can trace from Muslim and Arab groups today to the PLO and their corrupting influence, and back to the pivotal events of 1968, and most likely through that event to the influence and manipulations of the Soviet intelligence community.

Responding to Terror

I would now like to change the direction of this paper and write something about the reaction to terrorism by those who fight it. Before 1968 terrorism seemed to work because terrorists believed that civilized nations would not respond with unethical or illegal actions. That was indeed the thinking of Menachem Begin in Mandate Palestine. He believed that the British would be too "civilized" to do what was necessary to stop the Irgun.[41] However, since 1968 Begin's convictions about the West have yielded to new realities. Today, we see our society rapidly abandoning previously cherished principles and laws in the name of fighting terrorism.

First, torture has become acceptable to many people today. So-called soft forms of torture such as "enhanced interrogation" and harsher forms of outright torture have become acceptable within political circles and even among the general public.[42] In the popular imagination, torture has been glamorized by films such as *Zero Dark Thirty*, on the grounds that "it works." The irony is that it has been proven repeatedly that torture does not work on terrorists, especially religiously motivated terrorists, as

41. Hoffman, *Inside Terrorism*, 48–53.
42. Siems, "Inside the CIA's Black Site Torture Room"; BBC News, "CIA tactics."

seen in the work of Deuce Martinez,[43] Michel Khoubi,[44] and Matthew Alexander.[45] However, the fact remains that, in the face of internationalized terrorism, many people—leaders and the public alike—advocate torture techniques that would have horrified previous generations of civilized people.

In responding to terrorism, people often condone the adoption of outright brutality and human rights abuses. The phrase "collateral damage" has come to describe the increasing number of civilians and non-combatants whose harm has become more or less acceptable in the war on terror. In 2015, presidential candidate Donald Trump even called for US forces to "take out the families" of terrorists.[46] What may have been Trump's political rhetoric is, in fact, Russia's unofficial policy and strategy in the Caucasus. The families of terrorists are routinely targeted and subjected to what would, in previous times, be regarded as war crimes. This was made clear by a member of President Putin's "Human Rights Council," who justified the targeted killing of civilians by saying that terrorists' "relatives will be treated as accomplices."[47]

In recent times, while observing some of the Kurdish online chatter in Syria, I noticed that when the Russians intervened against the Islamic State/Daesh, many Kurds celebrated the imminent defeat of their enemy despite knowing that the Russians would act in ways that most civilized people would find repulsive.

I would also note the Russian response to Hezbollah kidnappings in Lebanon. Bergman recounts the story of Russians being kidnapped by Shiite terrorists in Beirut, after which Russian specialists kidnapped the terrorists' relatives, killed and mutilated them and left their strategically arranged body parts on the roadside. It is noted with some approval by people who fight terrorism that after this brutal intervention, there were no kidnappings of Russians in Lebanon.[48] However, I would ask, at what price to our humanity do we gain such a victory? Has the reaction to internationalized terrorism been so strong that people in our society are prepared to tolerate war crimes in response to terrorism? The popularity

43. Leonard, "Khalid Sheikh Mohammed: The interrogator who made him talk"; Shane, "Inside a 9/11 Mastermind's Interrogation."

44. Bowden, "The Dark Art of Interrogation."

45. Alexander, with Bruning, *How to Break a Terrorist*.

46. Taylor, "Trump Said He Would Take Out the Families of ISIS Fighters."

47. Kramer, "Russia Shows What Happens When Terrorists' Families Are Targeted."

48. Bergman, *The Secret War with Iran*, 98–100.

of Putin in Russia and the Middle East and the election of Trump in the USA would seem to indicate so.

Another significant development is the normalization of drone warfare against terrorists that has resulted in significant "collateral damage." President George W. Bush authorized approximately fifty drone strikes that killed 296 terrorists and 195 civilians. One may have expected better from a Nobel Peace Prize winner, but President Barack Hussein Obama authorized over 500 drone strikes that killed 3,040 terrorists and 391 civilians.[49] I have no statistics on the Trump Presidency, but would recall that the GBU-43/B "Massive Ordnance Air Blast" (Mother of All Bombs) that was recently dropped in Afghanistan was used not so much for its tactical utility, but for its value as performance violence. It is sobering to compare the strong reactions of Americans and Australians to unintended civilian casualties in Vietnam with the easily foreseeable civilian casualties in remote warfare/bombing carried out in the war on terror. One can argue that society has lost something of its soul in the reaction to international terrorism.

Having mentioned drone warfare, the neglect or violation of human rights in the war on terror has meant that it is now very easy to be placed on the drone target list. Leaked documents showed the ease with which an innocent civilian could be added to the US government's central terrorist database. This could happen even on the basis of a single uncorroborated social media post. In a 2014 court filing, the US government admitted that almost half a million people had been nominated in 2013 for inclusion on a government database of "known or suspected terrorists." Of these, only 4,900 were rejected.[50]

I argue that what was more consequential than the growth in the number of drone strikes or the number of people on "drone hit lists" was the Obama administration's efforts to institutionalize and normalize the practice. President Obama even made light of drone warfare and joked about it in 2010 at the White House Correspondents' Dinner. He said, "The Jonas Brothers are here; they're out there somewhere. Sasha and Malia are huge fans. But boys, don't get any ideas. I have two words for you, 'predator drones.' You will never see it coming."[51]

---

49. Zenko, "Obama's Embrace of Drone Strikes Will Be a Lasting Legacy."
50. Downie, "Obama's Drone War is a Shameful Part of His Legacy."
51. Fisher, "Obama Finds Predator Drones Hilarious."

I can't imagine President Truman making such jokes about nuclear weapons, nor can I imagine President Johnson joking about the bombing of North Vietnam during Operation Rolling Thunder. So what has just been written leads to the question that should be posed now: In response to internationalized terrorism, what happened to our culture that made us so tolerant of torture, mass killing revenge, and jokes about drones that kill multiple civilians? Have we become a culture in which it is acceptable to terrorize the terrorists and their loved ones? If that is the case, have we fallen for the temptation of which Friedrich Nietzsche warned us, "Whoever fights monsters should see to it that in the process he does not become a monster."[52]

Terrorists' "Self-Authorization"

An interesting interpretation of post-1968 terrorism comes from Cardinal Josef Ratzinger, now Pope Emeritus Benedict. 1968 saw the PLO switch from tactics that were more or less morally restrained to acts that could be authorized by no one other than the terrorists. Previous acts, if not approved of by a broader politic, were at least subject to international condemnation. Since the 1968 hijacking, terrorists see themselves as being outside of the normal laws of God and humanity. Ratzinger makes an excellent point about this way of thinking. "In the end, terrorism is also based on this modality of man's self-authorization, and not on the teachings of the Koran."[53]

Ratzinger's concept of "self-authorization" explains something of the mindset of terrorists, especially those who are religiously motivated. We have seen that since the internationalization of terrorism in 1968, such terrorists do not follow objective standards of truth or morality; they appoint themselves arbiters of political or religious truth. Politically, they seek not to conform to the will of the people or legitimate authority, but rather, they self-authorize their actions and seek instead to impose their own self-authorized positions on the people. They are self-authorized and accountable to no one, and as such, they see themselves as being above the law and even able to be judge, jury, and executioners of their victims. Ratzinger drives at the point that religious terrorists are now self-authorized in terms of their religious convictions. I would also argue that

52. Nietzsche, *Beyond Good and Evil*, Aphorism 146.
53. Ratzinger, "Cardinal Ratzinger on Europe's Crisis of Culture."

they are self-authorized in terms of their interpretation of law and politics, so that they fundamentally can justify acting contrarily to their faith. In reality, they are self-authorizing outlaws (in the most robust sense of that word) and also anti-democratic in their thinking and actions.

Self-authorization also ties into the self-image that terrorists have of themselves. There is the question of whether perpetrators of mass violence are genuine freedom fighters or immoral/unlawful terrorists. Martin Rudner makes the critical point that "there is the famous statement: 'One man's terrorist is another man's freedom fighter.' But that is grossly misleading. It assesses the validity of the cause when terrorism is an act. One can have a perfectly beautiful cause and yet if one commits terrorist acts, it is terrorism regardless."[54]

However, terrorists do not see themselves as terrorists; they do not perceive themselves in the way that others do. They view themselves as fighters taking up a necessary and just cause, as people fighting under the burden of a lack of viable alternatives, people fighting "a repressive state, a predatory rival ethnic or nationalist group, or an unresponsive international order."[55]

Ratzinger/Benedict's concept of "self-authorization" is thus a powerful tool for interpreting terrorism since 1968, and the concept would be well worth further research and elaboration. I would note that such self-authorization can come from a number of sources, but the most prominent one would seem to be a radical sense of victimhood. Such victimhood—or the mentality of grievance—is especially important, given the Soviet-Marxist influence on the PLO and other terrorist organizations. To see the impact of the victimhood mentality, we can compare efforts to exterminate the Holy Land's Jews during World War II and after the 1960s. During the Nazi era, the Grand Mufti of Jerusalem consorted with the Nazis in an effort to exterminate Jews, meeting Nazi leaders and recruiting Muslim soldiers to fight for or alongside the Third Reich.[56] However, the Grand Mufti did so not as a victim, but as a (foreseeable) victor. We see entirely different tactics being used (albeit with the same aim of killing Jews) in today's Holy Land. Armed, or prompted by a sense of victimhood and perpetual grievance, anti-Jewish organizations with no accountability to the rest of the world self-authorize any and all

---

54. Rudner, "One Official's 'Refugee' is Another's 'Terrorist.'"
55. Hoffman, *Inside Terrorism*, 22.
56. American–Israeli Cooperative Enterprise, "The Holocaust."

actions that they see necessary for their cause, even if those actions are considered to be abhorrent by the civilized world.

The Objectives of Terrorism

I would like to turn our attention to the objectives of terrorism noted by Hoffmann.[57] By distilling these objectives, Hoffman rejects the myth that terrorism is a senseless or thoughtless action. On the contrary, it is a consciously chosen and deliberate plan of action. The first objective is attention. This objective is realized not just by any sort of violence but by attention-grabbing violence that relies on publicity to shock and terrorize a target group by generating anxiety. The second objective is acknowledgment, which is an attempt to convert the attention created by the violence into an acknowledgment of the cause itself. Terrorists anticipate that acknowledgment can translate into some sort of sympathy for that cause. The third objective uses the outcomes of the first two objectives—i.e. attention and acknowledgment—to gain public recognition for the underlying cause for which the terrorists are fighting, seeking to establish the relevant terrorist group as the recognized representatives of that cause.

Importantly, some terrorist groups have attained these first three objectives. Only rarely, if ever, have terrorists attained the next two. The fourth objective is that terrorists intend to take the authority to change government or society. In the case of religious terrorists, they would seek the authority to mandate the observance of their religious views in their target culture. The fifth objective is taking full control of a state or a people, or in the case of religious terrorists, implementing a theocracy such as Sharia law.

With regard to these five objectives, I would argue that only the first two had been clearly achieved before 1968. However, after the pivotal changes in the nature of internationalized terrorism in 1968, terrorism went beyond attention and acknowledgment to the achievement of the third objective: public recognition of the cause. In the years that followed, the PLO and the IRA were able to achieve the fourth objective of taking authority in society. The degree to which any terror group has achieved the fifth objective of taking full control of a state is debatable. However, it does seem clear that terrorists would not have achieved more than the

---

57. Hoffman, *Inside Terrorism*, 255.

first two objectives were it not for the pivotal and radical changes to terrorism in 1968.

Concluding Comments

In this paper, I have described the changes in terrorism that occurred in 1968 and the years following. I have also argued that the nature of terrorism has changed and described some of the changes we have seen in response to terrorism in civilized society. Rather than summarize the paper, I would like to conclude with a short reflection.

Since 1968, terrorism has become utterly amoral. In previous years there were some sorts of restraints on terrorism, but since 1968, truth and ethics have given way to terrorist expediency. It has even led to the utter inversion of faith and values in different religious groups. However, terrorism is not alone in this regard. As we have seen, the fight against terrorism has sometimes shown an equal disregard for truth or ethics, so that one may argue that the fight against post-1968 terrorism has seen a corruption of Western society's values.

I would also raise a broader social question with regard to the ethical or moral compass of society. One could say that international terrorism's 1968 changes brought about the utter "amoralization" of guerrilla warfare. One can ask if this change is either analogous or coincident to the amoralization of ethics in other fields, like politics, the academy, or human sexuality? That is, is guerrilla warfare or terrorism alone in having previously been perpetrated or judged under strict ethical guidelines but having now become utterly amoral and performance-oriented?

The answer would seem to be in the affirmative. Other broad social movements have also abandoned truth and ethics. Whether we talk about the academy and the embrace of "grievance studies," the excesses of the sexual revolution, or the polarization of politics seen most recently in the Democrats' unethical and probably illegal attacks on Justice Kavanaugh, we may be left with the question of whether terrorists were alone in their paradigm shift. Does the amoralization of international terrorism stand alone, or does it reflect a broader social shift? It seems so, and I shall commit that question to further research.

Having said all that, I trust that this paper has shown something of the results of the PLO hijacking on July 22, 1968. With regard to terrorism, and whatever we think of terrorism and our counterterror culture, be it for or against, I would suggest that perhaps even if it is not the cause, most certainly the catalyst is found in the internationalization of terrorism by the PLO in the events of 1968.

BIBLIOGRAPHY

Al Jazeera News. "Erdogan Calls Netanyahu 'Tterrorist', Israel 'Terrorist State.'" *Al Jazeera*, April 2, 2018. https://www.aljazeera.com/news/2018/04/erdogan-calls-netanyahu-terrorist-israel-terrorist-state-180401140938404.html/.

Alexander, Matthew, with John R. Bruning. *How to Break a Terrorist*. New York: Free Press, 2008.

American–Israeli Cooperative Enterprise. "The Holocaust: The Mufti and the Führer." *Jewish Virtual Library*, 1998–2018. https://www.jewishvirtuallibrary.org/the-mufti-and-the-f-uuml-hrer.

Australian Government, Department of Veteran Affairs. "The Tet Offensive" (2017). https://anzacportal.dva.gov.au/history/conflicts/australia-and-vietnam-war/events/tet-offensive.

BBC News. "CIA Tactics: What Is 'Enhanced Interrogation'?" *BBC News*, December 10, 2014. https://www.bbc.com/news/world-us-canada-11723189.

———. "France Church Attack: Priest Killed by Two 'IS Militants.'" *BBC News*, July 26, 2016. http://www.bbc.com/news/world-europe-36892785.

———. "Syrian President Bashar al-Assad: Facing Down Rebellion." *BBC News*, September 3, 2018. https://www.bbc.com/news/10338256.

Bergman, Ronen. *The Secret War with Iran: The 30-Year Clandestine Struggle against the World's Most Dangerous Terrorist Power*. Translated by Ronnie Hope. New York: Free Press, 2008.

Bowden, Mark. "The Dark Art of Interrogation." *The Atlantic*, October 2003. https://www.theatlantic.com/magazine/archive/2003/10/the-dark-art-of-interrogation/302791.

Bukay, David. "The Religious Foundations of Suicide Bombings: Islamist Ideology." *Middle East Quarterly* 13.4 (2006). http://www.meforum.org/1003/the-religious-foundations-of-suicide-bombings.

Danan, Deborah. "Gaza's Millionaires and Billionaires—How Hamas's Leaders Got Rich Quick." *The Algemeiner*, July 28, 2014. https://www.algemeiner.com/2014/07/28/gazas-millionaires-and-billionaires-how-hamass-leaders-got-rich-quick.

Downie, James. "Obama's Drone War Is a Shameful Part of His Legacy." *The Washington Post*, May 5, 2016. https://www.washingtonpost.com/opinions/obamas-drone-war-is-a-shameful-part-of-his-legacy/2016/05/05/a727eea8-12ea-11e6-8967-7ac733c56f12_story.html?utm_term=.1cba541cd72e.

Eglash, Ruth. "Palestinian President Mahmoud Abbas Was Once a KGB Spy Code-Named 'Mole,' Report Claims." *The Washington Post*, September 8, 2016. https://www.washingtonpost.com/news/worldviews/wp/2016/09/08/palestinian-president-mahmoud-abbas-was-once-a-kgb-spy-codenamed-mole-report-claims/?noredirect=on&utm_term=.22b0cea76a26.

Fisher, Max. "Obama Finds Predator Drones Hilarious." *The Atlantic*, May 3, 2010. https://www.theatlantic.com/international/archive/2010/05/obama-finds-predator-drones-hilarious/340949.

Gladstone, Rick. "US Says Syria Has Used Chemical Weapons at Least 50 Times during War." *The New York Times*, April 13, 2018. https://www.nytimes.com/2018/04/13/world/middleeast/un-syria-haley-chemical-weapons.html.

Hamas. "The Covenant of The Islamic Resistance Movement—Hamas." 1988. https://www.memri.org/reports/covenant-islamic-resistance-movement-%E2%80%93-hamas.

Hoffman, Bruce. *Inside Terrorism*. Rev. ed. New York: Columbia University Press, 2006.

Jenkins, Michael. "The Study of Terrorism: Definitional Problems." Santa Monica: RAND Corporation, 1980. https://www.rand.org/content/dam/rand/pubs/papers/2006/P6563.pdf/.

Juergensmeyer, Mark. *Terror in the Mind of God: The Global Rise of Religious Violence*. Berkeley: University of California Press, 2000.

Khan, M. Muhsin. "Translation of Sahih Bukhari." Center for Muslim-Jewish Engagement, University of Southern California, (n.d.). http://www.usc.edu/org/cmje/religious-texts/hadith/bukhari.

Kramer, Andrew E. "Russia Shows What Happens When Terrorists' Families Are Targeted." *The New York Times*, March 30, 2016. https://www.nytimes.com/2016/03/30/world/europe/russia-chechnya-caucasus-terrorists-families.html.

Levi-Weinrib, Ela. "The Hamas Tycoons—How Much Are Khaled Mashal and Ismail Hania Worth?" *Walla!* (in Hebrew) (July 24, 2014). https://finance.walla.co.il/item/2768983/.

Leonard, Tom. "Khalid Sheikh Mohammed: The Interrogator Who Made Him Talk." *The Telegraph* (June 22, 2008). https://www.telegraph.co.uk/news/worldnews/northamerica/usa/2176359/Khalid-Sheikh-Mohammed-The-interrogator-who-made-him-talk.html.

McKernan, Bethan. "Assad 'Dropped 13,000 Barrel Bombs on Syria in 2016,' Watchdog Claims." *The Independent* (January 11, 2017). https://www.independent.co.uk/news/world/middle-east/bashar-al-assad-syria-president-regime-13000-barrel-bombs-rebels-aleppo-douma-2016-a7521656.html.

Middle East Media Research Institute. "Palestinian Authority TV Lauds President Abbas' Holocaust Denial PhD Thesis, Terror Attacks Launched from Lebanon." July 26, 2018. https://www.memri.org/reports/palestinian-authority-tv-lauds-president-abbas-holocaust-denial-phd-thesis-terror-attacks/.

National Review Editors. "Justice Prevailed." *National Review*, October 7, 2018. https://www.nationalreview.com/2018/10/brett-kavanaugh-confirmed-supreme-court-justice-prevailed/.

Nietzsche, Friedrich. *Beyond Good and Evil*. Translated by Helen Zimmern. 2013. Project Gutenberg EBook. https://www.gutenberg.org/files/4363/4363-h/4363-h.htm.

Pacepa, Ion. "Russian Footprints." *National Review*, August 24, 2006. https://www.nationalreview.com/2006/08/russian-footprints-ion-mihai-pacepa/.

Pacepa, Ion Mihai, with Ronald J Rychlak. *Disinformation: Former Spy Chief Reveals Secret Strategies for Undermining Freedom, Attacking Religion, and Promoting Terrorism*. Washington DC: WND Books, 2013.

Pluckrose, Helen, James A. Lindsay, and Peter Boghossian. "Academic Grievance Studies and the Corruption of Scholarship." *Areo Magazine*, October 2, 2018. https://areomagazine.com/2018/10/02/academic-grievance-studies-and-the-corruption-of-scholarship/.

Radwan, Ismail. "Reward and Honor Bestowed on Muslim Martyrs." Official Palestinian Authority TV (2001), video at *Palestinian Media Watch*. http://palwatch.org/main.aspx?fi=111&fld_id=111&doc_id=958/.

Ratzinger, Josef. "Cardinal Ratzinger on Europe's Crisis of Culture." Catholic Education Resource Center (2005). http://www.catholiceducation.org/en/culture/catholic-contributions/cardinal-ratzinger-on-europe-s-crisis-of-culture.html/.

Reeve, Simon. "Olympics Massacre: Munich—The Real Story." *The Independent*, January 22, 2006. http://www.independent.co.uk/news/world/europe/olympics-massacre-munich-the-real-story-5336955.html/.

Rudner, Martin. "One Official's 'Refugee' is Another's 'Terrorist.'" *National Post*, January 17, 2006.

Shane, Scott. "Inside a 9/11 Mastermind's Interrogation." *The New York Times*, June 22, 2008. https://www.nytimes.com/2008/06/22/washington/22ksm.html/.

Siems, Larry. "Inside the CIA's Black Site Torture Room." *The Guardian*, October 9, 2017. https://www.theguardian.com/us-news/ng-interactive/2017/oct/09/cia-torture-black-site-enhanced-interrogation/.

Taylor, Adam. "Trump Said He Would Take Out the Families of ISIS Fighters." *The Washington Post*, May 27, 2017. https://www.washingtonpost.com/news/worldviews/wp/2017/05/27/trump-said-he-would-take-out-the-families-of-isis-fighters-did-an-airstrike-in-syria-do-just-that/?noredirect=on&utm_term=.a8547fd77f03/.

Wildman, Wesley. "Review of *The Courage to Be* by Paul Tillich." *Paul Tillich Resources*. http://people.bu.edu/wwildman/tillich/resources/review_tillich-paul_couragetobe.htm (1994)/.

Yousef, Mosab. *Son of Hamas: A Gripping Account of Terror, Betrayal, Political Intrigue, and Unthinkable Choices*. Kindle ed. Carol Stream, IL: Tyndale Momentum, 2010.

Zenko, Micah. "Obama's Embrace of Drone Strikes Will Be a Lasting Legacy." *The New York Times*, January 12, 2016. https://www.nytimes.com/roomfordebate/2016/01/12/reflecting-on-obamas-presidency/obamas-embrace-of-drone-strikes-will-be-a-lasting-legacy/.

5

Narratives of Non-Violence
The Catholic Response to Italian Left-Wing Terrorism

Marco Ceccarelli

Throughout the 1970s, a type of radical left-wing terrorism took root in Italy. It was led by a violent organization named the Red Brigades. Urged on by a sense of dissatisfaction with what they saw as a corrupt and unjust Italian government, a number of young Italian men and women took their 1968 student protests and belief in popular radical ideologies a step further and opted for armed struggle against the state. Many of the individuals who took up arms had come from a Catholic upbringing. For those who turned their back on the teachings of the Church, it had become a matter of rejecting a set of "outdated principles" that they felt had become irrelevant in a world filled with malice and injustice. For others, it had been a matter of transition from the parish to the violent revolutionary organization; the sense of justice was still there, but the means by which to achieve it had changed. Witnessing a number of its subjects join the ranks of terrorist organizations, and called to take action by families of kidnapped victims or by kidnapped victims themselves, the

Catholic Church attempted to mediate with terrorists through methods of non-violence. This talk will analyze the Church's response to the extremist left-wing political violence in the so-called Italian "Years of Lead."

I am writing to you, men of the Red Brigades . . . you, unknown and implacable adversaries of this deserving and innocent man, on my knees I beg you, free Aldo Moro, simply and without conditions. —Pope Paul VI, letter to the Red Brigades, April 21, 1978[1]

Introduction

WHEN ANALYZING THE AFTERMATH of the 1968 protest movements within a context of Italian sociopolitical history, one cannot avoid documenting the terrorist violence which swept over Italy throughout the 1970s and, to a lesser degree, the 1980s. Led by the radical left-wing terrorist organization the Red Brigades, Italian terrorism primarily took aim at the Italian government yet often struck at the heart of Italian Catholicism in its political, religious, and intellectual forms. This presented a two-fold challenge for the Catholic Church. On the one hand, a number of Catholic politicians and journalists, presidents of Catholic organizations, and Catholic intellectuals came within the firing line of terrorists. On the other, some of the terrorists who planned attacks against state representatives came from a Catholic upbringing and had been schooled according to Catholic youth programs. In a move away from the non-violent teachings of their youth, they gravitated towards an ideology that conflated Marxist and Catholic beliefs and sought to bring about change through violence. As it witnessed these events with growing concern, the Church in Italy played an active and at times public role in stemming the political violence. This chapter will analyze the Church's response to the challenge of extremist left-wing political violence during the so-called Italian "Years of Lead."[2]

---

1. Paul VI, *Lettera del Santo Padre Paolo VI alle Brigate Rosse*. Unless otherwise noted, all translations are my own.

2. A reference to the bullets used throughout this period of frequent shootings in Italy.

Historical Context

By 1978, known as the year in which terrorism in Italy reached its apogee, the nation found itself in a state of crisis. Economically, Italy suffered from considerable inflation problems, low growth, capital shortages, and increased unemployment rates. On the political front, the Catholic-inspired Christian Democracy (*Democrazia Cristiana*) had been the most influential party of the last thirty years. It was led by former Prime Minister Aldo Moro, who in the second half of the decade had established an unpopular link with the Italian Communist Party (*Partito Comunista Italiano*). His attempt to form a coalition with this party, also known as the Historic Compromise, aimed at tackling the crisis of Italian democracy as the Christian Democrats were blamed for the economic and social downfalls Italy was experiencing. This political move lost the Christian Democracy strong support from traditional Catholic entities, making the ground on which it stood even shakier. As noted by Bartoli, at the beginning of the 1970s the Christian Democratic Party lacked coherence and power.[3]

In order to understand why terrorism broke out in the early years of this new decade there is a need to observe the development of social unrest in the student movements of 1968 and the student–worker movements of 1969. In her book *Autoritratto di gruppo,* historian Luisa Passerini offers a detailed overview of how she lived the creative and communicative explosion of 1968 in Italy. Through the reports of other individuals who shared a similar experience, Passerini explores themes regarding the construction of a political identity that spread among young people throughout the 1960s. Her discourse often returns to the concept of awareness. She affirms that throughout the nation "passed a desire to seek freedom and to mature the relationship with knowledge."[4] Passerini recalls how a desire to be politically aware and politically active matured among young people. Much of Italy's youth felt called to change society and to redefine the political and social *milieu* in which they found themselves.[5] Out of this great eruption of creativity and political awareness emerged the student movements of 1968. Mass demonstrations, protests against political entities, the refusal to be taught or examined by teachers and professors,

---

3. Bartoli, *Gli anni della tempesta*, 177.
4. Passerini. *Autoritratto di gruppo*, 50.
5. Passerini. *Autoritratto di gruppo*, 50

and the temporary occupation of schools and universities[6] would characterize a period of political and social upheaval.

The student protests of 1968 were as disruptive as they were contagious. In the years that followed, students influenced workers from large corporate factories such as Fiat, Sit-Siemens, Alfa Romeo, and Pirelli to join their protest and fight for workers' rights. As the decade of the 1960s closed and the student movements faded, many workers who had been encouraged to protest against their managers for improved working conditions and higher salaries had begun to fight for themselves. Thus, the turbulent autumn of 1969, also known as the Warm Autumn (*Autunno Caldo*) saw the birth of a worker–student movement. A participant in both the student and worker–student movements, Luigi Bobbio, later commented on this new strange set of circumstances:

> In the 1968–69 academic year there were [student protest] groups but the movement was no longer there. At the same time the worker struggles moved ahead. Thus, a type of attraction developed, something which we had tried to avoid. The pole shifted there. Then, after the collapse of the student movement in the university, it was as if the movement had produced militants that had nothing to do. We were political militants but had lost our objective. Eventually, we ended up concentrating our efforts towards Fiat[7].

Many young people like Bobbio stationed themselves in front of large factories inviting fellow "proletarians"[8] to seek better working conditions and rebel against company executives. This fuelled the growing resentment and distrust towards the government among both students and workers. A famous slogan that year—"Workers and Students United in Battle" (*Operai e studenti uniti nella lotta*)—signalled the strong alliance created between the two groups.[9] Defamatory campaigns were also frequently used to unveil the corrupt and illegitimate proceedings of the ruling elite. Subsequently, small radical left-wing political groups which

---

6. During these years of social unrest, it was customary for students to temporarily seize, or "occupy" buildings such as schools and universities in order to make requests to the ruling elite for improved conditions.

7. Passerini, *Autoritratto di gruppo*, 132.

8. The use of Leninist–Marxist language such as "proletarian" or "comrade" was common among left-wing student–worker circles of the 1970s.

9. Scalzone, *Biennio Rosso*, 30.

came to be known as proletarian youth movements[10] began forming, along with the extra-parliamentary Left[11] (*sinistra extra-parlamentare*), also known as "the autonomy" (*l'autonomia*).

The significance of extra-parliamentary circles for what would be the rise of terrorist groups was that they gave some organization and perspective to the sense of rebellion present among young Italians. Managed by intellectual leaders able to shape and remodel revolutionary ideas, these groups organized masses of students and workers to protest against the government and its way of ruling the country. Often seen as a pre-recruitment ground for those intending to move on to political violence, groups of the extra-parliamentary Left offered an education based on radical left-wing principles that helped young people mature their revolutionary ideals and impulses. Some of these left-wing organizations went by the name of Partisan Action Groups (*Gruppi D'azione Partigiana*), Metropolitan Political Collective (*Collettivo Politico Metropolitano*)—a group inside which the men and women who founded The Red Brigades operated—Worker's Power (*Potere Operaio*), Worker's Autonomy (*Autonomia Operaia*) and Continuous Struggle (*Lotta Continua*).[12] The latter seems to have been the most influential group. It was attended by nearly all of the young people that nursed a desire to progress onto political violence. In 1972, the group's national conference in the town of Rimini had assigned a relevant role to marshal bodies, stressing the need for revolutionary violence by both the "masses" and the "vanguard."[13]

The Catholic Church in the Firing Line

The years of terrorism in Italy were inaugurated by an infamous event which still remains shrouded in mystery. Seventeen people were killed and eighty-seven were wounded when a bomb placed in Milan's National Bank of Agriculture exploded during trading hours on December 12,

---

10. Proletarian youth movements, or youth groups, were loosely organized associations that organized protests and demonstrations and were known for their encouragement of rebellious behaviour among young people. Youth groups were found both on the left and right. For more information see Meade, *Red Brigades*, 25–26, 28–30.

11. Extra-parliamentary refers to groups which rejected the elected government and worked through different means ranging from mass demonstrations to acts of violence For more information see della Porta, *Social Movements*.

12. della Porta, *Social Movements*, 89–91.

13. della Porta, *Social Movements*, 92.

1969. The event would be named "The Tragedy of Piazza Fontana," a reference to the public square in which the bank was located. While no one claimed responsibility for the massacre, it is alleged that the attack was organized by a little-known right-wing organization named New Order (*Ordine Nuovo*). From this day on, the frequency of terrorist incidents was significantly heightened. Expropriations of boutiques, dispossessions, kneecappings,[14] assassinations, bombings in public places and on trains, shootouts with the police, kidnappings, and shootings amounted to more than fourteen thousand acts of political violence in the 1970s alone.[15] In the firing line were politicians and magistrates as well as journalists, policemen, security guards and low-ranking employees in the prison system, businessmen, and individuals who held any kind of executive function in factories or workplaces where workers could be exploited.[16] Driven by utopian ideals of freedom and sustained by left-wing philosophies, the ultimate goal of these terrorists was to cause a revolution.

Despite the scarcity of research surrounding the Catholic Church's role and response during these years, a significantly high number of victims were targeted not only because of their ties to the government, but also because they were Catholic. As Cingolani notes, the Christian Democracy was the primary target of a radical left-wing type of terrorism that became stronger and more aggressive as the 1970s went on.[17] An example of a carefully chosen Catholic victim is academic and politician Vittorio Bachelet, who was murdered on February 12, 1980 by an armed group of the Red Brigades. Bachelet had been president of Catholic Action (*Azione Cattolica*)—a prominent Roman Catholic lay association—and had been a close friend of Pope Paul VI. In a similar way, the journalist and writer Walter Tobagi was murdered on May 28, 1980 for his role as journalist in charge of the terrorism section of the newspaper *Corriere della Sera*. Tobagi was also a Catholic intellectual who had dedicated a part of his career to the Catholic newspaper *Avvenire*.[18] The headquarters of the Christian Democracy, of its newspaper *La Discussione*, and of the Catholic movement "Communion and Liberation"

14. The term "kneecapping" refers to the practice of shooting enemies in the legs. It became a way for terrorists to warn their opponents.
15. Meade, *Red Brigades*, 36.
16. Tarrow, "Crisis, Crises or Transition," 178.
17. Cingolani, *La destra in armi*.
18. Durand, "I Cattolici," 97.

(*Comunione e Liberazione*) were repeatedly firebombed in the 1970s, as was the Catholic-democratic Cooperative Library of Brescia, "the heart of democratic Catholicism and birth place of Pope Paul VI."[19] The twofold aim of the Red Brigades was to spread a sense of terror within the country and to cripple certain elements of Catholic culture.

The event that managed to put both the government and the Italian Church on high alert was the kidnapping and eventual execution by the Red Brigades of Christian Democracy President Aldo Moro. Moro was kidnapped on his way to parliament on the morning of March 16, 1978. He was on his way to celebrating the Historic Compromise, an event that would be his defining political achievement. Moro's vehicle and the accompanying vehicles of his bodyguards were rammed on Rome's Via Fani before five bodyguards were gunned down in cold blood. President Moro was taken away, held captive in the basement of a secret household for fifty-five days, and subjected to a mock-trial by the terrorists' own so-called "people's court." He was eventually gunned down and his body was discovered in the boot of a car on Rome's Via Caetani. For the duration of his captivity, the Red Brigades negotiated with the Italian government in order to have some of their fellow terrorists released from prison. Secretly, they were hoping that the Italian proletariat class would revolt against the state and begin its own "armed struggle." The years of Italian terrorism, in fact, also came to be known as the years of the Armed Struggle (*Lotta Armata*).[20]

Throughout his captivity, Moro called on help from his colleagues in the Christian Democracy and from his friends. Among the latter was Pope Paul VI. The two were lifelong friends and had known each other from their participation in the group Federation of Catholic University Students (FUCI). The central role that the Church was being asked to play in this time of upheaval was becoming more of a reality. "Only Your Holiness can bring the right to life and moral rationality to the attention of the State,"[21] Moro wrote to Paul VI, attempting to urge the Vatican into persuading statesmen to do more to save his life. He was convinced that the Pope's intervention would have made a difference in an environment of heightened tension.

---

19. Durand, "I Cattolici," 97.
20. This term was and is still being used by terrorists, journalists, and historians.
21. Macchi, *Paolo VI*, 26.

Paul VI did intervene, albeit not in the way that Moro had suggested. On April 21, 1979, he addressed the following open letter directly to the Red Brigades:

> I am writing to you, men of the Red Brigades: return the Honourable Aldo Moro to his freedom, to his family and to his civil life. I do not know you, and I have no means to contact you. For this I am writing to you publicly, taking advantage of this window of time which remains before the death sentence which you have bestowed upon him is up. He, a good and honest man, whom no one can accuse of having committed any crime, neither of having lacked any form of social sensibility nor service to the cause of justice and to peaceful civil coexistence. I have no mandate to speak to you, and I am not bound by any private interests in his regard. But I love him as a member of the great human family, as a friend of student days and by a very special title as a brother in faith and son of the Church of Christ.
>
> It is in this supreme name of Christ that I make an appeal that you will certainly not ignore. You, unknown and implacable adversaries of this deserving and innocent man. On my knees I beg you, free Aldo Moro, simply and without conditions, not so much because of my humble and well-meaning intercession, but because he shares with you the common dignity of a brother in humanity. Men of the Red Brigades, grant me, the interpreter of the voices of so many of our fellow citizens, the hope that in your heart will triumph feelings of humanity. In prayer, and always loving you, I await proof of that.[22]

Despite this emphatic attempt to save Moro's life, the appeal fell on deaf ears and on May 9, 1978, Moro was executed. The Church's request that Moro be released "without condition" surprised many, and raised a polemical debate in Italy about whether the Pope had in fact compromised any remaining attempts at negotiating with the terrorists.[23] What many in Italy saw as a feeble humanitarian appeal was said to have interfered with the prisoner exchange program that the government had considered but seemed more and more unwilling to pursue. Giovagnoli points out that the Pope's message was also seen by some as an act of surrender in front of an enemy trying to bring governing authorities to their knees.[24] Moro himself seemed dissatisfied with the Pope's intervention,

22. Paul VI, *Lettera del Santo Padre Paolo VI alle Brigate Rosse*.
23. Giovagnoli, *Il caso Moro*, 199.
24. Giovagnoli, *Il caso Moro*, 199.

as stated in a note later discovered by police: "the Pope has done very little."[25] Could an alliance between state and Church authorities have done more? Other attempts of the Church at gaining Moro's freedom are discussed in work by Giovagnoli.[26]

It is worth mentioning that this was not the first time that the Vatican had directed its attention to the Moro case; nor was it the first time it had intervened in a developing situation of terrorism. In an act reminiscent of Pope Paul VI's 1977 attempt to offer himself to the hijackers of a West German airliner in exchange for the eighty-six hostages on board, three Italian Bishops had offered themselves as prisoners in exchange for Aldo Moro.[27] These were Bishop of Ivrea and director of *Pax Christi* Monsignor Luigi Bettazzi; Bishop of Livorno, Monsignor Alberto Ablondi; and Auxiliary Bishop of Rome, Monsignor Clemente Riva.[28] The suggested request had the potential to be one of the Church's greatest acts of charity towards an Italian politician during the years of Italian terrorism. The Vatican eventually vetoed the risky exchange. Once again, this reveals how closely involved the Church was with the state in this moment of crisis. Part of this dedication to a peaceful resolution was linked to the sense of trust it had gained from both politicians and young activists. The Church was caught between a state unable to deal with the powerful political upheaval of student movements and an exasperated student body fixed in its distrust and scepticism of a corrupt government. As Durand claims, the Church sought to play the role of "*defensor civitatis*"[29] during this time of involvement in Italy's political affairs.[30]

Catholics Caught Up in the Violence

Of equal concern for the Church during the years of Italian terrorism was the number of individuals with a Catholic education who had joined the ranks of terrorist organizations. Many of the participants in the 1968 student protests had been members of Catholic groups and associations

---

25. Giovagnoli, *Il caso Moro*, 200.
26. Giovagnoli, *Il caso Moro*, 200.
27. *New York Times*, "Pope Restates Hostage Offer."
28. Durand, "I Cattolici," 99.
29. The term historically applied to the official created in the later Roman Empire as the defender of the city or people.
30. Durand, "I Cattolici," 98.

such as Catholic Action (*Azione Cattolica*), Catholic University Federation of Italy (*Federazione Universitaria Cattolica Italiana*), Christian Associations for Italian Workers (*Associazioni Cristiane Lavoratori Italiani*), and the Scout movement. By the same token, Berretta emphasizes that that the wave of protests in Italy had a religious dimension. Some of the first universities and faculties which became epicentres of the student protest were either Catholic universities like the University of the Sacred Heart of Milan (*Università Cattolica del Sacro Cuore di Milano*) or, like the Faculty of Sociology at Trent University, had been established by the Christian Democracy in the early 1960s.[31] Prominent Catholics—such as the rector of the University of the Sacred Heart and student leader Mario Capanna—often led the protests. Some of the most active protesters from Trent University were also Catholics: one of these, Margherita Cagol, would go on to become one of leaders of the Red Brigades. Student protests were regular and habitual and for some had become seamlessly intertwined with their religious life. There are records of an event in the main Cathedral of Trento in March 1968 where a group of students took part in Mass but at the moment of the homily stood up, processed to the square outside to take part in a protest, and re-entered the church to take the Eucharist. Meanwhile, in the same year, clashes with police became frequent. An incident in Lecce also saw a group from the Catholic University Federation of Italy temporarily occupy the university chapel to prevent the bishop from celebrating the Easter Mass.[32]

What pushed Catholic students to take such an active part in the protest movement? Orsini points to a growing hostility towards capitalism fuelled by the popularity of Leninist-Marxist ideology.[33] Intertwined with this was an increasingly popular literal interpretation of the Gospel and support for the Church's discourse against poverty in underdeveloped countries. Catholics looked to Pope Paul VI's Encyclical of the Development of Peoples, *Populorum Progressio*, which began with the following statement:

> The progressive development of peoples is an object of deep interest and concern to the Church. This is particularly true in the case of those peoples who are trying to escape the ravages of hunger, poverty, endemic disease and ignorance; of those who

---

31. Beretta, *Cantavamo dio è morto*, 14.
32. Durand, "I Cattolici," 92
33. Orsini, *Anatomy of the Red Brigades*.

are seeking a larger share in the benefits of civilization and a more active improvement of their human qualities; of those who are consciously striving for fuller growth.[34]

The dream of a new society loomed. For many people, the dream was based on a reconciliation between Catholicism and Marxism which did not exclude class struggle and, controversially, the use of violence. Not by chance was the revolutionary Columbian priest Camillo Torres, who died in his first combat experience in 1966, somewhat of an icon for a number of students.[35] In response to the momentum gained by this conflation of Marxist and Catholic ideals, some of which justified the use of violence, the Vatican began to make its position on the issue very clear. During a trip to Colombia in August 1968, Paul VI exhorted his listeners to "not put your trust in violence and revolution; these concepts are contrary to the Christian spirit, and they can delay that social improvement to which you legitimately aspire."[36] The Pope did not fail to emphasize that poverty, injustice, and oppression needed to be condemned, yet this needed to be done within the context of what he called a Christian "dynamism of love" within which there was no room for violence.

While the lack of oral history and academic work relating to the Church and Italian terrorism makes it difficult to conduct effective studies on the violent role played by Catholics, Peletier's portrayal of this moment as one of "Catholic crisis" and "Catholic dissent" offers valuable insights. The more popular and public terrorist organizations during the 1970s were radical left-wing organizations. The ideological makeup of these groups was Marxist, or a Marxism influenced by Leninism. It is to this intermingling of Marxist and Catholic culture and the shared ideals of solidarity and service to the poor and marginalized that we must look if we are to shed light on why many were led away from Catholic principles of nonviolence and towards radical left-wing ideals of political violence. As one ex-terrorist put it: "a certain type of violence could cohabit with these [catholic] principles, as long as it was used in defence of the weak."[37]

---

34. Paul VI, *Populorum progressio*.
35. Durand, "I Cattolici," 93.
36. Paul VI, *Discourse to the Colombian "Campesinos,"* 178–81.
37. Berretta, *Cantavamo*, 145–46.

The Church as Mediator

Another underreported aspect of the Church's role during the years of Italian terrorism is its social influence in the aftermath of the violence. Historically, one skill the Church has mastered in times of conflict and war is the ability to accompany people experiencing grief. It does this through counselling, opportunities for repentance, offering people closure, reconciliation, and in certain cases helping them in the process of forgiveness. The 1970s and particularly the 1980s spurred the Church into action as a number of people—victims, relatives of victims, and terrorists themselves—sought counsel from the Church in the wake of traumatic events. Proof of this can be found in the active participation of the Vatican throughout the Moro ordeal, in the appeals to reconciliation and forgiveness from the families of the victims, and in the work of Catholic chaplains working within those prisons that detained terrorists.

The Church even went as far as mediating between the terrorists and the Italian state, as an interview with one of the imprisoned founders of the Red Brigades, Alberto Franceschini, attests. Franceschini, who had participated in a hunger strike while in prison, indicated that the Church's human rights campaign during the hunger strikes was an important factor in his decision to eventually "dissociate from the armed struggle."[38]

> Perhaps we would have died, or they would have force fed us, I don't know. What I do know is that our change of perspective regarding the armed struggle and the ensuing decision to dissociate ourselves was strongly linked to that episode and to the Church's efforts to lay emphasis on human rights. In that condition we became aware of a nonviolent path to the affirmation of our rights. We were able to walk that path thanks to people such as Don Salvatore [the prison chaplain]. I am certain that terrorism's history would have been different if in Badu' and Carros, and in many other Italian prisons, there would not have been someone capable of welcoming our cry and transforming it into something positive.[39]

Franceschini's testimony suggests the Church was successful in its mediation efforts. He later claims to have found in the Church an

---

38. The expression "to dissociate oneself from the armed struggle" (*dissociarsi dalla lotta armata*) was frequently used by those terrorists who, often in prison, would renounce the willingness to use revolutionary violence.

39. Franceschini, as cited in Valle, *Parole, opere e omissioni*, 209.

interlocutor with whom his requests for a dignified treatment of imprisoned terrorists could be heard.[40] Much like the situation in twentieth-century terrorist violence in Ireland, the Church was seen as a powerful institution that terrorists turned to in the face of an immovable government. Furthermore, Franceschini's reaction demonstrates that the Church's approach to combating terrorism, based on dialogue and the respect of the human person, could in fact produce positive results.

Franceschini's declaration can be grouped with practical acts of dissociation from other Italian terrorists. In June 1984 a young man handed three suitcases filled with weapons to the secretary of the Archbishop of Milan Carlo Maria Martini.[41] When questioned about the rationale behind this act, Sergio Segio, a member of the terrorist organization responsible for the handover of the weapons, responded by defining the move as "a handover into the hands of the Milanese Church, and its Archdiocese, for the work of human and social, rather than political, reconciliation it undertook with all of us." Segio criticized the government's attempts to distort the deed and acknowledged the success of the Italian Church's humanitarian efforts during this time:

> They [the Italian state] also interfered on the handover of weapons. They said that this was yet another demonstration of our rejection of the state. Ours was interpreted as yet another subversive gesture. On the contrary, we recognised the Church as having a fundamental role of understanding and availability in our regards . . . there was a possibility of dialogue without immediate judgment and condemnation. With other forces of society, those of a left-wing nature included, condemnation always came before dialogue. Instead, with certain members who represented the Church, there was a reversed approach.[42]

The handing over of weapons, along with this testimony, confirms that the Church was one of the paths through which terrorists moved away from urban guerrilla warfare. This is also proof that the Church's pro-dialogue and nonviolent approach to terrorism could be effective.

Towards the end of the 1970s, and particularly after the kidnapping and killing of Aldo Moro, there was a significant drop in terrorist attacks in Italy. The Catholic Church, however, would go on to experience

---

40. Valle, *Parole, opere e omissioni*, 210.
41. Valle, *Parole, opere e omissioni*, 219.
42. Valle, *Parole, opere e omissioni*, 222.

political violence first hand when gunman Mahmet Ali Acğa attempted to shoot Pope John Paul II in St. Peter's square on the evening of May 13, 1981. This event led the Church to work on its own official condemnation of terrorism and eventually include a passage on this topic in the Catechism of the Church: "*Terrorism* which threatens wounds, and kills indiscriminately is gravely against justice and charity."[43] In the new millennium, the events of 9/11 and subsequent rise in terrorist attacks throughout the world brought the Church to an even more categorical judgment. Beginning with Pope John Paul II's statement on January 1, 2002, that terrorism is "itself a true crime against humanity,"[44] Popes have repeatedly condemned terrorism as a violation of human rights.

The Path towards Forgiveness and Reconciliation

Many lay and clerical Catholic figures remained close to the relatives of the victims of Italian terrorism in the aftermath of the assassinations. While the topic of forgiveness and reconciliation was a difficult one, the Church played a central role in bringing it to the fore as an option open to those grieving for lost loved ones. The reports emerging from some of the funeral masses for the victims demonstrate that some were helped by the Church in this process. For instance, Aldo Moro's wife, Elenora Moro, voiced this prayer during the mass celebrated only eight days after the discovery of her husband's body:

> For the instigators, the executors and the supporters of this horrible crime, we pray. For those who out of jealousy, cowardice, fear or stupidity, condemned an innocent man to death, we pray. For me and for my children, that the sense of desperation and rage that we feel now may be transformed in tears of forgiveness, we pray.

In a similar fashion, at the funeral of his father on February 14, 1980, Giovanni Bachelet expressed himself in this way:

> We want to pray also for those who struck my father because, without taking anything away from the process of justice which must triumph, on our mouths there will always be forgiveness, and never revenge, always life and never the desire for the death of others.

---

43. *Catechism of the Catholic Church*, 2297.
44. John Paul II, *No Peace Without Justice, No Justice Without Forgiveness*.

Conclusion

The Catholic Church struggled significantly during the years of Italian terrorism. Pope Paul VI passed away only three months after the death of Aldo Moro, raising questions as to just how much his friend's death weighed on him. The Church was caught in a predicament as it saw a number of its faithful targeted and killed because of who and what they represented, and another number abandon their Catholic beliefs to follow revolutionary ideologies and join the ranks of terrorist organizations. On this shaky ground, it attempted to tame national conflict by at times taking on the role of mediator between terrorists and statesmen. Sometimes called upon by both these groups to support and stand by their cause, the Church responded by emphasizing its message of nonviolence and by insisting that the dignity of the human person be respected, regardless of the circumstances. Despite its failures to stem the violence, the Church succeeded in its role as safety anchor for both grieving souls needing moral and spiritual support and for those who, disillusioned by revolutionary ideology, saw it as their only way towards repentance.

Bibliography

Bartoli, Domenico. *Gli anni della tempesta*. Milan: Nuova, 1981.
Beretta, Roberto. *Cantavamo dio è morto. Il '68 dei Cattolici*. Casale Monferrato: Piemme, 2008.
Catechism of the Catholic Church. Homebush: St Pauls, 1994.
Cingolani, Giorgio. *La destra in armi: Neofascisti Italiani tra ribellismo ed eversione 1977–1982*. Rome: Riunit, 1996.
Della Porta, Donatella. *Social Movements, Political Violence and the State: A Comparative Analysis of Italy and Germany*. Cambridge Studies in Comparative Politics. Cambridge: Cambridge University Press, 1995.
Drake, Richard. "The Red Brigades and the Italian Political Tradition." In *Terrorism in Europe*, edited by Yonah Alexander and Kenneth A. Myers, 102–39. London: Croom Helm, 1982.
Durand, Jean-Dominique. "I Cattolici di fronte alla violenza terroristica durante gli anni di piombo." In *Il libro degli anni di piombo: Storia e memoria del terrorismo Italiano*, edited by Marc Lazar and Marie-Anne Matard-Bonucci. Milan: Rizzoli, 2010.
Giovagnoli, Agostino. *Il caso Moro*. Bologna: Mulino, 2005.
John Paul II. *No Peace without Justice, No Justice without Forgiveness: Message for the Celebration of the World Day of Peace* (2002). http://www.vatican.va/holy_father/john_paul_ii/messages/peace/documents/hf_jpii_mes_20011211xxxv-world-day-for-peace_en.html. Sec 4.

Macchi, Pasquale. *Paolo VI e la tragedia di Moro. 55 giorni di ansie, tentativi, speranze e assurda crudeltà*. Milan: Rusconi, 1998.

Meade, Robert C. *Red Brigades: The Story of Italian Terrorism*. London: Macmillan Press, 1990.

New York Times. "Pope Restates Hostage Offer." *The New York Times*, October 20, 1977). https://www.nytimes.com/1977/10/20/archives/pope-restates-hostage-offer.html.

Orsini, Alessandro. *Anatomy of the Red Brigades: The Religious Mind-Set of Modern Terrorists*. Ithaca, NY: Cornell University Press, 2011.

Passerini, Luisa. *Autoritratto di gruppo*. Florence: Giunti Barbèra, 1988.

Paul VI, Pope. "Discourse to the Colombian 'Campesinos.'" In *Paolo VI pellegrino apostolico: Discorsi e messaggi*, edited by Romeo Panicro. Brescia-Rome: Istituto Paulo VI-Edizioni Sadium, 2001.

———. *Lettera del Santo Pader Paolo VI alle Brigate Rosse* (1978). https://w2.vatican.va/content/paul-vi/it/letters/1978/documents/hf_p-vi_let_19780422_brigate-rosse.html.

———. *Populorum progressio* (1967). http://w2.vatican.va/content/paul-vi/en/encyclicals/documents/hf_p-vi_enc_26031967_populorum.html.

Scalzone, Oreste. *Biennio Rosso*. Milan: Sugarco, 1988.

Tarrow, Sydney. "Crisis, Crises or Transition?" In *Italy in Transition: Conflict and Consensus,* edited by Peter Lange and Sydney Tarrow. Abingdon: Cass, 1980.

Valle, Annachiara. *Parole opere e omisisoni: La chiesa nell'Italia degli anni di piombo*. Milan: Rizzoli, 2008.

6

Christ in Hyperreality

Cultural Marxism, *Kulturkritik*, and Fake News

MATTHEW JOHN PAUL TAN

In this paper I will put forward a partial response to the derision of "Cultural Marxism" occurring in commentary—often Catholic commentary. I argue that despite the clear limitations of the Frankfurt School, Cultural Marxism in its technical usage has been a salient mode of interrogating the material foundations of what we now call postmodern culture, providing in particular an unusually insightful descriptor for contemporary forms of consumer behavior, including the consumption of images. More importantly I argue that some aspects of cultural critique describe consumer behavior as a form of soulcraft, thus providing a useful complement to a distinctly theological critique of postmodern culture as the normalization of idolatry. This becomes a particularly salient path of critique of what Jean Baudrillard called "The Age of the Simulacra," where simulation is now the primary reality by which consumers engage with and evaluate the world around them. The hallmarks of simulation include the rise of the phenomena of "fake news" and "alternative facts." To establish my case, I will outline the salient thread of *Kulturkritik* dealing with simulation, with particular reference to the work of Guy Debord and Jean Baudrillard. I will highlight how this thread of *Kulturkritik* not only provides a compelling description of a person's relationship to simulation, but also how simulations have significance in fusing divinity with history—a fusion that ends up dissolving the real for the sake of the simulation. Before concluding, I will also look at the limitations of this *Kulturkritik* which should temper theology's full partnership with this thread of the Frankfurt School, in spite of the useful evangelical inroads for the former carved out by the latter.

Introduction

THIS CHAPTER WILL LOOK into one of the great bogies mentioned with a clear air of disdain in Catholic online comboxes: Cultural Marxism. While the unrest of 1968 might make this disdain understandable, it must be remembered that the vice of wrath operates by taking an understandable response, blowing it out of proportion, and applying the response to things well beyond the original grievance. What this means is that nowadays, the term Cultural Marxism is used as a catchall label for anything that people dislike.

Everything that I do not like is Cultural Marxism—a mirror image of the equally unhelpful "everything I do not like is neoconservatism." In the process, people are mislabelled and histories are erroneously catalogued. More importantly, however, when the use of the term Cultural Marxism morphs from a way of analyzing the material processes underpinning consumer culture—what the Frankfurt School called *Kulturkritik*—to an all-encompassing conspiracy theory involving faceless men and their secret plans to destroy Western civilization, we ignore insights that understand the material processes taking place in contemporary culture. When Christians join in the derision of Cultural Marxism—and it is arguable that Christians make up the vast bulk of the voices of critique of it—they miss an opportunity to understand how those material processes can also be obstacles to the life of faith.

My aim is to tease out just one insight from two figures in the French strand of Cultural Marxism, which is distinct from but parallels the work of the Frankfurt School. The two figures are Guy Debord and Jean Baudrillard, who became known for their respective analyses of the cultural power of images in creating the cultural condition which Baudrillard would later call "hyperreality"; that is, the condition where images become more real than reality itself. In the course of this chapter I hope to do four things. First, I hope to outline Debord's and Baudrillard's warning to their readers that hyperreality is not only an immanent cultural problem to be endured but also a form of idolatry to be resisted. Secondly, I will bring these insights to bear on the contemporary cultural phenomenon of "alternative facts" or its more popular mirror image, "fake news." Third, while seemingly enthused by the insights, I will also highlight the limits of the full acceptance by Christians of the cultural critique of Cultural Marxism. Finally, I will articulate a liturgical site of resistance to hyperreality.

Commodity and Simulacrum

Before going further, we need to ask ourselves what our culture's relationship with images is. At its crassest level, we can say we are living in a cultural situation that has become saturated with images. Not a day goes by without one being bombarded by a graphic, a logo, or a flashing sign pushing a thing or a service into our collective face via billboards, sides of vehicles, or our phones. I cannot even respond to nature's call without the walls calling out to me with the latest offer I cannot refuse. A study conducted in 1994 indicated that the average American teenager was exposed to sixteen thousand images on any given day[1]—and this was before the age of the smartphone. A more recent study coming out of the University of Washington indicated that by age eighteen, a person would have been exposed to 350,000 images from television advertising alone (not including images seen in movies, computers, mobile devices, billboards, and schools).[2] Whether we are aware of it or not, or whether we like it or not, our world is awash with signs and symbols that are disseminated in every manner of social and private space—images which crash onto our collective imaginations at an ever-accelerating pace.

The *degree* of image saturation should lead us to the more interesting question of the cultural *effects* that this saturation can have, and this

---

1. Savan, *The Sponsored Life*, 1.
2. Teen Futures Media Network, "Media Literacy."

is where *Kulturkritik* comes in. At the heart of *Kulturkritik* is the analysis of the cultural effects of the modern process of commodification, the turning of things into a unit of exchange. At the risk of oversimplification, Marxist analysis sees modern commodities—the products of modern manufacturing—as entities sundered from the craftsman and communities that made them. In order to be saleable entities, commodities end up carrying a cultural capital that comes with industrial manufacture and commercial distribution. This cultural capital is an image of the commodity as having self-evident or self-contained value. For Marx, a commodity is thus a thing with an image fused to it.[3] But Marx goes further, arguing that this technique, rather than turning commodities into a sign of human control over things, actually requires a symbolic power to be asserted over its creator, instilling in that creator not only an image of the commodity, but also an image of the world around him or her. More specifically, the commodity "preinterprets" our lives before we enter into it, regardless of whether that part of our life is in turn part of an economic exchange.[4] Commodification emphasizes some aspects of the thing being commodified (usually surface features), hides other aspects (usually the conditions of the production of those surface features), and transforms our perceptions of the thing we behold (usually the meaning of those surface features). Commodification is the production of illusion, but Marx goes further to speak of this illusion as "religious." This link between religious and the commodified will become relevant and will be elaborated upon later.

Currently, we are talking about the production of tangible goods such as tables and chairs, though we must be aware that these "tangibles" also have "intangible" images attached to them. What happens, then, when the intangible good—the image—ends up becoming similarly turned into a commodity? It is here that our consideration of Baudrillard and Debord comes in. In 1967, Guy Debord published his landmark *The Society of the Spectacle,* which followed in the footsteps of another work in the tradition of the Frankfurt School, Herbert Marcuse's *One-Dimensional Man,*[5] which was first published in 1964. In *One-Dimensional Man,* Marcuse looks at the effects of commodities in what he calls "mass culture" (this is the postwar manufacturing boom), which flooded

3. On this see especially Miller, *Consuming Religion,* 36.
4. Miller, *Consuming Religion,* 37.
5. Marcuse, *One-Dimensional Man.*

the material world with cars, washing machines, hi-fi equipment, and the like at levels not seen in previous generations. Like Marx, Marcuse argues that commodities, and the processes that create these commodities (manufacturing, standardization, mass manufacture, and distribution, etc.) end up constraining man's freedom and agency rather than expanding it, with the standardizing of modes of economy activity simultaneously standardizing the horizons of thought. Commodities, as the embodiment of industrial technique, have come to frame the way people relate to the world and to each other.[6] This might all sound very similar to Marx, except for one thing. Consumers, says Marcuse, have come to identify so closely with what they consume that their metaphysical and even spiritual universe has become framed by commodities. Consumers, says Marcuse, "find their soul in their automobile, hi-fi set, split-level home, kitchen equipment."[7]

In 1967, Debord would take a similar path of *Kulturkritik* and apply it to the visual commodity. Paralleling Marcuse's observations of the colonizing power of commodities, Debord writes in *The Society of the Spectacle* that images as visual commodities have the mobilizing power they now have because "the commodity [in general] has attained the total occupation of social life. The relation to the commodity is not only visible, but one no longer sees anything but it: the world one sees is its world."[8] We start to see everything in terms set by commodities as a unit of exchange, and so every social interaction from our friendships, families, church, and personal life is demarcated in terms of trade and exchange, with accompanying cost–benefit analysis. Set in this context, images are not mere visual deception, a means to distract oneself from the real world. Rather, since they have become "a means of unification . . . . the focal point of all vision and consciousness,"[9] images have actually become the means by which one sees what counts as the real world.

As the 1980s began, Baudrillard would write another key work in this vein of cultural critique, namely *Simulacra and Simulation*, which builds on a project that he started with the 1968 publication of his doctoral thesis under the title *A System of Objects*. In *Simulacra and Simulation*, Baudrillard notes a further development in the condition that Debord

---

6. Marcuse, *One-Dimensional Man*, 3–21; 127–46.
7. Marcuse, *One-Dimensional Man*, 11.
8. Debord, *Society of the Spectacle*, 21.
9. Debord, *Society of the Spectacle*, 7.

describes in *Society of the Spectacle*. Recall that Debord argues that visual commodities have acquired great mobilizing power because commodities in general have had great mobilizing power. What is important to note is that back then, Debord's conception of the image still retained a presumed exchangeability between the image and the thing the image represented. In other words, the image got its power from the fact that it was a *placeholder* that could later be exchanged for a tangible reality. The sign was substantially linked to the signified. On the other hand, Baudrillard's analysis of the visual commodity is set against the backdrop of what he terms "the age of the simulacra." Why he uses this term becomes clear when you realize that by the time we get to the 1980s, visual media has become mainstreamed, and with this mainstreaming comes a greater degree of media saturation than what one would see in Debord's time. Awash with images, and with representations quickly outnumbering the things being represented, Baudrillard argues that the link between the sign and the signified starts to break down. In Baudrillard's words, the sign is "never exchanged for the real, but exchanged for itself, in an uninterrupted circuit without reference or circumference."[10] In other words, the sign can now be disconnected from the signified, and the image is no longer the facsimile of the real thing. It has become the *replacement* of the real thing. Reality is now being substituted by "a network of incessant, unreal circulation . . . an immense scenario and perpetual pan-shot."[11] Under such conditions "simulation is . . . the generation by models of a real without origin or reality: a hyperreal."[12] Baudrillard's notion of the "generation by models of a real without origin or reality" points to a very perverse twist about hyperreality, for in hyperreality, images are no mere *copy* of reality. According to Baudrillard, they have become *creators* of their own reality and have overtaken terrestrial reality by making the image and simulation the standard of reality to which the real world must conform.

God and the Hyperreal

At this point, a question needs to be asked: in what sense is this material problem of hyperreality also a theological problem? It is easy to point to

10. Baudrillard, *Simulacra and Simulation*, 6.
11. Baudrillard, *Simulacra and Simulation*, 13.
12. Baudrillard, *Simulacra and Simulation*, 1.

Marx's critique of the religious illusion surrounding commodities and simply dismiss that as so much atheism. To do so, however, would ignore a number of important insights that Debord and Baudrillard have made that are founded upon Marx's claim. In the remainder of this piece, my touchstone will be Chanon Ross's *Gifts Glittering and Poisoned*.[13] Ross's work is interesting because he takes up the material analyses of Debord and Baudrillard to produce a theopolitical manifesto. At the same time, however, Ross is also helpful in identifying shortcomings to the material fundamentalism of Debord and Baudrillard.

Ross begins his analysis by saying that images are not only presenting visuals, but also "focusing our gaze on a world that transcends our own immanent reality."[14] In saying this, Ross builds on Debord's argument that images are a "factitious God." The image, Ross argues, "moves the religious sensibility of heaven closer to us."[15] Going further, Ross argues that it is not just the image, but also the act of *gazing* on the image, that have great metaphysical and theological significance. This has escalated under the conditions of hyperreality outlined by Baudrillard. This is because, for Ross, sight is a unique faculty that blurs the divide between the material and the transcendent, just as the image itself blurs the divide between the transcendent and the temporal. Ross reminds us that images are not mere neutral instruments to help us *think of* a transcendent realm. Rather images actually have an ontology of their own and *are* a transcendent realm.

Ross cites John Ralston Saul's *Voltaire's Bastards*,[16] which explicitly touches upon the link between religion and imagery. In one passage, Saul says that "it is improbable that the image, which has played such a fundamentally religious . . . role for more than fifteen thousand years, could simply be freed of itself in the space of a few centuries to become a mere object of art."[17] Saul is more pointed in a passage later in the book concerning our age when he says:

> the death of God combined with the perfection of the image has brought us to a whole new state of expectation . . . the electronic image is man as God and the ritual involved leads us not to a

---

13. Ross, *Gifts Glittering and Poisoned. Kalos.*
14. Ross, *Gifts Glittering and Poisoned. Kalos*, 14.
15. Ross, *Gifts Glittering and Poisoned. Kalos*, 14.
16. Saul, *Voltaire's Bastards*.
17. Cited in Ross, *Gifts Glittering and Poisoned*, 84.

mysterious Holy Trinity but back to ourselves. In the absence of a clear understanding . . . these images cannot help but return to the expression of magic and fear proper to idolatrous societies.[18]

We can argue from Saul that a society marked by the death of God is not a society free of heaven; it has only put another heaven in its place. Heaven can be found in a number of places, but in the context of this work, "god" is to be found in the images and simulations that saturate our landscape, in the same way that Debord equates our in a sea of images with the worship of a "factitious god." Though not mentioning God by name, Baudrillard nonetheless alerts us to a more chilling effect of the age of the simulacra. Like gods, simulacra do not reflect reality but *create* reality in their own image. More accurately, they become the foundation of reality to which reality itself must realign. The creation of images that generate or reshape reality is known by the more commercially accepted term of "marketing." I remember sitting on a course in marketing in my undergraduate studies and being told that marketing is the creation of zones of activity, consumption, and profit that did not previously exist. Marketing is creation *ex nihilo*. More accurately, in the course of creating these simulated worlds, the world of the real—societies and bodies— must realign itself to the dimensions of the image in order that the former might enter into the lifeworld created by the latter and thereby savor the promises made by the image to its faithful consumers. In the Old Testament, treating something created—the image—as if it was the Creator had a name: "idolatry," and the Psalms mention twice that the creators of images will one day end up becoming like those images.[19] Another level of interest lies in Baudrillard's use of the term "simulacra," though this might not be intentional. In the Latin Vulgate, "simulacra" is the precise word that is used for "idols."[20]

Ross reminds us, however, that these observations are not new. Long before Saul, Augustine of Hippo launched a similar critique, only the images here were the images relayed through the spectacle of living bodies of slaves, victims of execution, and gladiators in the arena. Augustine is interesting because he was not primarily aiming at the ethics

---

18. Cited in Ross, *Gifts Glittering and Poisoned*, 84.

19. Ps 115:8; 135:18. "Those who make them will be like them as will all who trust in them."

20. See for example Ps 134(135):15. *Simulacra gentium argentum et aurum, opera manuum hominum.* (The idols of the nations are silver and gold, the work of man's hands.)

of the arena but at its metaphysics. Augustine speaks of the way in which the spectacles performed at the arena constituted a form of idolatry, going as far to say that seeing these images constituted "offering incense to demons within their hearts."[21] This for Ross is not just a rhetorical flourish to emphasize the ethical problems of the arena. Augustine is, for Ross, making a statement about the metaphysical status of the image, something Ross claims that the Marxists in the tradition that Debord and Baudrillard follow fail to explore in any depth, deliberately or otherwise.[22] The image, for Augustine, pierces the barrier between the earthly and the heavenly, occupying a metaphysical zone that traverses the temporal and the transcendent, which Augustine evaluates with this very pithy label of "the fellowship of demons," paraphrasing Paul's First letter to the Corinthians.[23] Relying on ancient Roman demonology, Augustine warns his congregation in a sermon about the dangers of idolatry. Idols, Augustine claims, are not mere human engravings, but also have demons "bound to these images" which "brought the souls of their worshippers into a wretched captivity, by forcing them into their fellowship."[24] The reason for this wretchedness is that, in Roman demonology, demons occupy a metaphysical zone that sits between the temporal and the transcendent. They enjoy an embodied immortality, but this supposed state of tranquillity is fused to the manifold passions of a diseased soul.[25] Thus, demons, driven by insatiable desire, are left in a state of permanent agitation as they move from one object of desire to another.

From the image, we must turn briefly to the act of gazing, for this is what activates the metaphysics of idolatrous images. While images blur the distinction between the sacred and profane, the act of gazing on an image also has a metaphysical effect on the gazer. In seeing the image, we are pulled into the image's metaphysical orbit. Our gaze instills in *us* a "desire to commune with a higher order of being" embodied in the image. In other words, Ross says that these simulations instill in us, wittingly or otherwise, a desire to be like gods ourselves. More specifically, we acquire within us the desire for the kind of godliness that the visual commodity has created and instilled. Under conditions of hyperreality,

21. Cited in Ross, *Gifts Glittering and Poisoned*, 56.
22. See especially Ross, *Gifts Glittering and Poisoned*, 76, 87.
23. 1 Cor 10:20
24. Cited in Ross, *Gifts Glittering and Poisoned*, 87.
25. Ross, *Gifts Glittering and Poisoned*, 79, 87.

we become willing to sacrifice our time, money, energy, bodies, libido, and relationships at the altar of images. In the name of hyperreality we manipulate, airbrush, objectify, render pornographic, cut up, and consume both ourselves and others—other people, other communities, other countries—just so that we might have share in that divine life promised by the image, a life of transcending the grind of normality, ourselves, and others.

God and Fake News

If hyperreality is, as Debord and Baudrillard argue, the material foundation for idolatry, then we can start to look at a specific media phenomenon: the idolatry that is at work in the use of images to produce fake news or alternative facts. It must be noted that the image here refers to both pictorial and textual content, since both are interwoven in the production of any image. Indeed, with digital code underpinning a lot of images, pictorial content at its heart is really more text than picture. Under the conditions of hyperreality, the news is now a zone of production in which images generate reality rather than reflect it.

Like marketing, the news is the trade of image commodities packaged under the label of "information," only the "information" under conditions of hyperreality need not have any correlation with what is actually happening. Instead, the "information" peddled by the news becomes the generator of worlds of plausibility. "Information" in hyperreality inverts the order of reality, for actual reality is no longer a check on fantasy. Rather, reality is the raw material that builds the alternate worlds that are generated by the fantasy. One can make any claim with a visual commodity to which all facts must conform so long as the headline is prefaced with a seal of authorization commonly marked by the preface "research has shown that . . ."—and it must be noted that research is just as much a commodity as any other source of information. This news can be anything: breaking news from a stockmarket that sparks a panic sell-off; the banding and segregating of individuals via religion, race, or clothing; the propagation of flat or young-earth societies; military mobilization for or against another nation; the mobilization of churches for or against papacies—the list goes on.

This is all idolatry, not only because the image is playing the role of the creator of worlds of plausibility, but also because we participate in these images to varying degrees. We do so by consuming and indulging in the commodity of the image, spurred on by a sense of frustration or helplessness in our lives, whilst we are either unaware of or trying to ignore the fact that it was the world that produced the image in the first place. To apply Ross's analysis, our consumption of images becomes the means by which we indulge, even if unwittingly, in our desire to transcend the limitations imposed by our concrete circumstances. Moreover, the images that relay alternative facts also serve a transcendental function, because they are taken to be higher forms of knowledge which others cannot or will not access. The consumer of alternative facts occupies a level of being higher than other people, who they see as lemmings bowing to the propaganda generated by the image. Such people fail to see that this superior status comes as a result of following, lemming-like, the propaganda generated by other images.

Whilst Debord and Baudrillard provide a material inroad to identify the idolatry of the image, they are severely limited in coming up with an antidote for it. According to Ross, the key to the problem is their refusal to analyze the metaphysics of the image and their subsequent refusal to come up with an alternative. Indeed, Ross locates the problem with the analyses of Debord and Baudrillard in their saying that the problem with images lies with metaphysics itself (which is also equated with the religious fog surrounding the commodity). As a result, Debord and Baudrillard are saying that the solution is in casting out metaphysics to excise the idolatrous aura of commodities and seeing things for what they really are.[26]

The problem is not merely that Cultural Marxism throws the baby out with the bathwater, but also that a call to the kind of material fundamentalism suggested by Debord and Baudrillard is pastorally inadequate. It is inadequate for the same reason that it is inadequate for the Christian to say that the solution is to be more rational and to fortify our cognitive faculties against the fantasy world of the image. The reason for the inadequacy is, if Ross is correct, that the phenomenon of images will always carry with them the transcendental freight we mentioned above, no matter how much the Marxist may deny it. Furthermore, and more importantly, images will always smuggle that idolatrous metaphysics past

---

26. See for example Ross, *Gifts Glittering and Poisoned*, 70.

the Christian's cognitive defences by accessing the Christian's affective substratum.[27]

The answer to the idolatry of the image, for Ross, lies in the metaphysics of the true image in the Eucharistic logic of the Passion of Jesus Christ. Ross says that the Eucharist does not negate the divinizing desire to consume the image, since in His Passion, Christ "overaccepts [the] malformed desire to consume and presents himself as a gift."[28] Having met us where we are affectively, Christ then redirects that desire to transcend others. First, the image joins the spectator to the spectacle, the consumer of the body of Christ is incorporated *into* the body of Christ, the true image—the image of the unseen God. This image does not continue the idolatrous disconnect of hyperreality. Instead, the body of Christ counters hyperreality, where the signified is disconnected from the signifier. This is because, if one is to take the Eucharistic doctrine of the real presence seriously, the signified and the signifier come together in real space and time. Rather than follow the logic of hyperreality, where reality enjoins a disengagement from real space and time, the Eucharist, because it extends the logic of the incarnation, extends in turn God's commitment to "so love the world" by plunging into the depths of the world. By being joined to that incarnational logic through our consumption of the Eucharist, we are committed to also commit to real space and time.

Conclusion

I have outlined in this chapter how some of the seeds of resistance sown in 1968 can be rehabilitated to give voice to the Church's own resistance to the powers and principalities of this world, in particular those that have control of the media we consume. With reference to the thought of Debord on spectacle and Baudrillard on the hyperreal, I have sought to provide a vocabulary for postmodern diagnosis of the age-old problem of idolatry in consumer culture. With reference to the theological thought of Ross, I have sought to bring out the deficiencies of an exclusive reliance on these two thinkers in resisting the idolatry of the image, and I have highlighted the need for theology to avoid the prospect of the Church being outflanked by the subtle distortions of theology built within the artifacts of postmodernity. With particular reference to Ross's work on

27. For more on this, see Smith, *Desiring the Kingdom*, 37–74.
28. Ross, *Gifts Glittering and Poisoned*, 41.

the Eucharist, this chapter has outlined the beginnings of a site of resistance to the idolatry of the image by positing Christ as the true image that redeems our idols. Being asked in the liturgy to "behold the Lamb of God" is not a spiritual nicety but a crucial part of our worship, for such a beholding forms the locus of resistance to the irresistible dominance of hyperreality.

Bibliography

Baudrillard, Jean. *Simulacra and Simulation*. Translated by Sheila Faria Glaser. Ann Arbor: University of Michigan Press, 1994.

Debord, Guy. *Society of the Spectacle*. London: AK Press, 2006.

Marcuse, Herbert. *One-Dimensional Man: Studies in the Ideology of Advanced Industrial Society*. 2nd ed. New York: Routledge, 2002.

Miller, Vincent J. *Consuming Religion: Christian Faith and Practice in a Consumer Culture*. New York: Continuum, 2003.

Ross, Chanon. *Gifts Glittering and Poisoned: Spectacle, Empire and Metaphysics*. Kalos 3. Eugene, OR: Cascade Books, 2014.

Saul, John Ralston. *Voltaire's Bastards: The Dictatorship of Reason in the West*. New York: Random House, 1992.

Savan, Leslie. *The Sponsored Life: Ads, TV, and American Culture*. Culture and the Moving Image. Philadelphia: Temple University Press, 1994.

Smith, James K. A. *Desiring the Kingdom: Worship, Worldview, and Cultural Formation*. Grand Rapids: Baker Academic, 2009.

Teen Futures Media Network. "Media Literacy." *Teen Health and the Media* (n.d.). http://depts.washington.edu/thmedia/view.cgi?section=medialiteracy&page=fast facts.

7

Stonewalling?

The Catholic Church and the Gay Liberation Movement

Philippa Martyr

The Stonewall Inn riots in New York in mid-1969 were the crucible of the gay liberation movement, building on the unrest of the previous year. What did gay liberation really bring to same-sex attracted Catholics? There is a mass of publicly available historical evidence to show that the Church's capacity in the 1960s and 1970s to create a genuinely pastoral response to same-sex attracted people was neutralized by specific bishops, senior clergy, and religious. Most of these individuals were also directly involved in the cover-up of clerical child sexual abuse. So what became of those same-sex attracted Catholics who wanted genuine gay liberation—who wanted the Church's help to live chastely, with or without a change in orientation? Who helped them, and how?

THE STONEWALL INN RIOTS in New York in mid-1969—when police raids on a gay bar led to violent street clashes with patrons and other supporters—were the crucible of the gay liberation movement, building on the global unrest of the previous year. References to "Stonewall" became a shorthand term for every gay rights conflict in the following years. But "to stonewall" is also a term for refusing to engage with another person or organization by using uncooperative and sometimes delaying tactics. It is almost always a sign of a dysfunctional relationship.

What did gay liberation really bring to same-sex attracted Catholics? There is now a mass of evidence to show that in the 1960s and 1970s specific bishops, senior clergy, and religious (nuns and brothers) neutralized the Church's capacity to create a genuinely pastoral response to same-sex attracted people in the pews. Many of those who neutralized the response were also directly involved in the cover-up of clerical child sexual abuse.[1]

This review of the Church's difficult recent history of engagement with gay liberation is timely. In May 2018, after years of pressure and public speculation, the Catholic bishops in Chile offered their resignations over a sexual abuse cover-up involving both male minors and young adult seminarians.[2] Then at the end of June 2018, Cardinal McCarrick, former Archbishop of Washington DC, who was rumored to have had numerous adult male sexual encounters with seminarians in his archdiocese, was credibly accused of assaulting a male minor. It transpired that for years, "everyone knew" about McCarrick's tendency to prey on his own seminarians, but no one said or did anything because minors were apparently not involved.[3] The McCarrick scandal also offered a master class in keeping secrets: homosexuality in the clergy has been routinely covered up by a tightly-locked network of fellow clerical offenders, and in this case a docile US media that was happy to play along with the cardinal because of his liberal political views.[4]

The full-blown breaking of the McCarrick scandal in the United States came precisely at the fiftieth anniversary of the promulgation of *Humanae vitae*. The rejection of *Humanae vitae* effectively split sexual union from procreation in the Western Catholic mind, and from there, all other types of non-procreative sex became harder to argue against.[5] Sexual decision-making became a purely personal choice made in the

---

1. Likoudis, *AmChurch Comes Out*; Hidalgo, *Sexual Abuse*; Berry and Greeley, *Lead Us Not into Temptation*; Martyr, "Sexual abuse," 22–26.
2. Lawler, "The Chilean Bishops Crisis."
3. Douthat, "#MeToo Comes for the Archbishop."
4. Mattingly, "Using the Journalism TARDIS?"
5. Martyr, "Gay Marriage and Australian Catholicism."

privacy of one's own mind, with results that were obvious enough to draw comment from openly gay New York City-based writer, blogger, and radio host Xorje Olivares. In 2017 Olivares said in an interview that:

> *I never felt this call to be celibate. I was surrounded by straight people and all the good kids were going to church, but you knew they were having sex anyway. So why do they get a pass but people like me don't? I thought, well if he said God created me this way, then what issue would be taken with however way I choose to express myself? Now that I've become part of the particular church group that I'm in, this conversation about how unrealistic it is for LGBTQ+ people to be called to the celibate life when no one else is adhering to that.*[6]

We may never know how many US bishops were (and are) same-sex attracted—we have only their criminal records to show what may be the tip of a rather large iceberg.[7] But we do know that some of those who have been identified through their sexual acting out and subsequent exposure—like Archbishop Rembert Weakland of Milwaukee—used their authority to nurture gay liberation movements in their dioceses that were completely at odds with what the Catholic Church taught on homosexual attraction and behaviour.[8] Some of those who have been similarly accused or identified—like the late Thomas Dupre of Springfield,[9] John Nienstedt of Minneapolis-St Paul,[10] and Scotland's Cardinal Keith O'Brien[11]—did not support those ministries, and delivered consistently Catholic teaching on same-sex relationships.

So where did this leave ordinary same-sex attracted Catholics who wanted genuine liberation—who wanted assistance to be set free from painful lifelong burdens, or at least to carry them with greater dignity? And where does this put us as a Church now? I believe this is where the real stonewalling has been in evidence. I should clarify that I do not think the term "stonewalling" applies to the Church's overall relationship with people who experience same-sex attraction. To them, the Church has always responded in the same terms they offer to everyone else: repent

---

6. Sciambra, "Drag Queen."
7. Lawler, "The McCarrick Scandal & The Gay Lobby."
8. Abbott, "Operation iGuardian."
9. BishopAccountability.org, "Dupre, Thomas."
10. BishopAccountability.org, "Nienstedt, John."
11. BishopAccountability.org, "O'Brien, Keith."

and believe in the Gospel. However, history and experience show that theology is one thing, and pastoral practice is another.

I want to talk in this paper about three things:

1. Catholic gay liberation support groups in the US in the late 1960s and early 1970s.
2. How and why this movement was absorbed into the mainstream of the US Catholic Church.
3. Where this leaves the Church and same-sex attracted Catholics today.

I will focus on the US because it is the biggest laboratory for this social experiment, and because the US Catholic Church is, and is likely to remain, the most influential voice in the Catholic Anglosphere.

The Science of Same-Sex Attraction?

First, we need to talk about the modern history of homosexuality, so that we understand exactly what we are talking about in terms of the Church and gay liberation. Homosexual behaviour is as old as humanity: it has had many names and has been defined mostly by the performance of specific sexual acts. In the centuries when marriage in the West was not based primarily on psychological compatibility, it seems to have been more common to have intimate, affectionate, lasting friendships with people of the same sex.[12] It is usually not possible to discuss these in terms of the present understanding of homosexuality, because not enough evidence is available to indicate that these relationships were understood by their participants or by observers in that way.[13]

Same-sex acts, however, were different: these were consistently understood as always morally wrong, and their practice was not limited to people who we would today call homosexual. Local church documents such as penitentials had differing views about how same-sex acts should be punished.[14] Ultimately, they were less interested in why people did these acts; what mattered was that they *had* done them, and now they were repentant. Broadly speaking, male-on-male sexual acts were usually

12. Caine, *Friendship*.
13. Hannon, "Against Heterosexuality." I am indebted to Thomas Meagher for pointing out this article to me.
14. McCann, "Transgressing the Boundaries of Holiness."

punished quite severely. Female-on-female sexual acts were usually not punished as severely because they were not taken as seriously, for many reasons.[15]

Same-sex acting out was a known problem in monastic communities before celibacy became mandatory for all clergy in the Latin Church. There are ample writings from the desert and monastic fathers on how to manage individuals who acted out sexually. Whether the sexual temptations were heterosexual or homosexual did not seem to matter as much as the struggle to overcome them and live chastely. This was the real goal of monastic life: to subsume these desires to live more closely united to Christ. When celibacy finally became mandatory for the diocesan priesthood in the Western Church in the eleventh century, St. Peter Damien was able to describe and condemn the problem of sexual misconduct among diocesan clergy and bishops in vivid detail.[16]

What we call homosexuality today is different. It is a construct made up of many influences, starting from the mid-nineteenth century in Europe with the work of German sexologist Richard von Kraft-Ebbing (1840–1902).[17] He and his successors, notably British sexologist Havelock Ellis (1859–1939), saw homosexuality as an unfortunate but innate inversion of human sexuality, which meant that it was cruel to legislate against it and to punish people for acting on these desires. This was a paradigm shift: a move from the idea of a standard-issue human being who happens to commit a series of sexual acts, to the idea that a different type of human being—one with inverted sexual desires—is perhaps doing what comes naturally to them.

Psychology and the sciences now began to ask two principal questions:

1. Who or what is this different type of human being that is same-sex attracted? and;

2. How did they get that way?

The initial secular scientific response was to classify them as mentally disordered, notably in the first two versions of the *Diagnostic and Statistical Manual of Mental Disorders* (DSM-I and DMS-II). With the birth of a much more vocal and public gay liberation movement in the

---

15. Brown, *The Body and Society*, 30, 308, 438.
16. Hoffman, *The Book of Gomorrah*.
17. Drescher, "Out of DSM: Depathologizing Homosexuality," 565–75.

US by 1970, protesters rallied at the 1970 and 1971 American Psychiatric Association (APA) conferences on the platform that homosexuality was a normal variant of human sexuality. The APA removed homosexuality as a diagnosis in the seventh and last printing of DSM-II.[18]

As a research subject, same-sex attraction is a fascinating and elusive phenomenon. Its development and expressions are complex and individual, and its etiology is still contested.[19] Although extensive, the research is littered with methodological flaws, including selective use of widely varying findings and small and/or self-selected samples of participants.[20] There is also an additional layer of politicization, which means that even robustly secular studies with unpopular findings can be discredited through other channels and even suppressed.[21]

The two hardest things to prove in scientific research, especially in naturalistic settings, are causality and directionality: if two things happen at roughly the same time, does one cause the other, and if so, which came first? We can often point to a correlation between two phenomena, but that is not the same as finding a cause or direction. Probably one of the most difficult elements to control for in this research area is the ever-present threat of social desirability bias, which may skew any form of self-reporting because the participants give the answer they believe they should give rather than what they really think or believe.[22] These issues have hindered research into a range of issues affecting the gay community—such as domestic violence—where there is a high degree of self-protectiveness against perceived stigmatization.[23]

---

18. Spitzer, "The Diagnostic Status of Homosexuality In DSM-III," 210–15; American Psychiatric Association, *Homosexuality and Sexual Orientation Disturbance*.

19. Ashley, "The Science on Sexual Orientation," 175–82; Rekers, "Development of Homosexual Orientation," 62–84; Diamond and Rosky, "Scrutinizing Immutability," 363–91.

20. Cameron and Cameron, "Psychology of the Scientist," 259–74.

21. Spitzer, "Can Some Gay Men and Lesbians Change Their Sexual Orientation?" 403–17; Spitzer, "Reply," 469–72; Spitzer, "Spitzer Reassesses," 757; Littman, "Rapid-onset Gender Dysphoria."

22. van de Mortel, "Faking it," 40–48.

23. Ahmed et al., "Perceptions of domestic violence," 250–60.

The Two Paradigms

In terms of what the Catholic Church and the world believe about same-sex attraction, we have two very different paradigms. On the one hand, we have the Catholic Church, whose teaching on same-sex attraction can be summarized as follows:

- All human beings are made in the image and likeness of God.
- They are created male and female.
- They are fallen and inclined to sin.
- Same-sex acts are sinful; they are not part of the natural order.
- If you do them, and you repent, God's mercy is always there for you.

On the other hand, we have a conglomerate of ideas within what we might call "the world"—a mix of constantly evolving science, popular culture, and social movements, whose beliefs about same-sex attraction might be summarized as follows:

- All human beings evolved from lower animals.
- They are male and female, mostly.
- Sin does not exist.
- Same-sex acts are the normal sexual expressions of a certain percentage of the population.
- Sexual identity and autonomy are paramount concerns.

These two paradigms are effectively incompatible, so there is always going to be conflict between them. Between the two paradigms is an ideological and scientific battleground which has been littered with unsolved problems since the late nineteenth century:

- What causes same-sex attraction?
- Is it nature, or nurture, or both?
- What percentage of the population has same-sex attraction?
- Is it an orientation or a preference?
- Can sexual orientation or preference change during a person's lifetime, or are they fixed?

- Is it right to want to change sexual orientation or preference? Should you see a psychologist to talk you into this (as in DSM-II), or to talk you out of this (as in DSM-V)?
- Why do people with same-sex attraction experience higher levels of comorbidities with mental disorders, substance misuse, and lifestyle diseases, even in liberal and gay-friendly societies?
- Should we define ourselves and other people by their sexual orientation or preference?

There are multiple theories and points of view here, but the science is not settled. This is the intellectual background against which the Church was operating—and gay liberation began to make its voice heard—at the end of the 1950s.

The Seedbed in the 1950s

Taken at face value, a person who looked from the outside at how gay liberation hit the Church would tell a very romantic story. A stuffy, conservative American Catholic Church—already shaken up by the Second Vatican Council and by the failure to receive *Humanae vitae*—was hit with another body blow from the rapidly advancing field of human sexuality. Increasingly confident gay people began to challenge and question its authority, calling for love and understanding, and inclusion, and eventually marriage.

With the benefit of hindsight, especially in the light of the sexual abuse crisis, the story is quite different. An already compromised US episcopate, with an unknown proportion of same-sex attracted bishops and priests, welcomed the gay liberation movement. They encouraged it to work within the Church to convince ordinary Catholics that same-sex attraction—or being gay or being homosexual—was a normal variation on being human, and that this kind (or indeed any kind) of sexual activity should not be a problem.

The clergy sexual abuse scandals have been producing an evidence trail in the public domain since at least the mid-1980s. They show that from at least the late 1950s, individual US dioceses and bishops created enclaves of sexually active, same-sex attracted clergy. These clergy held senior positions in these dioceses and were often involved in seminary formation, and they actively recruited sexually active, same-sex attracted men to the diocesan priesthood. These dioceses also welcomed Catholic gay liberation groups and ministries and later founded their own diocesan ministries, which varied greatly in their interpretation of the Church's teaching on same-sex attraction.[24]

An example of this process can be found in the Archdiocese of Seattle under Archbishop Raymond Hunthausen (1975–1991), a political and doctrinal liberal whose archdiocese was subject to apostolic visitation in 1983 due to doctrinal misrule, with a coadjutor archbishop appointed in 1989. In 1978, Hunthausen appointed Fr. David Jaegher as Archdiocesan Seminary Director. Jaegher was ordained in 1969, and from 1990 to 2001 he was assigned to AIDS Ministry, and then Pastoral Care and Inclusion Ministry Resources. Jaegher admitted to improperly touching eight to ten boys at a CYO camp in the 1970s, and two claims were settled financially by his archdiocese. He was voluntarily laicized in 2005 and died in 2014. During his time as seminary director, Fr. Jaegher recruited Paul Conn, who successfully completed his seminary training and was ordained for Seattle in 1985. Just three years later, Fr. Conn was convicted of molesting six altar boys between the ages of eleven and thirteen. He also admitted to the abuse of other boys of whom the police knew nothing. Conn was sentenced to four years in prison and was laicized.[25]

Another example is that of Archbishop Rembert Weakland of Milwaukee, who appointed Fr. James Arimond as chaplain to the local branch of Dignity. Arimond said on US television in 1988 that "the teachings of the church's hierarchy [on homosexuality] do not conform to reality." It later emerged that Arimond had molested a boy in the same year.[26] He served eighteen months of a custodial sentence and was laicized, turning to counselling as a profession until ordered to surrender his licence in 2003.[27]

Gay Liberation and the Church

In 1968, explosive public events took place which made that year a critical one in the West. The gay liberation movement, like so many other social movements in the 1960s, already existed, but it was underground in

---

24. Likoudis, *AmChurch Comes Out*, xii-xv; Rose, *Goodbye, Good Men*.
25. Likoudis, *AmChurch Comes Out*, 25–26.
26. Abbott, "Operation iGuardian"; BishopAccountability.org, "Arimond, James."
27. BishopAccountability.org, "Arimond, James."

the US and in other Western countries, where sexual acts between males were still illegal. Gay liberation adopted the same type of networking and agitation as other social movements.

The Stonewall riots of June 1969 consolidated the movement and brought it out into the open. Within a month, there was a recognizable gay liberation movement in the US, and this spread quickly to the UK, Canada, Australia, and New Zealand. It was an out-of-control Stonewall anniversary party on Oxford St. in Sydney, Australia in June 1978 that was the origin of today's Sydney Gay and Lesbian Mardi Gras festival.[28]

The Christian churches, including the Catholic Church, had been actively involved in civil rights issues, where priests like the Berrigan brothers had achieved fame (or notoriety) through the anti-war movement.[29] There was and still is no explicit Catholic teaching on many political issues, so individuals who felt strongly enough about these issues could become involved with them in good conscience. But homosexuality was different: there was and is explicit Catholic teaching on sexual acts between people of the same sex. Now there was a movement calling for the repeal of legislation which criminalized those acts, and an interesting and colourful marginalized community apparently in need of help. In these exciting times, there was going to be a problem distinguishing between the sinner and the sin.

In 1969 in Los Angeles, Fr. Patrick X. Nidorf, an Augustinian priest and psychologist, began a ministry which he called Dignity, saying that, "The Catholic gay people whom I had met were frequently bothered by ethical problems and identity with the church. It seemed obvious that the church wasn't meeting the needs of the gay community."[30] The nature of those ethical problems became more evident with the Dignity mission statement in 1970, which stated that:

> We believe that homosexuality is a natural variation on the use of sex. It implies no sickness or immorality. Those with such sexual attraction have a natural right to use their power of sex in a way that is both responsible and fulfilling . . . and should use it with a sense of pride.[31]

---

28. Sydney Gay and Lesbian Mardi Gras, "History."
29. O'Brien, "The Berrigans," 87–92.
30. Lefebvre and Hannum, "Pride and Prejudice," 12–17.
31. Lefebvre and Hannum, "Pride and Prejudice," 12–17.

Fr. Nidorf was asked to step down by Los Angeles Archbishop Timothy Manning, but Dignity continued as a lay-led ministry. Nidorf—now known affectionately as Pax Nidorf by his followers—left the priesthood in 1973 to marry, becoming a psychotherapist and artist.

What followed over the next two decades was a confusing game of push-and-pull between the US bishops, various gay ministries, and Rome. In 1974, the National Federation of Priests' Councils and the National Coalition of American Nuns adopted a platform supporting gay civil rights, and in 1975 Dignity was able to meet with representatives of the US Bishops Conference.[32] However, in that same year, the Holy See issued a declaration on sexual ethics, clarifying that homosexual acts were disordered and could not be approved of, and the US Bishops' document *To Live in Christ Jesus*, s.52, essentially took the same approach.[33]

In 1968 in New York, Fr. John McNeill SJ published three articles on homosexuality in *Homiletic and Pastoral Review*.[34] In 1964 McNeill had fallen in love with a man, and his experience personally convinced him that same-sex attraction and acts were a moral good. He helped found a chapter of Dignity in New York in 1972.[35] In 1976 the Jesuits gave McNeill permission to publish his book *The Church and the Homosexual*, which was hugely influential: it equated same-sex acts with opposite-sex acts and argued that they should be judged by the same standards. However, by 1978 McNeil had been officially silenced. He was dismissed from the Jesuits in 1987, married his same-sex partner in 2008, and died in 2015.[36]

In the mid-1970s, Bishop Francis Mugavero of Brooklyn invited Sister Jeannine Gramick and Father Robert Nugent to find a new way to minister to self-identified gay and lesbian Catholics.[37] Gramick and Nugent set up New Ways Ministry in 1977, and in 1981 they held their first national symposium. Archbishop James Hickey of Washington DC opposed New Ways vigorously and warned other bishops not to send delegates to the symposium, with some success. In 1984 the Vatican asked Gramick and Nugent to disassociate themselves from New Ways

---

32. Lefebvre and Hannum, "Pride and Prejudice," 12–17.
33. National Conference of Catholic Bishops, *To Live in Christ Jesus*.
34. Lefebvre and Hannum, "Pride and Prejudice," 12–17.
35. Rothaus, "The Rev. John J. McNeill."
36. Woo, "Rev. John McNeill Dies At 90."
37. Burkeman, "$300m Lawsuit."

Ministry. Despite this, in 1992 Bishops Thomas Gumbleton of Detroit, Kenneth Untener of Saginaw, Michigan, and William Hughes of Covington, Kentucky, conducted workshops at the third annual New Ways Ministry's national symposium. In 1999 the Congregation for the Doctrine of the Faith permanently banned Sister Jeannine Gramick and Father Robert Nugent from pastoral work involving same-sex attracted people.[38]

Courage and the Rise of the Diocesan Gay Ministries

In 1980, psychologist Fr. Benedict Groeschel CFR recommended his fellow priest—psychologist Fr. John Harvey (1918–2010) to Cardinal Terrence Cooke of New York, to help Cooke set up a ministry to same-sex attracted Catholics that would represent Church teaching authentically.[39] Harvey was a moral theologian of considerable experience and founded the Courage ministry with five goals for its participants:

1. **Chastity:** To live chaste lives in accordance with the Roman Catholic Church's teaching on homosexuality.

2. **Prayer and Dedication:** To dedicate their lives to Christ through service to others, spiritual reading, prayer, meditation, individual spiritual direction, frequent attendance at Mass, and the frequent reception of the sacraments of Reconciliation and Holy Eucharist.

3. **Fellowship:** To foster a spirit of fellowship for sharing thoughts and experiences, and so ensure that no one will have to face the problems of homosexuality alone.

4. **Support:** To be mindful of the truth that chaste friendships are not only possible but necessary in a chaste Christian life; and to encourage one another in forming and sustaining these friendships.

5. **Good Example/Role Model:** To live lives that may serve as good examples to others.[40]

In the 1980s, the tide seemed to be turning against the gay liberationists. The first cases of AIDS were beginning to be reported, and the first public exposures of the clergy sexual abuse scandal were beginning to appear in the US. In 1980, the Archdiocese of Chicago Association of

---

38. Lefebvre and Hannum, "Pride and Prejudice," 12–17.
39. Lefebvre and Hannum, "Pride and Prejudice," 12–17.
40. Courage International, "About Courage."

Priests named Dignity Chicago as their chosen organization of the year. However, six years later the Congregation for the Doctrine of the Faith issued a *Letter to the Bishops of the Catholic Church on the Pastoral Care of Homosexual Persons*,[41] asking bishops to remove support and funding from ministries that were not authentically Catholic. In the late 1980s, various US bishops moved Dignity chapters out of church buildings and disallowed meetings on church property.[42]

In 1994, the newly released *Catechism of the Catholic Church* (English translation) contained three paragraphs on same-sex attraction that summarized Catholic teaching and recommendation for pastoral care:[43] the long history, uncertain origins, and intrinsic disorder of homosexuality (§2357); the need for respect and compassion for people with these attractions (§2358); and the universal call to chastity, helped by the sacraments and disinterested friendship (§2359). Three years later, the US bishops issued *Always Our Children: A Pastoral Message to the Parents of Homosexual Children*, the initial version of which had to be modified to accurately reflect Catholic teaching.[44]

In the 1980s and 1990s, there were strong and repeated top-down clarifications of Catholic teaching, and better articulation of those teachings. But at the local level in the US, it was a different matter. Individual bishops had already acted where they were the most powerful—that is, in their own dioceses—to set up their own ministries, appoint their own people, and mainstream their own variations on Catholic teaching. The first was in 1976 in Richmond, Virginia, and then in 1987 Archbishop Roger Mahony of Los Angeles established an archdiocesan gay and lesbian ministry. These were followed by Oakland, California; Trenton, New Jersey; St. Augustine, Florida; and Seattle, Washington. By 2001 there were also diocesan ministries in Cleveland, Ohio; Cincinnati, Ohio; Orlando, Florida; Charlotte, North Carolina; and Rochester, New York.[45] Today, there are very active diocesan gay ministries in the Archdioceses

---

41. Congregation for the Doctrine of the Faith, *Letter to the Bishops of the Catholic Church*.

42. Lefebvre and Hannum, "Pride and Prejudice," 12–17.

43. *Catechism of the Catholic*, §2357–2359.

44. US Conference of Catholic Bishops, *Always Our Children*; Bishop Fabian Bruskewitz, "On *Always Our Children*"; Lefebvre and Hannum, "Pride and Prejudice," 12–17.

45. Lefebvre and Hannum, "Pride and Prejudice," 12–17.

of New York, Los Angeles, and San Francisco, none of which promote chastity for same-sex attracted Catholics.[46]

"Gay Priests" and Sexual Abuse?

On March 3, 2002, an article appeared in the *New York Times* speculating about why a large proportion of clergy abuse victims were teenage males—not a typical presentation of pedophile offences.[47] The author, Melinda Henneberger, quoted psychiatrist and Vatican spokesman Dr. Joaquin Navarro-Walls, who questioned whether same-sex attracted men should be ordained. This immediately became a full-scale media outcry against perceived homophobia and the victimization of gay Catholic priests.

Just two months later, in May 2002, the Weakland scandal broke in earnest. Archbishop Rembert Weakland in Milwaukee resigned when it became known that he had spent nearly half a million dollars to pay off a former male lover who was now allegedly blackmailing him. The media response—in the age of Monica Lewinsky—was to demonize Weakland's lover, a former theology student called Paul Marcoux who had originally gone to Weakland for help with vocation discernment.[48]

This was the first warning for American Catholics that some of their bishops might be personally compromised in the sexual abuse crisis, and that the crisis might be a larger one than the abuse of minors. The following month, in June 2002, the US bishops signed the Dallas *Charter for the Protection of Children and Young People* and the policy norms for dealing with cases of sexual abuse. The term "clergy" was removed from the original draft and replaced with "priests and deacons," thus exempting the US bishops from the same degree of scrutiny and censure because the drafting committee decided that the bishops were "beyond the purview of this document." One of the architects of the Dallas Charter was Theodore McCarrick.[49]

Dignity approached the US Catholic Bishops Conference in November of the same year, urging them to make a public statement that

---

46. Sciambra, "High-heels and Hubba Hubba."
47. Henneberger, "Vatican Weighs Reaction."
48. Shapiro and Spillane, "The Witch Hunt Against Archbishop Weakland."
49. Flynn, "McCarrick, The Bishops, and Unanswered Questions."

would "stop blaming gay priests."[50] Finally in 2005 a clear directive came from Rome that same-sex attracted men were not to be ordained to the priesthood.[51] Anecdotally, this directive appears to have been ignored, minimized, or interpreted locally to ensure that many seminaries in the US and elsewhere remained open to same-sex attracted men.[52]

Where Are We Now?

What became of Dignity? In 2010, Call to Action, DignityUSA, Fortunate Families, and New Ways Ministry formed Equally Blessed, which they described as "a coalition to support full equality for LGBT people in the church and civil society."[53] Today, there are around forty-eight chapters of Dignity in the US, with mixed presentation, affiliations, practices, and organization.[54] Their membership seems to be small and made up largely of over-fifties same-sex attracted singles and couples. New Ways, meanwhile, hosts an online directory of LGBT-friendly parishes.[55] There are currently 110 chapters of Courage in the US, as well as multiple chapters in Central and South America, Europe, South East Asia, and Australia.[56] Again, anecdotal evidence indicates a wide variety of membership size and makeup across Courage internationally, but small numbers.

The US episcopate's integrity has been dramatically compromised by recent events, which have also cast suspicion on the 2002 decision to exempt themselves from the same level of scrutiny and discipline applied to priests and deacons.[57] The high proportion of accused US bishops may indicate a higher rate of alleged offending, or it may reflect better reporting and a more sensitive legal system: there has historically been a culture of non-reporting of clergy sexual offenses in some European countries.[58] At the time of writing, using a count and review of the in-

    50. Lefebvre and Hannum, "Pride and Prejudice," 12–17.

    51. Congregation for Catholic Education, *Instruction Concerning the Criteria for the Discernment of Vocations with regard to Persons with Homosexual Tendencies.*

    52. McDonough and Fr. Martin, "The Vatican and Gay Priests."

    53. Lefebvre and Hannum, "Pride and Prejudice," 12–17.

    54. DignityUSA, "Dignity USA Chapters"; "Jubilee Discussions—the Voice of our Communities."

    55. New Ways Ministry, "LBGT Friendly Parishes and Faith Communities."

    56. Courage International, "Find a Courage Site Near You."

    57. Daly, "Confrontation Time: Cardinal McCarrick and Me in 2002."

    58. Collins, "Lesson from the McCarrick Case"; Dreher, "Cardinal McCarrick Is a

formation provided on accused (but not necessarily convicted) bishops on the website BishopAccountability.org, the following estimates can be produced (Table 1).[59]

Table 1. Bishops accused of sexual misconduct as of September 2018

	Worldwide	US
Total number of Catholic bishops—Western and Eastern	5,100	428
Of whom are accused this number	90 (2%)	34 (8%)
Of those accused:		
Number accused of abusing males	61 (67%)	25 (74%)
Number accused of abusing minor males	40 (44%)	17 (50%)
Number accused of abusing both minor and adult males	49 (54%)	21 (62%)
Number accused of targeting altar boys, seminarians, or other clergy	17 (19%)	9 (26%)

There is now an unarguable (and growing) data set to support the argument that clergy sexual abuse, at least in Western countries, is a largely male-on-male problem, and one predominantly involving teenage rather than pre-pubescent boys. The John Jay Report of 2004 confirmed that in the US, 81 percent of all victims of reported clergy abuse were male.[60] In the early 2000s, the Archdiocese of Chicago opened up records for all 2,252 of its priests over the past forty years, which apparently showed that the majority of complaints about sexual incidents with clergy involved fifteen- to sixteen-year-old boys.[61] In Australia, the report of the recent

---

Molester"; "Cardinal McCarrick: Everybody Knew"; "How Uncle Ted's Tribe Thrives."

59. BishopAccountability.org, "Bishops Accused of Sexual Abuse and Misconduct." I compiled the data from the contemporaneous data set on that website, so the table caption dates it to September 2018.

60. John Jay College of Criminal Justice, *The Nature and Scope of Sexual Abuse of Minors*, 6.

61. Miller, "Compassion, Secrecy and Scandal"; Yaccino and Paulson, "In Files, a History of Sexual Abuse by Priests in Chicago Archdiocese."

Royal Commission into institutional child sexual abuse found that 74 percent of all Church-related sexual abuse victims were male.[62]

But What about Ordinary Catholics?

Where does this leave ordinary faithful Catholics with same-sex attraction, and their families? Ironically, those who were intended to be helped by gay liberation coming to the Church are the ones who have been the most hindered by it. These individuals have struggled to get the support they need to live authentically Catholic lives. Many have been held back by a profound sense of secrecy, shame, guilt, and loneliness. Poor advice or no advice in the confessional on the management of moral issues, especially sexual addiction and acting-out, is very common. They have experienced pressure from peers, family, and sometimes clergy to identify as gay, and to come out. Some have done so, only to find that this has brought them greater unhappiness, hurt, and confusion. Where there are comorbidities like depression and post-traumatic stress from child sexual abuse, it is also difficult for them to find appropriate psychological help that incorporates their religious beliefs.[63]

Added to this is confusion caused by evangelical Protestant movements such as Exodus (in its original form) who claim to have "prayed away the gay," and who insist on attraction change and preferably marriage as proof that the person is now "healed" of their same-sex attractions.[64] The subsequent damage to, and sometimes collapse of, some "ex-gay" marriages through same-sex infidelities is generally left unacknowledged and unpublicized. Protestant theologians maintain a different position from the Church on salvation, regeneration, and concupiscence, which means that they are largely unable to accept a paradigm in which inclinations and attractions are not sinful in themselves. The Protestant approach sees the attraction or inclination towards the same sex as sinful and in need of eradication or conversion, whereas the Catholic approach distinguishes between the temptation to sin and the voluntary

---

62. Australia, Royal Commission into Institutional Responses to Child Sexual Abuse, *Final Report*.

63. Gershom, "After the Desert"; Hrbacek, "Living with Same-Sex Attraction"; Miller, "Finding Courage."

64. Steffan, "After Exodus."

participation in sinful acts.⁶⁵ This misunderstanding and lack of agreement can hold back ecumenical efforts to support believing Christians who are same-sex attracted.

Individuals can and have found help through Courage groups, books like Fr. John Harvey's *The Homosexual Person* and *Truth about Homosexuality*,⁶⁶ word of mouth about trustworthy priests, and informal networks. Social media has also helped to connect many people with Catholic writers and thinkers who experience same-sex attraction, and who write about it with frankness and practical advice. This has not always been smooth sailing; for example, writer and blogger Eve Tushnet has attracted criticism from some conservative Catholics for seeing her attraction as a gift from God and a force for good in the Church and the world.⁶⁷ Other Catholic same-sex attracted writers like David Morrison take a different view from Tushnet.⁶⁸ Some, like Joseph Sciambra, have documented their personal and ongoing struggles with destructive gay ministries and apparently stone-deaf diocesan bureaucracies. Others like Daniel Mattson have shared why it is that they as same-sex attracted men are not suited to the ordained ministry, providing an unparalleled insider's view of the real struggles involved in living chastely.⁶⁹

The struggle towards self-care and healing has also allowed same-sex attracted Catholics to connect with a wider movement of clear and often beautiful articulations of the theology of true friendship, and the merits of the chaste single life.⁷⁰ A phenomenon known informally as the Spiritual Friendship movement, to which many of these writers and thinkers belong in varying degree, has also not escaped criticism.⁷¹ However, its existence is a sign of hope that the Church's strong emphasis on supporting marriage in the last fifty years might gradually be expanding to encompass the unmarried and the divorced who try to live chastely. Efforts

---

65. Burk and Butterfield, "Learning to Hate Our Sin Without Hating Ourselves." I am indebted to James Parker for sending me this article.

66. Harvey, *The Homosexual Person*; Harvey, *The Truth About*.

67. Tushnet, "About"; Lu, "'Spiritual Friendship.'"

68. Morrison, *Beyond Gay*.

69. Mattson, "Why Men Like Me Should Not Be Priests."

70. Altenberger, "Single Life Is More Fundamental for Christianity"; Keating, "Celibacy at 30."

71. Lu, "Spiritual friendship."

to develop a healthier theology of singleness and celibacy beyond the limited concept of the "single vocation" appear to be making inroads.[72]

Summing Up

The landscape today is a daunting one. We have what could be called a "chequerboard church"—a patchwork quilt of individual priests, parishes, and dioceses completely at odds with each other over pastoral approaches to same-sex attraction. This became very obvious in the recent debate in Australia over the legalisation of same-sex marriage.[73] This is both a cause and a symptom of a wider confusion over issues of sexual morality in the Church that has flourished since 1968, compounded by poor or non-existent catechesis and deliberate undermining by individuals with vested interests in not proclaiming the full liberating truth of the Gospel to those who needed it the most.[74]

As gay liberation became part of the mainstream of most Western liberal democratic societies, it created a climate of media silence on clergy sexual offending involving male adults, because of the fear of being branded as homophobic. This has compounded the problem by delaying the exposure of the issue for years. The sexual revolution has ended in the #MeToo movement, which is now starting to bite into years of silence and complicity, and the Church is not exempt from this.

On balance, the gay liberation movement had nothing to offer the Church—an institution that already saw people as equals, as individuals before God, but with different types of temptations. The Church has always acknowledged that scientific knowledge about same-sex attraction is in its infancy, and there is plenty of room to move. The 1986 instruction on pastoral care for homosexual persons said at its outset:

> The Church is thus in a position to learn from scientific discovery but also to transcend the horizons of science and to be confident that her more global vision does greater justice to the rich reality of the human person in his spiritual and physical dimensions, created by God and heir, by grace, to eternal life.[75]

---

72. Bonacci, "Is the Single Life a Vocation?"
73. Martyr, "Gay Marriage and Australian Catholicism."
74. Amodeo, "Redefining Courage."
75. Congregation for the Doctrine of the Faith, *Letter to the Bishops of the Catholic Church on the Pastoral Care of Homosexual Persons*, 2.

Gay liberation did not offer any kind of real spiritual liberation. Its philosophical underpinnings—with little real scientific basis—effectively labelled same-sex attracted people as a different type of human being. This is why the process of coming out has the potential to constrict a person into a predetermined self-identification that extends far beyond their sexual life and which can be very hard to escape.[76] There is also increasing public exposure of intersectoral fissures in the non-heteronormative movement, in the form of biphobia (hostility of both heterosexuals and gay/lesbian people to perceived bisexuals),[77] and the furor between transwomen and lesbian rights activists.[78] Above all, the fact that so many teenage boys and young men were sexually abused by Catholic clergy, who either concealed their sexual orientation or exposed it and were ordained anyway, is a stark reality which the Church must face if it is ever to heal.

Whenever the Church in the West has tried to align with the spirit of the age, it has always done so just a little too late and then become paralyzed: there have been some egregious examples of this in the liturgy. There is a risk that the same thing is taking place here: loud voices are trying to formalize a relationship with the more extreme aspects of a gay culture that is already disappearing into the broader middle class.[79] At the very point at which more and more people in the West are questioning the idea that homosexuality is innate—given the obvious fluidity of sexual desires when there are fewer social inhibitions to worry about[80]— disproportionately powerful individuals in the Western Church are trying once again to tether it to a will o' the wisp. The tiny numbers of self-identified sexually active gay men and women who are also practicing Catholics is telling: for most of them, the Church is simply irrelevant.

However, because of the incursion of gay liberation into the American Catholic Church, a broader and more humane vision of the homosexual person was proclaimed in response. This can and does offer liberation, integration, and peace to anyone who wants to pursue it, while not requiring any change of sexual preference. This is still the greatest strength of the Courage ministry, especially in the light of the current

76. Milioti, "Why I Reject Popular Gay Culture."

77. Shreiber and Hausenblas, "Why So Many Bisexuals Are Victimised."

78. Fleming, "The Gender Identity Movement Undermines Lesbians"; Glover, "Why It's Time to Take Out the T From LGBT."

79. Sullivan, "The End of Gay Culture."

80. McArdle, "Why It's Time."

backlash against "conversion therapies."[81] As the dust settles and we count the cost of the sexual revolution, a more positive discussion about the deeper theology of singleness and chastity is now becoming possible. The impact of the transgender movement on the already fragile political alliances within the gay liberation movement is also, paradoxically, helping to unpick ideas of innate and unchanging sexual preferences.

All human beings have that rich reality described by the Congregation for the Doctrine of the Faith: all are created by God, and all are heir by grace to eternal life. Chastity in singleness and in marriage is never achieved once and for all; it is a work in progress for every individual. The sufferings and witness of those Catholics who live with sexual problems of all kinds in a hypersexualized world, and who nonetheless strive to remain faithful, is a secret gift to the Church. It is in these lives that we can see the recognition of that rich reality which is the true liberation, offered by Jesus himself to each human person regardless of their unique temptations and failures.

Bibliography

Abbott, Matt. "Operation iGuardian; Weakland's Filthy Legacy Continues to Haunt Milwaukee (My Birthplace)." *RenewAmerica*, July 17, 2013. http://www.renewamerica.com/columns/abbott/130717.

Ahmed, Ali et al. "Perceptions of Gay, Lesbian, and Heterosexual Domestic Violence among Undergraduates in Sweden." *International Journal of Conflict and Violence* 7 (2013) 250–60.

Altenburger, Michael. "Single Life Is More Fundamental for Christianity than both Married and Religious Life." *Church Life Journal*, November 29, 2017. http://churchlife.nd.edu/2017/11/29/single-life-is-more-fundamental-for-christianity-than-both-married-and-religious-life.

American Psychiatric Association. *Homosexuality and Sexual Orientation Disturbance: Proposed Change in DSM-II, 6th Printing, page 44 Position Statement (Retired)* (November 1973). http://displus.sk/DSM/subory/dsm2_revision.pdf.

Amodeo, Joseph. "Redefining Courage: What the New Apostolate for LGBT Catholics Gets Wrong." *Huffington Post*, March 6, 2012. https://www.huffingtonpost.com/joseph-amodeo/courage-apostolate-for-lgbt-catholics_b_1186725.html.

Ashley, Kenneth. "The Science on Sexual Orientation: A Review of the Recent Literature." *Journal of Gay & Lesbian Mental Health* 17 (2013) 175–82.

Australia, Royal Commission into Institutional Responses to Child Sexual Abuse. *Final Report*, vol. 16 (2017). https://www.childabuseroyalcommission.gov.au/religious-institutions.

Berry, Jason, and Andrew Greeley. *Lead Us not into Temptation: Catholic Priests and the Sexual Abuse of Children*. New York: Doubleday, 1992.

81. Munsey, "Love's not Sex."

BishopAccountability.org. "Arimond, James." http://bishop-accountability.org/priestdb/PriestDBbylastName-A.html.
———. "Bishops Accused of Sexual Abuse and Misconduct." http://www.bishop-accountability.org/bishops/accused/global_list_of_accused_bishops.htm.
———. "Dupre, Thomas." http://www.bishopaccountability.org/assign/Dupre_Thomas_L.htm.
———. "Nienstedt, John." http://www.bishop-accountability.org/bishops/accused/global_list_of_accused_bishops.htm#NIENSTEDT.
———. "O'Brien, Keith." http://www.bishop-accountability.org/bishops/accused/global_list_of_accused_bishops.htm#OBRIEN.
Bonacci, Mary Beth. "Is the Single Life a Vocation?" *Catholic Exchange*, March 2, 2006. https://catholicexchange.com/is-the-single-life-a-vocation.
Brown, Peter. *The Body and Society: Men, Women, and Sexual Renunciation in Early Christianity*. New York: Columbia University Press, 2008.
Bruskewitz, Bishop Fabian. "On *Always Our Children*." *Social Justice Review* (March/April 1998). https://www.catholicculture.org/culture/library/view.cfm?recnum=448.
Burk, Denny, and Rosaria Butterfield. "Learning to Hate Our Sin without Hating Ourselves." *The Public Discourse* (July 4, 2018). http://www.thepublicdiscourse.com/2018/07/22066.
Burkeman, Oliver. "$300m Lawsuit Claims Catholic Bishop Covered Up for Paedophile Priests." *The Guardian*, October 17, 2002. https://www.theguardian.com/world/2002/oct/17/usa.oliverburkeman.
Caine, Barbara, ed. *Friendship: A History*. New York: Routledge, 2014.
Cameron, Paul, and Kirk Cameron. "Psychology of the Scientist: LXXXV. Research on Homosexuality: A Response to Schumm (and Herek)." *Psychological Reports* 92 (2003) 259–74.
Catechism of the Catholic Church. Vatican City: Libreria Editrice Vaticana, 1994.
Collins, Charles. "Lesson from the McCarrick Case: Pay Attention to Misconduct with Adults." *CruxNow*, July 2, 2018. https://cruxnow.com/news-analysis/2018/07/02/lesson-from-mccarrick-case-pay-attention-to-misconduct-with-adults.
Congregation for Catholic Education. *Instruction Concerning the Criteria for the Discernment of Vocations with regard to Persons with Homosexual Tendencies in View of Their Admission to the Seminary and to Holy Orders* (2005).
Congregation for the Doctrine of the Faith. *Letter to the Bishops of the Catholic Church on the Pastoral Care of Homosexual Persons* (1986). http://www.vatican.va/roman_curia/congregations/cfaith/documents/rc_con_cfaith_doc_19861001_homosexual-persons_en.html.
Courage International. "About Courage." https://couragerc.org/about.
———. "Find a Courage Site Near You." https://couragerc.org/courage.
Daly, Peter. "Confrontation Time: Cardinal McCarrick and Me in 2002." *National Catholic Reporter*, August 20, 2018. https://www.ncronline.org/news/accountability/parish-diary/confrontation-time-cardinal-mccarrick-and-me-2002.
Diamond, Lisa, and Clifford Rosky. "Scrutinizing Immutability: Research on Sexual Orientation and US Legal Advocacy for Sexual Minorities." *Journal of Sex Research* 53 (2016) 363–91.
DignityUSA. "Dignity USA Chapters." https://www.dignityusa.org/chapters.
———. "Jubilee Discussions—the Voice of Our Communities." https://www.dignityusa.org/page/jubilee-discussions-voice-our-communities.

Douthat, Ross. "#MeToo Comes for the Archbishop." *New York Times*, June 23, 2018. https://www.nytimes.com/2018/06/23/opinion/sunday/cardinal-theodore-mccarrick-metoo-archbishop.html.
Dreher, Rod. "Cardinal McCarrick: Everybody Knew." *American Conservative*, June 20, 2018. http://www.theamericanconservative.com/dreher/cardinal-mccarrick-everybody-knew.
———. "Cardinal McCarrick Is a Molester." *American Conservative*, June 20, 2018. http://www.theamericanconservative.com/dreher/church-cardinal-mccarrick-is-a-molester.
———. "How Uncle Ted's Tribe Thrives." *American Conservative*, June 29, 2018. http://www.theamericanconservative.com/dreher/uncle-ted-mccarrick-catholic-church-thrive/.
Drescher, Jack. "Out of DSM: Depathologizing Homosexuality." *Behavioral Sciences* 5 (2015) 565–75.
Fleming, Pippa. "The Gender Identity Movement Undermines Lesbians." *The Economist*, July 3, 2018. https://www.economist.com/open-future/2018/07/03/the-gender-identity-movement-undermines-lesbians.
Flynn, J. D. "McCarrick, The Bishops, and Unanswered Questions." *Catholic News Agency*, July 23, 2018. https://www.catholicnewsagency.com/news/mccarrick-the-bishops-and-unanswered-questions-87927.
Gershom, Steve. "After the Desert: A Faithful Catholic's Reflection on Same-Sex Attraction." *Our Sunday Visitor*, November 2, 2011. https://www.osv.com/Article/TabId/493/ArtMID/13569/ArticleID/683/After-the-desert-A-faithful-Catholics-reflection-on-samesex-attraction.aspx.
Glover, Katie. "Why It's Time to Take Out the T From LGBT." *The Independent*, September 10, 2015. https://www.independent.co.uk/voices/why-its-time-to-take-the-t-out-of-lgbt-10493352.html.
Hannon, Michael. "Against Heterosexuality." *First Things*, March 2014. https://www.firstthings.com/article/2014/03/against-heterosexuality.
Harvey, Fr. John. *The Homosexual Person: New Thinking in Pastoral Care*. San Francisco: Ignatius Press, 1987.
———. *The Truth about Homosexuality: The Cry of the Faithful*. San Francisco: Ignatius, 1996.
Henneberger, Melinda. "Vatican Weighs Reaction to Accusations of Molesting Clergy." *New York Times*, March 3, 2002. https://www.nytimes.com/2002/03/03/us/vatican-weighs-reaction-to-accusations-of-molesting-by-clergy.html.
Hidalgo, Myra. *Sexual Abuse and the Culture of Catholicism*. Oxford: Haworth, 2007.
Hoffman, Matthew. *The Book of Gomorrah and St. Peter Damian's Struggle against Ecclesiastical Corruption*. Ite Ad Thomam, 2015.
Hrbacek, Dave. "Living with Same-Sex Attraction: Five Catholics Describe Joys, Struggles of Embracing Chastity." *St. Anthony's Catholic Church*, October 19, 2012. http://www.stanthonysely.org/blog/view/Living-With-Same-sex-Attraction-Five-Catholics-describe-joys-struggles-of-embracing-chastity.
John Jay College of Criminal Justice. *The Nature and Scope of Sexual Abuse of Minors by Catholic Priests and Deacons in The United States 1950–2002*. Washington, DC: United States Conference of Catholic Bishops, 2004.

Keating, Jessica. "Celibacy at 30 is not Just an Empty Holding Pattern." *America: The Jesuit Review*, September 8, 2016. https://www.americamagazine.org/faith/2016/09/08/celibacy-30-not-just-empty-holding-pattern.

Lawler, Philip. "The Chilean Bishops Crisis." *First Things*, May 2018. https://www.firstthings.com/web-exclusives/2018/05/the-chilean-bishopscrisis.

———. "The McCarrick Scandal & the Gay Lobby: A Problem the Bishops Won't Address." *Catholic Culture*, July 6, 2018. https://www.catholicculture.org/commentary/otn.cfm?id=1296.

Lefebvre, Elizabeth and Kristen Hannum. "Pride and Prejudice: A History of the Relationship Between Gay and Lesbian Catholics and Their Church." *US Catholic* 77 (2012) 12–17. http://www.uscatholic.org/church/2012/02/pride-and-prejudice-history-relationship-between-gay-and-lesbian-catholics-and-their-.

Likoudis, Paul. *AmChurch Comes Out: The US Bishops, Pedophile Scandals and the Homosexual Agenda*. Petersberg, IL: Roman Catholic Faithful, 2002.

Littman, Lisa. "Rapid-Onset Gender Dysphoria in Adolescents and Young Adults: A Study of Parental Reports." *PLoS ONE* 13 (2018) e0202330. https://doi.org/10.1371/journal.pone.0202330.

Lu, Rachel. "'Spiritual Friendship' and Ministering to the Same-Sex Attracted." *Catholic World Report*, October 15, 2015. https://www.catholicworldreport.com/2015/10/15/spiritual-friendship-and-ministering-to-the-same-sex-attracted-2.

Martyr, Philippa. "Gay Marriage and Australian Catholicism." *Quadrant* 61 (December 2017). https://quadrant.org.au/magazine/2017/12/fault-lines-sex-marriage-catholic-church.

———. "Sexual Abuse: Where the Church Erred." *Quadrant* 61 (April 2017) 22–26. https://quadrant.org.au/magazine/2017/04/sexual-abuse-catholic-church-went-wrong.

Mattingly, Terry. "Using the Journalism TARDIS: Why Was Cardinal McCarrick such a Critical News Source?" *GetReligion*, July 24, 2018. https://www.getreligion.org/getreligion/2018/7/24/using-the-journalism-tardis-why-was-cardinal-mccarrick-such-a-crucial-news-source.

Mattson, Daniel. "Why Men Like Me Should not Be Priests." *First Things*, August 17, 2018. https://www.firstthings.com/web-exclusives/2018/08/why-men-like-me-should-not-be-priests.

McArdle, Megan. "Why It's Time to Retire the 'Born This Way' Argument for LGBT Rights." *Sydney Morning Herald*, June 24, 2017. https://www.smh.com.au/lifestyle/why-its-time-to-retire-the-born-this-way-argument-for-lgbt-rights-20170618-gwtnbp.html.

McCann, Christine. "Transgressing the Boundaries of Holiness: Sexual Deviance in the Early Medieval Penitential Handbooks of Ireland, England and France 500–1000." Thesis, Seton Hall University, 2010. http://scholarship.shu.edu/theses/76.

McDonaugh, William, and Fr. James Martin. "The Vatican and Gay Priests." *Commonweal*, January 9, 2006. https://www.commonwealmagazine.org/vatican-gay-priests-0.

Milioti, Stephen. "Why I Reject Popular Gay Culture (Or: What to Know before Setting Me Up with Your Other Gay Friend)." *Columbia Journal of American Studies* (n.d.). http://www.columbia.edu/cu/cjas/may_reject.html.

Miller, Karl. "Finding Courage as a Same-Sex Attracted, Catholic Man." *America: The Jesuit Review*, April 19, 2018. https://www.americamagazine.org/faith/2018/04/19/finding-courage-same-sex-attracted-catholic-man.

Miller, Peter. "Compassion, Secrecy and Scandal in the Archdiocese of Seattle." *Seattle Catholic*, April 11, 2002. http://www.seattlecatholic.com/article_20020411_Seattle_Archdiocese.html.

Morrison, David. *Beyond Gay*. Huntington, IN: Our Sunday Visitor, 1999.

Munsey, Christopher. "Love's Not Sex." *American Psychological Association: Monitor on Psychology*, February 2007. http://www.apa.org/monitor/feb07/lovesnot.aspx.

National Conference of Catholic Bishops. *To Live in Christ Jesus*. Washington, DC: Publications Office US Catholic Conference, 1976.

New Ways Ministry. "LBGT Friendly Parishes and Faith Communities." https://www.newwaysministry.org/parishes.

O'Brien, David. "The Berrigans: History, Witness, Memory." *American Catholic Studies* 114 (2003) 87–92.

Rekers, George. "The Development of a Homosexual Orientation." In *Homosexuality and American Public Life*, edited by Christopher Wolfe. Dallas: Spence, 1999.

Rose, Michael. *Goodbye, Good Men: How Liberals Brought Corruption into the Catholic Church*. Washington, DC: Regnery, 2002.

Rothaus, Steve. "The Rev. John J. McNeill, Jesuit Priest Who Became Famed LGBT Activist, Dies at 90." *Miami Herald*, September 24, 2015. https://www.miamiherald.com/news/local/community/gay-south-florida/article36352038.html.

Sciambra, Joseph. "Drag Queen in Charge of Archdiocese of NY LGBT Ministry Puts On Wig in Front of Tabernacle." Joseph Sciambra, May 30, 2018. http://josephsciambra.com/drag-queen-in-charge-of-archdiocese-of-ny-lgbt-ministry-puts-on-wig-in-front-of-tabernacle.

———. "High-heels and Hubba Hubba: How the Archdiocese of San Francisco Accompanies 'Gay' Catholics." Joseph Sciambra, October 27, 2016. http://josephsciambra.com/high-heels-and-hubba-hubba-how-the-archdiocese-of-san-francisco-accompanies-gay-catholics.

Shapiro, Bruce, and Margaret Spillane. "The Witch Hunt against Archbishop Weakland." *Salon*, May 25, 2002. https://www.salon.com/2002/05/25/church_4.

Shreiber, Katherine, and Heather Hausenblas. "Why So Many Bisexuals Are Victimised." *Psychology Today*, October 25, 2016. https://www.psychologytoday.com/au/blog/the-truth-about-exercise-addiction/201610/why-so-many-bisexuals-are-victimized.

Spitzer, Robert. "Can Some Gay Men and Lesbians Change Their Sexual Orientation? 200 Participants Reporting a Change from Homosexual to Heterosexual Orientation." *Archives of Sexual Behavior* 32 (2003) 403–17.

———. "The Diagnostic Status of Homosexuality in DSM-III: A Reformulation of the Issues." *American Journal of Psychiatry* 138 (1981) 210–15.

———. "Reply: Study Results Should not Be Dismissed and Justify Further Research on the Efficacy of Sexual Reorientation Therapy." *Archives of Sexual Behavior* 32 (2003) 469–72.

———. "Spitzer Reassesses His 2003 Study of Reparative Therapy of Homosexuality." *Archives of Sexual Behavior* 41 (2012) 757.

Steffan, Melissa. "After Exodus: Evangelicals React as Ex-Gay Ministry Starts Over." *Christianity Today*, June 21, 2013. https://www.christianitytoday.com/ct/2013/

june-web-only/exodus-international-alan-chambers-apologize-for-exgay-past.html.

Sullivan, Andrew. "The End of Gay Culture." *New Republic*, October 24, 2005. https://newrepublic.com/article/61118/the-end-gay-culture.

Sydney Gay and Lesbian Mardi Gras. "History—Sydney Gay and Lesbian Mardi Gras." https://www.mardigras.org.au/history.

Tushnet, Eve. "About." *Eve Tushnet*. http://www.patheos.com/blogs/evetushnet.

US Conference of Catholic Bishops. *Always Our Children: A Pastoral Message to the Parents of Homosexual Children* (1997). http://www.usccb.org/issues-and-action/human-life-and-dignity/homosexuality/always-our-children.cfm.

van de Mortel, Thea. "Faking It: Social Desirability Response Bias in Selfreport Research." *Australian Journal of Advanced Nursing* 25 (2008) 40–48.

Woo, Elaine. "Rev John McNeill Dies At 90; Gay Priest, Author Expelled by Jesuits." *Los Angeles Times*, September 29, 2015. http://www.latimes.com/local/obituaries/la-me-john-mcneill-20150929-story.html.

Yaccino, Steven, and Paulson, Michael. "In Files, a History of Sexual Abuse by Priests in Chicago Archdiocese." *New York Times*, January 21, 2014. https://www.nytimes.com/2014/01/22/us/chicago-archdiocese-records-of-abuse-complaints.html/.

8

1960s Psychologists

Beguiling Ideologues and Smiling Assassins

Wanda Skowronska

The growth of cultural Marxism in the West during the 1960s is usually associated with iconic Frankfurt School figures—Marcuse, Fromm, Adorno, and Horkheimer—who saw psychologists Sigmund Freud and Erich Fromm as allies. But few analyses of this period see the smiling assassins of Western culture, psychologist Carl Rogers and his peers, as equally deadly examples of the Frankfurt School, Critical Theory, its ideas and methods. Even fewer know that there were Christian psychologists who confronted the spread of this seductive, political/psychological influence. This paper will look first at how Rogers's thought, even more than that of Freud, was a natural, effective evolution of the Frankfurt School; and second, how this was resisted by a solidarity of Christian psychologists and in particular Paul Vitz, who from the late 1960s challenged the entire cultural Marxist project. Vitz was to psychology what Dawson was to history. Both clarified, exposed, and deconstructed twentieth-century ideologies in perceptive analyses that have outlasted their delusions.

OF THE MYRIAD INFLUENCES which created the utopian conflagration of the 1960s, one of the most significant was that of the *Institut für Sozialforschung* at Goethe University, Frankfurt, the first Marxist-oriented research center affiliated with a major university in the West. It was established in 1923 and had a major impact on European and American thought by presenting Marxist visions of a world rid of its Western culture—as if this were a natural evolution. And its ideas were propelled covertly into Western psychology by respected scholars, never identifying themselves as Communists, who beguiled the media and educational and cultural institutions. These ideas found their home not so much in Freudian but rather in Rogerian/humanistic psychology, whose ideas were challenged by an American psychologist, Paul Vitz. What Christopher Dawson is to Western history, Paul Vitz is to Western psychology. But let us briefly review what happened.

After Lenin's failed military attempt to conquer Poland in 1919, the failed Communist revolution in Munich in 1918–19, and the failed military action in Hungary in 1920, the idea of a non-military way of attacking the West was conceived at the Moscow Marx-Engels Institute in 1922. It was to be a way of confronting, as Chad Kautzer states, "national cultural forces that inhibited revolutionary praxis."[1]

The Frankfurt Institute came into existence with the financial help of the Soviet Comintern and also with the help of Félix José *Weil*, a Jewish–German–Argentine Marxist who had inherited wealth and who described himself as a "salon Bolshevik"—what we might nowadays call an "armchair revolutionary" or a "Chardonnay socialist."

While the term "Western Marxism," as Douglas Kellner explains, was first used by Soviet Communists to disparage the turn to more Hegelian, i.e. philosophical, critical forms of Marxism in Western Europe, it was soon adopted by Frankfurt School thinkers like Lukács, Horkheimer, Korsch, and Gramsci to describe a more "independent and critical Marxism"—more independent, that is, than the pure focus on the economic and so-called "scientific" Marxism of the Second and Third Internationals.[2] The special form of social critique that came into being was called Critical Theory; that is, a critique of society, specifically Western society,

1. Kautzer, "The Influence of Marx on the Early Frankfurt School," 49.
2. Kellner, "Western Marxism," 154–58.

which the Frankfurt Institute promoted as unique and apparently urgently needed in a capitalist world beset with problems. Critical Theory did not aim to tear down the economic base of Western society itself, which was inevitably going to collapse anyway. It aimed rather at tearing down the cultural superstructure which supposedly reflected the powerful controllers of the economic system, and this would facilitate the collapse of Western civilization.[3] Critical theory included a critique of bourgeois ideology, alienated labour, art, and mass culture, and was particularly prevalent in the humanities. Marx had called for ruthless critique, the abolition of the family, and the destruction of everything existing.[4] As de Toledano put it, "[t]hat destruction would wipe out religion, the family, morality, the free interplay of men and economic forces, human relationships, and everything that made Western civilization."[5]

Italian Marxist Antonio Gramsci (1891–1937) specified that the institutions of civil society to be taken down—namely religion, marriage, notions of democracy, and individualism—were linked to and reflected capitalist economic hegemony. There might be debates as to what constituted culture or Hegelianism, or how economic systems were changing, but the overriding broader focus was not transforming but eliminating Western culture and reinstating a new narrative. As John Fonte describes it, the past century had been a battle between Gramsci and de Toqueville, between transmitting Western culture or transforming it; recognizing objective truths or opting for historical context determining truth; imposing a new mass hegemony, preferably Marxist-style, or preserving individual freedoms. One could add to this the battle between a secular anthropology as opposed to a Christian anthropology.[6] These battles of political and linguistic engineering during the twentieth century affected every cultural, education, and media organization in the West.

Why were Frankfurt theorists so effective? In analyzing entire societies, they tapped into an ideologicalWestern *Zeitgeist* which paralleled the loss of Christian belief and the need for something to replace it. Nineteenth-century world-builders had an obsession with melding state,

---

3. Some of the major figures involved in the Moscow conspiracy of 1920 at the Marx-Engels Institute were Karl Radek, Vladimir Lenin, Felix Djerzinsky, György Lukács, and Willi Münzenberg, the latter being the Comintern's organizational mastermind in the West.

4. Marx, "For a Ruthless Criticism of Everything Existing," 15.

5. de Toledano, *Cry Havoc!*, 7.

6. Fonte, "Why There Is A Culture War."

culture, and religion in the wake of the cracks and dissolution of sovereigns, states, and faith. In this, they tapped into the sense of an unstoppably changing world. As Russell Hittinger observed:

> No project was too big for the human mind, whether the conquest of nations, the civilizing of colonial peoples, the creation of new religions, and the invention of most every -ism worth fighting about. Auguste Comte's proposal that the earth's elliptical path be changed to a circular orbit to moderate climatic extremes was emblematic of a culture in which the state, science, and religion pledged their energies to eschatological visions.[7]

The Frankfurt School theorists had access to academic institutions and were welcomed as pioneering researchers in Berlin, London and America, especially Columbia University. As deToledano noted, their main chance of success was in "seducing the intellectuals, always ... the most dissatisfied element in any society."[8] Another reason they were so effective was that they tuned into and validated the alienation of individuals lost in postindustrial, overwhelming, mass cultures. Other institutions, secular and religious, had not always recognized nor addressed the psychologically destabilizing effect of the industrial era. And in tuning in to the angst, some Frankfurt theorists—in particular Herbert Marcuse, who moved to America and was to become a guru of the radical 1960s counterculture—incorporated into Critical Theory a burgeoning interest in psychology.

German-born Marcuse, who studied with Husserl and Heidegger, came to America to flee Hitler's Germany in 1934.[9] He published *Reason and Revolution*, a dialectical work studying Hegel and Marx, in 1940, while he was working in US government service for the Office of Strategic Services as part of an analyst team directing information to the US government. After the war Marcuse taught at Columbia, Harvard, and Brandeis and became what many called the "father of the New Left."

Marcuse leapt onto the academic stage with his work *Eros and Civilization* (1953), melding his Marxist views with Freudian psychology. At first glance this political–psychological alliance does not make sense. First, Freud was focused on the personal dynamics of family life, whereas

---

7. Hittinger, "The Churches of Earthly Power," para 2.

8. de Toledano, *Cry Havoc!*, 43.

9. *Standford Encyclopedia of Philosophy* gives a synthesis of Marcuse's life and thought.

the Frankfurt School was concerned with the broad historical sweep of entire societies, seeing the family in Marxist terms. Second, while Freud observed infantile sexuality and other forms of it, he did not advocate its unrestrained expression as did the Frankfurt School theorists such as Marcuse and William Reich before him. Third, Freud never engaged in any serious social critique of his society; he was rather a settled, successful member of it. The Frankfurt School, however, focused intensely on Critical Theory, on critiquing Western society and destroying it. So how could these seeming contradictions be resolved?

Again, one has to delve into the attunement of political activism with the psychological mood of the times in order to understand what was happening. During the nineteenth century, as Edward Shorter explains, the psychologist could be experimenter or healer, the former representing a more Enlightenment stance and the latter a more Romantic one.[10] It was the latter path, that of healing, that had a wide appeal—with the wealthier, for example, using spas to ease their ailments. But ordinary people, dislocated by the angst of the industrial and postindustrial eras, war, and rapid social change, found their relief—their ideological "spa"— in Marcuse's articulation of their dislocation, unhappiness, and unrest. Marcuse gave the alliance of psychology and politics a certain academic credibility in addressing societal discontent; he allied the social/political critique of Western capitalism to the psychology of Freud by *reinterpreting* many of Freud's ideas and giving them a Marxist twist, thus creating a kind of psychopolitics. As Kellner says in his introduction to the 1998 edition of Marcuse's *Eros and Civilisation*:

> Marcuse shows both how a Marxian critique can correct and radicalize Freud, and how Freud can in turn be used in developing a radical psychology, theory of socialization, and anthropology of liberation—all of which Marcuse believes a critical theory of society needed and could not discover in Marx.[11]

Marcuse saw in Freud an extension of Marx, in that he envisioned a nonrepressive society and depicted Western culture as an oppressive class structure on the political and personal level (and this at a time when the Soviet gulags held millions in the Marxist "paradise"). From the first chapter of *Eros and Civilization*, he states that existing capitalist culture constrains not only each person's societal existence but also

---

10. Shorter, *A History of Psychiatry*, 30.
11. Kellner, Preface to Marcuse, *Eros and Civilisation*, iv.

their biological existence: that is, human instinctual structure itself. Thus, Freud's notion of individual repression is welded to Marx's notion of the capitalist subjugation of us all.

Marcuse explained that civil society plunges us all into a destructive dialectic: the perpetual restrictions on Eros ultimately will restrain our true selves, our spontaneity, and all our instincts from expressing themselves and will impede the triumph of the proletariat. He nevertheless recognized that repression of instincts served a purpose in stopping us from commiting murder, robbery, and genocide. He asserted, however, that if our destructive instincts were let go in the right way, we would become destructive in the right way in eliminating Western culture, which *needed* to be destroyed. One upbeat Marcusian suggestion to facilitate this was the psychoanalytic liberation of memory, which would help us understand our repression, help us break out of the status quo, and help us acquire mature consciousness for a new mature civil order.

This harnessing of psychopolitical forces, purportedly to liberate Western society, synchronized with or helped intensify other calls for liberation at the time. For example, Margaret Sanger's growing American Birth Control League, established in 1921, was focused on liberating women from perceived patriarchal control over their sexuality. Joyce Milton points out that Margaret Mead and Ruth Benedict presented to the American public the concept of cultural moral relativity in the 1930s and 1940s.[12] And then there was the work of Alfred Kinsey, who officially began sexual research in 1941 and in 1947 founded the Kinsey Institute for Sex Research, now known as the Kinsey Institute, at Indiana University. Kinsey's "research" on children would have had him arrested and put away for life today.[13]

Seemingly innocuous yet sinister in its effects was the *Humanist Manifesto* of 1933, which American psychologists and founders of humanistic psychology Carl Rogers and Abraham Maslow had eagerly signed. This manifesto rejected the Judeo-Christian worldview and praised human potential, insisting on social transformation, indeed revolution, in its seemingly benign way. Thus Maslow and Rogers absorbed this ambience of cultural revolution from many sources, including the rising stars of the Frankfurt School—Marcuse, Horkheimer, Adorno, and Fromm—and the concomitant rise of the *Humanist Manifesto*. Timothy

---

12. Milton gives a comprehensive account of the times in *The Road to Malpsychia*.
13. A useful account of this can be found in Branch, "Alfred Kinsey."

Leary represented the wild side of the influencers, while humanist guru John Dewey was a more respectable and academically validating representative. Dewey's book *A Common Faith* had revealed the secular humanist hegemony to be absorbed by the West as its new "faith," and the humanistic psychologists took to it like ducks to water. One could say that humanistic psychology absorbed such ideas and infiltrated intellectual domains much more successfully than Freud ever did. Thus humanistic psychology became the transmitter of cultural Marxism—more so than Marcuse's Freudian–Marxist theories. It became highly effective in implementing the Frankfurt School's aim of destroying the West's culture and its superstructure. It was less theoretical and much more hypnotic and inviting: the perfect Kool-Aid for a utopia-seeking age.

Rogers, perhaps the best-known and most beguiling of the humanistic psychologists, saw a totally new philosophical anthropology replacing the old Judeo–Christian one, describing the future of a "new person" in terms of what he termed the "new revolution" which humanistic psychology represented, and saying that from it would emerge "a new kind of person, thrusting up through the dying, yellowing, putrefying leaves and stalks of our fading institutions."[14] Perhaps this was a bit more Keatsian than Marxist. But one can easily imagine Rogers's gentle, poetic, mellifluous voice lulling his students into a Frankfurtian view of a Western world needing destruction in order to give way to smiling psychologists selling wellbeing in a morally relativist world. He was the smiling assassin par excellence in expressing these revolutionary notions. Maslow, in *Toward a Psychology of Being* (1962), had also reached for grand phrases, if not the hyperbolic stratosphere, and described humanistic psychology as "a general *Weltanschauung*, a new philosophy of life, a new conception of man, the beginning of a new century."[15] In emphasizing the revolutionary nature of their conception of the human person, they were the mouthpiece of Critical Theory's ideas.[16] They were the apotheosis of the Frankfurt Institute's aims. They duped intellectuals, most significantly Christians, with an alluring philosophical anthropology that praised human potential—welcome after the war years. They rejected behaviorism's

---

14. Rogers, *Carl Rogers on Personal Power*, 262.

15. Maslow, *Towards a New Psychology of Being*, iii.

16. Bugental commented at the time, "I think we are on the verge of a new era in man's concern about man which may—if allowed to run its course –produce as profound changes in the human condition as those we have seen the physical sciences bring about in the past century." Bugental, "Third Force Psychology," 563.

rigidities, and yet like behaviorism, they totally ignored the human person as a spiritual seeker. While Frankfurt School psychopolitics is more associated with Freud in academic literature, Rogers and his humanistic school were much more effective because they were not bogged down by theories of Marx and Freud, as was Marcuse. Rogers and the humanistic school moved away from theoretical intensity and rational discourse itself and propelled their views via a "feel-good" state through which their hapless followers were seduced into thinking the West was bad and replacing all religions and theories with the new worldview of wellbeing. Of course there was a political underbelly that supported the society of wellbeing, and it was "totalitarian," as Del Noce says, for it rejected all theories as irrelevant, even fascist, while rigidly controlling its subjects under the banner of an illusory democratic liberalism.[17]

Kent Clizbe, speaking from the point of view of an ex-CIA agent adept in covert operations, says that the infiltration of Marxist notions into the West of is one of the most effective influence operations of all time.[18] Of course there is more to it, including the Soviet agents of influence within the US government, the cover-up of such influence, and its later morphing into other politically correct causes. But humanistic psychology departments were a particularly effective conduit to the media, educational institutions, and cultural organizations—the three branches of society mentioned by Clizbe that need infiltration for such an effective takeover. The mellifluous repetitions of the need for "tolerance" and "equality" to achieve a better society were not unlike the Communist utopia proposed by the older Marxists.

The new triumvirate of Western education was to become self-esteem, recycling, and *Heather Has Two Mommies*. It all happened seamlessly as the smiling assassins put their projects into place, since no one would deny the need for tolerance and wellbeing, and that is what the psychopolitical, newer cultural Marxism promised. As a psychologist I saw this infiltration into the area of educational psychology, where the normalization of homosexuality and transgenderism was seen as social and intellectual openness, tolerance, and progress—and where to question the need to teach children this was seen as primitive, fascist, repressive, and anti-progress.

17. Del Noce, *The Age of Secular*, 22.
18. See Clizbe, *Willing Accomplices*.

But you may ask whether anyone saw through this mass infiltration of cultural Marxism in psychology departments at the time. The answer is yes. American psychologist Paul Vitz, unique in his era, saw the massive cultural sleight of hand that was happening around him from the sixties onwards and followed his inborn critical instinct. Like a fearless mythbuster, he took to questioning the prevailing psychological verities invading Western society, launching a powerful critique—his own critical theory of Critical Theory—in his book *Psychology as Religion: The Cult of Self-Worship* (1977). In this incisive, analytical discourse on the ideas purveyed by Marxist, Marcusian, Freudian, Rogerian, Maslovian, and other fashionable theorists, he may not have mentioned them all by name but he did attack their ideas.[19] And in critiquing hyperindividualism, which rejects its past and the West's cultural and religious roots seeks to create its own world with total reliance on the self, Vitz was in effect critiquing the ideas of Marcuse and the Frankfurt School. Vitz turned his hermeneutic of suspicion to question whether the deconstruction of the West and the reconstruction of a personal utopia would create a happy society.

While Abraham Mowrer (*The Crisis in Psychiatry and Religion*, 1961) and Thomas Oden (*Kerygma and Counseling*, 1966) had previously critiqued some aspects of the new psychology, Vitz's book was the first sustained book-length critique of humanistic psychology to emerge from a Christian psychologist. As such it was a landmark work and laid the basis of much of his later writing on the subject, and also the writing of other critical psychologists. Vitz was as deconstructionist as Derrida, as postmodern as Foucault, as demythologyzing as Bultman. But who wanted to listen? It was as popular as spitting on Elvis or the Beatles. It certainly was followed by other critiques in time, but the salient point here is that it appeared at a time when Vitz found few around him who echoed his concerns about this popular, humanistic "child of the sixties." Vitz has stated he felt very alone at this time, and he wrote in 2010:

> At the time (1975–77) I did not know any other critics of humanistic psychology. In the summer of 1976 as I was completing the ms Tom Wolfe published an influential article titled "The Me Generation" which had some of my perspective and in 1978 Christopher Lasch published his influential book "The Culture

---

19. See in particular Chapter 6 in Vitz, *Psychology as Religion*, 66–82.

of Narcissism." Neither of these are/were psychologists and they each took a more cultural point of view.[20]

Vitz recognized the cultural war and saw his own field of psychology as a successful weapon in it—not only from the direction of Freud but much more so from the humanistic worldview. Vitz saw through the Rogerian/humanistic promises of endless liberation from all fetters, of whatever type they were; he saw through its easy promises of self-fulfilment; and most importantly he detected its anti-rationalism, to be transmitted by the comforting path of the counselling psychologist. In fact, Vitz's critique is a model for those confronting postmodernism: know the ideology and go on an academic charm offensive against it with logic, humor, and clear explanations. Vitz actually preceded another psychological mythbuster, Canadian Jordan Peterson, by over three decades! Like Peterson, Vitz looks you straight in the eye, as it were, and asks if the sacred deconstructionist cows are all they are cracked up to be. He asks whether the dismantling of family, religious, and social structures will really bring wellbeing, or whether they will instead bring personal suffering and social disaster for generations to come.

Nowhere is Vitz's critique more telling than when he challenges Rogers's lack of clear definition of the person. Rogers built a quasi-theory of the person without having a clear idea of what a person is, except for some vaguely outlined, self-satisfied, comfortable sort of being. Vitz points out that Rogers utterly failed to distinguish the "self" from the "person"—a distinction which has long perplexed Western philosophy—and that Rogers's language is opaque, incomprehensible, if not tortuous at times. For example, Rogers says of the self: "It is a gestalt, which is available to awareness though not necessarily in awareness. It is a fluid and changing gestalt, a process, but at any given moment it is a specific entity which is at least partially definable in operational terms."[21] Rogers says of the person: "a person is a fluid process, not a fixed and static entity, a flowing river of change, not a block of solid material; a continually changing constellation of potentialities, not a fixed quantity of traits."[22] Do not worry if you cannot understand this. Very few can. Vitz highlights the vagueness of Rogers's definitions in a somewhat milder version of

---

20. Personal communication with the author, January 19, 2020.
21. Rogers, "A Theory of Therapy, Personality and Interpersonal Relationships," 200–3.
22. Rogers, *On Becoming a Person*, 122.

Chaplin's *The Great Dictator* (1940), in which Chaplin sent up the repetitive and vague speeches through which Hitler had seduced millions. Vitz identified Rogerian psychobabble as philosophical smoke and mirrors, saying:

> When Carl Rogers titles his well-known book *On Becoming a Person*, he is simply wrong. Instead he has written a book on becoming an individual, in particular, an autonomous, self-actualizing, independent individual. An individual is created by separating from others . . . by concentrating psychological energy and effect on the self instead of on God or others. The founders of modern psychology clearly knew this.[23]

Vitz himself has shown a broad historical and philosophical understanding of the Western notion of the person, going to Greek, Roman, and ultimately Christian understandings of the term.[24] He praises Ratzinger's and von Balthasar's syntheses of the Western understanding of the person, making sure his students understood that.[25] As a scholar, formerly at New York State University and now Emeritus Professor at the Divine Word University in Virginia in the US, he has not only escaped but soared high above the postmodern academic miasma, and—unlike most of his peers—has given detailed historical, philosophical, and theological contexts to his study of psychology.

In deconstructing Rogers and the humanistic psychologists, Vitz deconstructed the psychopolitical aims of the Frankfurt School. He attacked the latter's endless calls for anti-institutionalism and its calls for liberation, which can mean anything you want it to mean—political, economic, sexual, psychological, and religious—as long as you are liberated from the straw-man, the evil oppressor that is Western society. As Stefan Daniel observed, the deconstructionists of 1968 wanted liberty, which meant "the creation of self-determining monads" for whom "almost every kind of limit, prescription, or definition is an instrument of domination."[26] Vitz saw early on that this anti-institutional frenzy bred an unrealistic autonomy in the independent, mobile, metrosexual individual,which in turn bred dissatisfaction and narcissism. As Vitz

---

23. Vitz, "A Covenant Theory of Personality," 95.

24. Vitz, "From the Modern Individual to the Transmodern Person," 109.

25. von Balthasar, "On the Concept of Person"; Ratzinger, "Concerning the Notion of the Person in Theology."

26. McDaniel, "Gaul Divided," para 3.

says, it leads to the glorification of the self—a self which fears principled thought as a threat to power—and becomes so entrenched that "the entire world is devoid of interest except in so far as it offers him an opportunity to experience his own superiority, power and splendour."[27] It destabilizes a person in building an overarching desire to control all objects, even objectifying the self, making it imperative to reject conscience, that "voice within," for thought itself is too overwhelming and panic-inducing. In opposition to this, Vitz points out quite simply that the human person was always and remains a spiritual seeker and will never cease to be one, and he reasserts the need for a spiritual dimension to be seriously accounted for in psychological studies.

Vitz also hurled logical spanners at Rogers's counselling method, which was based particularly on the three qualities of congruence, unconditional positive regard, and empathic understanding. Regarding the first quality—congruence—Rogers said personal change is facilitated when the psychotherapist's relationship with his client is genuine and without façade. In reply, Vitz asks if this is not a Heraclitan, utopian ideal which posits the therapist as having perfect understanding. But is this ever possible?

Regarding the second quality, Rogers saw unconditional positive regard as an acceptant attitude, facilitating change. Vitz asked whether it is "simply a transformation of the devout believer's conviction of God's unconditional love for him" into a form of self devotion and hence a "cult of self worship."[28] He pointed out the lurking, disguised power and manipulation of the counsellor. Rogerian purported nondirectiveness was in Vitz's view a pronounced directiveness—an authoritarianism. Such pretended nondirectiveness ignored metaphysical content hidden under subtle, amiable guises; for example, why was congruence or nondirectiveness good, and indeed, what does "good" mean in this context? It certainly contained a rejection of any positive regard for Christianity's legacy of thought on such matters. It also ignored the issue of how to deal with immoral and amoral stances. Can one listen with unconditional positive regard to a client relating pedophiliac experiences, or to a client expressing a desire for imminent suicide?

As to the third vaunted Rogerian quality—empathic understanding—Rogers said this was "when someone understands how it feels and

---

27. Vitz and Gartner, "The Vicissitudes of Original Sin," 11.
28. Vitz, *Psychology as Religion*, 79, 105.

seems to be me, without wanting to analyze me or judge me."[29] Again, Vitz asks, is the sense of being fully received by the therapist borrowing from Christian theology and replacing the sense of being fully accepted by God? Again, does this not imply an omniscience usually attributed to God Himself?[30] Vitz points out that in this view, there may have been some emotional empathy referred to, but there was no empathy for the Judeo–Christian understanding of the human person.

Of course, these three counselling qualities are desirable to some extent, but Vitz highlights their absolutization and how they became political and hypnotic tools for destroying inherited wisdom and for the deconstruction of Western society. They discarded the Judeo–Christian notion of flawed humanity, of original sin. The absence of evil in this worldview of humanistic psychology finally got through to Rogers's peer, Zollo May, who eventually, in 1982, questioned Rogers's failure to deal with the existence of evil.[31] Rogers ignored the issues of moral restraint and undeserved suffering about which Western culture, particularly Christianity, has much to say.

The humanistic psychologists were like a covert Frankfurt School psych-ops team, poised to sell disengagement from Judeo–Christian values to the West. The Comintern would have been proud of them all, but especially proud of Rogers, who roped in psychology students by the millions and made them dissatisfied with any institutions and doctrinal fetters, thus helping pave the way for postmodernism, cultural Marxism, and its variants.

Vatican II's *Gaudium et Spes* had warned about a false humanism, "a total emancipation of humanity wrought solely by human effort" open to totalitarian control.[32] Pope Paul VI, quoting de Lubac, said:

> A narrow humanism closed in on itself and not open to the values of the spirit and to God who is their source, could achieve apparent success for man . . . But "closed off from God [it] will end up being directed against man. A humanism closed off from other realities becomes inhuman."[33]

---

29. Rogers, *On Becoming a Person*, 62.
30. Vitz, *Psychology as Religion*, 79.
31. May, "The Problem of Evil," 10.
32. *Gaudium et spes*, para 10.
33. Paul VI, *Populorum progressio*, para 42.

Vitz predicted that the new humanism, with its Pelagian and Gnostic dimension of wellbeing, would ultimately backfire, saying, "it is an irony of course that the Enlightenment tradition has systematically evolved into today's nihilist, relativist and deconstructionist theories," adding that they have nowhere to go, but to become like a snake "eating its own tail."[34] Vitz points out the significant resurfacing of the study of the virtues, resilience, and common sense in facing life's inevitable injustice and suffering.[35] He points out psychology's genealogy, its openness to spiritual realities, and its rich philosophical heritage, as evidenced by people's never-ending search for a spiritual meaning.

Just as history had Dawson, psychology had Vitz. Both Dawson and Vitz—mythbusters of their time—had immense courage in creating a resistance, a solidarity in the face of the cultural Marxist utopias, linguistic mangling, and a plethora of delusions that surrounded them. They directly or indirectly influenced other writers and triggered increasing critiques of the Frankfurtian ideologues and irrational deconstructionists in their fields. Vitz in particular focused on the good in the Western legacy; the use of reason in evaluating that good; the lack of reason in the Marcusian/Gramscian calls for deconstruction, placing their utopian view of human progress among other utopian dustbins of history. He pointed out the hidden authoritarian fist underlying postmodern calls for "tolerance" and "equality" and salvaged the Western understanding of the human person from pervasive ideological linguistic rubble.

Vitz turned his hermeneutic of suspicion back on the humanistic psychologists. His deconstruction of the humanistic, Frankfurtian, and Gramscian ideas has been followed by many other critiques arising from a creative solidarity of psychologists, mainly Christian, now numbering several thousands. Like Vitz, they continue to transmit critical observations and the Western legacy of psychology to the increasing number of survivors of the sixties' illusions.

Bibliography

Abbott, Walter, ed. *Documents of Vatican II*. London: Chapman, 1966.
Balthasar, Hans Urs von. "On the Concept of Person." *Communio* 13 (Spring 1986) 18–26.

---

34. Vitz, "Escaping the Secular Enlightenment," 23.
35. Vitz, "Psychology in Recovery," para 14.

Bragg, Raymond, et al. "Humanist Manifesto 1." https://americanhumanist.org/what-is-humanism/manifesto1.

Branch, Alan. "Alfred Kinsey: A Brief Summary and Critique." *The Ethics and Religious Liberty Commission* (May 2014). https://erlc.com/resource-library/articles/alfred-kinsey-a-brief-summary-and-critique.

Bugental, James. "Third Force Psychology." *Journal of Humanistic Psychology* 4.1 (1964).

Clizbe, Kent. *Willing Accomplices: How KGB Covert Influence Agents Created Political Correctness, Obama's Hate-America-First Political Platform, and Destroyed America*. No city: Andemca, 2011.

Daniel, Stefan. "Gaul Divided." *First Things*, February 2016. https://www.firstthings.com/article/2016/02/gaul-divided.

de Toledano, Ralph. *Cry Havoc! The Great American Bring-Down and How It Happened*. Washington, DC: Anthem, 2006.

Del Noce, Augusto. *The Age of Secularization*. Translated by Carlo Lancellotti. McGill-Queen's Studies in the History of Ideas. Montreal: McGill University Press, 2017.

Fonte, John. "Why There Is a Culture War: Gramsci and Tocqueville in America." *Policy Review*, December 1, 2000. https://www.hoover.org/research/why-there-culture-war.

Gaudium et spes (The Pastoral Constitution on the Church in the Modern World). In *Documents of Vatican II*, edited by Walter. M. Abbott SJ. London: Chapman, 1966.

Hittinger, Russell. "The Churches of Earthly Power." *First Things*, June 2006. https://www.firstthings.com/article/2006/06/the-churches-of-earthly-power.

Kautzer, Chad. "The Influence of Marx on the Early Frankfurt School." In *The Palgrave Handbook of Critical Theory*, edited by Michael J. Thompson. Political Philosophy and Public Purpose. New York: Palgrave Macmillan, 2017.

Kellner, Douglas. Preface to Herbert Marcuse, *Eros and Civilisation*. London: Routledge, 1998.

———. "Western Marxism." In *Modern Social Theory: An Introduction*. Edited by Austin Harrington. Oxford: Oxford University Press, 2005.

Marx, Karl. "For a Ruthless Criticism of Everything Existing." In *The Marx–Engels Reader*, edited by Robert C. Tucker. New York: Norton, 1978.

May, Rollo. "The Problem of Evil: An Open Letter to Carl Rogers." *Journal of Humanistic Psychology* 22.3 (1982) 11.

Maslow, Abraham. *Towards a New Psychology of Being*. New York: Van Nostrand, 1968.

McDaniel, Stefan. "Gaul Divided." *First Things*, February 2016. https://www.firstthings.com/article/2016/02/gaul-divided.

Milton, Joyce. *The Road to Malpsychia: Humanistic Psychology and Our Discontents*. New York: Encounter, 2003.

Mowrer, Hobart. *The Crisis in Psychiatry and Religion*. Princeton: Van Nostrand, 1961.

Oden, Thomas. *Kerygma and Counseling*. Philadelphia: Westminster, 1966, 1978.

Paul VI. *Populorum progressio (On the Development of Peoples)*. Boston: Pauline Books and Media, 1967.

Ratzinger, Joseph. "Retrieving the Tradition: Concerning the Notion of Person in Theology." *Communio* 17 (1990).

Rogers, Carl. *Carl Rogers on Personal Power*. New York: Dell, 1977.

———. *On Becoming a Person: A Therapist's View of Psychotherapy*. Boston: Houghton Mifflin, 1961.

---. "A Theory of Therapy, Personality and Interpersonal Relationships, as Developed in the Client-Centered Framework." In *A Study of a Science: Formulations of the Person in the Social Context*, edited by Sigmund Koch, 184–256. New York: McGraw-Hill.

Shorter, Edward. *A History of Psychiatry: From the Era of the Asylum to the Age of Prozac*. New York: Wiley, 1997.

Standford Encyclopedia of Philosophy. "Herbert Marcuse." https://plato.stanford.edu/entries/marcuse.

Vitz, Paul. "A Covenant Theory of Personality: A Theoretical Introduction." In *The Christian Vision: Man in Society*, edited by Lynne Morris, 75–99. Hillsdale, MI: Hillsdale College Press, 1984.

---. "Escaping the Secular Enlightenment—but Slouching toward Yugoslavia: A Response to Watson." *International Journal for the Psychology of Religion* 3.1 (1993) 21–24.

---. "From the Modern Individual to the Transmodern Person." In *The Person and the Polis: Faith and Values within the Secular State*, edited by Craig Steven Titus, 109–31. John Henry Cardinal Newman lectures 1. Arlington, VA: Institute for the Psychological Sciences Press, 2006.

---. *Psychology as Religion: The Cult of Self-Worship*. Grand Rapids: Eerdmans, 1977.

---. "Psychology in Recovery." *First Things*, March 2005. http://www.firstthings.com/article.php3?id_article=170.

Vitz, Paul, and John Gartner. "The Vicissitudes of Original Sin: A Reply to Bridgman and Carter." *Journal of Psychology and Theology* 17 (1989) 9–12.

9

Moral Maximalism

Seeds for the Renewal of Moral Theology

Helenka Mannering

Following the promulgation of *Humanae vitae*, the reappraisal of the authority of the Magisterium in matters of morality by a significant number of moral theologians led to confusion and a general crisis in moral theology. Arguably, the crisis provided theologians seeking to be faithful to Christian revelation with the impetus to rearticulate the foundations of Christian moral life. The themes embraced by these writers, including Saint John Paul II, Servais Pinckaers OP, Joseph Ratzinger, and Hans Urs von Balthasar, can be analyzed as the renewal of a perennial Christian moral maximalism. In this paper, I will firstly introduce the concept of moral maximalism as defined by a team of Polish sociologists and outline the four criteria required for behavior to be considered morally maximalist. Secondly, I will show how this definition fits the Christian context and provides a schema that accords with biblical morality. Finally, aspects of the thought of the above-listed theologians will be analyzed in light of this framework, with the hope of highlighting some of the seeds for a renewal of moral theology with which we have been gifted over the past fifty years.

IN 1968, MORAL THEOLOGY was facing a complex series of challenges and developments that were exacerbated by the release of Pope Paul VI's *Humanae vitae* and the polarizing reactions it generated. One of the most significant trends in moral theology at that time was an approach referred to as situation ethics, which questioned the existence of moral absolutes, the authority of the magisterium to rule in moral matters, and traditional conceptions of the natural law. The introduction of the first oral contraceptive—Enovid-10—in 1960, and the 1965 *Griswold v. Connecticut* Supreme Court ruling allowing for the use of birth control by married couples, corresponded to a rise in popularity of situation ethics in North America. This approach gained further momentum in popular culture in response to the promulgation of *Humanae vitae*, as many sought to articulate a perspective which would permit them to dissent from magisterial teaching prohibiting contraception. This paper interprets situation ethics as contributing to a crisis in moral theology that erupted after 1968 and was manifested in the widespread dissent from the papal encyclical *Humanae vitae*, a crisis that has not yet been resolved. Simultaneously, however, the crisis acted as a stimulus for the rearticulation of a morality firmly grounded on the Gospels and modelled on the words of Christ. This paper will begin with a brief account of the nature of the crisis in Catholic moral theology, particularly through the lens of contemporary attitudes to contraceptive practice among Catholics. Following this, the dominant themes of situation ethics, which created the landscape for the reception of *Humanae vitae*, will be examined. Finally, we will turn to other significant voices in the field of moral theology over the past fifty years, particularly focusing on John Paul II's encyclical *Veritatis splendor*. It will be claimed that situation ethics, which grew out of a reaction against legalistic minimalism, itself falls prey to another species of minimalism, and that the renewed Gospel morality of the last fifty years, in contrast to situation ethics, proposes a genuine "moral maximalism."

The Crisis

The contemporary crisis in moral theology has been recently articulated by Charles Curran. He writes of a "huge gap between the teaching of the hierarchical magisterium and the practice of the faithful"[1] on this issue. This discrepancy is not a new phenomenon, but rather the continuation of a trend which began in the late sixties. Curran refers to a study conducted by Andrew M. Greeley, William C. McCready, and Kathleen McCourt, according to which "45 percent of American Catholics approved of artificial contraception for married couples in 1963, whereas by 1973, 83 percent of American Catholics approved of artificial contraception."[2] He also reports that "A 1969 survey . . . found that only 13 percent of priests refused absolution to a penitent practicing contraception."[3] Just over ten years later, in 1980, Archbishop John R. Quinn, president of the US Conference of Catholic Bishops, addressed the International Synod on the Family in Rome and pointed out that "90 percent of American Catholic women were using artificial contraception in their marriage, and that many theologians and priests disagreed with the teaching that every use of contraception is intrinsically evil."[4] Recent statistics demonstrate a continuation of the significant opposition to magisterial teaching on this issue. According to the 2016 Pew Research Centre report, only 8 percent of American Catholics regard the use of contraceptives as morally wrong, 41 percent view it as morally acceptable, and 48 percent claim that it is not a moral issue. Narrowing down the field to Catholics who attend mass at least on a weekly basis, the numbers remain similar: only 13 percent regard contraceptive use as morally wrong, 45 percent view it as morally acceptable, and 42 percent claim that it is not a moral issue.[5]

There are a number of possible causes that may account for the large number of Catholics who disagree with papal teaching on this issue, including ignorance, misunderstanding, and deliberate dissent. While most Catholics are not ignorant of the Church's stance on contraception, they may be ignorant that the issue has moral implications, or of the reasons undergirding the Church's prohibition. Given that the media frequently chide the Church for its position on contraception, complete invincible ignorance on this issue is highly unlikely.[6] Furthermore, ac-

---

1. Curran, "*Humanae vitae*," 537.
2. Curran, "*Humanae vitae*," 535. Cf. Greeley, McCready, and McCourt, *Catholic Schools in a Declining Church*, 35.
3. Curran, "*Humanae vitae*," 531.
4. Curran, "*Humanae vitae*," 529.
5. Pew Research Center, "Where the Public Stands on Religious Liberty."
6. Some recent articles include "The Guardian View on the Catholic Contraceptive Ban," and McClain, "How the Catholic Church Came to Oppose Birth Control."

cording to Curran, following the recent issue of the HHS mandate in the US, most North Americans are aware of the Catholic Church's stance on contraception. Curran writes that the mandate, which was opposed by the US Catholic bishops, "reinforced the public recognition of the Catholic teaching condemning artificial contraception for spouses."[7] The second possible cause—misunderstanding—may be present among the faithful, although it is likely to stem from the deliberate dissent of theologians or pastors of the laity. In other words, while very few Catholics may genuinely misunderstand the Church's teaching on contraceptive practice—once again, the media may be thanked in this regard—there may be confusion because their pastors consistently preach an alternative morality to that expressed by the magisterium and decried by the media. Hence it is possible to interpret the *modus vivendi*—according to which in 1969, 87 percent of priests would extend absolution to penitents practicing contraception—as an act of dissent by the priest, contributing to misunderstanding and confusion among the faithful.

The systematic disposition of deliberate dissent from magisterial teaching on the issue of contraception has been present among many clergy and laity, including theologians, since the publication of *Humanae vitae*. Curran recounts his own role in the earliest dissent from the encyclical:

> I was the primary organizer, drafter, and spokesperson for the statement coming from this group, which has often been called by others "The Washington Statement." This statement was made public at a news conference on Tuesday morning, July 30. Eighty-seven theologians, as a result of phone calls throughout the night, agreed to sign the statement. Ultimately over 600 signed the statement.[8]

Curran recognizes that the ensuing debates over *Humanae vitae* intensified the divide between "revisionist" theologians and "more traditional-minded thinkers."[9] According to John A. Gallagher, "the decisive

---

7. Curran, "*Humanae vitae*," 530.

8. Curran, "*Humanae vitae*," 522.

9. Curran, "*Humanae vitae*," 533; Curran, "*Humanae vitae*," 525 writes, "As is well known ... the 'lively debate' set off by *Humanae vitae* developed into a broad theological discussion of the issues raised by and connected with *Humanae vitae*. A very large group of theologians supported the legitimacy of dissent from noninfallible teachings when there are sufficient reasons for so doing and disagreed with aspects of the accepted Catholic teachings in the area of sexuality as well as on natural law, absolute

moment in the transition from neo-Thomist to revisionist moral theology has usually been associated with the publication of Paul VI's encyclical *Humanae vitae* and the theological debate which it engendered."[10] The main representatives of the revisionist theologians, according to Gallagher, included Curran, Bernard Häring, Karl Rahner, Richard McCormick, Joseph Fuchs, and Bruno Schüller. All these theologians dissented from the magisterial teaching in *Humanae vitae*: Curran was the primary organizer of the dissenting theologians, Häring published a book in 1973 in which he supported contraception,[11] and Rahner wrote that a Catholic who conscientiously decided to use contraception "need not fear that he has incurred any subjective guilt or regard himself as in a state of formal disobedience to the Church's authority."[12] McCormick, Fuchs, and Schüller also dissented from the pope's teaching on contraception.

The debate over *Humanae vitae* touched upon not only the issue of contraception but also the authority of the magisterium, the existence of moral absolutes, and the correct interpretation of natural law. Curran writes, "*Humanae vitae* itself involves not only the moral question of artificial contraception, but also the ecclesial issue of the teaching authority of the hierarchical magisterium,"[13] and, furthermore, "The ecclesial aspect has moved the matter beyond a debate among moral theologians and has solidified the divisions between those who uphold the teaching and those who question it, sometimes called 'revisionist' theologians."[14] These themes had already been widely promulgated among American theologians in the form of situation ethics before the promulgation of *Humanae vitae*. This was recognized by Gallagher, who wrote:

> The foundations of [the theologians'] response [to *Humanae vitae*] can only be adequately assessed in relation to the discussion of situation ethics in the 1940s, 1950s and 1960s. The question of moral absolutes, the nature of the natural law and the binding force of the ordinary i.e. non-infallible, papal magisterium had been heatedly discussed among theologians and commented on

moral norms, intrinsic evil, and conscience."
10. Gallagher, *Time Past, Time Future*, 223.
11. Häring, *Medical Ethics*.
12. Rahner, "On the Encyclical *Humanae vitae*," 285.
13. Curran, "*Humanae Vitae*," 533.
14. Curran, "*Humanae Vitae*," 533.

by the papal magisterium prior to the publication of *Humanae vitae*.[15]

Rather than causing "massive apostasy and . . . a notable decline in religious devotion and belief,"[16] at most, *Humanae vitae* acted as a stimulus for the transposition of situation ethics from a debate among specialists into mainstream culture, and as a catalyst for the widespread acceptance of the major tenets of a radical interpretation of situation ethics among American Catholics.

Because situation ethics dictated to such a high degree the theological response to *Humanae vitae*, it is now necessary to explore its main tenets.

Situation Ethics

Situation ethics was an approach to moral theology that originated in Germany. In an article published in 1950, Karl Rahner referred to two tendencies among Catholics: situation ethics, which he referred to as *situationsethik*, and "sin mysticism."[17] These were not "philosophical theories, but rather lived, existential approaches to moral problems."[18] According to Rahner, the emerging *situationsethik* was: "an extreme existential philosophy which holds that where spirit, person, and freedom are present, no universal essence of man and his affairs ought to determine the moral decision; there are no universally binding norms, there are only non-deducible individual decisions which are in no way instances of a universal norm."[19] It is necessary to recognize that *situationsethik* arose out of the recognition of important shortcomings of the prevalent approach to moral theology. Alice and Dietrich von Hildebrand identify three contributing factors to the development of *situationsethik*. First, they claim that "worldly standards . . . crept into the moral code by which [Christians] live,"[20] thereby contributing to a "heresy of ethos."[21] Hence,

---

15. Gallagher, *Time Past, Time Future*, 223–24.
16. Greeley, McCready, and McCourt, *Catholic Schools in a Declining Church*, 153.
17. Rahner, "Situationsethik Und Sündenmystik."
18. von Hildebrand, *Morality and Situation Ethics*, 5.
19. Rahner, "Situationsethik Und Sündenmystik," 331. As translated by Gallagher, *Time Past, Time Future*, 230.
20. von Hildebrand, *Morality and Situation Ethics*, 6.
21. von Hildebrand, *Morality and Situation Ethics*, 5.

"the origin of circumstance ethics and of sin mysticism is certainly linked to a reaction against this bourgeois, conventional deformation of Christianity."[22] The second factor was the dominant legalistic model of moral theology: "Circumstance ethics reacts further against the tendency to substitute legality for morality, to replace moral values by *rights*, to adapt morality to the juridical sphere, and to make of the juridical sphere the *causa exemplaris* of morality—a tendency that can be found among many Christians and sometimes even in Christian textbooks."[23] The third factor was an overemphasis on abstractions and the failure of moral theories to engage with the whole concrete personality.[24]

These three factors were problematic trends in moral theology during the first half of the twentieth century. Of the three, legalism was most strongly recognized and opposed.[25] According to Servais Pinckaers OP, legalism was bequeathed to moral theology by nominalism, which led morality to be "understood basically as the relation of the free act to the law that determines obligation."[26] Pinckaers recognized that a morality dominated by a legalistic approach is necessarily minimalist. He wrote that "At the heart of [a legalistic] moral system is the idea and feeling of obligation or duty . . . We are no longer looking at a morality of the virtues, where the tendency toward a certain perfection is of the essence. Rather, the determination of the legal minimum now predominates."[27] In another article written six years later, he similarly claimed, "Legal obligations bear directly on exterior acts and determine 'that without which no virtue is possible' or the minimum required of everyone."[28] However, while *situationsethik* rightly appreciated that a moral vision limited by worldliness, legalism, and unrealistic generalizations cannot do justice to a Christian gospel morality, by the middle of the twentieth century it was recognized that the solution it proposed was inadequate. Pope Pius XII, in a 1952 address to the Catholic World Federation of Young Women, stated that *situationsethik* was so foreign to the Catholic faith and principles that "even a child, if he knows his catechism, will realize it and

---

22. von Hildebrand, *Morality and Situation Ethics*, 6.
23. von Hildebrand, *Morality and Situation Ethics*, 7.
24. von Hildebrand, *Morality and Situation Ethics*, 7.
25. Outka, "The New Morality," 45.
26. Pinckaers, "A Historical Perspective on Intrinsically Evil Acts," 216.
27. Pinckaers, "Conscience and Christian Tradition," 336.
28. Pinckaers, "Conscience and the Virtue of Prudence," 352–53.

will feel it."²⁹ The theory also failed to gain traction in North America in the forties and fifties. Thus, commenting on the European theological landscape, John J. Lynch SJ wrote, "none of our Catholic theologians in this country have attempted—or even been tempted I would presume to say—to defend any theory of situational morality."³⁰

A change of fortune for situation ethics in North America took place in the sixties with the publication of John A. T. Robinson's *Honest to God* in 1963³¹ and Joseph Fletcher's *Situation Ethics: The New Morality* in 1966.³² It is interesting to note the correspondence between the rise in popularity in situation ethics among American Catholic theologians, the invention of the first oral contraceptive, and legalization of contraceptive use for married couples. An underlying factor that may have contributed to the rise in popularity of situation ethics could have been that it provided a reasonable justification for those engaging in contraceptive practice, as, according to Curran, "even before the encyclical a great number of married Catholics used artificial means of contraception, but the subject was not widely discussed publicly."³³ Another possible contributing factor to the rise in popularity of situation ethics was proposed by Gene H. Outka, namely "a widespread, popular antagonism to what is regarded as legalism in all its forms. This antagonism has been directed at everything from sexual mores to standards of dress and etiquette."³⁴ Third, it is likely that "50 years of increasingly interiorized authority and agency, made possible by both individually appropriated 'mysticism' (including the liturgical movement) as well as communal action"³⁵—which Stephen R. Schloesser SJ identifies as contributing to the reception of *Humanae vitae*—also contributed to the theological climate in which situation ethics could flourish. Given that situation ethics was strongly influenced in its development and reception by the "cultural mood"³⁶ out of which it grew, it is unsurprising that it has recently been evaluated by Robin

---

29. Pius XII, "Address soyez les bienvenues"; "l'éthique nouvelle est tellement en dehors de la foi et des principes catholiques, que même un enfant, s'il sait son catéchisme, s'en rendra compte et le sentira."

30. Lynch, "Notes on Moral Theology," 168.

31. Robinson, *Honest to God*.

32. Fletcher, *Situation Ethics*, 1

33. Curran, "*Humanae vitae*," 535.

34. Outka, "The New Morality," 44.

35. Schloesser, "1918–1968–2018," 490.

36. Outka, "The New Morality," 44.

Gill as "time-bound in the whimsical and individualistic 'All You Need is Love' version of the 1960s."[37]

The main implications of situation ethics for moral theology in the sixties were the questioning of the existence of moral absolutes, of the authority of the magisterium to rule in moral matters, and of traditional conceptions of the natural law.[38] Gallagher writes:

> Key to the entire situation ethics debate was the question of moral absolutes. The neo-Thomist tradition had contended that such absolute moral norms could be known in either of two manners: through an apprehension of the natural law or through the magisterium of the church. The sort of considerations which led a growing number of theologians to deny the existence of concrete moral absolutes also impelled them to rethink their basic conceptions of the natural law and the binding force of the ordinary papal magisterium.[39]

Unsurprisingly, these issues took center stage in many discussions on moral theology in the journals of the time. The position which argued for the denial of moral absolutes was summarized well by Francis Sullivan fifteen years after *Humanae vitae*, in his book *Magisterium*, where he claimed that "the more common opinion among Catholic moralists" was that there are no moral absolutes because there is no such thing as "a norm which, at some point in history, can be so irreversibly determined that no future development could possibly call for the substantial revision of this determination."[40] An influential book published on moral theology in 1968 was Curran's *Absolutes in Moral Theology?*[41] A contemporary review of that book claimed that it was "most helpful in the present

---

37. Gill, "Cult Books Revisited: Joseph Fletcher's *Situation Ethics*," *Theology* 120, no. 2 (2017), 98.

38. Both Robinson and Fletcher proposed a moderate form of situation ethics which Frankena referred to as "summary rule" or "modified act-agapism." In "Love and Principle in Christian Ethics," 212, Frankena explains: "This admits rules but regards them as summaries of past experience, useful, perhaps almost indispensable, but only as rules of thumb. It cannot allow that a rule may every be followed in a situation when it is seen to conflict with what love dictates in that situation. For, if rules are to be followed only in so far as they are helpful as aids to love, they cannot constrain or constrict love in any way. But they may and perhaps should be used."

39. Gallagher, *Time Past, Time Future*, 240–1.

40. Sullivan, *Magisterium*, 151.

41. Curran, *Absolutes in Moral Theology?*

controversy on the encyclical *Human Life*. It bears witness to the erosion of moral absolutes even in Roman Catholic scholarly circles."[42]

The denial of moral absolutes was often argued on the basis of a consequentialist approach to morality, of which situation ethics is a form. "Consequentialism" was a term coined by Elizabeth Anscombe in her 1958 paper *Modern Moral Philosophy*, in which she claimed: "consequentialism . . . marks [Sidgwick] and every English academic moral philosopher since him. By it, the kind of consideration which would formerly have been regarded as a temptation . . . was given a status by moral philosophers in their theories."[43] The argument against moral absolutes in Catholic moral theology usually includes consequentialist considerations. It is assumed that the consequences of an act measure its goodness, rather than the classic trivariate of object, end, and circumstance. Revisionist theologians have claimed that since it is impossible to foresee all possible consequences of a particular action for future societies and cultures, the magisterium should refrain from pronouncements that certain acts are intrinsically evil or disordered. In particular, as it is impossible to foresee historical changes which may make acceptable what seems to be legitimately inappropriate today or may make unacceptable what seems appropriate today, the Church should refrain from proclamations of moral absolutes.[44] All we can do to discern whether an act is morally good is foresee the possible consequences of the act for us, within our own particular milieu. Daniel C. Maguire, in a 1968 article "Morality and Magisterium," had recourse to this method of argumentation in his claim that "to say in advance that no circumstance whatever could every justify a particular action implies a foreknowledge of the ethical import of all possible circumstances. The epistemological problem here should be obvious. In actions involving other human beings history should have

---

42. Wassmer, "Absolutes in Moral Theology?" 267. Wassmer explains: "In the essays included in this volume, these theologians insist that moral principles are necessary, and absolutely so; but the principles themselves in virtue of the findings of history, psychology, sociology and phenomenology are not always and necessarily absolute. It would seem plausible to introduce here something analogous to the insight of G. E. Moore, who in his reflections on intrinsic good held that such intrinsic good is known by everyone but is undefinable. The same might be said of intrinsic evil: that everyone knows what it is, but it is undefinable": "Absolutes in Moral Theology?" 265–6.

43. Anscombe, "Modern Moral Philosophy," 12.

44. In "History Shows the Church Has Changed Its Moral Teachings," Curran claims "history shows the church has changed its moral teachings," giving examples such as slavery and usury.

taught us that the unpredictable and imponderables should not be adjudicated in advance."[45]

The existential application of a moral approach that denies moral absolutes leads to the minimization of the possibility of mortal sin and the denial that freely chosen actions can impact one's salvation. One particular proposal regarding the former was articulated by Kevin F. O'Shea, an Australian Redemptorist, in 1968. He proposed a distinction between serious and mortal sin, where "serious" sin may not necessarily act as an impediment towards that person's salvation, even if not confessed and forgiven sacramentally. O'Shea gave the following example of a person committing "serious" sin: "He wants to take a very radical position against God right now, and he does, but at the same time he does not want to be that kind of person for good and all. He stands back from involving himself as a person in the drive to sin-death which such an act really does lead to by its own intrinsic implication."[46]

O'Shea maintains:

> the position he has taken is merely "serious" sin, and the character he has assumed by committing it, do not really tell what he is in the deepest center of his personality. They are rather false symptoms of it. Precisely because his sin was "only" "serious" and not "mortal," we would hope that he preserves a real state of personality which, when unveiled to him in his final decision, would lead him to repentance and to God.[47]

This minimization of many acts which have been classically regarded as mortal sins into "serious" sin is connected with the denial that freely chosen actions in this life can have an impact on one's salvation. In O'Shea's words, "Sin (in the biblical sense) can happen only in the framework of *human life* in its totality, not in the framework of any single human act."[48]

This method of approaching morality has been variously expressed but can be categorized under the label "fundamental option." In 1966, this approach to theology was lauded by McCormick as "one of the most fruitful areas of recent scientific analysis."[49] The theory was described by McCormick as follows:

45. Maguire, "Morality and Magisterium," 49.
46. O'Shea, "The Reality of Sin," 250.
47. O'Shea, "The Reality of Sin," 250.
48. O'Shea, "The Reality of Sin," 255.
49. McCormick, "Current Theology," 70.

> The term "fundamental option" is used by theologians to refer to the free determination of oneself with regard to the totality of existence, the fundamental choice between love of self and love of the saving Lord. Because man's eternal salvation, his basic position for or against the God of salvation, is at stake in such choices, they must involve a man's total disposition of himself, out of the radical center of his being. Since this is the case, these choices will involve a depth of the person's being beyond formulating (or reflex) consciousness, and hence will escape adequate conceptual formulation.[50]

While discouraged by John Paul II in the 1993 encyclical *Veritatis Splendor*, in 1968, "fundamental option" theory was an exciting theory in moral theology. Hence, for example, we read in an article written by John W. Glaser in 1968:

> Because of the nature and depth of the fundamental option, this degree of freedom's engagement must have a considerable stability and therefore excludes the possibility of rapid fluctuation between affirmation and rejection. When external acts of the individual seem to contradict this, the source of these acts must be seen as arising from a more peripheral level of freedom, insofar as these are genuine human acts.[51]

In the radical version of "fundamental option" theory, we see a disconnect between one's freely chosen acts and the interior disposition of faith for or against God. If one can claim that freely chosen acts on a daily basis remain at the peripheral level, and one's center is not altered by them, one can legitimately hold, or at least intimate, the position that freely chosen sinful actions in this life may have no connection with one's final end.

Closely connected with the debate over moral absolutes was the radical questioning of the authority of the magisterium to pronounce judgments on matters of morals. In a 1968 article which both compiled leading positions on magisterial authority and offered a thoroughly developed original perspective, Daniel C. Maguire suggested that a serious re-evaluation should take place of the "Church's authentic teaching competence in [the] area [of morality]."[52] He argued that it is insufficient to

---

50. McCormick, "Current Theology," 70–1.
51. Glaser, "Transition between Grace and Sin," 274.
52. Maguire, "Morality and Magisterium," 42.

speak of the Church's infallible teaching in the area of morality.[53] Hence he claimed:

> As often happens in any science, certain aspects of a truth might be overly stressed due to cultural and polemical factors, with the result that other elements are neglected and an imbalance ensures. Regarding the ecclesiastical office, theological science should be especially wary. There is a deep-rooted tendency observable in man's religious history to magnify the role of religious authority figures and to view their teachings as oracular.[54]

Maguire suggested that an adequate alternative to this approach would be recognizing multiple "*Magisteria* of the Church." He elaborates:

> We would then consider not just the papal and episcopal magisterial but the equally authentic magisterium of the laity and the magisterium of theologians. Each of these has a role of creative service to the truth; none can be considered as having a juridical power to stifle or invalidate the other. Rather, each magisterium must be seen as open to the corrective influence of the other magisteria.[55]

In practical terms this means that for Maguire the ordinary magisterium no longer demands a *religiosum obsequium* in matters of morals but may be freely critiqued and dissented from by the laity, including theologians, who, in dissenting, are interpreted as exercising a "corrective influence" over the papal magisterium.

Maguire used this approach to defend dissent from papal teaching on the use of contraception. He commented on an article written by John J. Reed in 1965, where Reed had argued for the "possibility that someone, exceptionally qualified in some aspect of the question upon which the conclusion depends, may have grave reason to think that the proposition is not certainly true,"[56] a possibility that in itself is "a rather extraordinary thing."[57] However, for Maguire, on the issue of contraception, "given the wide publicity afforded important studies on the subject

---

53. Maguire, "Morality and Magisterium," 47: "the term 'infallible' does not in fact aptly describe the nature or function of the moral magisterium and . . . we should discontinue using that term in discussing the moral magisterium."
54. Maguire, "Morality and Magisterium," 54.
55. Maguire, "Morality and Magisterium," 62–3.
56. Reed, "Natural Law, Theology, and the Church," 59.
57. Reed, "Natural Law, Theology, and the Church," 60.

and the deep convictions of the persons and groups with whom we are in dialogue ... the number of those 'exceptionally qualified' to dissent could be quite large."[58] Furthermore, whereas Reed recognized an "obligation not to contradict the doctrine in public speech and writing,"[59] Maguire claimed that this assertion "is hardly defensible today."[60]

Maguire's position was not unique in 1968 but can be interpreted as representative of a larger trend. For example, Cardinal Heenan wrote, "The decline of the magisterium is one of the most significant developments in the post-conciliar Church,"[61] while Richard McCormick wrote, "assent, as the immediate proportionate response to authentic noninfallible teaching, could be a product of an overly juridical notion of the Church."[62] These reflections offered by the theologians of the time led many to believe that dissent from magisterial moral teaching was a viable option and led to the widespread rejection of papal teaching on contraception in *Humanae vitae*.

While situation ethics, with its denial of moral absolutes and questioning of magisterial authority, initially developed as a response to the moral minimalism of a legalistic mentality marked by worldliness and unrealistic generalizations, it in turn fell prey to another species of moral minimalism. Although Robinson and Fletcher's articulations of situation ethics may have sought to introduce nuanced versions of the theory to North America, its popular interpretation meant that most acts were justified as long as the motivating factor was "love," and often "love" was interpreted as the all-consuming, passionate, but ultimately selfish *eros* of Hollywood. It is unsurprising that popular interpretations of what was meant by "love" in the sixties often differed from Johannine or Augustinian interpretations of love. Hence the popular mentality, influenced by a simplified form of situation ethics, justified practices which conformed to social and cultural currents, demanded minimal cost or sacrifice, and even served self-interest in the name of "love." All these are marks of a moral minimalism that seeks the path of least resistance. It is little wonder that when *Humanae vitae* was promulgated, it almost suffocated in such a noxious atmosphere. The encyclical proposed an alternate, maximalist,

---

58. Maguire, "Morality and Magisterium," 57.
59. Reed, "Natural Law, Theology, and the Church," 59.
60. Maguire, "Morality and Magisterium," 56.
61. Heenan, "The Authority of the Church," 243.
62. McCormick, "Current Theology," 205.

vision of morality, based on beauty, truth, and goodness, which contrasted uncomfortably with the minimalist *modus operandi*. The current crisis, which consists of a chasm between the magisterium and common practice, is an extension of this conflict between a minimalist *modus operandi* and maximalist Church teaching. Hence while Curran claims that "the generally received wisdom today is that the people of God as a whole have not received or accepted this teaching,"[63] it is necessary to question whether this true wisdom or whether it is conformity to this world (something against which St. Paul sternly warned).

Moral Maximalism

While recognizing the gravity of the present crisis, it is necessary not to overlook the fact that every crisis is an opportunity for growth. Livio Melina writes: "for the Christian, above all, the word "crisis" cannot have a meaning unequivocally negative in character: it refers to a "judgement," to a "putting to the test" on the part of God that reveals the secrets of the heart and brings the truth to light. If a well-balanced paradigm (of crisis) is the subject of discussion, it amounts to a challenge for a purer perception of value, for the search for new and more adequate models."[64] The contemporary crisis of morals in the Catholic Church can likewise be interpreted as an opportunity for growth and for the reassessment of some of the theological approaches of the last century. Rather than placing the blame on the magisterium for setting the bar too high, it is necessary to look inwards and recognize within each of our hearts the temptation towards ease and comfort, even at the expense of truth and goodness. Rather than claiming that it is the "discerning consciences" of Catholics which have "led them not to observe the teaching [of *Humanae vitae*],"[65] it is necessary to ask whether Catholics have become so entrenched in worldly "culture" that many are no longer able to live according to the culture of the Incarnation, which is in the world but not of it. Perhaps, over and above the minimalist path of least resistance that is so easy to follow, the magisterium has served as a constant reminder of the radical and demanding reality of gospel morality. This gospel morality can be imagined as a "moral maximalism" which contrasts against the

63. Curran, "*Humanae vitae*," 521.
64. Melina, *Sharing in Christ's Virtues*, 15.
65. Curran, "*Humanae vitae*," 537.

minimalist inclinations of our own hearts, of legalistic casuistry, and of situation ethics.

Although moral maximalism is not a term that has been explicitly used by moral theologians, there have been gestures in its direction. In *Veritatis Splendor*, John Paul II emphasized that Christian morality is not about meeting a minimum requirement, but about striving constantly to surpass all limits through a perfection of charity. He wrote, "Jesus shows that the commandments must not be understood as a minimum limit not to be done beyond, but rather as a path involving a moral and spiritual journey towards perfection, at the heart of which is love (cf. Col 3:14),"[66] and similarly, "the commandment of love of God and neighbor does not have in its dynamic any higher limit, but it does have a lower limit, beneath which the commandment is broken."[67] While moral maximalism has not been defined theologically, it is a term that was used by a team of Polish sociologists in 2010. They defined it according to four criteria:

1. it goes beyond standard social expectations;
2. it pursues universal human values rather than self-interest;
3. it requires relatively high individual costs and sacrifices;
4. it is not a consequence of the fear of breaking the law.[68]

The remainder of this paper will explore the applicability of these criteria to moral theology and claim that moral maximalism summarizes the approach of a Gospel morality which far surpasses legalistic and situational minimalism. Due to limitations of space, only the first three criteria will be analyzed. An adequate discussion of the fourth criterion would require extended reflection on various interpretations of the natural law and the New Law of the Gospel, which is enough subject matter for at least a whole essay in itself. By using the concept of moral maximalism, it is hoped that some trends for the renewal of Catholic moral theology and for the healing of the current crisis may be uncovered.

The first criterion of moral maximalism is that it exceeds social expectations. To be morally maximalist, one must cultivate a faith-informed vision that pierces through the social fabric and hence bear a countercultural witness. While Curran claims that the magisterium should adjust its

---

66. John Paul II, *Veritatis splendor*, 15.
67. John Paul II, *Veritatis splendor*, 52.
68. Oleszkowicz, Czyzowska, and Bak, "Moral Maximalism."

teaching to correspond with the *modus vivendi* of most Catholics on the issue of contraception, arguing that "the church as a whole has already tacitly changed its teaching, at least on the pastoral level,"[69] the morally maximalist approach proposes that Catholics are invited to enter deeper into their faith so that they can transcend prevalent social practices, not be corrupted by worldly desires, and become "participants in the divine nature" (2 Peter 1:4). In John Paul II's words, "it is urgent then that Christians should rediscover *the newness of the faith and its power to judge* a prevalent and all-intrusive culture."[70] Christians partake of an alternate eucharistic economy,[71] and realize an alternate incarnational metaphysics that subverts the secular culture. According to Chanon Ross, "participation in the Eucharist requires the cultivation of a *new metaphysical vision.*"[72] In the words of David Bentley Hart, Christian optics: "is a way of seeing that must be learned, because it alters every perspective upon things; and to learn it properly one must be conformed to what one sees. Vision here is inseparable, even indistinguishable from practice: faith, which is the form this Christian optics must take, lies in the surrender of one's actions to the form of Christ."[73] While it is undeniable that our culture influences the way we think and perceive, we are not completely conditioned by our secular world culture. John Paul II explains: "it must certainly be admitted that man always exists in a particular culture, but it must also be admitted that man is not exhaustively defined by that same culture. Moreover, the very progress of cultures demonstrates that there is something in man which transcends those cultures."[74]

Transcendence of moral social expectations has been a mark of authentic Christian living since the beginning of Christianity. The Gospels and the Letters of Paul are filled with exhortations for Christians not to be conformed to this world but be transformed by the renewing of our minds (Rom 12:2). However, the requirement placed on Christians to go beyond standard social expectations and strive for moral perfection

---

69. Curran, "*Humanae vitae.*"

70. John Paul II, *Veritatis splendor*, 88.

71. Cavanaugh, *Theopolitical Imagination*, 120: "The consumer of the Eucharist begins to walk in the strange landscape of the body of Christ, while still inhabiting a particular earthly place. Now the worldly landscape is transformed by the intrusions of the universal body of Christ in the particular interstices of local space."

72. Ross, *Gifts Glittering and Poisoned*, 92.

73. Hart, *The Beauty of the Infinite*, 337.

74. John Paul II, *Veritatis splendor*, 53.

would seem impossibly idealistic were it not for the grace won for us by Christ's death and resurrection, and the indwelling of the Holy Spirit in the souls of the baptized. John Paul II writes:

> *Only in the mystery of Christ's Redemption do we discover the "concrete" possibilities of man.* It would be a very serious error to conclude . . . that the Church's teaching is essentially only an "ideal" which must then be adapted, proportioned, graduated to the so-called concrete possibilities of man, according to a "balancing of the goods in question." But what are the "concrete possibilities of man"? And of *which* man are we speaking? Of man *dominated* by lust or of man *redeemed by Christ?* This is what is at stake: the *reality* of Christ's redemption. *Christ has redeemed us!* This means that he has given us the possibility of realizing *the entire* truth of our being; he has set our freedom free from the *domination* of concupiscence. And if redeemed man still sins, this is not due to an imperfection of Christ's redemptive act, but to man's will not to avail himself of the grace which flows from that act. God's command is of course proportioned to man's capabilities; but to the capabilities of the man to whom the Holy Spirit has been given; of the man who, though he has fallen into sin, can always obtain pardon and enjoy the presence of the Holy Spirit.[75]

Christians are enabled to realize a moral maximalism because they have been given the Spirit of Christ, and thus are able to exceed social expectations with a power that comes not from them alone, but from a synergy with God himself.

The second criterion of moral maximalism is that it pursues universal human values rather than self-interest. This seems vague unless properly contextualized within Christianity. In particular, the word "universal" is problematic, evoking images of Kantian ethics. In fact, the formulation itself seems distinctly Kantian, in that Kant sought to establish a universal moral code accessible by reason alone, without reference to religion or faith.[76] Roger Crisp summarizes Kant's moral project as follows: "Kant develops a morality of universal principles with . . . a basis in reason, so that moral principles present requirements on action that are valid for any rational agent (regardless of their desires and ends)."[77] This

---

75. John Paul II, *Veritatis splendor*, 103.
76. See Rowland, *Catholic Theology*, 82.
77. Crisp, *The Oxford Handbook of the History of Ethics*, 443.

Kantian preoccupation with a universal morality accessible to all rational agents, with no reference to their religious faith or paradigmatic assumptions, was taken up by a number of Catholic theologians who sought to ground their moral theory in a natural law that made no reference to an eternal or evangelical law.[78] Livio Melina, referring to the moral theology projects of the 1970s and 1980s in general, has written that among other things:

> The heavy emphasis on the rational and universal character of morality . . . led to a bracketing, if not an outright elimination of the specifically Christian element in morality. What occurred was a "secularization of morality," which was cut off from the determinative influence of faith: its epistemological character as a specifically theological science was undermined in both its sources and its methods.[79]

This, according to Melina, has been "the most prevalent drift in postconciliar moral theology."[80]

Yet while a de-Christianized universal morality became the fashionable approach amongst Catholic moral theologians—note the paradox here—in the seventies and eighties, it was by no means the only approach. For example, Hans Urs von Balthasar proposed that the person of Jesus Christ is the "universal" norm that forms the foundation for morality, thus moving beyond the destructiveness of a strict separation of faith and reason, and of a morality of obligation that underlies a Kantian approach.[81] This ensures that morality, on the one hand, remains authenti-

---

78. One such group, known as proponents of the "New Natural Law," combined, according to Rowland, "the two-tiered account of nature and grace and faith and reason typical of Strand One-type Neo-Thomism, coupled with some Kantian elements borrowed from Strand Two-type Neo-Thomism . . . and a novel Humean element not found in any other variety of Thomism." Rowland, *Catholic Theology*, 75.

79. Melina, "Christ and the Dynamism of Action," 124.

80. Melina, "Christ and the Dynamism of Action," 120.

81. Similarly, Joseph Ratzinger has written clearly against both Kantian and Jansenist tendencies. Of these two tendencies, Rowland writes, "The Kantian emphasis upon duty and the notion of the moral as that which is done out of a sense of obligation rather than for the satisfaction of any affection, or even in accordance with any tradition, shares a logical affinity with Jansenism, a quasi-Calvinist heresy which infected the Church in France, Ireland, and countries of the New World where Irish missionaries (who had themselves been infected by the influx of Jansenist clergy from France in the eighteenth century) were deployed. The two movements (Jansenism and Kantianism) arose in different centuries and in different intellectual cultures, and although Kantian ethics is based on an exaltation of the faculty of reason, and it appears

cally Christian, and, on the other, does not become an esoteric or gnostic mystery available only to the elect. Balthasar writes:

> The norm of the concrete existence of Christ is both personal and universal, because in him the Father's love for the world is realized in a comprehensive and unsurpassable way. This norm, therefore, embraces all men in their different ethical situations and unites all persons (with their uniqueness and freedom) in his Person. As the Holy Spirit of freedom it also hovers over all men in order to bring them to the Kingdom of the Father.[82]

Balthasar does not hesitate to use Kantian terminology, thus transforming Kant's own inner logic from within. He writes that "Jesus Christ is the concrete categorical imperative"; that is, both a "formal, universal norm of moral life, which can be applied to everyone" and also a "concrete and personal norm."[83] The strength to act in union with Christ's filial obedience to the Father is given to every human person, and thus is universally accessible, by virtue of "his suffering for us and the Eucharistic giving up of his life for us as well as his handing it on to us (*per ipsum et cum ipso*)."[84] Hence, Balthasar presents a universal morality based not on a rational abstraction that is static and limited, but based on a dynamic relationship of love that is open to all, yet remains intensely personal. By keeping the essential relationship between God and the human person

---

to be the dialectical opposite of Jansenism with its intensely pessimistic outlook for the capacities of fallen human nature, the two movements share the property of making obedience to a legislator (even if in Kant's case the legislator is reason itself) the driving force behind moral action. They also share the dialectical affinity for fostering a humanism without religion (the project of Kant), and a religion without a humanism (the effect of Jansenius)." Rowland, *Ratzinger's Faith*, 68. Rowland continues, "Ratzinger has shown that he both understands and is disturbed by the spiritual pathologies which Kantian and Jansenist tendencies have generated among the faithful. After the Council, when a majority of avant-garde theologians seemed to believe that there are no moral absolutes, the hitherto sharp focus on right moral conduct tended to blur. The point which Ratzinger and von Balthasar made was that there could not have been such an implosion of Catholic moral practices within such a short frame of time unless there was something deeply flawed about the motivations behind the pre-conciliar practices. They concluded that people in the pre-conciliar era had a tendency to live prescriptively, not because they believed that the moral injunctions were life-giving, not because they could see truth, goodness, and beauty in the practices themselves, but because of a fear of eternal damnation. Once the fear was eliminated the motivation holding up the practice dissipated." Rowland, *Ratzinger's Faith*, 68–9.

82. von Balthasar, "Nine Theses in Christian Ethics."
83. von Balthasar, "Nine Theses in Christian Ethics," Thesis 1.1.
84. von Balthasar, "Nine Theses in Christian Ethics," Thesis 1.1.

at the heart of all moral action, Christian morality is recognized as universal; that is, open to anyone who wishes to follow it. Furthermore, it does not allow for a preoccupation with self-interest—it has no room for a self-serving *eros*, but only for an *eros* that rises "'in ecstasy' towards the Divine, to lead us beyond ourselves," and thus that "calls for a path of ascent, renunciation, purification and healing."[85]

The third criterion of moral maximalism is that it requires high individual costs and sacrifices. According to this criterion, the Christian who adheres to a gospel morality is engaged in a constant struggle against the world, the flesh, and the devil, rather than seeking the path of least resistance. Yet, present in every human heart is the temptation to succumb to a minimalistic morality which does not call for sacrifice. John Paul II proposes that an often-overlooked cause of this temptation is the realization that, on our own, we cannot live up to the commandments of God. Due to our inadvertent continual moral shortcomings, we are more inclined to adopt the attitude of the Pharisee rather than the poor sinner. John Paul II writes that, in our own day, the attitude of the Pharisee:

> is expressed particularly in the attempt to adapt the moral norm to one's own capacities and personal interests, and even in the rejection of the very idea of a norm. Accepting, on the other hand, the "disproportion" between law and human ability (that is, the capacity of the moral forces of man left to himself) kindles the desire for grace and prepares one to receive it.[86]

This attempt to "adapt the moral norm to one's own capacities and personal interests" is evident in the situation ethics approach to morality, whereby all moral acts are judged according to the situation as it appears to the individual, and hence moral absolutes which derive from an external source no longer exist. This is the motive which underpins much of the dissent from magisterial teaching on the issue of contraception, and hence also the contemporary crisis in Catholic morality.

Against such a stance, John Paul II repeatedly sought to draw our attention to the witness of the martyrs, who clearly show the high individual costs of faithfulness to Christian life. He wrote, "Martyrdom, accepted as an affirmation of the inviolability of the moral order, bears splendid witness both to the holiness of God's law and to the inviolability

---

85. Benedict XVI, *Deus caritas est*, 5.
86. John Paul II, *Veritatis splendor*, 105.

of the personal dignity of man, created in God's image and likeness."[87] He continues: "Martyrdom rejects as false and illusory whatever "human meaning" one might claim to attribute, even in "exceptional" conditions, to an act morally evil in itself. Indeed, it even more clearly unmasks the true face of such an act: *it is a violation of man's "humanity,"* in the one perpetrating it even before the one enduring it."[88] While not all Christians are called to be martyrs, of all Christians is required a radical witness and readiness for martyrdom in the defence of moral truth. John Paul II writes, "there is . . . a consistent witness which all Christians must daily be ready to make, even at the cost of suffering and great sacrifice."[89] Martyrdom is ultimately a witness to a moral truth that exceeds the individual human person, and remains, in all situations, absolute. This moral truth cannot be justified or rationalized through situational analysis, but lies always above human judgment, based as it is in the relation between God and the human person, the relation that constitutes the human person's very essence.

It is impossible to know how moral theology would have developed over the past fifty years without the significant dissent following *Humanae vitae*. However, it is clear that *Humanae vitae* acted as a "paramount catalyst" for the popularization of a situation ethics mentality, which led many Catholics to question the existence of moral absolutes and reappraise "the very authority of the Magisterium in matters of morality."[90] This, in turn, contributed to the creation of a crisis that consists of a chasm between magisterial teaching and popular Catholic practice. Underlying the widespread dissent from the encyclical it is possible to discern a minimalist mentality that has infected both situation ethics and the worldly legalistic moralism situation ethics was seeking to overcome. Marks of this mentality are conformity to current social expectations, and a moral approach that seeks to avoid high individual costs and sacrifices. Against such moral minimalism, John Paul II sought to renew a gospel Christian morality that goes beyond social expectations, does not pursue self-interest, and requires high personal costs and sacrifices. Hence, the crisis in Catholic morality has provided an impetus for the rearticulation of the foundations of the Christian life, and an encouragement for Christians to

87. John Paul II, *Veritatis splendor*, 92.
88. John Paul II, *Veritatis splendor*, 92.
89. John Paul II, *Veritatis splendor*, 93.
90. Pinckaers, "Revisionist Understandings of Actions in the Wake of Vatican II," 237.

remain ever-faithful to the words of Christ, "Be perfect, therefore, as your heavenly Father is perfect" (Matt 5:48).

Bibliography

Anscombe, G. E. M. "Modern Moral Philosophy." *Philosophy* 33/124 (1958) 1–19.
Balthasar, Hans Urs von. "Nine Theses in Christian Ethics." *International Theological Commission* (1974). http://www.vatican.va/roman_curia/congregations/cfaith/cti_documents/rc_cti_1974_morale-cristiana_en.html.
Benedict XVI. *Deus caritas est: Encyclical Letter on Christian Love*. Vatican: Libreria Editrice Vaticana, 2005. http://w2.vatican.va/content/benedict-xvi/en/encyclicals/documents/hf_ben-xvi_enc_20051225_deus-caritas-est.html.
Cavanaugh, William T. *Theopolitical Imagination: Discovering the Liturgy as a Political Act in an Age of Global Consumerism*. London: T. & T. Clark, 2002.
Crisp, Roger. *The Oxford Handbook of the History of Ethics*. Oxford Handbooks. Oxford: Oxford University Press, 2013.
Curran, Charles. *Absolutes in Moral Theology?* Washington, DC: Corpus, 1968.
———. "History Shows the Church Has Changed Its Moral Teachings." *The Irish Times*, May 3, 2005. https://www.irishtimes.com/opinion/history-shows-the-church-has-changed-its-moral-teachings-1.437230.
———. "*Humanae vitae*: Fifty Years Later." *Theological Studies* 79 (2018) 520–42.
Fletcher, Joseph. *Situation Ethics: The New Morality*. Philadelphia: Westminster, 1966.
Frankena, William K. "Love and Principle in Christian Ethics." In *Faith and Philosophy*, edited by Alvin Plantinga, 203–25. Grand Rapids: Eerdmans, 1964.
Gallagher, John A. *Time Past, Time Future: An Historical Study of Catholic Moral Theology*. Mahwah, NJ: Paulist, 1990.
Gill, Robin. "Cult Books Revisited: Joseph Fletcher's *Situation Ethics*." *Theology* 120.2 (2017) 93–99.
Glaser, John W. "Transition between Grace and Sin: Fresh Perspectives." *Theological Studies* 29 (1968) 260–74.
Greeley, Andrew M., William C. McCready, Kathleen McCourt. *Catholic Schools in a Declining Church*. Kansas City, MO: Sheed & Ward, 1976.
"The Guardian View on the Catholic Contraceptive Ban: A Historic Mistake." *The Guardian*, July 26, 2018. https://www.theguardian.com/commentisfree/2018/jul/25/the-guardian-view-on-the-catholic-contraceptive-ban-a-historic-mistake.
Häring, Bernard. *Medical Ethics*. Edited by Gabrielle L. Jean. London: St. Paul, 1972.
Hart, David Bentley. *The Beauty of the Infinite: The Aesthetics of Christian Truth*. Grand Rapids: Eerdmans, 2004.
Heenan, John. "The Authority of the Church." *The Linacre Quarterly* 35 (1968) 243–48.
Hildebrand, Dietrich, and Alice von Hildebrand. *Morality and Situation Ethics*. Chicago: Franciscan Herald, 1966.
John Paul II. *The Splendor of Truth: Veritatis splendor: Regarding Certain Fundamental Questions of the Church's Moral Teaching*. Washington DC: USCCB, 1993.
Lynch, John J. "Notes on Moral Theology." *Theological Studies* 19 (1958) 168.
Maguire, Daniel C. "Morality and Magisterium." *Cross Currents* 18.1 (1968) 41–65.

McClain, Lisa. "How the Catholic Church Came to Oppose Birth Control." *Huffington Post*, June 16, 2018. https://www.huffingtonpost.com/entry/how-the-catholic-church-came-to-oppose-birth-control_us_5b4cd603e4b02538dbcaf463.

McCormick, Richard A. "Current Theology: 1965." In *Notes on Moral Theology: 1965 through 1980*. Washington, DC: University Press of America, 1981.

———. "Current Theology: Notes on Moral Theology: January–June,1968." *Theological Studies* 29 (1968) 679–85.

Melina, Livio. "Christ and the Dynamism of Action: Outlook and Overview of Christocentrism in Moral Theology." *Communio* 28 (2001) 112–40.

———. *Sharing in Christ's Virtues: For a Renewal of Moral Theology in Light of Veritatis Splendor*. Translated by William E. May. Washington, DC: Catholic University of America Press, 2001.

Oleszkowich, Anna, Dorota Czyzowska, and Olga Bak. "Moral Maximalism: In Search for the Types of Behavior Meeting the Definition Criteria (Maksymalizm Moralny: Poszukiwanie Zachowan Spelniajacych Kryteria Definicyjne)." *Studia Socjologiczne* 2.197 (2010) 109–26.

O'Shea, Kevin F. "The Reality of Sin: A Theological and Pastoral Critique." *Theological Studies* 29 (1968) 241–59.

Outka, Gene H. "The New Morality: Recent Discussion within Protestantism." In *The Future of Ethics and Moral Theology*, 44–77. Chicago: Argus, 1968.

Pew Research Center. "Where the Public Stands on Religious Liberty vs. Non-discrimination." *Religion & Public Life*, September 28, 2016.

Pinckaers, Servais. "Conscience and Christian Tradition." In *The Pinckaers Reader: Renewing Thomistic Moral Theology*, edited by John Berkman and Craig Steven Titus, 321–41. Washington, DC: Catholic University of America Press, 2005.

———. "Conscience and the Virtue of Prudence." In *The Pinckaers Reader: Renewing Thomistic Moral Theology*, edited by John Berkman and Craig Steven Titus, 342–58. Washington, DC: Catholic University of America Press, 2005.

———. "A Historical Perspective on Intrinsically Evil Acts." In *The Pinckaers Reader: Renewing Thomistic Moral Theology*, edited by John Berkman and Craig Steven Titus, 185–235. Washington, DC: Catholic University of America Press, 2005.

———. "Revisionist Understandings of Actions in the Wake of Vatican II." In *The Pinckaers Reader: Renewing Thomistic Moral Theology*, edited by John Berkman and Craig Steven Titus, 236–72. Washington, DC: Catholic University of America Press, 2005.

Pius XII. "Address Soyez Les Bienvenues to the Catholic World Federation of Young Women." 18 April 1952. https://w2.vatican.va/content/pius-xii/fr/speeches/1952/documents/hf_p-xii_spe_19520418_soyez-bienvenues.html.

Rahner, Karl. "On the Encyclical *Humanae vitae*." In *Theological Investigations*. Vol. 11, *Confrontations*, 263–87. New York: Seabury, 1974.

———. "Situationsethik und Sündenmystik." *Stimmen der Zeit* 145 (1949–50) 320–42.

Reed, John J. "Natural Law, Theology, and the Church." *Theological Studies* 26 (1965) 40–64.

Robinson, John A. T. *Honest to God*. Philadelphia: Westminster, 1963.

Ross, Chanon. *Gifts Glittering and Poisoned: Spectacle, Empire, and Metaphysics*. Kalos 3. Eugene, OR: Cascade Books, 2014.

Rowland, Tracey. *Catholic Theology*. Doing Theology. London: Bloomsbury T. & T. Clark, 2017.

———. *Ratzinger's Faith: The Theology of Pope Benedict XVI.* Oxford: Oxford University Press, 2008.

Schloesser, Stephen R. "1918–1968–2018: A Tissue of Laws and Choices and Chance." *Theological Studies* 79 (2018) 487–519.

Sullivan, Francis. *Magisterium: Teaching Authority in the Catholic Church.* New York: Paulist, 1983.

Wassmer, Thomas A. "Absolutes in Moral Theology? (Book Review)." *America*, September 28, 1968, 265–67.

10

Two Freedoms

Herbert Marcuse and Romano Guardini

Lawrence Qummou

In the 1966 political preface to *Eros and Civilization*, Herbert Marcuse notes that "Today, the fight for life, the fight for eros is the political fight." This call to arms, taken up by the student radicals of 1968, was formulated upon Marcuse's conception of freedom and his emphasis upon an unrestrained individual authenticity. For Marcuse, the technological advancements of industrial society, manifested clearly in mass consumerism, usher in the voluntary servitude of the modern man. To overcome this self imposed false consciousness, Marcuse stresses not only economic liberation (à la Marx) but more importantly the recovery of psychological freedom, namely the ability to identify, pursue, and fulfill one's true desires unencumbered. In a similar critique of modern society and technological prowess, yet with a radically different diagnosis, Romano Guardini offers a notion of freedom centered upon the return to a "spiritual consciousness," grounded in the relationship of the human person with the transcendent source of being. For Guardini, the autonomous self (cut off from the "I–Thou" relationship with God) is unable to escape the servitude of a seemingly meaningless existence. Thus against the more promethean conception of the self offered by Marcuse, Guardini presents man's freedom as the ability to participate in the authenticity of God through relationship. This paper will seek to explore the rival conceptions of freedom in the thought of both Herbert Marcuse and Romano Guardini. More specifically, the anthropological presuppositions of both thinkers will be examined in light of their respective intellectual descendants and the degree of hope each can provide to the human person in the twenty-first century.

THE CULTURAL SHIFT IN attitude toward authority and self-determination that was expressed in the student protests of 1968 is difficult to attribute to one single factor or historical event. However, a particular understanding of "freedom" is clearly central to this watershed moment of the twentieth century. Hardly an unambiguous term, used equally as emphatically by both the Jacobins of the French Revolution and the Civil Rights leaders in the 1960s, one's understanding of what it means to be "free" is inextricably connected to how one understands what it means to be a human person. The purpose of this chapter will be to offer an outline of two rival conceptions of freedom in the thought of two individuals who influenced the twentieth century and beyond for entirely different reasons. Although sharing legitimate concerns for human freedom in a society dominated by technological progress, both Herbert Marcuse (1898–1979) and Romano Guardini (1885–1968) offered fundamentally different pictures of what freedom means. After surveying their key features and presuppositions, each conception will be examined in terms of their import for contemporary culture today.

Herbert Marcuse

In commenting on the rebellious social movements of the 1960s, the British historian Eric Hobsbawm (1917–2012) noted that the only individual to exert more influence than Che Guevara on the student activists of 1968 was the German-American philosopher Herbert Marcuse.[1] Described by Alasdair MacIntyre as the "intellectual patron saint" of the New Left,

---

1. Abromet and Cobb, *Herbert Marcuse*, 2.

Marcuse's thought provided a theoretical framework for understanding the suppression of the human subject in advanced industrial society.[2] His methodology involved a welding together of Marxist and Hegelian categories with the psychoanalysis of Freud in an attempt to explain the presence of human alienation in a society so seemingly prosperous. In his analysis, advancements in technology and production—inherent to advanced capitalism—promote and maintain the dominant structures of oppression that compel the human subject into voluntary servitude. This bondage, aided by the onslaught of mass consumption and manipulated culture, result in the effect of a "one-dimensional man," a term used by Marcuse to describe the hollowing out of human choice and individuality in a fully administered society.[3] In this way, one's thoughts and deeds are both enclosed within and dictated by the very structure of the established order. The result is not only the restriction of one's freedom but, more critically, its absence from conscious thought.

Marcuse's edifice of freedom, and consequently his understanding of the human person, combines elements of Marxist humanism, Freudian psychoanalysis, and Epicurean hedonism.[4] A developed account of Marcuse's vision of human freedom can be found in his two most famous works: *Eros and Civilization* (1955) and *One-Dimensional Man* (1964). Both works played a pivotal role in establishing Marcuse, alongside Theodor Adorno (1903–1969) and Max Horkheimer (1895–1973), as one of the most culturally significant thinkers of the Frankfurt School. The earlier of the two works, *Eros and Civilization,* focused specifically on a reworking of the life and death drives in Freud's psychoanalytic theory.[5] Marcuse's objective was to place Freud's theory of instinctual repression—that is the sacrificing of the pleasure principle for the reality principle—into historical context and show how the requirement to suppress instinctual gratification is not an absolute prerequisite for

---

2. MacIntyre, *Marcuse*, 68.

3. Marcuse, *Eros and Civilization*, xiii.

4. Valiavicharska, "Herbert Marcuse, the Liberation of 'Man,' and Hegemonic Humanism," 808. In this sense, Marxist humanism refers to the earlier works of Marx such as the *1844 Manuscripts* and the developed critique that Marx makes of Hegel's idealistic response to existential themes such as alienation, objectification, human emancipation, and freedom. Central figures in the rise of Marxist humanism were Theodor Adorno (1903–1969) and György Lukács (1885–1971). See also Scruton, *Fools, Frauds and Firebrands*, 116–77.

5. Freud's primary work on the *Eros* and *Thanatos* instincts is outlined in his seminal work *Beyond the Pleasure Principle*, first published in 1920.

civilization. Rather, instead of viewing the need to repress personal pleasure as a necessary trade-off for societal harmony, Marcuse sought to show that the scarcity of resources often blamed for the repression of pleasure is in fact an inbuilt feature of late capitalism with the objective of social domination.[6] Marcuse used the term "surplus repression" to refer to those additional controls imposed by society beyond those necessary for civilized human association.[7] These added restrictions operate to maintain the domination of the ruling system by subduing the attainment of personal pleasure. Marcuse's utopian optimism can be gleaned from his rejection of Freud's assertion that a trade-off between pleasure and reality is necessary for society to function optimally. Marcuse challenges Freud by framing the notion of scarcity and repression as historically contingent, and thus envisions a future where not only is the possibility to pursue uninhibited pleasure actively promoted, but also the ability to totally refashion human nature itself is enabled. In his 1967 lecture titled the *End of Utopia*, Marcuse stated: "What is at stake is the idea of a new theory of man, not only as theory but also as a way of existence: the genesis and development of a vital need for freedom and of the vital needs of freedom—of a freedom no longer based on and limited by scarcity and the necessity of alienated labour."[8]

In arguably his most famous work, *One-Dimensional Man*, Marcuse turned his attention to the way in which modern industrial society effectively uses the fruits of capitalism to generate the conditions for total social domination. This is achieved through the ability of technology to fundamentally restructure both labour and leisure. Marcuse noted that this restructuring results in a critical integration between the individual and the plethora of consumer goods offered by late capitalism. In this way, mass consumerism, entertainment, and material comfort transform the individual into a docile subject disinterested in challenging the status quo. An example of this is the conflation of a person's needs and desires with the productive output that the technological machine generates. Marcuse stated that "the people recognise themselves into their commodities; they find their soul in their automobile, hi-fi set, split level home, kitchen equipment."[9] The effect of this conflation between sub-

---

6. Marcuse, *Eros and Civilization*, 36–38. See also Cho, "Thanatos and Civilization," 32.

7. Marcuse, *Eros and Civilization*, 37.

8. Marcuse, *Psychoanalyse Und Politik*, 16.

9. Marcuse, *One-Dimensional Man*, 12.

jective identity and the goods produced is the fabrication of false needs and the negation of any critical capacities for emancipation. What Marcuse claimed is that this totally administered society uses technology in a way that "invades" and "whittles down" the inner freedom of the human person so that an effective mimesis between the individual and society is actualized.[10] For Marcuse, the most sinister aspect of this entire system is the inability of this "one-dimensional" mode of thought to ever reflectively negate this state of being and envision authentic freedom. Central to Marcuse's thought—and that of Critical Theory more broadly—is the ability to overcome the coercion of oppressive systems and identify one's true needs.[11] However, the inability of the human person to identify true needs and resist the coercion of the establishment is not solely the result of the docility and distraction afforded by consumerism. Central to this restrictive framework, according to Marcuse, are the prevailing forms of rationality that inhibit creative thought and behaviour. Marcuse developed themes in both Hegel and Marx to contrast dialectical thinking—that is the ability to think critically and envisage other modes of existence—with the dominant technological rationality concerned only with a certain scientific pragmatism in a bid to control both nature and human action.[12] Thus individual rationality, critical reason, creative thinking, and freedom itself are sacrificed for an instrumental rationality that cannot escape its own political ends. Marcuse noted that "Nature, scientifically comprehended and mastered, reappears in the technical apparatus of production and destruction which sustains and improves the life of the individuals while subordinating them to the masters of the apparatus."[13] Hence, technological rationality, whilst claiming to operate in a value-neutral space, has in fact been used as an inbuilt feature of capitalism to administer thoughts and desires to man. Reducing knowledge and understanding to its instrumental benefit only (in a productive sense) incapacitates the ability for the individual to uncover true needs. Marcuse claimed that there need not necessarily be a trade-off between a more comfortable standard of living afforded by technology on the one

10. Marcuse, *One-Dimensional Man*, 12.
11. Geuss, *The Idea of Critical Theory*, 55.
12. Marcuse notes, "The principles of modern science were *a priori* structured in such a way that they could serve as conceptual instruments for a universe of self-propelling, productive control; theoretical operationalism came to correspond to practical operationalism." *One-Dimensional Man*, 162.
13. Marcuse, *One-Dimensional Man*, 26.

hand and the accompanying exploitation through instrumental rationality on the other. In other words, no essential link exists between the advanced productive system and social domination. Ironically, Marcuse envisioned a future where advancements in technology could indeed be used toward a "life-affirming ethos."[14] This positive use of technology would, amongst other things, "end the competitive struggle for existence; abolish poverty and reconstruct a social and natural environment that is a peaceful, beautiful universe."[15] Therefore, this life-affirming use of technology, ordered toward human liberation, would untie man from the realm of necessity and open up the space for a more authentic pursuit of happiness.[16]

For Marcuse, freedom is achieved once the human person is able to break free from the chains of capitalism and live as an authentic individual, unaffected by any impositions or intrusions from outside of the self. According to this understanding, the domination of a fully administered society permeates into every aspect of one's existence and to break free, one must reject the false needs imposed by the ruling class. In order to discover one's true needs, the individual must revolt against the status quo and engage in what Marcuse referred to as the "Great Refusal," that ultimate act of rebellion that he described as "the protest against unnecessary repression, and the struggle for the ultimate form of freedom."[17] A concise picture of what this form of ultimate freedom would look like in a concrete sense is not always clear or consistent in Marcuse's writings. What is clear, however, is Marcuse's insistence upon a radical qualitative change deep within the individual. Echoing Nietzsche, Marcuse calls for a "transvaluation of values" together with a restructuring of the instinctual and biological elements within the human subject.[18] Although utilizing the physiological language of "biology" and "vitality," Marcuse's reference is to those existential needs or desires which if left unsatisfied would result in the alienation and "dysfunction of the organism."[19] The pursuit of instinctual gratification without guilt—epitomized by the "Free Love" and hippie movements of the 1960s—is held up by Marcuse as an

14. Feenberg, "Radical Philosophy of Technology," 209.

15. Marcuse, *An Essay on Liberation*, 280.

16. Marcuse, *One-Dimensional Man*, 3. See also Valiavicharska, "Herbert Marcuse, the Liberation of Man," 810.

17. Marcuse, *Eros and Cizilization*, 149; *One-Dimensional Man*, 256.

18. Marcuse, *Essay on Liberation*, 6.

19. Marcuse, *Essay on Liberation*, 1.

example of how a vitality towards freedom could be materialized through an open rebellion against the status quo. This emphasis upon freedom as a biological necessity stems from Marcuse's attempt to contribute to the early work of Marx, which offered a material basis for the reality of human alienation.[20] Agreeing with Marx's claims in the *Paris Manuscripts of 1844* that the locus of this alienation is the fact that true fulfillment cannot be attained by workers in the capitalist system, Marcuse sought to ground authentic humanism not in any idealistic or transcendent foundations but rather by driving downward into the material nature of man: "Liberation seems to be predicated upon an opening and activation of a depth of human existence, this side and underneath the traditional material base: Not an idealistic dimension, over and above the material base, but a dimension even more material than the material base, a dimension underneath the material base."[21]

The needs and satisfactions of Marcuse's liberated man are tied to those traits that he defined as the distinguishing features of the human person, namely the presence of a free and creative subjectivity.[22] Rather ironically, this vision of freedom is reliant upon an advancement in technology that is capable of radically altering the demanding nature of work placed on the human person. By focusing technology upon the affirmation of life and pleasure as opposed to profit and production, the burden of necessity can be finally overcome. Replacing this would be what Marcuse described as a "sensuous and aesthetic society," largely focused upon the recapturing of imagination and creativity.[23] Not too different from the Marxist epigram of the man being free to engage in the full gamut of human experiences throughout the day, Marcuse's sensuous man would guide the reconstruction of "a society devoid of ugliness, enforced togetherness, pollution, and rich with tranquillity, joy, pacifism and pleasure."[24] In this way production, rather than being focused upon profit and accumulation, would instead be united with a sensuous imagination focused on creativity and spontaneity.

Together with this new sensuous imagination is Marcuse's undeniable emphasis upon sexual gratification as a manifestation of personal

20. Balibar, *The Philosophy of Marx*, 18.
21. Marcuse, "Liberation from the Affluent Society," 183.
22. Marcuse, *One-Dimensional Man*, xxviii.
23. Marcuse, *Eros and Civilization*, 223.
24. Marcuse, *Essay on Liberation*, 8.

freedom. Marcuse equates the eroticization of the whole human person as one of the fruits of a society emancipated from oppression. Once the burden of an administered society disappears, the whole being can be transformed into a conduit of pleasure and, as Marcuse claimed, return to a "pre-genital polymorphous sexuality."[25] As a result, institutions that formerly organized personal relationships such as the patriarchal and monogamous family would be disintegrated, and a new free play of individuals would be developed. Against those that claimed that this would be nothing more than a total explosion of sexual maniacs, Marcuse answered quite ambiguously that what would occur would be a "libidinizing of all activity."[26]

In his analysis of the obstruction of freedom in the advanced society, Marcuse's thought represents an interplay between protest and pleasure centred upon the dominant theme of self-determination and radical subjectivity.[27] Whilst the importance of self-determination for human freedom is evident in alternate pictures of freedom to that of Herbert Marcuse, what is striking in Marcuse's vision is the strict refusal to ground self-determination in any transcendent or idealistic foundations. In contrast, we now turn to a thinker equally concerned about the notion of freedom in the administered society but boldly prepared to herald the transcendent source of human self-determination.

Romano Guardini

Despite retiring prematurely due to the rise of the Third Reich and never holding a teaching position in a theology faculty, Romano Guardini's writings greatly influenced both the Second Vatican Council and numerous influential Catholic theologians of the twentieth century, most notably Joseph Ratzinger.[28] A deeply prolific writer, Guardini's thought

---

25. Marcuse, *Eros and Civilization*, 206.

26. Malinovich, "On Herbert Marcuse and the Concept of Psychological Freedom," 171.

27. Kellner, "Marcuse and the Quest for Radical Subjectivity," 3–4. Kellner notes that "Marcuse posits a bodily, erotic, gendered, and aestheticized subjectivity that overcomes mind–body dualism, avoids idealist and rational essentialism, and is constructed in a specific social milieu and is challenged to reconstruct itself and emancipate itself from limited and oppressive forms."

28. Krieg, "Romano Guardini's Theology of the Human Person," 458. See also Rowland, *Catholic Theology*, 34.

can be categorized as an attempt to present a unified picture of "Christian existence." This existence is characterized by a fundamental relationship with Jesus Christ, a relationship that anchors both personhood and, subsequently, human freedom. Guardini's writings reveal an aversion to the modern tendency to fragment elements of existence and modes of thought. The inclination to separate spheres of knowledge into compartments where they can be studied in isolation from one another is considered by Guardini as incapable of viewing the world as the gift of creation and thus distorting an authentic understanding of the human person.[29]

Importantly, Guardini attempted to dialogue with modernity by highlighting the deficiencies of a progressive society devoid of any metaphysics of transcendence. In his view, a world blind to its supernatural foundation is unable to provide any meaningful understanding of one's existence. Subsequently, Guardini's criticisms of the commodification of man by technology is predicated upon a particular vision of the human person and reality itself. Eight years prior to Herbert Marcuse's critique on the effect of technology on human individuality, Guardini noted the following: "The rise of technology is creating a radically different sociological type and attitude. The new man finds the ideal of the self-made and creative personality inimical; he refuses to grant that the autonomous subject is the measure of human perfection."[30] Guardini wrote this passage in his 1956 work *The End of the Modern World*, with the objective of tracing the disintegration of the human person and the rise of the "mass man."[31] For Guardini, the "mass man" represents the progeny of a world no longer connected to nature in a cosmic sense. This picture of nature, now seen purely for its instrumental and exploitive value, leaves the human person in a fractured cosmos lacking any critical unity.[32] In this new world, the human person loses what Guardini terms "real existence" through a rejection of transcendence and a belief that scientific rationality and technology are the only gateways to truth. Equally problematic for Guardini is the loss of individuality, substituted now for the banality of group conformity.[33] In a strikingly similar observation that Marcuse

29. Guardini, *Freedom, Grace, and Destiny*, 9.
30. Guardini, *The End of the Modern World*, 58.
31. Guardini, *The End of the Modern World*, xx.
32. Guardini, *The End of the Modern World*, 69.
33. Guardini, *Freedom, Grace, and Destiny*, 24.

would make almost a decade later in *One-Dimensional Man*, Guardini laments the alienation caused by the tendency in the modern world for man's identity to be absorbed into the fruits of technology and the emphasis upon the use of instrumental reason abstracted from concrete existence.[34] Whilst both Guardini and Marcuse critique the problematic elements of technology for its capacity to inhibit the freedom of the individual, Guardini's picture of freedom is underpinned by a radically different understanding of what it means to be a human person.

A comprehensive account of Guardini's understanding of the human person can be found in his 1939 work *The World and the Person*.[35] Guardini's overarching theme relating to personhood is its ontological reliance upon relationship. After categorizing numerous elements that make up personhood—including form, individuality, and personality—Guardini noted that one's personhood begins at the moment of subjective self-awareness.[36] In this way, the term "person" reflects a particular mode of existence, a subject capable of knowing, acting and creating, and a mode which arrives constantly at a meeting point that elicits "existential wonder."[37] Guardini wrote: "To the question 'What is your person?' I cannot answer 'my body, my soul, my reason, my will, my freedom, my spirit.' All this is not as yet the person but, as it were, the stuff of which it is made; the person itself is the fact that it exists in the form of a being which belongs to itself."[38]

Importantly, Guardini stressed that this critical moment of self-positing that is necessary for personhood, the recognition of one's own self, is only one half of the equation. The fullness of personhood is only realized through an encounter with another person. Guardini notes that this encounter is not simply the relationship between a subject and its object but rather a vulnerable moment when both persons accept each other as they truly are and reciprocate the function of being toward one

---

34. Guardini, *The End of Modern World*, 58. See also Guardini, *Letters from Lake Como: Explorations in Technology and the Human Race*, 111: "Our attention today is claimed for rational and utilitarian tasks in such a way that we can no longer pay attention to that other dimension of our existence."

35. First published in German as *Welt Und Person*. The English translation is *The World and the Person*. The book is a collection of three essays: "The World," "The Person," and "Providence." In the English translation, "Providence" appears as a section within the essay "The Person."

36. Guardini, *The World and the Person*, 120.

37. Guardini, *The World and the Person*, 119.

38. Guardini, *The World and the Person*, 118.

another: "In the measure in which I release the being which at first I regarded only as an object, and consider it as a self meeting me from its own centre, permitting it to become my 'Thou,' I pass from the attitude of a using or fighting subject into that of the 'I.'"[39]

Overcoming the vulnerability of this critical meeting point in the "I–thou" relationship are two indispensable features that Guardini claimed as decisive for the spiritual health of persons in relationship: justice and love. Through a recognition of justice, the person acknowledges a certain intrinsic character to all of reality and as such laws reflective of this are to be upheld and preserved. In a similar way, love enables the individual to perceive the value in another personal being and thus enables one to move out from a space of self-centredness and begin to experience what Guardini referred to as the "truest self."[40]

Guardini's rejection of the construal of the human person as an isolated self-contained being necessitates an account of human freedom that navigates between two poles: on the one hand a promethean sense of self, characterized by the negation of any external authority upon one's will, and on the other hand a heteronomy that dictates upon the individual particular modes of thought and behaviour from outside of the self, such as the forced restrictions of totalitarian regimes.[41] In outlining a way through this, Guardini claimed that "the phenomenon we know as freedom is realized only in right action in concrete circumstances."[42] This was in response to what he considered to be a truncated modern view of freedom, namely the tendency to "abstract" freedom from any true object and envision freedom as simply a floating concept, applied arbitrarily by the subject to a myriad of finite ends incapable of providing any lasting fulfillment. In contrast, Guardini conceives of freedom as being centred upon an innate desire within the human person to conform to the truth of existence. This conformity to the truth of one's existence is reflected in what Guardini considers to be the qualitative determinant of freedom; an assent toward the Good. In choosing to conform with the Good and act in accordance with one's nature, freedom is guarded against both an unconstrained will and a mere pragmatism.[43] Therefore free action

---

39. Guardini, *The World and the Person*, 128–29.
40. Guardini, *The World and the Person*, 118.
41. Krieg, "Theology of the Human Person," 464.
42. Guardini, *Freedom, Grace, and Destiny*, 47.
43. Guardini, *Freedom, Grace, and Destiny*, 50–51.

manifests itself only when it is correctly ordered toward a desire that is intrinsic to man's very being. This ontological desire, pointing toward a true understanding of reality and by extension free action, enables man to conform to his true self by attaching his actions toward the proper object of freedom.[44] Critically, this attachment to freedom's true object requires a recognition of the spiritual character of the human person. Guardini stresses that a purely mechanical or materialistic conception of the human person would be imprisoned within the self and he thus identifies the reality of the spirit as that which enables the human person to identify God as creator and to recognize the gift of God's unique call to each person. He noted, "Spirit is that reality by which man is able to comprehend God—as befits the nature of the creature, not in a manner proper to God, but by all those acts and ways in which man lays hold of God as an object, as a measure, as a prerequisite, within the limits defined by his human existence."[45]

Thus, for Guardini, what makes freedom possible is the attachment of the proper subject—the spiritual nature of the person—with its proper object: God. Importantly, the spirit is not to be viewed as an element or aspect contained within the human person but rather is to be understood as man himself. The relationship of the body and spirit is one of synergy, expression, and interdependence; however, Guardini emphasized that "without the spirit the body disintegrates."[46] It is only this spiritual-corporeal man that is capable of freedom. Tying together Guardini's account of both the subject and object of freedom is a Christocentric thread expressed as a relationship conferred by grace. This crucial relationship is manifested in an encounter whereby the human person is granted its perfect "thou" with the very source of one's being. In approaching man and allowing man to receive Him, God opens the space for man to discover himself and enter into full possession of himself.[47] The freedom made capable by this "I–thou" relationship is possible only due to the Trinitarian nature of the Christian God. Through the gift of grace, the human person is able to respond to the call of encounter and enter into what Guardini termed the "existentiality of Christ's existence."[48] Importantly,

44. Scola, "Freedom, Grace, and Destiny," 454; Guardini, *Freedom, Grace, and Destiny*, 81–82.
45. Guardini, *The Focus of Freedom*, 156.
46. Guardini, *Freedom, Grace, and Destiny*, 64.
47. Guardini, *Freedom, Grace, and Destiny*, 128.
48. Guardini, *World and Person*, 156.

man does not stand face to face with Christ, but rather enters into Christ and follows Christ in facing toward the ultimate "thou" and saying "I."[49] This does not result in a blotting out of one's self and a loss of autonomy but rather is an opening up of one's true self through the indwelling of Christ. This interweaving with the life of the Trinity is completed through the Holy Spirit, who through Baptism enables the human person to die with Christ and live as a new creation.[50]

We may describe the basic outline for Guardini's conception of human freedom as comprising of four elements. Firstly, freedom is made possible only when one is able to live and act in accordance with the true reality of their nature. Secondly, one's true nature is characterized by a spiritual personhood which comprises two elements: a subjective awareness of one's self and the recognition that the subjective self is made whole only in the encounter with the other.[51] Thirdly, by virtue of creation, the proper object of the human subject is none other than the ultimate source of one's being, the Trinitarian God. Fourth and finally, it is only with Christ, who shares human existence in every respect, and through the Holy Spirit that the human person is able to come face to face with the Father and thus realize who he or she really is.[52] In this way, the finite freedom of man is united to the infinite freedom of the Trinity and as a result unveils the true destiny of the human person.

Italian theologian Angelo Scola, in an essay sharing the title of Guardini's famous work *Freedom, Grace, and Destiny*, emphasized the attainment of human freedom as a function of sharing in this Trinitarian relationship. Scola writes, "The difference between finite freedom and infinite freedom is therefore an image of the holy and infinite difference within the mystery of God himself. I mean the difference between the hypostases of the Father and the Son, a difference kept open and sealed by the fecundity of the Holy Spirit who proceeds from them both."[53]

---

49. Krieg, "Theology of the Human Person," 473.

50. Guardini, *World and Person*, 157; *Freedom, Grace, and Destiny*, 129; 2 Cor 5:17.

51. Guardini, *Freedom, Grace, and Destiny*, 123. "Man's historical character denotes also that he comes into act not only from himself but also in an encounter with others.... It means that man comes into spiritual contact with things, that he knows and assesses them, adopts an attitude towards them and uses them, fashions them and creates with them. His capacities unfold and his personality expresses itself in the process, or, on the other hand, they may be restricted and destroyed."

52. Guardini, *World and Person*, 155.

53. Scola, "Freedom, Grace, and Destiny," 460.

In Guardini's thought, this attachment to the mystery of the Trinity as the source of one's self-determination and the subsequent understanding of freedom is not to be viewed as a descent into a form of heteronomy so repudiated by the modern man. Rather, in acknowledging God as the source of all existence, the human person is able to act in accordance with their true nature and, through seeking knowledge, love, and creativity, come to discover true freedom.[54]

Guardini's and Marcuse's Conceptions of Human Freedom

In both Guardini's and Marcuse's conceptions of human freedom, the importance of self-determination is clear. What differs substantially, however, is where each of them locates the starting point for determining one's self and how this relates to freedom. Marcuse sought to ground freedom by driving downward into the depth of one's self and seeking pleasures that invariably differ from individual to individual. More crucially, what is required for true freedom is a total rejection of any standards, norms, or distractions which would inhibit the fulfillment of desires considered necessary for authentic existence. Consistent with his understanding of the human person is the importance placed on the unrestrained will. The descendants of Marcuse's picture of human freedom manifest themselves in the popular culture of Western society. The notion of freedom as nothing more than the atomised self and the free exercise of one's will seeking pleasure is writ large not only in popular culture but also in the framing of political issues in Western liberal democracies.[55] Nowhere is this more obvious than in the sexualized consumer culture of the twenty-first century and the consequences of the sexual revolution more broadly. The current aversion to any restriction upon pornographic content and the movement toward a total refashioning of sexual identity is evidence of the championing of choice, pleasure, and the commodification of the human body. If true freedom is to be grounded in a promethean conception of radical subjectivity, whereby relationships with other persons are simply an incidental aspect of existence itself, a strong argument against any external restrictions on one's personal choices becomes difficult to justify. In what appears to be

---

54. Guardini, *Freedom, Grace, and Destiny*, 80.
55. Kalb, *The Tyranny of Liberalism*, 55.

a succint encapsulation of a Marcusian understanding of the primacy of freedom as the unbridled will, David Bentley Hart notes:

> It is in the will—in the liberty of choice—that we place primary value, which means that we must as a society strive, as far as possible, to recognize as few objective goods outside the self as we possible can. Of course, we are prepared to set certain objective social and legal limits to the exercise of the will, but these are by their very nature flexible and frail, and the great interminable task of human liberation—as we tend to understand it—is to erase as many of these limits as we safely can.[56]

In contrast to a modern secular understanding of freedom, the spiritually conscious notion of freedom promoted by Romano Guardini seeks to orientate freedom upward and emanating from outside of the self and into relationship. This understanding of freedom views personal autonomy not as an end in itself but rather as a mechanism to move toward the authentic life of relationship with one's creator and in the ability to freely choose actions that conform to one's true nature. This picture of freedom squares with the reality that human beings enter into existence not as enclosed blocks of individuality, but rather as beings ontologically linked to relationship.

The indispensable theme of relationship so crucial to Guardini's vision of freedom is emphasized in the writings of Joseph Ratzinger/Pope Benedict XVI. In an essay titled "Truth and Freedom," Ratzinger used the example of a mother and her child to emphasize the notion of human-connectedness as intrinsic to one's nature and thus foundational to an authentic understanding of freedom.[57] When this relational character to freedom is jettisoned, Ratzinger notes that not only is a liberation from authority demanded, but more destructively, a liberation from one's true essence is seen to be the ultimate frontier of freedom.[58] This pairing of relationship and freedom is further connected to moral conviction of an assent toward the Good in Benedict XVI's 2007 encyclical *Spe salvi*.[59]

---

56. Hart, *In the Aftermath*, 88.

57. Ratzinger, "Truth and Freedom," 26.

58. Ratzinger, "Truth and Freedom," 28. For a comprehensive outline of Ratzinger's writings on freedom see McGregor, "Joseph Ratzinger's Understanding of Freedom," 352–53. McGregor notes, "For Ratzinger, one cannot understand freedom as long as one sees the human person in his or her individuality, without reference to the other person and to the whole of mankind," 354.

59. Benedict XVI, *Spe salvi*.

Benedict notes that social structures alone cannot guarantee freedom, but rather what is required is a "community animated by convictions."[60] Through a community united by love, the moral conviction to assent towards the Good can be achieved. As a result, the true essence of human nature can be revealed, and authentic freedom safeguarded. Finally, Ratzinger notes that Christianity itself is to be seen as a philosophy of freedom. In his *Introduction to Christianity* he stated: "the explanation of all reality as a whole is not an all-embracing consciousness or one single materiality; on the contrary, at the summit stands a freedom that thinks and, by thinking, creates freedoms, thus making freedom the structural form of being."[61]

Bibliography

Abromeit, John, and W. Mark Cobb. *Herbert Marcuse: A Critical Reader.* New York: Routledge, 2004.

Balibar, Etienne. *The Philosophy of Marx.* Translated by Chris Turner. London: Verso, 2017.

Benedict XVI. *Spe salvi.* Encyclical Letter. Vatican website (November 20, 2007). http://www.vatican.va/edocs/ENG0141/_INDEX.HTM.

Cho, Daniel. "Thanatos and Civilization: Lacan, Marcuse, and the Death Drive." *Policy Futures in Education* 4 (2006) 18–32.

Cooper, David. *The Dialectics of Liberation.* London: Verso, 2015.

Feenberg, Andrew. "Radical Philosophy of Technology." *Radical Philosophy Review* 12 (2009) 199–217.

Geuss, Raymond. *The Idea of Critical Theory: Habermas and the Frankfurt School.* Cambridge: Cambridge University Press, 1981.

Guardini, Romano. *The End of the Modern World.* Delaware: ISI Books, 1956.

———. *The Focus of Freedom.* Translated by Gregory Roettger OSB. Baltimore: Helicon, 1966.

———. *Freedom, Grace, and Destiny: Three Chapters in the Interpretation of Existence.* London: Harvill, 1961.

———. *Letters from Lake Como: Explorations in Technology and the Human Race.* Translated by Geoffrey W. Bromiley. Grand Rapids: Eerdmans, 1994.

———. *The World and the Person.* Translated by Stella Lange. Chicago: Regnery, 1969.

Hart, David Bentley. *In the Aftermath: Provocations and Laments.* Grand Rapids: Eerdmans, 2009.

Kalb, James. *The Tyranny of Liberalism: Understanding and Overcoming Administered Freedom, Inquisitorial Tolerance, and Equality by Command.* Wilmington, DE: ISI Books, 2008.

---

60. Benedict XVI, *Spe salvi*, 24.
61. Ratzinger, *Introduction to Christianity*, 157–58.

Kellner, Douglas. "Marcuse and the Quest for Radical Subjectivity." In *Herbert Marcuse: A Critical Reader*, edited by John Abromeit and W. Mark Cobb. New York: Routledge, 2004.
Krieg, Robert A. "Romano Guardini's Theology of the Human Person." *Theological Studies* 59 (1998) 457–74.
MacIntyre, Alasdair. *Marcuse*. London: Fontana, 1970.
Malinovich, Myriam Miedzian. "On Herbert Marcuse and the Concept of Psychological Freedom." *Social Research* 49 (1982) 158–80.
Marcuse, Herbert. *Eros and Civilization*. Boston: Beacon, 1966.
———. *An Essay on Liberation*. Boston: Beacon, 1969.
———. "Liberation from the Affluent Society." In *The Dialectis of Liberation*, edited by David Cooper. London: Verso, 2015.
———. *One-Dimensional Man*. Abingdon, UK: Routledge, 1964.
———. *One-Dimensional Man: Studies in the Ideology of Advanced Industrial Society*. 2nd ed. New York: Routledge, 2002.
———. *Psychoanalyse und Politik*. Hamburg: Europaische Verlagsanstalt, 1972.
McGregor, Peter John. "Joseph Ratzinger's Understanding of Freedom." *Radical Orthodoxy* 2 (2014) 335–78.
Ratzinger, Joseph. *Introduction to Christianity*. Translated by J. R. Foster. San Francisco: Ignatius, 2004.
———. "Truth and Freedom." Translated by Adrian Walker. *Communio* 23 (Spring 1996) 16–34.
Rowland, Tracey. *Catholic Theology*. New York: Bloomsbury, 2017.
Scruton, Roger. *Fools, Frauds and Firebrands: Thinkers of the New Left*. London: Bloomsbury, 2015.
Scola, Angelo. "Freedom, Grace, and Destiny." *Communio* 25 (Fall 1998) 439–61.
Valiavicharska, Zhivka. "Herbert Marcuse, the Liberation of 'Man,' and Hegemonic Humanism." *Theory and Event* 20 (2017) 804–27.

11

Rahner's Last Gambit

The Idea of Christianity in a World of Pure Ideas

MADDISON JAY REDDIE-CLIFFORD

This paper explores the extent to which Rahner's *Foundations of Christian Faith* can be read as a response to the rise of French post-structuralist postmodernism in the German universities. It examines the historical development of postmodernism that culminates in the 1967 symposium at Johns Hopkins University in dialogue with the history of the development of *Foundations*.

Introduction

RAHNER'S FOUNDATIONS OF CHRISTIAN *Faith: An Introduction to the Idea of Christianity* is one of the most controversial of the influential theologian's writings. Published in 1972, the text had a tortuous journey towards publication. According to the editors of the project at Herder, the project died more than once.[1] This paper aims to explore the extent to which the alternative creeds found in *Foundations* were a response to

1. Batlogg, Michalski, and Turner, *Encounters with Karl Rahner*.

a particular phenomenon of the late 1960s: postmodernism. We contend that the theological creed represents an attempt to define the most essential dogma of the Catholic faith relationally rather than definitionally; that the theological creed emphasizes the relationships that are essential to Catholic theology, from God to Christ, from Christ to man, and from man back to Christ. We contend that this attempt to define these most important truths is a probable consequence of the encounter in the late 1960s of two divergent notions of *symbol*: Rahner's concept of *RealSymbol* and the post-structuralist concept of the linguistic *sign*.

To fully explicate the significance of Rahner's argument we will first examine a divergent path of theory on the nature of the linguistic *sign*, and how semiological structuralism gave rise to post-structuralism. We will then contrast this with how Rahner's transcendental theology, mediated by both his theology of the *RealSymbol* and the historical phenomena surrounding *Foundations of Christian Faith*, culminated in the theological creed found in *Foundations*. It is our hypothesis that by understanding these two divergent historical developments in the notion of the symbol, we may come to a more favorable hermeneutic for understanding Rahner's intention in composing the material found in *Foundations*.

The Semiology of Ferdinand de Saussure

Ferdinand de Saussure, in his revolutionary lectures, outlined several key qualities inherent to the process of human communication. As he rightly identified, understanding how human language functioned was a deeply important activity for those engaged in the human sciences.[2] The key theme of Saussure taken up by the humanities was the relationship between the word that is the act of speech and the meaning of the word. As Saussure outlines, language is comprised of three principal elements: *sign, signified, signifier*. To understand what he meant by these three elements we must appreciate that Saussure developed his understanding as a way of understanding the linguistic sign: "The linguistic sign unites, not a thing and a name, but a concept and a sound image. The latter is not the material sound, a purely physical thing, but the psychological imprint of the sound, the impression that it makes in our senses."[3] This definition

---

2. Saussure, *Course in General Linguistics*.
3. Saussure, *Course in General Linguistics*, 66.

of the linguistic sign did not suffice to elucidate the nuance of Saussure's analysis: "I call the combination of a concept and a sound-image a *sign*, but the current usage of the term generally designates only a sound-image, a word."[4] Saussure instead redefined the relationship between *concept* and *word*: "I propose to retain the word *sign* [*signe*] to designate the whole and to replace *concept* and *sound-image* respectively by *signified* [*signifie*] and *signifier* [*signifiant*]; the last two terms have the advantage of indicating the opposition that separates them from each other and from the whole of which they are parts."[5] By defining the sound-image and the concept in opposition to each other, Saussure was able to determine two basic principles that defined the relationship between the *signified* and the *signifier*, the first principle—the arbitrary nature of the bond between the *signified* and the *signifier*—being the most relevant for our purposes.

As Saussure explains, the arbitrary relationship of this bond is self-evident. Consider the *signifier* "tree." We identify this with the mental concept of the tree because that is what we affirm it to identify with. If we were to use Latin, the *signified* we communicate by the concept would be the *signifier* "arbour" instead. This reveals two things: first, that the *signified* is only related to the *signifier* by the act of human affirmation, and secondly, that human communications rely upon an external arbiter to provide stability of meaning and thus communication. As Saussure exposits, "In fact, every means of expression used in society is based, in principle, on collective behaviour or—what amounts to the same thing—on convention. Polite formulas, for instance, though often imbued with a certain natural expressiveness (as in the case of a Chinese who greets his emperor by bowing down to the ground nine times), are nonetheless fixed by rule; it is this rule and the intrinsic value of the gestures that obliges one to use them."[6]

Because there is no intrinsic property that links the *signified* to the *signifier* for the act of communication, we must rely upon a set of shared meanings and definitions to facilitate our communications. However, these shared expectations of meanings cannot be truly noticeable as a part of the act of speaking. Though we have a dependence on meanings that we share communally, this codependence of context and expression is not readily accessible to the human person in their daily life. As Saussure

---

4. Saussure, *Course in General Linguistics*, 67.
5. Saussure, *Course in General Linguistics*, 67.
6. Saussure, *Course in General Linguistics*, 68.

notes, "The first thing that strikes us when we study the facts of language is that their succession in time does not exist insofar as the speaker is concerned. He is confronted with a state. That is why the linguist who wishes to understand a state must discard all knowledge of everything that produced it and ignore diachrony. He can enter the mind of speakers only by completely suppressing the past. The intervention of history can only falsify his judgement."[7] That is to say, individuals when they speak are not particularly aware of the significance that their language developed historically. Similarly, we must be aware that being mindful of the historical development of concepts introduces the risk that we see our communicative actions as entirely formed consequent to history; that we are *structured* by the past in such a way that our future is determined.

The inevitable consequence was the school of humanities scholarship that we call structuralism. Heavily influenced by Marxist theories on the nature of how society is ordered, structuralism suggests that fundamentally, society acts as the structural framework that makes possible many of the intricacies of human life. In this way, we as people form the society, but the society also structures who and what we are as individuals. This contingent relationship is why we have an obligation to the society every bit as necessary as our society's obligation to us. A mutual dependence is the consequence.

Time has shown that Saussure's semiology has limits that one reaches under certain conditions. Jacques Derrida and Roland Barthes were two scholars who noticed this.

From Structuralism to Post-Structuralism

The inevitable conclusion of the post-structuralist critique of truth was that in all spheres—not just literature—we could not state with certainty the absolute of meaning. This was a disastrous turning point in the history of twentieth-century philosophy. A critique of whether it would be possible within the limits of the fields of human communications for *truth* itself to be possible undermines the very substance of the modernist consensus, be it Marxist, liberal, or realist. Jacques Derrida, in 1967, presented a lecture at the John Hopkins Symposium on Structuralism that laid bare the implicit contradiction of the definition of transcendental properties of analysis.

---

7. Saussure, *Course in General Linguistics*, 81.

Derrida's Critique of Finality

Derrida begins his commentary with some observations about the methodological claims of structuralist anthropologist Claude Levi-Strauss: "When Levi-Strauss says in the preface to *The Raw and the Cooked* that he has 'sought to transcend the opposition between the sensible and the intelligible by placing (himself) from the very beginning at the level of signs,' the necessity, force, and legitimacy of his act cannot make us forget that the concept of the sign cannot in itself surpass or bypass the opposition between the sensible and the intelligible."[8] According to Derrida, there is a fundamental problem with a methodological approach that attempts to define a definitive or total system or analysis. Derrida rejects Levi-Strauss's attempt as being damaging to the legitimacy of the semiological theories that underpin Levi-Strauss's theoretical framework. Undoing the radical opposition between *signified* and *signifier* is a self-defeating endeavor. As Derrida explains, "The concept of the sign is determined by this opposition: through and throughout the totality of its history and by its system. But we cannot do without the concept of the sign, for we cannot give us this metaphysical complicity without also giving up the critique we are directing against this complicity, without the risk of erasing difference (altogether) in the self-identity of a signified reducing into itself its signifier or, what amounts to the same thing, simply expelling it outside itself."[9]

For Derrida, the attempt to dissolve the intrinsic point of differentiation between the *signifier* and the *signified* is to begin the process of invalidating the theory of the *sign* in and of itself. The key element of the *signifier* is not that it is a word, but that it is the phenomena of experience, the sound-image, or in terms of writing, the physical word on the page. For Derrida, the only thing we communicate through the word (which maintains the linguistic *sign*) is the radical difference between the *signifier* and the *signified*. When you attempt to fix both elements of an individual *sign* permanently, you are making yourself a victim of an intrinsic paradox: "The paradox is that the metaphysical reduction of the sign needed the opposition it was reducing. The opposition is part of the system, along with the reduction."[10] In a sense, Derrida is illustrating the point

---

8. Derrida, "Structure, Sign and Play in the Discourse of the Human Sciences," 250.

9. Derrida, "Structure, Sign and Play in the Discourse of the Human Sciences," 250–51.

10. Derrida, "Structure, Sign and Play in the Discourse of the Human Sciences,"

that Maurice Blondel made in the 1890s: that all things occur in reaction to other things.[11] This dialectic ensures that it is impossible to move towards a finalization of discourse without a recourse to the infinite. While Blondel concludes the philosophical necessity of God, Derrida concludes that definitive *truth* is itself beyond the ability of any scholarship to reach.

Turning to philosophy, Derrida points out how the shared inheritances of syntax necessary for meaningful communication trap metaphysics in a destructive cycle, with a reliance upon metaphysics so as to be capable of denouncing it. Derrida illustrates this with reference to three significant contributors to contemporary philosophy: Friedrich Nietzsche, Sigmund Freud, and Martin Heidegger:

> But all these destructive discourses and all their analogues are trapped in a sort of circle. This circle is unique. It describes the form of the relationship between the history of metaphysics and the destruction of the history of metaphysics. *There is no sense* in doing without the concepts of metaphysics to attack metaphysics. We have no language—no syntax and lexicon—which is alien to this history; we cannot utter a single destructive proposition which has not already slipped into the form, the logic and the implicit postulations of precisely what it seeks to contest.[12]

For Derrida, it is almost impossible to avoid the circular trap implicit within the examination of a metadiscourse. Metaphysics, particularly, falls prey to this cycle:

> But there are many ways of being caught in this circle. They are all more or less naïve, more or less empirical, more or less systematic, more or less close to the formulation or even to the formalization of this circle. It is these differences which explain the multiplicity of destructive discourses and the disagreement between those who make them. It was within concepts inherited from metaphysics that Nietzsche, Freud, and Heidegger worked, for example. Since these concepts are not elements or atoms and since they are taken from a syntax and a system, every particular borrowing drags along with it the whole of metaphysics. This is what allows these destroyers to destroy each other reciprocally—for example, Heidegger, considering Nietzsche, with as much lucidity and rigour as bad faith and misconstruction, as

251.

11. Blondel, *L'Action*.

12. Derrida, "Structure, Sign and Play in the Discourse of the Human Sciences," 250.

the last metaphysician, the last "Platonist." One could do the same for Heidegger himself, for Freud, or for a number of others. And today no exercise is more widespread.[13]

For Derrida, the very process of attempting to define the structures that govern the dialogue simply extends the dialogue. The very act of definition does not reach a universal totality; it extends the totality itself until the next critique similarly extends the totality. With such a process, how can we ever say we have the *Truth* if rather than state the *Truth* all we can do is extend the contents of *Truth*. A definitive undertaking becomes not just impossible but entirely senseless. What benefit can be reached when the very act of stating the metaphysical truth merely expands the content that needs to be stated?

Barthes's Critique of Agency

While Roland Barthes presented a paper at the 1966 John Hopkins Symposium, we will instead focus on a paper he published in 1968. This paper, entitled *The Death of the Author*, is symptomatic of a second characteristic of post-structuralism: the attack on the agency of the individual. The title of this paper has since become idiomatic, but the paper is based on Barthes's interesting insight that in the fulfillment of the act of being an author, the author facilitates their own negation: "As soon as a fact is narrated no longer with a view to acting directly on reality but intransitively, that is to say, finally outside of any function other than that of the very practice of the symbol itself, this disconnection occurs, the voice loses its origin, the author enters into his own death, writing begins."[14]

Barthes observes that the act of writing is an act of creation. Like most creative acts the creator loses control over how the creation utilizes its agency as part of the intrinsic activity of creation. However, Barthes is also minimizing the reality of the creative trajectory inherent to the act of writing. The author is not merely creating *ex nihilo*, but is, in fact, part of a dialectical process; their inspirations, their influences shaping and conditioning the trajectory into which their writing act is acting. For Barthes, however, this process is irrelevant to the written text.

---

13. Derrida, "Structure, Sign and Play in the Discourse of the Human Sciences," 251.

14. Barthes, "The Death of the Author," 142.

Barthes objects to the fetishization of the author as determinative of the meaning of a text: "The *explanation* of a work is always sought in the man or woman who produced it, as if it were always in the end, through the more or less transparent allegory of the fiction, the voice of a single person, the *author* 'confiding' in us."[15] According to Barthes, this view reflects the tyrannical impulses of positivism as an ultimate celebration of the nobility of the human person. For Barthes, though, this was a poor reality, and it was better for one to exalt language than to exalt the author. Barthes's concept of the author is as a creature of their psychology, irrelevant and unrelated to the phenomena of his writings. This reveals that Barthes is operating with a deficient anthropology. He would have us suspicious of any claim to intrinsic dignity, instead focusing on the primacy of language as a medium beyond us as individuals.

What we can briefly conclude is that postmodernism was born out of the post-structuralist critiques of Derrida—whereby the impossibility of the grasping of a totality of discourse renders truth unreachable—and Barthes, who reduces human agency to a fallacy of positivist modernism and elevates the product stripped of all connection to the author. These critiques assume a conception of knowledge that finalizes a totality of a particular discourse. When Derrida finds that it is impossible to finalize a static knowledge that totalizes a discourse, he concludes that *truth* is impossible. Similarly, Barthes concludes that the writer in producing a product renders a new creation into being. In this act, agency transfers from the writer to the text. For Barthes, this transfer does not occasion the transfer of a direction, intention, or purpose, because the text has now become the *other* of the writer, and thus fulfils his total negation. This conclusion for Barthes is a necessary consequence of the denial of the absolute. It is a subversion of the Hegelian concept of self-negation by the fact of its denial of God as the absolute.

What is clear is that the post-structuralist project arises out of a crisis of both major strands of modernist thought. Because both the liberal and Marxist traditions insist on a singular notion of definitive truth, they have sought to derive singular static truths that are definitive to a discipline. Because these traditions argue for a utopic human existence, they deny the absolute within the dialectic. Both require the reaching of perfection within the aegis of human activity. This requires a refutation

---

15. Barthes, "The Death of the Author," 143.

of the absolute as the end and in Barthes reaches the death of agency as a requirement for agency itself.

Foundations as Negation

As we have shown above, postmodernity is born out of a particular problem inherent to modern understandings of the dialectic and a static theory of truth. Considering that Barthes's and Derrida's influence became most potent in the European Academies in the late 1960s and early 1970s, it seems appropriate to examine the core text written by Karl Rahner during this period: *Foundations of Christian Faith*. It is our hypothesis that the alternative theological creed found in *Foundations* was written at least in part as a means of formulating a Christian response to the crisis of *truth* that the emergence of post-structuralism had created.

We would propose that the key to understanding *Foundations* is to understand the intellectual development of Karl Rahner himself. Rahner was never so arrogant as to want to propose foundations for Christianity. Instead, he sought to present an argument that was an apologetic for the very intellectual concept of Christianity, hence the subtitle of "An Introduction to the Idea of Christianity." *The Foundations of Christian Faith* may be the explicit title of the text, but it is the subtitle that explains what the text aims to achieve. In *Hortes des Wortes* (*Hearer of the Word*), Rahner explores the extent to which every act of human knowledge occurs through the connection between affirming outward and receiving inward. Rahner draws on the Hegelian notion of negation to propose that the very act of human knowledge relies upon on an externalizing self-emptying, resembling Hegel's notion from *Phenomenology of Spirit*: "Further, the living Substance is being which is in truth Subject, or, what is the same, is in truth actual only in so far as it is the movement of positing itself, or is the mediation of its self-othering with itself."[16]

One should read *Foundations* in the Hegelian sense as a dialectical negation. We propose that by exposing the historical circumstances that culminate in *Foundations* we can examine the context that engendered its creation. This is particularly relevant for any reading of the alternative theological creed, as this would constitute identifying the question that this alternative creed is supposed to be an answer to. To achieve this, we need to assess two primary categories. The first is the history of ideas

16. Hegel, *Phenomenology of Spirit*, 10.

that culminates in the writing of *Foundations*. The second involves the examination of how reading this history of ideas when engaged with the developments in the understanding of truth in philosophy in the 1960s can provide us with a best reading of the alternative theological creed.

The Constitutive Foundations of the Text

We contend there are three constitutive elements to *Foundations* as text. Firstly, the metaphysical system of transcendental theology that Rahner developed from Jesuit neo-Thomist philosophy. Secondly, Rahner's lifelong interest in the theology of the symbol. And finally, the particular circumstances that Rahner encountered at the University of Munich from 1966 to 1968.

Neo-Thomism

A categorical requirement to understanding Rahner's reaction to post-structuralism is a brief understanding of Jesuit neo-Thomism. Jesuit neo-Thomism was a movement in response to Leo XIII's *Aeterni patris*. This encyclical called for understanding the philosophy of St. Thomas Aquinas in relationship to modern philosophy. Jesuit neo-Thomism, one of the responses to *Aeterni patris*, seeks to demonstrate how the philosophy of St. Thomas Aquinas provides an effective antidote to Immanuel Kant's critique of metaphysics.

The Belgian Jesuit Joseph Marechal and the French Jesuit Pierre Rousselot wrote the first texts of transcendental Thomism at the turn of the twentieth century. Primarily concerned with the encounter between modern philosophy and the scholastics, they devoted considerable time and effort to the theory of knowledge. Marechal believed that the Thomistic theory of knowledge pre figured Immanuel Kant's notion of transcendental knowing. Comparing St. Thomas's concept of doubt with Descartes, Marechal expresses, "The purpose of St. Thomas is not, as with Descartes to reach as soon as possible among all other possible "truths" a privileged one, which is indubitable, well defined and capable of serving as a constructive starting point. His intention is not so particularized, the scope of his doubt is wider and, paradoxical though it may sound, it is more thoroughly 'modern.'"[17] According to Marechal, the fundamen-

---

17. Maréchal, *A Maréchal Reader*, 89.

tal goal of doubt for St. Thomas Aquinas contrasts with Descartes. St. Thomas "aims for nothing less than setting up a general critique of truth as such. That is why the first results of the methodological doubt will not be the same in Thomism and Cartesian metaphysics. The latter reaches the intuitive evidence of the ontological Ego (will it not be imprisoned in it?). The former concludes to the objective necessity of *Being* in general."[18]

It is in the Thomistic first principles of metaphysics that one finds a basis to engage with modern philosophy. Whereas Cartesian metaphysics leads inevitably towards the nihilistic primacy of doubt, Thomistic metaphysics as presented by Marechal reveals the fundamental possibility of being. While we can have doubts about the character and the nature of our knowledge, it is thoroughly beyond us to deny that there are things that exist and that we can ostensibly know about them. There remains as a basic premise the absolute necessity of *beings*, no matter how subjective our experience of these *beings* may be at the phenomenological level. This means that at the categorical level we must assume that *being* exists no matter how much we come to doubt the ontology of that *being*. Marechal takes this Thomistic basis and synthesizes a transcendental method of knowing based on a Thomistic concept of being. The ultimate purpose for this was to demonstrate the necessary affirmation of God as part of every intellectual act. Anthoney Matteo has summarized the logic of Marechal's argument as follows: "transcendental analysis shows that a finalistic dynamism underlies all our cognitive operations . . ."[19] We can demonstrate that there is a finalistic movement or action inherent to all cognitive operations. Things that begin naturally possess an end and all cognitive operations possess a beginning. Therefore, because there is the inner movement towards an absolute finality, we can say that "since no conceivable finite or contingent achievement could possibly satisfy this dynamism, its ultimate end must be the absolute, necessary being or God . . ."[20] As all operations of the intellect are occurring into the infinite of the dialectical action, can we fully have an end to cognitive operations within our life? Surely our subjective teleology will reveal an orientation towards an ultimate destination, "thus, our striving for the this being qualifies as a necessary a priori condition for the possibility of cognition as such, and every intellectual act by which we comprehend some finite

18. Maréchal, *A Maréchal Reader*, 89.
19. Matteo, *Quest for the Absolute*, 110.
20. Matteo, *Quest for the Absolute*, 110.

entity must be seen as a subordinate movement towards absolute being . . ."[21] Every cognitive act aims towards the cognition of the immediate subject while possessing its own finality. However, this is but a contingent part of the broader and deeper continuing finality of the cognitive act. We can thus argue that the subjective intellection towards finality reveals a shared objective quality, that "the fundamental striving toward God, which is the necessary precondition for cognition as such, implies that God is possible . . ."[22] Because all cognition occurs as part of a dynamic action towards the absolute ipso facto, the absolute itself must be a possible end that can be reached. If we are talking about the possibilities of the ends of cognitive action, it is impossible to undertake an action which has a beginning that does not also possess an end. Therefore, we can extend this principle to the final premise of Marechal's logical structure: "in the case of God alone—the necessary being whose existence grounds the possibility of everything else that 'is'—possible existence entails actual existence."[23] This final element reveals the profound insight that was at the heart of the neo-Thomist project: that as part of every cognitive act we affirm God, not in the particulars of His qualities but by the necessity of His relationship to us. We first find God in our turn to ourselves as subject and because we find Him in this turn to ourselves, we find Him at the centre of all creation. The relationship between God as the total end of our subjective self and the God of every other subjective self represents the moment in which we can know the objective reality of God, not from a definitional argument of "He must exist" but rather from a relational argument of "I find God when I find my own subjective end."

This ontological argument forms one of the constitutive elements to Rahner's entire transcendental system. It gives rise to Rahner's notion of the pre-thematic experience of God that is necessary for the cognitive act. In this way, these basic epistemic principles are the foundations of Rahner's transcendental theology. Rahner was not content with just demonstrating how the relationship between thought and finality demonstrated the intrinsic requirement for God. Rahner instead sought to illustrate how the particularity of human history demonstrated the fundamental necessity of the theology of the Christian faith. This attempt was made with his theology of the *RealSymbol*.

21. Matteo, *Quest for the Absolute*, 110.
22. Matteo, *Quest for the Absolute*, 110.
23. Matteo, *Quest for the Absolute*, 110.

The RealSymbol

The *RealSymbol* is one of the most potent notions to occur in Rahner's theology. While it is not as universally known as the concepts of the *Transcendental Existential*, *Vogriff auf en esse*, or *Anonymous Christianity*, the *RealSymbol* is one of the most subversive elements of Rahner's theology, intended to answer a fundamental question of faith; that is, what is Jesus Christ the man to the Christian living today in witness?[24] The *RealSymbol* is present in Rahner's theology from the early 1930s until the end of his life. We find an early example of this theme in the conclusion of his doctoral thesis *E Latere Christi*[25]. Written during the early 1930s, quite probably before he began his PhD in philosophy at Freiburg in 1934, *E Latere Christi* provides a rare insight to Rahner's earliest theological processes. In this rarely examined work, Rahner explores how the scriptural accounts of the life of Christ contained further truths than the explicit event would allow. For Rahner, it was critical that theology develop an understanding of the ontological significance of the life of Christ in the life of the Christian, beyond a mere pious reflection. According to Rahner, the life of Christ contains several symbolic meanings that we can find in scripture. Rahner takes as his example John 19:34, and how this passage of scripture connects to the development of the doctrine of the Church as the "New Eve" from the pierced side of Christ ("The New Adam"). According to Rahner this prefiguration of later soteriological practices of the early Church demonstrates that the life of Jesus contains rich *types* that demonstrate the revelatory significance of the life of Jesus for the ongoing self-reflection of the Church. *E Latere Christi* was not a complete work in its own right. Rahner identifies two additional projects necessary to fully demonstrate the symbolic significance of the life of Jesus for the Church. He observes a general ontology of human historicity,[26] and the application of this general ontology of human historicity to the life of Jesus to demonstrate that the events of his life "are not merely symbols of the supratemporal work of a saving Logos in the life of a Christian, 'But rather that they *are* such "symbols" through their positing by a historical

---

24. This question was first asked rhetorically by Rahner in his doctoral thesis, *E Latere Christi*.

25. Rahner, *E Latere Christi*.

26. I would contend that *Hearer of the Word* was written to fulfill this requirement.

person in advance.' The events in Jesus's life are posited 'in advance' as an address to a later person."[27]

In this way, the symbolic nature of the events of the life of Christ are particularly historical. They are deliberate interventions into human history to achieve particular consequences at a later point in human history. These symbols are thus more than mere symbols of language as Saussure articulates, but represent locus points in which human history is uniquely determined in the present to speak to a person in a moment in the future. These symbols thus become the relational reference between the moments of revelation and the development of Christian doctrine.

After the Second World War Rahner returned to the exploration of theological symbols with his article *Theology of the Symbol*.[28] First published in 1959, this article endeavors to outline the meaning of the word *symbol* for theology, using the specific instance of the theology of devotion to the heart of Jesus.[29] In *Theology of the Symbol*, Rahner outlined two basic principles of an ontology of symbolism: "Our first statement, which we put forward as the basic principle of an ontology of symbolism, is as follows: all beings are by their nature symbolic, because they necessarily 'express' themselves in order to attain their own nature."[30] That is to say that all *beings* are symbolic because they first ground their reality in the act of the expression of the other. As James F. Buckley summarizes, according to Rahner, "man *is* insofar as he gives himself up" or "letting of one's self go is certainly the essence of man." "Self-possession" is attained through "self-expression."[31] As Buckley continues, "One way to interpret such remarks is that it is of the very essence of human subjects to 'express themselves in the other,' to utter a performative 'I love you' to God and neighbour, to be a *RealSymbol*."[32] These truths and observations find themselves explicitly stated by Rahner in his second principle of the basic ontology of the symbol: "The symbol strictly speaking (symbolic reality) is the self-realization of a being in the other, which is constitutive of its essence."[33]

---

27. Buckley, "On Being a Symbol," 459.
28. Rahner, "The Theology of the Symbol," 221–52.
29. Rahner, "The Theology of the Symbol," 221–52.
30. Rahner, "The Theology of the Symbol," 224.
31. Buckley, "On Being a Symbol," 468.
32. Buckley, "On Being a Symbol," 468.
33. Rahner, "The Theology of the Symbol," 234.

Rahner envisioned the being of the *RealSymbol* as a being that is acting to express itself, acting to express itself in relationship to an *other*. This development from *E Latere Christi*'s symbolic relationship between the events of the life of Jesus and the life of the Christian shows a similar development to the logic of Marechal's affirmation of God. As Anthony Matteo summarizes, "Marechal concludes that 'we may state in strictest logic, that the possibility of our subjective last end presupposes logically the existence of our object last end, God. Thus, in every intellectual act, we affirm implicitly, the existence of an absolute Being.'"[34] For Marechal, the affirmation of God was a necessary contingent component based on the relationship of the intellectual act. Because it is necessary that it is possible that we can reach a subjective last end, it is necessarily possible for there to *be* an objective last end. Because of this, every act of thought, which is an act reaching towards the fulfillment of the subjective end also, must at the very least carry an *implicit* affirmation of the objective last end, i.e. God. Or to express it more simply, if it is possible to reach a subjective conclusion, we ipso facto affirm the possibility of an objective conclusion, by way of the relationship between the objective and the subjective.

Rahner in the 1960s

In 1966, after the conclusion of the Second Vatican Council, Rahner accepted the call to the Romano Guardini Chair of Philosophy of Religion at the University of Munich. Seeing an opportunity to engage with the Council's call for an openness toward modernity, Rahner wrote several new courses, one of which was entitled "An Introduction to the Concept of Christianity."[35] In this course, Rahner sought to outline the reasons why Christianity was not simply a matter of faith but was also a serious intellectual project worth engaging with. Rahner's lectures at Munich were not a success. Unlike Guardini, Rahner was not inclined to steep his lectures in popular literature.[36] His course "An Introduction to the Concept of Christianity" was designed to answer a theological agenda that was called for by the Second Vatican Council. By engaging with the

---

34. Matteo, *Quest for the Absolute*, 109.
35. Dych, *Karl Rahner*.
36. Turner and Batlogg, "A Towering Figure of Theology in the 20th Century," 81–89.

concepts of Christian faith as concepts, Rahner believed he was facilitating the first object of necessary reform in ecclesiastical studies: "a better integration of philosophy and theology."[37] Rahner further assumed that those who would attend his lectures would be "educated to an extent" and willing to "wrestle with an idea."[38] As we explored earlier, this particular time period also happened to coincide with the growing influence of the post-structuralist critique of truth in the European universities. A final contributing historical factor was that it was between 1966 and 1969 that Rahner experienced the fatal breakdown of several hitherto close friendships and associations with his contemporary theologians—in particular, Hans Urs von Balthasar and Joseph Ratzinger. These factors and the increasing toxification of the faculty politics at Munich led to Rahner accepting the call to Münster in 1969.[39] There is no doubt that Rahner would have had to have been engaged with students at Munich who were acting under the influence of the new ideas of Derrida and Barthes. Considering both the courses that Rahner taught and the expectations left by Guardini, we can assume that many of his students would have read the pioneering work of Derrida and Barthes. Further, we can ascertain from several of his interviews on German radio in the early 1980s that Rahner believed that the linguistic turn in philosophy provided a particular threat to the language of theology because he believed "that a really radical separation between pure theology and pure philosophy is presumably not at all possible."[40] For Rahner, the linguistic turn revealed that even in the act of vocalizing, the impossibility of the particular expression communicated a possibility: "Exactly. I believe that when Wittgenstein says that one should not speak about that about which one cannot speak clearly, then with this statement, no doubt, he has virtually spoken once more about something, and, furthermore, he had no choice but to speak."[41]

It is therefore apparent that the post-structuralist conclusions about truth and authorship are, in fact, saying something about truth and authorship. We suggest that this view of the axiomatic nature of such discourse reflects that for Rahner *truth* was not something embedded within

37. Rahner and Dych, *Foundations of Christian Faith*, 3.
38. Rahner and Dych, *Foundations of Christian Faith*, 3.
39. Several of Rahner's associates, students and friends provide their accounts of this time period in Batlogg, Michalski, and Turner, *Encounters with Karl Rahner*.
40. Rahner, "The Language of Science and the Language of Theology, 304.
41. Rahner, "Interdisciplinary Dialogue and the Language of Theology, 315.

an utterance, but it was something more dynamic that came categorically from the encounter. We conclude that *Foundations* is an encounter between a dynamic concept of mind that in the act of intellection affirms reality and encounters God (a God who has made Himself a *RealSymbol* in human history to condition and facilitate a lived encounter ever afterwards) and a world that has turned against the modernist conception of truth.

Theological Creed against the Doubt of Truth

So let us finally turn to the subject of our inquiry: the alternative theological creed. We know that Rahner's *Foundations of Christian Faith* is a segmented text. A study of interviews with the primary editors and research assistants who contributed to the text reveals that the major chapters and organization of the work took place segmentally.[42] Therefore we can reliably examine the theological creed in exclusion to other elements of the text. If we consider the creed itself, "The incomprehensible term of human transcendence, which takes place in man's exitentiall[sic] and original being and not only in theoretical or merely conceptual reflection, is called God, and he communicates himself in forgiving love to man both existentielly[sic] and historically as man's own fulfilment. The eschatological climax of God's historical self-communication, in which this self-communication becomes manifest as irreversible and victorious is called Jesus Christ."[43]

Our study of Rahner's theology of *symbol* and our brief exploration of the epistemic system which informed Rahner's notion of *truth* should make several points obvious. We find God within the transcendence of man's original and existential being. This truth statement resembles the Marechalian insight that the act of the intellect must affirm God. Further, it is not presenting a direct or static fact. Both the concept of God and man's being are necessarily dynamic. They form in the act of being by their expression into the other, as Rahner further put forth in his concept of the *RealSymbol*.

God communicates his existence in both our interior lives and in the shared history of humanity. This does not actually rely on a definitive statement. Man's "existentiall" is not a fixed concept, but rather a fluid

---

42. Batlogg, Michalski, and Turner, *Encounters with Karl Rahner*.
43. Rahner and Dych, *Foundations of Christian Faith*, 454.

notion that reflects the experience of humanity. Further, we find the historical nature of God's communication in a history, the history scripture communicates, and in a person: Jesus Christ.

Finally, the climax of the communication of God to man in history is in the incarnation of Jesus Christ, and this makes the communication irreversible and victorious. Once more there is nothing here that is necessarily static as per the Derridan objection to *truth*. Jesus Christ is not a mere concept or a notion: he is a man, and like men, he is a dynamic being with relationships that define and proclaim him. This is the genius of the theological creed. There is not a single proposition here that can truly fall victim to the post-structuralist critique.

In his creed Rahner has not sought a demonstrable, definitive, total definition: he has rather demonstrated the constitutive nature of the relationship between us as human beings, Jesus as man and God, and God as the architect of both our being and the teleology of our reality. The only point that is left to critique remains the moment of the incarnation, and it is a rare man indeed who tries to claim there was not a man called Jesus, who came from Nazareth, and whom history has called the Christ.

Conclusion

As the French philosopher Maurice Blondel opined in his doctoral thesis, *L'Action*, "Action is inevitable. It happens not because of us, but in spite of us."[44] In recognition of this reality, we suggest that *Foundations* needs to be read not as positing a radical new way of being a Christian, but as an apologetic that defends the claim of Christian truth from the implacable assault on truth and meaning that we now call postmodernism.

We have shown that Rahner actively attempts to develop a language that explains the atemporality of the eschatological moment, and that this one can only do this by a recourse to truths that exist not in the substance of their premise, but in their relationship with each other. Unlike the modern truth that the post-structuralists repudiated, Rahner's truth was not based on a single static moment, but instead proposed a relationship between multiple dynamic constituents. This was a natural evolution of the epistemic foundations that formed Rahner's understanding of the world, his cosmology.

---

44. Blondel, *Action (1893)*, 1.

If we consider that the development of postmodernism reached its critical mass at the time that Rahner was in a German philosophy faculty, it seems only right that the encounter between his work on a theology of symbol and the postmodern moment would have been significant. We conclude that this context is the appropriate hermeneutic to engage for understanding several of the consequences of this encounter, and the question whether *Foundations* provides an appropriate response to the crisis in the modern concept of *truth* begs further investigation. We would suggest that to date there has not been a sufficient examination of this moment of encounter.

To conclude by way of historical analogy: If the Ottomans are at the gates of Vienna, it is hardly useful for John III Sobieski and his Polish hussars to ride on Constantinople. When we cannot take the very possibility of a Christian *truth* for certain, be it for historical, philosophical, cultural, or political reasons, then it is necessary for one to defend the possibility of truth before one can assert the truth. The success of Rahner's gambit to defend the truth of Christian faith has not yet been determined. We hold the Battle of Vienna to be the moment in history when Christianity stopped the Islamic invasion of Europe by the Ottomans. Looking at the chronology, the end of the Ottoman invasions came sixteen years later. Similarly, we are to this day still engaged in the war for *truth* that began in the turbulent 1960s. Therefore, similarly, we must await the resolution of the conflict for *truth* before we can properly appraise all contributions to it. Perhaps we may yet see that Rahner's gambit has won.

Bibliography

Barthes, Roland. "The Death of the Author." In *Image Music Text*, edited and translated by selected and translated by Stephen Heath, 142–49. New York: Noonday, 1977.

Batlogg, Andreas R., Melvin Michalski, and Barbara Turner, eds. *Encounters with Karl Rahner: Remembrances of Rahner by Those Who Knew Him*. Marquette Studies in Theology 63. Milwaukee: Marquette University Press, 2009.

Blondel, Maurice. *Action (1893): Essay on a Critique of Life and a Science of Practice*. Translated by Oliva Blanchette. Notre Dame, IN: University of Notre Dame, 2004.

Buckley, James J. "On Being a Symbol: An Appraisal of Karl Rahner." *Theological Studies* 40 (1979) 453–73.

Derrida, Jacques. "Structure, Sign and Play in the Discourse of the Human Sciences." In *The Structuralist Controversy: The Languages of Criticism & the Sciences of Man*, edited by Richard Macksey and Eugenio Donato, 147–64. Baltimore: Johns Hopkins University Press, 1970.

Dych, William V. *Karl Rahner*. London: Chapman, 1992.

Hegel, Georg Wilhelm Friedrich. *Phenomenology of Spirit.* Edited by John N. Findlay. Translated by A. V. Miller. Oxford: Oxford University Press, 2013.

Maréchal, Joseph. *A Maréchal Reader.* Edited by Joseph Donceel. New York: Herder & Herder, 1970.

Matteo, Anthony M. *Quest for the Absolute: The Philosophical Vision of Joseph Marechal.* De Kalb: Northern Illinois University Press, 1992.

Rahner, Karl. *E Latere Christi.* In *Sämtliche Werke.* Vol. 3, *Spiritualit und Theologie der Kirchenvater.* Translated by Brandon R. Peterson, Freiburg: Herder.

———. "Interdisciplinary Dialogue and the Language of Theology: Interview with Joachim Schickel of North-German Radio (NDR), Hamburg (November 22, 1981)." In *Karl Rahner in Dialogue: Conversations and Interviews, 1965-1982,* edited by Paul Imhof and Hubert Biallowons, 307-15. Translated by Harvey D. Egan and William Hoye. New York: Crossroad, 1986.

———. "The Language of Science and the Language of Theology: Interview with Joachim Schickel of North-German Radio (NDR), Hamburg (November 22, 1981)." In *Karl Rahner in Dialogue: Conversations and Interviews, 1965-1982,* edited by Paul Imhof and Hubert Biallowons, 302-8. Translated by Harvey D. Egan and William Hoye. New York: Crossroad, 1986.

———. "The Theology of the Symbol." In *Theological Investigations.* Vol. 4, *More Recent Writings.* Translated by Kevin Smyth. London: Darton, Longman & Todd, 1966.

———. *Foundations of Christian Faith: An Introduction to the Idea of Christianity.* Translated by William V. Dych. London: Darton, Longman & Todd, 1978.

Saussure, Ferdinand de. *Course in General Linguistics.* Edited by Charles Bally and Albert Sechehaye. Translated by Wade Baskin. New York: Philosophical Library, 1959.

Turner, Barbara, and Andreas R. Batlogg, eds. "A Towering Figure of Theology in the 20th Century: In Conversation with Raymund Schwager, SJ." In *Encounters with Karl Rahner: Remembrances of Rahner by Those Who Knew Him,* 81-89. Milwaukee: Marquette University Press, 2009.

12

A Curran Affair

The Triumph of the Liberal Model of the Academy in Catholic Higher Education

Thomas V. Gourlay

The 1960s were a tumultuous time in the world of Catholic higher education, and the events occurring during this time have had a significant impact on the nature of Catholic higher education the world over. 1967 saw the issuing of the "Land O' Lakes Statement,"[1] which effectively dissociated Catholic universities from the institutional Church, and the faculty strike at the Catholic University of America in 1968 witnessed hitherto inconceivable displays of public dissent from papal teaching by Catholic theologians, priests, bishops, and even bishops conferences. The promulgation of Paul VI's encyclical on June 29, 1968, was followed the subsequent day with a "Statement of Dissent" led by Fr. Charles Curran and many of his colleagues at the Catholic University of America. This brought to a head the overwhelming tensions operative within the Catholic academy

---

1. "Land O'Lakes Statement."

in the US around academic freedom and the role of the Catholic magisterium.

This paper will explore competing conceptions of the nature and purpose of Catholic institutions of higher education in light of the events of 1968. Using the theological critique of David L. Schindler, it will seek to examine the two key conceptions of the role of Catholic higher education vis-à-vis the secular–liberal academy and offer something of a third way that enables the Catholic university to fulfill its mission from the heart of the world whilst maintaining its centre in the Church.

1968 SAW TREMENDOUS CHANGES across the world and in the Catholic Church in a wide variety of often unexpected areas. While much has been made of the changes in Catholic moral theology that came to a head during this time,[2] it seems that insufficient attention has been given to the impact of what came to a head in Catholic academy in the late 1960s outside of the realm of moral theology and beyond the reductive tribal labels of liberal/progressive or conservative/traditional.

The explosive events that occurred in the realm of Catholic higher education in the US in 1968—particularly, as we shall see, at the Catholic University of America (CUA)—are sometimes examined superficially, as though they emerged *ex nihilo*, with few historical antecedents. I will argue, however, that these events were merely manifestations of a latent problem pertaining to the situation of Catholicism within the sphere of higher education in the US and within the American civil project more broadly, and that these events should give rise to a thoroughgoing examination of the nature and purpose of Catholic universities on the part of those charged with the leadership of such institutions.

The burden of this paper, then, is to demonstrate that the unprecedented events that were brought to the surface in 1968 within the realm of Catholic higher education were manifestations of this latent problem. This problem has been present in the US for some time and continues to haunt Catholic higher education and the institutional Catholic Church in the US to this day.

---

2. See the chapters in this volume by Giertych, Rowland, Mannering, and Chua.

A Curran Affair

On July 25, 1968, Pope Paul VI released the long-awaited encyclical *Humanae vitae: On Human Life*. The encyclical was long awaited because, having read the leaked reports of the Papal Commission on Problems of the Family, Population, and Natality, many people had assumed that the longstanding Catholic teaching prohibiting artificial birth control would finally be overturned. The argument of the majority opinion of the commission was that as new methods of contraception did nothing to the physical act of marital embrace, they were to be considered as morally permissible. It was argued that the newly available hormonal methods such as the oral contraceptive pill were unlike previously available forms of contraception such as the barrier method and, as these new hormonal methods did not interfere with the physical act of the marital embrace, they were considered to be of a different moral order.

The negative reaction to the encyclical, particularly in North America, was swift, forceful, and wholly unprecedented. Fr. Charles Curran, who was at that time professor of moral theology at the Catholic University of America (CUA), recounted that "the reaction of American theologians was focused in the statement released in Washington DC on July 30, 1968 in the name of eighty-seven American theologians. That statement by Catholic theologians was ultimately endorsed by more than 600 Catholic academics qualified in the sacred sciences, including moral theologians, canon lawyers, philosophers, biblical scholars, and teachers in related specialties."[3]

This statement by Catholic theologians was instigated by the afore mentioned Fr. Charles Curran, who was to become the central figure of the controversy and who led the public dissent from papal and magisterial teaching which was to unfold over the course of that fateful year. Fr. Charles Curran began teaching at CUA in 1965. At that time, according to Curran, "The School of Theology, in which all of the faculty members before 1968 were priests, had an especially conservative reputation."[4] Curran's first altercation with ecclesial authority occurred in 1967 when, after a few years on CUA's faculty, the school's trustees—comprised of a select committee of US bishops—decided not to renew his contract. The manner in which this was done admittedly did lack transparency and the bishops, somewhat threatened by what they had perceived as *at*

---

3. Curran and Hunt, *Dissent in and for the Church*, viii.
4. Curran, *Loyal Dissent*, 28.

least flirtations with dissenting views on perennial Catholic teaching on a variety of moral issues pertaining particularly to sexual ethics, thought that they would be able to let Fr. Curran's contract lapse and dismiss him quietly. Fr. Curran, who was thirty-three years of age at the time, was given no reason for his dismissal and subsequently sought not only to appeal the decision, but also to force the hand of the bishops to reinstate him.

The actions of the trustees to deny Curran's application for tenure and let his contract lapse prompted a response by way of a massive protest by staff and students of the university which effectively shut the university down for five days. Within a week of the campus boycott, Fr. Curran was reinstated and given academic tenure along with a promotion.

The intricacies of these events have been detailed meticulously in Peter M. Mitchell's *The Coup at Catholic University: The 1968 Revolution in Catholic Education*. Mitchell's careful historical scholarship describes the events as they unfolded, showing that the authoritarian, clericalist, and neoscholastic "old guard" of the American Catholic bishops who made up the board of trustees of CUA were not particularly well placed to incorporate the fullness of the teaching of the Second Vatican Council, chiefly in the areas of the Church's relationship to culture/the world. The actions of the bishops were met with significant agitation amongst the modern progressive liberal movement at the university, whose understanding of the Council saw the Church as having taken a far more open and accommodationalist stance vis-à-vis the world. Led by Fr. Charles Curran, this progressive liberal movement sought to see the institution of CUA measured against the standards of the (modern/liberal) American Association of University Professors (AAUP).[5]

Empowered by his defeat of the bishops, evidenced not only in his reinstatement but also his promotion as well as the granting of his academic tenure, Fr. Curran's teaching and publications grew increasingly out of step with authoritative magisterial teaching. His work took on a new and emboldened character, as we have mentioned, with the promulgation of Paul VI's encyclical *Humanae vitae* and the subsequent statement of dissent orchestrated by Curran, which saw the eventual kowtowing of the US bishops to the liberally minded university faculty.

---

5. The Council's openness to the world is a theme much discussed in the years that followed. For a detailed study of the lack of critical engagement with the culture of modernity evident in the conciliar documents, see Rowland, *Culture and the Thomist Tradition*.

The significance of this massive display of public dissent from definitive papal teaching is difficult to overstate. Never before had there been such brazen disregard for authoritative papal teaching by those charged by the bishops with disseminating it. What made this perhaps so shocking was the fact that this dissent came from within the ranks of predominantly priest-professors in the paid employ of Church institutions—and the fact that this was led from within the bishop's own university was even more stunning.

However, this is no simple story of rapscallion dissent against legitimate authority; nor is it a story of the heroic defiance of a young and brilliant scholar against the overbearing authoritarianism of anachronous bishops. Indeed, the story touches on far deeper issues pertaining to the position of Catholicism, not only in the realm of higher education in the US, but also within the context of the American liberal project more generally. As we will see, the North American (liberal) context within which all this was played out is of tremendous importance, particularly because these issues were primarily fought and ultimately won by the dissenters on the grounds of academic freedom, as conceived of from within the context of the modern American liberal academy.

Lusting after Modernity: The Drift of the Catholic Academy

In his magisterial work *Contending with Modernity: Catholic Higher Education in the Twentieth Century*, Philip Gleason writes that "Even before the Council ended in 1965, commentators on Catholic higher education were beginning to point out that a new formulation of its fundamental reason for being was needed in the light of the growing acceptance of 'secularity' and increasing discontent over academic weaknesses, authoritarian procedures, and forms of thought widely regarded by Catholic intellectuals as outmoded and embarrassingly parochial."[6]

Fr. Theodore Hesburgh CSC was one such academic unsatisfied with the pre-conciliar model of the Catholic university. Appointed as president of Notre Dame in 1952, a position that he held until his retirement

---

6. Gleason, *Contending with Modernity*, 318.

in 1987, Fr. Hesburgh exercised enormous influence over Catholic higher education in the US and further afield.[7]

In 1967, under the leadership of the Fr. Hesburgh, a blue-ribbon commission of the International Federation of Catholic Universities (IFCU) met to discuss the nature of the Catholic university in the modern world. Fr. Hesburgh, who was the president of the IFCU at that time, brought together a group of twenty-six leaders from some of the most prestigious and influential Catholic universities in the US and Canada. The commission eventually issued what has come to be known as the "Land O' Lakes Statement." Under the overall title "The Idea of the Catholic University," the statement set out a vision of Catholic education that, I will argue, takes as its ideal the secular liberal model of the university, adding to it a concern that at Catholic universities, "Catholicism is perceptibly present and effectively operative."[8]

Some common critiques of the "Land O' Lakes Statement" identify the document to be the reason for the secularization of those Catholic colleges and universities who were signatories to the document, and the others who followed suit. They identify the increased participation of lay Catholics in the respective boards of governance of Catholic colleges and universities with the eventual and in some cases total secularization of these institutions. While these developments are worthy of attention, such approaches are simplistic and fail to grasp the essence of the underlying issues at play.

The "Land O' Lakes Statement" gave voice to the rising sentiment amongst the Catholic intelligentsia leading up to and following the Second Vatican Council that the Church needed to be more open to the world. What this meant for seemingly the vast majority of these voices was that the Church needed to accommodate itself to the world. Perhaps the most significant element of the "Land O' Lakes Statement" is that it reads effectively as a statement of institutional independence for the signatory universities from "any authority of whatever kind, lay or clerical,

---

7. Hesburgh was awarded 150 honorary degrees from colleges and universities around the world, even from such faraway places as Australia. The University of Notre Dame Australia conferred this honor upon him in 1997, to honor him and formally acknowledge his influence on that institution and Catholic education more broadly. Cf. Tannock, *The Founding and Establishment of the University of Notre Dame Australia 1986–2014*.

8. "Land O' Lakes Statement."

external to the academic community itself."⁹ In declaring such freedom, the architect of this document (Fr. Hesburgh) along with its signatories appropriate for themselves a model of radical autonomy that is novel in the history of Catholic universities; however, common critiques of the statement often fail to recognize the relative freedom and self-governance of even the very first (Catholic) universities in the Middle Ages.

Institutional autonomy and the coincident academic freedom that was being sought in these maneuvers was, and in many ways remains, the neuralgic point within Catholic institutions of higher education, especially though not exclusively as it pertains to issues related to the faith and moral teachings of the Catholic Church. This goes to the very heart of what it is to be a Catholic institution in a modern liberal state. Upon examination, it is evident that Catholic universities as envisioned by the "Land O' Lakes Statement," and perhaps more articulately in the writings of Fr. Hesburgh elsewhere, sought to adopt the putatively metaphysically neutral, secular liberal model of the university within their own institutions.

A University with Catholicism

In the introduction to a volume that he edited entitled *The Challenge and Promise of a Catholic University*, Hesburgh outlines key elements of his vision for Catholic higher education, articulately presenting his vision of the modern Catholic university. He states:

> The church did not create the modern university world as it had helped create the medieval university world. Moreover, the church does not have to be present in the modern world of the university, but if it is to enter, the reality and the terms of this world are well established and must be observed. The terms may be complicated and unlike those operative within the church itself. The reality of the university world may make the church uneasy at times; nevertheless, all university people throughout the world recognize this reality and its terms as essential to anything that wishes to merit the name of university in the modern context. One may add descriptive adjectives to this or that university, calling it public or private, Catholic or Protestant, British or American, but the university must first and foremost be a

---

9. "Land O' Lakes Statement."

university, or else the thing that the qualifiers qualify is something, but not a university.[10]

Elsewhere, Hesburgh argues:

> The Catholic university has too often been looked upon by many Catholics as Catholic first and university second. University is the substantive noun in this combination, and the world judges clearly enough whether or not an institution, whatever else it claims to be, is in fact a university in the commonly accepted meaning of the word. One can similarly speak of a Catholic person, but he must be a person before he can become a Catholic. Catholic here is an adjective. So, too, in the case of a Catholic university.[11]

It is evident here that for Hesburgh, the defining structure of the university is set prior to any engagement from the Church or any other defined set of metaphysical or value-based systems. As such, Hesburgh argues that any ecclesial engagement with the world of higher education and research must be determined in advance by the putatively neutral structure of the modern university.

It is important to note Hesburgh's prioritization of the secular form of the university over and above its Catholic character. For Hesburgh and those who have followed his approach in Catholic higher education, the university is a pre-existing and neutral structure that is devoid of any metaphysical and moral content. As such, it can be filled, from without, with Catholic content, or with content of another sort—Protestant, American, English, etc. The academic project of David L. Schindler is useful here, as he shows that despite the putative neutrality of the structures of liberal modernity, such structures are always and already imbued with a logic and a metaphysic that is mechanistic and atomistic and, therefore, at odds with the Gospel.[12]

---

10. Hesburgh, *The Challenge and Promise of a Catholic University*, 4.

11. Hesburgh, "Preface," in McCluskey, *The Catholic University*, x.

12. See Schindler, *Heart of the World*. Cf. also Healy and Schindler, *Being Holy in the World*.

The Purpose of the Catholic University: The Formation of the Catholic Mind

What is evident here in the two approaches—from Fr. Hesburgh at Notre Dame and the IFCU on the one hand, and the US bishops at CUA on the other—are two radically different conceptions of the nature and purpose of Catholic higher education in the modern world. Fr. Hesburgh's vision for Catholic higher education, as has been seen, was to achieve something of a rapprochement of Catholic higher education and its secular, liberal, and pluralistic counterpart. For Hesburgh, the modern university has a form that precedes its confessional character, and this is what must be adopted by Catholic universities if they are to enter the discussion, so to speak, with their secular counterparts. This accommodationalist perspective, offered and ultimately implemented by Hesburgh, was a radical departure from the previous, pre-conciliar notion of Catholic higher education which was exemplified in the behavior of the trustees of CUA at the time of the Curran crisis. The approach of the bishops was in many ways sectarian, authoritarian, and slavishly dogmatic.

Both approaches, the extrinsicist and the accommodationalist, are caricatures of the stance of the Church vis-à-vis the world prior to and following the Second Vatican Council. American philosopher and theologian David L. Schindler, however, argues that neither the Hesurghian accommodationalism characteristic of much of the post-conciliar Church nor the theological extrinsicism of the bishops at CUA characteristic of the pre-conciliar Church are sufficiently adequate for the Catholic university to fulfill its mission as a Catholic university from the heart of the world with its centre in the Church.

Schindler argues that if a university must be concerned with the formation of the mind, a Catholic university must be concerned with the formation of the Catholic mind. Its Catholicity must be effective in its very essence as a university, and must not exist only as a descriptive adjective or as an extrinsic moralism. This conception of a Catholic university is understandably difficult to measure or quantify, as the faith by its very nature cannot simply be reduced to a mere checklist of factors that distinguish Catholic identity. Schindler argues:

> Catholic universities may have theology departments that are faithful to the teaching of the Church, dormitory life that is a model of morality, campus chapels that are full of prayerful worshippers, and community organizations that energetically

serve the most vulnerable and most afflicted in our society. All of these things are indispensable for a college or university that would be vibrantly Catholic. But the point is that none of them yet informs us what specifies a Catholic institution *as a university*. To have a Catholic university, in other words, it is necessary (also) to develop a Catholic *mind*.[13]

For a university to be adequately "Catholic" according to Schindler it must, in all areas of its teaching and research, be affected by the relational onto-logic of sanctity/holiness.[14] It is the formation of the Catholic mind that is the key task of the Catholic university. This, it must be remembered, is primarily intellectual work, despite the fact that it cannot be done in isolation from prayer, the sacraments, faithful adherence to the Church's magisterium, or without considerable attention to and practice of both the spiritual and corporal works of mercy.

Schindler is a sharp critic of the model of the Catholic university proposed and ultimately realized by Fr. Hesburgh, arguing that "The sense of the priority [that] Fr. Hesburgh accords to the form of the university in relation to Catholicism . . . already commits him, as a matter of principle, to a priority of a university that is liberal in character . . . [So] either we reformulate Fr. Hesburgh's conception of a Catholic university, or we must resign ourselves to achieving what is at best a Catholic version of a liberal university."[15] The Catholicity of the Catholic university must not merely be a moral gloss on what would otherwise be any other kind of university. The Catholic university, argues Schindler, must "be concerned to be Catholic in its *mind*, and not merely to couple a secularized mind with a Catholic will."[16]

If, as Schindler argues, sanctity is to provide the inner *form* of the intellectual life "in a way that affects both the methods and the content of the modern academy,"[17] then the Catholic university must be characterized by a deeply profound integration of faith and reason in a way that radically grounds all academic inquiry in an onto-logic of holiness. Such a logic of being sees reality as gift, and therefore as given, and constitutively related to God as well as to the rest of creation through God the Son. This

13. Schindler, *Heart of the World*, 147.
14. Cf. Schindler, "Faith and the Logic of Intelligence"; Schindler, "Catholicity and the State of Contemporary Theology."
15. Schindler, *Heart of the World*, 155.
16. Schindler, "Faith and the Logic of Intelligence," 179.
17. Schindler, *Heart of the World*, 207.

stands at odds not only with the neo-scholastic thinking prevalent on the campuses of Catholic universities prior to the Second Vatican Council, but also with the liberal accommodationism of Fr. Hesburgh and most of the American Catholic academy.

A Perpetual Problematic

The tension that exists within Catholic higher education in the US seems to be deeply embedded. The Curran affair, as detailed above, was a particular manifestation of the hard shift from extrinsicist authoritarianism to liberal accommodationism. Hesburgh's articulation of the nature and purpose of the modern Catholic university in the "Land O' Lakes Statement" and elsewhere has been in ascendency for the most part at least since the promulgation of that document, notwithstanding efforts to hold Catholicism at the heart of Catholic colleges and universities across North America and elsewhere.

That this tension continues to exist was seen somewhat recently with the decision taken by the University of Notre Dame to confer upon then-President Barack Obama the award of honorary Doctor of Laws at its 164th University Commencement Ceremony in May of 2009. Fr. Jenkins, president of Notre Dame, stated in his address and citation of President Obama that "The primary reason for the invitation was thus to honor Obama, America's first African-American president, while using the event also as an opportunity for 'further positive engagement' and 'dialogue' regarding differences in the 'life' issues."[18]

The controversy surrounding the Notre Dame decision to honor President Obama with the honorary Doctor of Laws was significant, with over eighty US Catholic bishops, including Bishop D'Arcy of Fort Wayne, Indiana, whose diocese encompasses the Notre Dame campus, publicly denouncing the decision to honor the avowedly pro-abortion president. Bishop D'Arcy himself boycotted the ceremony, which he would usually have attended, and instead led a prayerful demonstration outside with members of ND Response, a student-led pro-life group. In a public statement announcing his dismay at the decision, D'Arcy, citing the US Catholic Bishop's Conference document of 2004, explained that "The Catholic community and Catholic institutions should not honor those who act in defiance of our fundamental moral principles. They should

---

18. Schindler, "President Obama, Notre Dame, and a Dialogue that Witnesses," 8.

not be given awards, honors or platforms which would suggest support for their actions."[19]

David L. Schindler also wrote in response to the decision to confer such an award on President Obama. His paper is carefully nuanced, providing on the one hand a strong criticism of the decision and on the other providing a careful appeal to Fr. Jenkins to revisit his own undertanding of the mission of the Catholic university within the broader mission of the Church vis-à-vis the world.

For Schindler, Fr. Jenkins's reasoning was marred by a failure to account for the fact that "his invitation to the President already helps define the basic terms and horizon of the intended dialogue. The fact of the invitation itself begins a conversation the terms of which already reflect a proportional ordering of social–moral issues much like that of the President himself."[20] For Schindler, this is the classic pitfall of a Catholic engagement with liberalism. Fr. Jenkins's invitation, given putatively in the spirit of dialogue, succumbs to a logic which is already imbued with an order that already "pre-empts the debate."[21]

As Schindler points out, the issues surrounding the Obama invitation which gave rise to the controversy—specifically his avowed support for abortion, embryonic stem-cell research, and the like—are at a level of moral gravity such that the kind of dialogue which must surround them should bear the form of *witness*. "A grave unconditional moral good can be properly defended only with the gesture of one's whole being and in the flesh, and only with a reason exercised from inside this more comprehensive testimony," Schindler writes. "Indeed, it is reason intrinsically tied to witness in this sense that is the *raison d'être* of any adequately conceived university, especially a Catholic university and especially in our time."[22]

Schindler's critique of Notre Dame is strong, not in a malicious way but, as he points out, "The university [Notre Dame] plays an important role in articulating the reasonable nature of Catholic higher education, not to mention the cultural meaning of Catholicism in America."[23] To

19. Bishop D'Arcy's comments were reported in a Catholic News Agency article, dated March 24, entitled "Bishop D'Arcy will not attend Notre Dame commencement featuring Obama." See also "Catholics in Political Life."
20. Schindler, "President Obama, Notre Dame, and a Dialogue that Witnesses," 9.
21. MacIntyre, *Whose Justice? Which Rationality?*, 394.
22. Schindler, "President Obama, Notre Dame, and a Dialogue that Witnesses," 10.
23. Schindler, "President Obama, Notre Dame, and a Dialogue that Witnesses," 12.

have invited President Obama on such an auspicious occasion as the solemn commencement ceremony and to have conferred an honorary degree upon him at this time does not adequately provide the witness to the truth which Schindler argues is required of a university, let alone a Catholic university.

Schindler argues that the university is called to be a faithful witness to the truth *in love*, and also of love *in truth*. This does not marginalize reason; quite to the contrary, such witness is impossible should it be divorced from reason as such. The university is, then, a privileged place where "we will realize Pope Francis's call for a renewal of merciful love only proportionately to our ability to live radically obedience to the truth as the word of God's love: to live radically obedience to the truth *in love* and love *in truth*."[24] For Schindler, "Only a missionary task so understood bears the principled capacity for reintegrating ideas and reality that is adequate to the words of *Lumen gentium*: we are called to share love with our whole heart and our whole soul and our whole mind (40), to proclaim it to all human beings, and to include every aspect of each human being, so that God and his love might be in all (cf. 1 Col 15:28)."[25]

Conclusion

Like so much that seemed to explode around the world in 1968, the events of that year at CUA were little more than the manifestation of much that had been simmering just below the surface of the awareness of those living through that moment. In this instance it was the culmination of the longstanding uncomfortable situation of Catholicism within the context of modernity in its dominant liberal form. The previously ascendant mode of engagement of the Church, in this instance exemplified by the US Catholic Bishops, was marked by an extrinsicism and authoritarianism whereby the teaching of the faith was to be protected in a kind of hermetically sealed environment—kept away from the pollutants of the culture, and therefore unaffected by various cultural developments. What seemed radical and revolutionary in the moral theology of Fr. Curran and in the organized dissent from magisterial teaching was, in fact, modeled after particular understandings of the Church's openness to the world taught by the Second Vatican Council and exemplified here not only by

24. Schindler, "'In the Beginning Was the Word,'" 773.
25. Schindler, "'In the Beginning Was the Word,'" 773.

Fr. Curran but particularly by Fr. Hesburgh and the presidents of other Catholic colleges and universities who followed Hesburgh's leadership. This new mode of engagement, in stark opposition to that previously employed by the bishops, was one of radical openness to the culture, such that even the truths of the faith are positioned by cultural norms. Sadly both these models failed to adequately represent the Church in the context of the modern world, particularly within this context of higher education. Relying on the work of David L. Schindler, this paper sought to demonstrate that the events of 1968 at CUA involving Fr. Charles Curran were not isolated or merely the result of one troublesome moralist riding the tide of popular opinion, but rather the outworking of the longstanding uncomfortable position of Catholicism within the context of the American civic project.

Schindler argues that the liberal model of the university adopted by Hesburgh and others provides both the form and content of a secularized mode of thinking "blocking the arrival of authentic Catholicism." He argues that the Catholic university's role is the formation of a Catholic mind, and that to achieve this, Catholic universities must undertake a thoroughgoing a desecularization of their intellectual outlook, and that this will involve a reassertion of—or, better, a conversion to—an ontologic of holiness or sanctity that will "provide the inner form of the intellectual life, in a way that affects both the methods and the content of the modern academy."

As Schindler sees it, the liberal–Catholic attempt to "bracket out" Christ "from one's thinking or one's formation of and participation in cultural institutions (with the intention, of course, of reintroducing it at the appropriate moment, namely when moral questions come to the fore) betrays at once a false understanding of Christianity and a false understanding of understanding."[26] This bracketing out of Christ and His Church is precisely what is effected (however unwittingly) by the adoption of the liberal mode of the academy by Catholic institutions of higher education, as advocated by Hesburgh and others. At stake here, then, is a radical reduction of the Catholic faith itself to a voluntaristic moralism or a simple set of propositional dogmatic formulations which sit outside of reasonable discourse. This positions the faith as extrinsic to the life of the mind—to reason. And such an understanding not only damages the Catholicity of a Catholic university, but does violence to one's conception

---

26. Schindler, "Beauty and the Holiness of Mind," 7.

of reason as such. Again, as D. C. Schindler (son of David L. Schindler) argues, "If we do not see that the Christian logos transforms what we commonly mean by time, space, matter, and motion, we will not in fact be receiving it as a logos, but rather as a moral inspiration or isolated and so inconsequential truth claim."[27]

This is what is at stake in what unfolded across Catholic higher education in 1968, and perhaps again in 2009 with the Obama controversy. The conception of reason as ultimately given form in the logos of Jesus Christ, which is the mark of the Catholic mind, simply cannot be present in the university that has taken the liberal model of the academy as its own, as was done at the majority of Catholic institutions of higher education in the 1960s. This is despite even the most heroic attempts to foster an active liturgical life, a faithful theological faculty, prioritized student recruitment from marginalized communities, and active charitable outreach programs.

The events of 1968 at CUA drive home the need for a clearly articulated vision for the nature and purpose of the Catholic university with respect to the broader liberal academy and the world more generally. Schindler describes a twofold missionary task for the Catholic university which provides a unique third way, overcoming the authoritarianism and extrinsicism of preconciliar models, and the liberal accomodationalism that became ascendant following the Second Vatican Council most particularly after the proclamation of the "Land O' Lakes Statement" and the Curran affair. First, according to Schindler, the Catholic university is to demonstrate "from within each discipline and in the terms proper to each discipline, how that discipline is being guided by a worldview—in the case of liberalism by mechanism and subjectivism." And, second, "to show how a Catholic worldview (of the cosmos as created in the image of Christ's [eucharistic] love, hence of a cosmos wherein order and love are mutually inclusive) leads to a more ample understanding of evidence and argument, already within the terms proper to each discipline."[28]

Bibliography

Catholic News Agency. "Bishop D'Arcy Will not Attend Notre Dame Commencement Featuring Obama." http://www.catholicnewsagency.com/news/bishop_darcy_will_not_attend_notre_dame_commencement_featuring_obama.

27. Schindler, "Beauty and the Holiness of Mind," 4.
28. Schindler, *Heart of the World*, 171–72.

Curran, Charles E. *Loyal Dissent: Memoir of a Catholic Theologian*. Washington, DC: Georgetown University Press, 2006.

Curran, Charles E., and Robert E. Hunt. *Dissent in and for the Church*. New York: Sheed & Ward, 1969.

Gleason, Philip. *Contending with Modernity: Catholic Higher Education in the Twentieth Century*. New York: Oxford University Press, 1995.

Healy, Nicholas J., and D. C. Schindler, eds. *Being Holy in the World: Theology and Culture in the Thought of David L. Schindler*. Grand Rapids: Eerdmans, 2011.

Hesburgh, Theodore M., ed. *The Challenge and Promise of a Catholic University*. Notre Dame, IN: University of Notre Dame Press, 1994.

———. "Preface." In *The Catholic University: A Modern Appraisal*, edited by Neil G. McCluskey. Notre Dame: University of Notre Dame Press, 1970.

"Land O' Lakes Statement on the Nature of the Contemporary Catholic University." Notre Dame Archives, Updated July 23, 1967. http://archives.nd.edu/episodes/visitors/lol/idea.htm.

MacIntyre, Alasdair. *Whose Justice? Which Rationality?* Notre Dame, IN: University of Notre Dame Press, 1988.

McCluskey, Neil G., ed. *The Catholic University: A Modern Appraisal*. Notre Dame: University of Notre Dame Press, 1970.

Mitchell, Peter M. *The Coup at Catholic University: The 1968 Revolution in American Catholic Education*. San Francisco: Ignatius, 2015.

Rowland, Tracey. *Culture and the Thomist Tradition: After Vatican II. Radical Orthodoxy*. London: Routledge, 2003.

Schindler, D. C. "Beauty and the Holiness of Mind." In *Being Holy in the World: Theology and Culture in the Thought of David L. Schindler*, edited by Nicholas J. Healy and D. C. Schindler. Grand Rapids: Eerdmans, 2011.

Schindler, David L. "Catholicity and the State of Contemporary Theology: The Need for an onto-Logic of Holiness." *Communio* 14 (1987) 426–50.

———. "Faith and the Logic of Intelligence: Secularization and the Academy." In *Catholicism and Secularization in America*, edited by David L. Schindler. Huntington, IN: Communio Books, Our Sunday Visitor, 1990.

———. *Heart of the World, Centre of the Church: Communio Ecclesiology, Liberalism and Liberation*. Grand Rapids: Eerdmans, 1996.

———. "'In the Beginning Was the Word': Mercy as a 'Reality Illuminated by Reason.'" *Communio* 41 (2014) 751–73.

———. "President Obama, Notre Dame, and a Dialogue that Witnesses: A Question for Fr Jenkins." *Communio* 36 (2009) 7–12.

Tannock, Peter. *The Founding and Establishment of the University of Notre Dame Australia 1986-2014*. Fremantle, Western Australia: University of Notre Dame, 2014.

United States Conference of Catholic Bishops. "Catholics in Political Life." http://www.usccb.org/issues-and-action/faithful-citizenship/church-teaching/catholics-in-political-life.cfm.

13

Ratzinger and Del Noce on 1968 and Beyond

Michael Liccione

In a recent article in *Commonweal*, Carlo Lancellotti presents the unusual and prescient perspective of Italian-Catholic philosopher Augusto Del Noce on the social and political trends that manifested themselves across the West in the tumultuous events of 1968. In this paper I shall support Del Noce's thesis in two ways. First, I shall summarize then-Professor Joseph Ratzinger's reactions to 1968 and relate them to the conclusions of Del Noce and others Lancellotti cites. While Lancellotti does not cite Ratzinger, what motivated the latter's shift away from "progressivism" toward a more conservative reception of Vatican II well illustrates Del Noce's thesis. I shall then argue at greater length than Lancellotti, whose purpose is primarily expository, that Del Noce's perspective, while needing qualification and expansion in light of what has happened since his death, is essentially correct.

Most of us who had at least achieved puberty by 1968 will remember what a tumultuous year it was, particularly for American Catholics. In the US, sometimes-violent protests against the war in Vietnam and the military draft escalated on college campuses, most notably Columbia

University. (When I started attending college there four years later, administrators were still traumatized by the event.) The assassination of black civil-rights activist Dr. Martin Luther King in March sparked race riots in dozens of American cities, including Washington itself. The June assassination of presidential candidate Robert F. Kennedy, brother of the previous president (who had also been assassinated) further stoked already considerable turmoil within the Democratic Party. That helped generate an ugly, riotous atmosphere at the party's election-year convention held a few months later in Chicago, where police used massive force to remove kicking-and-screaming protesters. That in turn generated, among American voters, both sympathy for and backlash against the student-led "New Left" that would soon gain such influence in the party. Politically, it was a very polarizing time. And so it was theologically.

For I also recall my parents and their friends, on the eve of said convention, arguing vociferously about the encyclical *Humanae vitae*,[1] which Pope Paul VI had just published in July to the great displeasure of many theologians and rank-and-file laity. People had been led to believe that change was in the offing and were furious when it did not come. That dispute took place in the context not only of the so-called "sexual revolution" but also of the generally vertiginous context of the immediate post-Vatican II years. It seemed to many people then that everything about Catholicism, not just the drastically changing liturgy, was up for grabs. It still seems that way to many Catholics who came of age at that time, and to the relatively few young people today who take progressive Catholicism seriously. By any measure, 1968 was one of the most significant years of the twentieth century, at least in the Western world.

Now to Europe. At that time, Joseph Ratzinger was in his second year as a professor at the University of Tübingen, the home of what had long been the most prestigious theology faculty in Germany. He had been personally recruited to said faculty by Hans Küng as a fellow "progressive." Ironically, when I met Küng in New York fifteen years later, he had recently been stripped of his pontifical license to teach theology by Ratzinger, who was by then head of the Sacred Congregation for the Doctrine of the Faith—the key Vatican dicastery which, at its founding in the sixteenth century, was called "The Supreme Sacred Congregation of the Roman and Universal Inquisition." I was quite amused to hear from Küng how well he and Ratzinger had got on during the Council and

---

1. Paul VI. *Humanae vitae*.

its immediate aftermath, despite their differences in temperament and thought. Before 1968, it was still quite possible for moderate progressives like Ratzinger to sympathize with more radical ones like Küng.

But the events of 1968 in France and Germany, as tumultuous in their own way as those in the US, alarmed and repelled Ratzinger, who experienced some of the tumult among his own students. They so shook him that, even as pope almost forty years later, he characterized "the pause [*caesura*] in 1968" as "the beginning or 'explosion'—I would dare to call it—of the great cultural crisis of the West."[2] He decided back then that there was something seriously wrong not just with the European Left in general, but also with progressive Catholicism in particular. In 1969, he left Tübingen for the University of Regensburg, a new and obscure foundation of the Bavarian state—presumably to find some peace and space to be the quiet, civil, irenic scholar he was.

Specifying just what he thought went wrong brings to the fore certain themes that were also being sounded and developed by the unjustly neglected Italian philosopher Augusto Del Noce, who died in 1989, shortly after the Berlin Wall fell. In my view, Del Noce's incisive, substantively correct account of the origin and significance of those themes shows how they continue to play themselves out today, both culturally and politically. 1968 was indeed, I submit, the key spiritual bellwether for 2018. Ratzinger and Del Noce together enable us to understand why.

In the preface to the 2004 English edition of his *Introduction to Christianity*, a book first published in 1968, then-Cardinal Ratzinger wrote: "The year 1968 is linked to the rise of a new generation, which not only regarded the work of reconstruction after the Second World War as inadequate, full of injustice, egoism and the urge to possess, but conceived the whole evolution of history, beginning with the era of the triumph of Christianity, as an error and a failure."[3] That perception is what led to the "great refusal" of 1968, expressed in the disruption and violence on the Parisian barricades and the campuses of West German universities. The whole exercise had distinctly Marxist overtones, though most of its leaders were not sympathetic to Soviet Communism. Thus "the Revolution" was supposed to sweep away all the error and failure and yield a kind of utopia. The new order, whose outlines were necessarily vague because it would be such a radical break with the past, would

---

2. Meeting with the clergy of the dioceses of Belluno-Feltre and Treviso, July 2007.

3. Ratzinger, *Introduction to Christianity*, ix.

indeed be a "classless society." God, already viewed largely as a mystification of concrete, pre-existing "power relations," would be completely "immanentized" so that human beings could fully flourish. People would all be mutually supportive coequals having no need of a transcendent God. So if God existed, there would, in Ratzinger's words, "be nothing for him to do."

Just as important was the "sexual revolution" then kicking into high gear throughout the West thanks to the contraceptive pill, whose advent had prompted *Humanae vitae*. Rationalized by such thinkers as Wilhelm Reich and Herbert Marcuse, and welcomed even by some Catholic theologians, that revolution was supposed to be as complete and necessary a liberation as any strictly economic or political development. Marriage and family—at least as traditionally understood in hierarchical terms that would soon be called "sexist"—were to become obsolete.

At the time, Ratzinger had little to say about such matters. Indeed, in his memoir he confesses his rather tepid initial response to *Humanae vitae*: "It was certainly clear that what it said was essentially valid, but the reasoning, for us at that time, and for me too, was not satisfactory. I was looking for a comprehensive anthropological viewpoint. In fact, it was [Pope] John Paul II who was to complement the natural-law viewpoint of the encyclical with a personalistic vision."[4] But by 1989, the end of the decade in which St. John Paul II developed that vision in a long series of public audiences,[5] Ratzinger could argue, correctly, that the now-standard "progressive" objections to Church teaching on contraception, homosexuality, communion for the divorced-and-civilly-remarried, and women's ordination arose together from a now-familiar view of conscience and freedom that is fundamentally incompatible with Catholic theological anthropology.

For the sake of exhibiting the connection between his theme and Del Noce's, it is worth quoting his argument at length:

> The concept "norm"—or what is even worse, the moral law itself—takes on negative shades of dark intensity: an external rule may supply models for direction, but it can in no case serve as the ultimate arbiter of one's obligation. Where such thinking holds sway, the relationship of man to his body necessarily changes too. This change is described as a liberation, when compared to the relationship obtaining until now, like an opening up to a

---

4. Benedict XVI, *Last Testament*, 157.
5. John Paul II, *Man and Woman He Created Them*.

freedom long unknown. The body then comes to be considered as a possession which a person can make use of in whatever way seems to him most helpful in attaining "quality of life." The body is something that one has and that one uses. No longer does man expect to receive a message from his bodiliness as to who he is and what he should do, but definitely, on the basis of his reasonable deliberations and with complete independence, he expects to do with it as he wishes. In consequence, there is indeed no difference whether the body be of the masculine or the feminine sex; the body no longer expresses being at all; on the contrary, it has become a piece of property. It may be that man's temptation has always lain in the direction of such control and the exploitation of goods. At its roots, however, this way of thinking first became an actual possibility through the fundamental separation—not a theoretical but a practical and constantly practiced separation—of sexuality and procreation. This separation was introduced with the Pill and has been brought to its culmination by genetic engineers so that man can now "make" human beings in the laboratory. The material for doing this has to be procured by actions deliberately carried out for the sake of the planned results, which no longer involve interpersonal human bonds and decisions in any way. Indeed, where this kind of thinking has been completely adopted, the difference between homosexuality and heterosexuality as well as that between sexual relations within or outside marriage have become unimportant.[6]

The notion of the human body as property to dispose of via complete self-determination, not as a manifestation of an objective moral order to which we should conform ourselves, had already taken firm hold in the West by the 1970s. Unlike most Catholic intellectuals at the time, Del Noce saw that, calling it part of the "technological society" that is logically equivalent to the "consumer" or "affluent" society. And because said notion is more influential than ever forty years later, Del Noce was also quite prescient.

In his remarkable essay "The Ascendance of Eroticism,"[7] Del Noce noted that the intellectual stage for the sexual revolution had already been set by Wilhelm Reich, especially in his book The Sexual Revolution: Toward a Self-Regulating Character.[8] Although Reich died half-forgotten in an American prison in 1957, he would soon become a hero of the

6. Ratzinger, "Difficulties Confronting the Faith in Europe Today."
7. Republished in *The Crisis of Modernity* as ch.10, 157–87.
8. Reich, *The Sexual Revolution*.

sexual revolution that was about to occur. As a scientistic materialist, he took for granted that there is no given order of values, rooted in a transcendent God and handed on by tradition, to which we ought to conform ourselves. Fascism and all other forms of authoritarianism went hand-in-hand with sexual repression, the elimination of which would release vital energy in the way necessary for freedom and happiness, and thus render militarism obsolete. It is easy to understand the appeal of such a view to the beatniks and hippies who were soon to follow.

Reich believed that the concept and expression of sexuality must be separated from procreation to achieve the kind of liberation he advocated. And that is the point of connection with what I have been quoting from Ratzinger. The "scientistic-materialistic level" is exactly what remains—even and especially after the failure of "the Revolution" to create the "new man" of Marxism—and dominates Western culture even more now than it did when Reich was alive and Del Noce was writing. It is only at that level that the sexual revolution makes such sense as it does.

Needless to say, the sexual revolution has not led to what Reich, and much of the generation that came of age in the 1960s and 70s, thought it would. Already, much disorder and disillusionment was setting in.[9] And in Ratzinger's estimation, the fall of the Soviet empire had already proved to be a great disillusionment. Thus:

> Marxism had been conceived in these terms: a current that augured justice for all, the advent of peace, the abolition of unjustified relations of man's dominance over man, etc. . . . To reach these noble objectives, it was thought that one had to give up ethical principles and that terror could be used as the instrument of good. When the time came that all could see, if only on the surface, the ruins caused in humanity by this idea, people preferred to take refuge in a pragmatic life and publicly profess contempt of ethics.[10]

Yet the failure of the god called "the Revolution" did not occasion a resurgence of the Christian faith and values that had given European civilization its inspiration and shape. Instead, as Del Noce rightly argued, Marxism underwent a "decomposition"[11] into two main elements that

9. See Eberstadt, *Adam and Eve after the Pill*, especially ch. 8.

10. Ratzinger, *Introduction to Christianity*, 12.

11. The word and the concept appear at various points in *The Crisis of Modernity*, especially in Chapter 4, "The Latent Metaphysics in Contemporary Politics," originally published as "La metafisica latente nella realtà politica contemporanea," 61–76.

can be summarized as "technocracy"—in which scientism undergirds a practical materialism but without the engine of the Marxian dialectic—and "nihilism," by which he seems to mean a cynical relativism in which ethics is absorbed into politics without any overarching vision of humanity and its place in the scheme of things.

In his introductory essay for *The Crisis of Modernity*, his collection of some of Del Noce's key essays, Carlo Lancellotti expounds Del Noce's thesis of decomposition:

> On the one hand, with Marxism, modern secular thought made itself an (atheistic) religion and reached the masses, thus shaping modern history as the history of the expansion of atheism. On the other, Marxism's success coincided with its decomposition: instead of producing universal liberation, it opened the way to the affluent society, "the society that succeeds in eliminating the dialectic tension that sustains the revolution by pushing alienation to the highest degree" (Del Noce, *Il problema dell'ateismo*, 314). Decades before the end of the Soviet Union, at a time when large segments of the Western intelligentsia still embraced Marxism as "the philosophy of our time," Del Noce understood that Marxism had been fundamentally defeated because history had refuted its fundamental metaphysical assumption, namely the revolutionary transition to the "new man." However, by infusing Western culture with historical materialism and an attitude of radical rejection of religious transcendence, Marxism had succeeded in its *pars destruens* (CM, 9).

From one angle, the attitude described above can be understood as a neo-gnostic "rejection of being," in the sense of a resentful rejection of limits. Del Noce discusses what that means in an essay that Lancellotti includes in his collection.[12] It is how the sexual revolution dovetails with the decomposition of Marxism and its replacement by a technocratic, bourgeois brand of materialism. As evidenced first by widespread contraception and abortion, then by artificial procreation, and now by the transgender movement, treating our bodies as instruments of sexual expressions that need not be bound by their given structure is precisely what the sexual revolution consists in. It is not just that what we do sexually is now a matter of individual predilection limited only by the principle of mutual consent. It is also that what we *are* as sexual beings is primarily a matter of individual self-understanding, which one might

---

12. Especially "Violence and Modern Gnosticism," *The Crisis of Modernity*, ch. 2.

or might not experience as freely chosen. But freely chosen or not, it is a form of violence to the human person inasmuch as it signifies a radical rejection of naturally given limits. The technocratic, bourgeois society of the contemporary West, in which "choice" is enshrined in consumerism and libertinism, is as materialistic and neo-gnostic as Marxism and just as destructive of the exigencies of the human person. And it depends on the disappearance of "religious transcendence" already described. Marxism might seem different and worse inasmuch as it relativized ethics in terms of power: Whatever promotes the Revolution is right, whatever inhibits it is wrong. But the "technocratic" society also relativizes ethics in a different way.

As Ratzinger said in his homily to the conclave that was about to elect him pope:

> Today, having a clear faith based on the Creed of the Church is often labeled as fundamentalism. Whereas relativism, that is, letting oneself be "tossed here and there, carried about by every wind of doctrine," seems the only attitude that can cope with modern times. We are building a dictatorship of relativism that does not recognize anything as definitive and whose ultimate goal consists solely of one's own ego and desires.[13]

Instead of the dictatorship of the proletariat, we have the exaltation of individual choice untrammeled by nature itself. But why is such relativism dictatorial? Is it not instead the raising of individual freedom to the highest moral level possible?

As Del Noce recognized,[14] the kind of society that survives, and in some ways thrives, in the West is totalitarian to the degree that its assumptions are scientistic and its moral norms justified in scientific as well as political terms. Now strictly speaking, scientism is the belief that the only publicly accessible form of knowledge is scientific knowledge. If that belief be taken literally, it is performatively self-refuting, for the truth of scientism cannot be established scientifically. So ordinarily, scientism takes the form of people's *choosing* to privilege scientific knowledge over such other forms of knowledge as they admit. Usually, such reasons arise from resentment of traditional religion—and thus the accompanying morality—as oppressive. That attitude goes hand-in-hand with a grand narrative according to which the only genuine human progress is

---

13. Ratzinger, Homily at the Mass *Pro Eligendo Pontifice*, 2005.
14. Cf. Del Noce, *The Crisis of Modernity*, 86–91.

and will be constituted by the progress of science, largely by how such progress contributes to individual freedom understood as complete self-determination. That suggests to many people, without logically entailing, that those aspects of religion and morality which cannot be made cogent in what they recognize as scientific terms are obstacles to such progress.

Hence, despite the survival of Judaeo-Christian thought and morality among many in the West—albeit often in deracinated form, as sympathy for victims of every kind—resistance to complete sexual "liberation" has largely and swiftly collapsed. What once seemed like divine commands securely rooted in human nature are now seen as irrational and arbitrary prejudices. For example, abortion and contraception, once thought of as abominations, are now seen as necessary for women's agency and fulfillment. Artificial procreation is now seen as a right for those who want and can afford it. Same-sex "marriage," inconceivable until a few generations ago, is now law. And in the Anglosphere, governments now treat gender "transitioning" as a necessary health measure.

Even the concept of human nature becomes suspect, precisely to the degree that it specifies a *telos* with moral significance that would set limits on self-determination. The loss of any teleological view of nature, which began with the scientific revolution of the seventeenth century, is now complete. But it has not left a vacuum. It has been replaced by an ideology of indefinite progress toward a society in which people will be equipped by technology to be what they wish and do as they wish with apparently minimal interference from others. The "transhumanist" movement is simply the vanguard of ideas that are already and very much at work in society at large. Though some of the details are dated, Aldous Huxley's *Brave New World* (1932) and C. S. Lewis's *The Abolition of Man* (1943) were prophetic, and their vision of said world totalitarian. That is the world now taking shape in the West.

The totalitarianism that develops apace in the West is enforced by what I call the "normalization of Bulverism," especially in political discourse. Bulverism is a toxic hybrid of the fallacies of *petitio principii* and *ad hominem*: one assumes one's opponent is wrong, so obviously wrong that some unflattering explanation must be found for their error in terms other than those they themselves would give. That has always been a tool of polemics. But despite their considerable differences in thought and style, Marx, Freud, and their grandchildren in critical theory and postmodernism have together taught people how to turn it into an instrument for advocating an entire explanation of human behavior—economic in

Marx's case, usually sexual in Freud's, and now a mixture of the two, with race thrown in. Of course, that kind of critique is not fallacious when one's opponent denies obvious facts, such as the truths of arithmetic or the sphericity of the Earth. But certain debatable assumptions of the secular, progressive worldview are now taken by our cultural elites as so obviously true that dissent can only be explained in terms quite unflattering to the dissenters, who are thereby socially discredited and marginalized. That's a tool of totalitarianism.

The totalitarianism Del Noce saw is also nihilistic in two ways. On the front end, and as has already been pointed out, it is a neo-gnostic rejection of "given" limits on human nature and action. Only those enlightened by scientific knowledge, as opposed to religious "obscurantists" and "bigots," can escape those limits as all should. On the back end, it is doomed to ultimate disillusionment just as Marxism was. It has no overarching account of what man is for, which seems *prima facie* to make space for the complete fulfillment of human freedom as science progresses. But as Lewis saw, the power of man over nature inevitably becomes "the power of some men exercised over other men with nature as its instrument."[15] Hence, despite ever-increasing scientific and material progress—good in itself, in many ways—political freedom is not increasing, wars continue to rage, multinational corporations dominate markets, and life becomes increasingly standardized. That has led to a cynicism whose growth is palpable and fed by instant, global, round-the-clock "news," usually negative, via the Internet.

Neither Del Noce nor Ratzinger, however, took enough account of what I see as a third element of the decomposition of Marxism: the morally earnest concern for historically "oppressed" groups that now expresses itself in multiculturalism, political correctness, and leftist identity politics. Those manifest what is sometimes called "cultural Marxism": the extension of classic Marxist critique from economic class alone to race, gender, and sexual orientation too. But they are right about the other two elements described above. The third element I am describing represents the survival of Christian moral passion in secular form: the same passion from which Marxism itself drew much of its energy, as both thinkers recognized. That is why one of Del Noce's favorite themes, the "heterogenesis of ends"[16] that he thought would lead to Marxism's complete self-

---

15. Lewis, *The Abolition of Man*, 22.
16. Del Noce, *Crisis of Modernity*, 11.

negation, is not entirely on point. The moral passion driving Marxism's original, quasi-messianic utopianism did survive—just not in quite the form that unreconstructed Communists would recognize as such.

That element of moral passion fits in with the other elements of "decomposition" insofar as invidious distinctions among groups according to income, race, gender, and sexual orientation are seen to have no scientific basis. From that standpoint, and just as in old-fashioned Marxism, members of less-privileged groups are necessarily seen as oppressed by their evil overlords even now, and thus in need of liberation. But it too is plagued by the lack of any notion of a distinctively human *telos* beyond self-fulfillment conceived in primarily material terms.

The specifically theological aspect of the aforesaid developments is where the concerns of Ratzinger and Del Noce mostly directly intersect. It began in part with the fact that during the generation following the Second World War, progressive theologians in both the Catholic and the Protestant communities persisted in the illusion that "true" Marxism could not only be reconciled with Christianity but also be reconceived as an authentic expression thereof. That was a primary manifestation of "secularization theology" about which both thinkers had much to say.

Some of Ratzinger's students at Tübingen in 1968, for example, decided to take their inspiration not from him but from the aged Ernst Bloch, the gravamen of whose work was the illusion I have just described. All one had to do was strip out the mythical elements of Christianity and emphasize the biblical theme of casting down the mighty and lifting up the lowly—the primary theme of Bloch's books *The Principle of Hope* (1954) and *Atheism in Christianity* (1968). The former book strongly influenced Jürgen Moltmann's *Theology of Hope*, first published in 1964. In turn, and also to Ratzinger's chagrin, Moltmann's book strongly influenced German Catholic graduate students and teaching assistants in theology soon after it was published. And in 1968, in Latin America, Gustavo Gutierrez organized and held a major conference called "Toward a Theology of Liberation," which formed the basis of his seminal 1971 book *A Theology of Liberation*.[17]

All these closely related ideas formed the intellectual climate of the Catholic *avant garde* from the mid-1960s through the mid-1980s. Among older Jesuits and Franciscans, and the dwindling number of students they influence, it still does, mostly—just without the *avant-garde* cachet.

---

17. Gutierrez, *A Theology of Liberation*.

Indeed, thanks to the martyrdom (and now canonization) of Archbishop Oscar Romero, the remnants of the climate persist in Latin American Catholicism and among left-wing Catholics elsewhere. And that despite Ratzinger's largely negative assessment of liberation theology in the Sacred Congregation for the Doctrine of the Faith (CDF) *Instruction* on the topic.[18] The whole thing constitutes a dream that refuses to die.

In his magnum opus *Il problema dell'ateism*, published in 1964,[19] Del Noce explained why it can remain only a dream. For one thing, and as recent history has verified, the notion that Marxism and Christianity are in any way mutually compatible was always illusory. There is no need to rehash tired old debates about the relation of actual Communist regimes to "true" Marxism; on Marx's own premises, there is no essence of Marxism other than its concrete historical embodiments. By general agreement, it was essential to Marx's thought that allegedly objective, transcendent ideas and values are always mystifications of—masks for—underlying power relations based on people's concrete economic roles, in which some classes necessarily exploit others. If that is the case, then there is nothing of permanent value for something called "tradition" to hand on, so that there is no religious or moral tradition worth preserving and defending anymore. For the revolution to occur, ethics had to be subsumed into politics. From all that, it follows that atheism is essential to Marxism. Man no longer *discovers* a transcendental order of being and value, with a creator God at its apex, to which he must learn to conform himself; rather, he makes and remakes himself, thus overcoming his own alienation. *Homo faber* replaces *homo sapiens*, and thus has no need of God, whom Marx's progenitor Feuerbach saw as the supreme expression of man's old alienation.

That is why, when the fall of the Soviet empire unmasked the failure of the revolution, so many Europeans turned not to their ancestral Christian faith but to a corrosive relativism that can culminate only in nihilism. Having accepted the "hermeneutic of suspicion"—a methodology that Marx and Freud had largely introduced (without calling it that) and which critical theory and postmodernism went on to extend to race, gender, and even language as well as to class—such Europeans had nothing solid with which to replace Marxism as a font of inspiration. In my

---

18. Ratzinger, *Instruction on Certain Aspects of the Theology of Liberation*.
19. Del Noce, *Il problema dell'ateism*.

observation, that is increasingly true of secular-minded American and Australian academics as well.

Of course, some theologians did not see the essential role of atheism in Marxism as a problem because they did not see atheism *tout court* as a problem. In the mid-twentieth century, it was a passing fashion to hold that atheism can be understood as a development or expression of Christianity if treated as a kind of iconoclastic precondition for spiritual maturity and earthly progress. Hence "death-of-God" theology. But that idea is dying the death it deserves—ironically enough, partly under the cruel knife of the hermeneutic of suspicion. As Del Noce suggested, the efforts of progressive-Catholic thinkers to secularize and demythologize Catholicism can only produce a new and more virulent form of clericalism, in which the enlightened few, preferably but not necessarily ordained, ridicule and marginalize believers who cling stubbornly to the old-fashioned religion. That mirrors what happened under Communism, in which the putative subject and beneficiary of the revolution, the proletariat, is too *lumpen* to serve as the engine thereof, and so must yield that role to a more enlightened party of intellectuals. Both lead eventually and at best to an oppressive hypocrisy that inevitably undermines its own theoretical and practical supports.

What remains of the dream is the idea of the equal and inherent dignity of every human person, which of course is a fundamentally Judaeo–Christian idea. Leaving aside the Left's negativity toward tradition in general, long evoked by the hermeneutic of suspicion, the idea of equal dignity is what now sustains the moral passion driving much of the contemporary Left in the West, both secular and religious. But secular progressivism detaches said idea from its metaphysical and theological foundations. And it is at precisely at that point that Del Noce's explicit reaction to 1968 becomes most informative.

In a recent article,[20] Lancellotti presents and expands on Del Noce's reaction to a very revealing debate that took place in 1969 between two well-known Catholic intellectuals at the time: Jean-Marie Domenach, who in 1957 had succeeded Emmanuel Mounier as editor of *Esprit* and *de facto* flag-bearer of "progressive" French Catholicism, and Thomas Molnar, the distinguished Hungarian–American philosopher and historian (and a regular *Commonweal* contributor for years before his death). According to Lancellotti, who translated it, Del Noce in 1970 turned the

---

20. Lancellotti, "The Dead End of the Left."

Domenach–Molnar debate into a short book whose Italian title was a phrase Domenach had used in French: in English, "The Dead End of the Left."[21] Del Noce started the book with his own substantial, introductory essay "A New Perspective on Right and Left." We should begin with what all three men agreed was the meaning of the book's title.

Already apparent by 1968, the "crisis of the Left," in Del Noce's words: "takes the form of a split into two opposite developments. One is adaptation to reality, which ultimately leads to submission to the 'reality principle.' Reality, however, is no longer ordered toward values but rather coincides with pure power. The other is pure unrealism, which, however, objectively becomes an accomplice of the first attitude in the global rejection of all values."[22]

The "pure unrealism" to which he refers has several aspects deriving, ultimately, from the neo-gnostic "rejection of Being" already discussed. The inevitable limitations of human life, which make perfect justice and complete individual freedom impossible, cause a resentment that, for a certain sort of temperament, makes working toward some ill-defined future utopia seem like a moral imperative. That utopia would consist in liberation from all "repressive" constraints, sexual and cultural as well as economic, since the traditional norms and values allegedly justifying such constraints are merely instruments of oppression.

According to Domenach, Molnar, and Del Noce, that manifested itself in the "great refusal" of May 1968 in France and elsewhere. But its justified rejection of Soviet-style communism, coupled with its extension of the hermeneutic of suspicion to all allegedly objective values, deprives contemporary leftism of any firm philosophical basis for upholding any values other than those which now characterize our "technocratic" society: namely, scientism, eroticism, and for religious progressives, the theology of secularization. Hence the "adaptation to reality" that coexists with the pure unrealism.

Secular progressives are strongly motivated to be scientistic because for them, the social sciences in particular "demystify" traditional values as masks for will-to-power. Since Del Noce's death, the group whose will-to-power is thus masked has come to be seen not merely as an economic

---

21. I am unable to locate the original pamphlet.

22. Del Noce, "A New Perspective on Left and Right" in *The Crisis of Modernity*, 229. Del Noce's essay was first published as "Un discorso 'nuovo' su destra e sinistra," *L'Europa* 4, no. 10 (1970), 24–28, republished in *Rivoluzione Risorgimento Tradizione*, 171–86.

class—the capitalists—but more broadly as the hegemonic white, Christian, "heteronormative" patriarchy, which largely invented capitalism. That stance had already begun to take shape with the "New Left" of the late 1960s, which came to wield an ever-stronger influence within left-wing parties in Europe and America.

For the contemporary Left, complete sexual autonomy is also necessary, albeit not itself sufficient, for "liberation" and "justice." Del Noce saw that coming in 1968. It did not take more than a generation thereafter for consent to become the sole moral criterion for sexual activity, and individual experience the sole criterion for sexual identity. Hence the rejection of heteronormativity and the proliferation of "genders" that are really sexual preferences taken as constitutive of personal identity. But because of the prestige of science, and the success of regular technological progress that contributes to such prestige, the Left lacks a critique of the globalist elites who aim to rule technocratically, through enlightened "experts." Those elites aim to rule in the name of science and progress while fully supporting the new dogma of sexual autonomy. Not many on the Left today question that—or if they do, they don't seriously propose giving up the arrangements that make affluence possible. Thus does the revolutionary spirit of the Left become the opposite of revolutionary. We have reached "the dead end of the Left."

With the effective and mostly unquestioned rule of scientism and sexual autonomy (which latter Del Noce called "eroticism") in today's Western-globalist technocracy, the only outlets for moral passion on what del Noce called "the Left" are the drive for the *equality* of the sexes, of different cultures, and of racial and ethnic groups. Thus the insistence on women participating in every sphere of life on the same terms as men, and the charge of "racism" leveled against those who oppose open borders and favor the equal enforcement of laws on all within a given jurisdiction. The problem for the Left is that despite its laudable passion for the equal dignity of each and every human person, its overall philosophical anthropology cannot support that idea, and therefore the passion for it, rationally. It is freighted with a purely negative conception of individual freedom as freedom from whatever hinders individual self-definition and the corresponding pursuit of an individualistic, bourgeois sense of wellbeing in terms of that identity. That is now what the "dignity of the human person" is thought to consist in. But it is a formula for the brave new world where "human dignity" will be flattened, instrumentalized, and thus rendered incoherent.

Because they accept secularization, and thus practical atheism, as an inevitable development of modernity and progress, religious progressives lack the resources to resist the sort of secular progressivism I have been describing—hence the collapse of mainline Protestantism and the willingness of most of the Catholic Left to accept the technocratic society and economic globalism while sharing the aforesaid moral passion of the secular Left. The moral capital built up by the religious idea of the dignity of the human person for centuries is being spent and not replaced.

The process that has brought the Left to its dead end, beginning in the 1960s and accelerating even today, hinges on a mistaken anthropology that takes the essence of personhood simply as the capacity for exercising agency in self-determination. That is to mistake the part for the whole: It neglects how human personhood is constituted by relationship, and thus in part by reception of certain "givens" that function as limits. It is why Del Noce was so prescient when he noted that *homo faber* has replaced *homo sapiens* in leftist thought.[23] On that view, we are what we freely make ourselves to be; there is no prior "human nature," a concept that is only a mystifying mask for will-to-power. And of course, the religious dimension of human life is thereby dissipated. That same mistake underlies what Ratzinger has called the dictatorship of relativism—a phrase that is only superficially paradoxical, since the full force of government coercion is now being brought to bear to enforce the aforesaid anthropology in Western countries. That is the final dead end of freedom as conceived by most of the Left today. We are fortunate to have thinkers who saw it coming.

Bibliography

Benedict XVI. *Last Testament: In His Own Words*. New York: Bloomsbury, 2016.
Benedict XVI. Meeting with the Clergy of the Dioceses of Belluno-Feltre and Treviso, Church of St. Justin Martyr, Auronzo di Cadore, July 24, 2007. http://www.vatican.va/content/benedict xvi/en/speeches/2007/july/documents/hf_ben-xvi_spe_20070724_clero-cadore.html.
Del Noce, Augusto. *The Age of Secularization*. Translated and edited by Carlo Lancellotti. McGill-Queen's Studies in the History of Ideas. Kindle Edition, 2016.
———. *The Crisis of Modernity*. Translated and edited by Carlo Lancellotti. McGill-Queens University Press, Kindle Edition, 2014.

---

23. Del Noce developed that theme in many places. Cf. the essay "Technological Civilization and Christianity" in *The Age of Secularization*, especially 74–75.

———. "La metafisica latente nella realtà politica contemporanea." In *Cultura del dare e dultura dell'essere* [Culture of Doing vs Culture of Being]. Rome: Japadre, 1988.

———. *Il problema dell'ateismo*. Il Mulino, Bologna 1964. 2nd ed., 2010.

Eberstadt, Mary. *Adam and Eve after the Pill: Paradoxes of the Sexual Revolution*. San Francisco: Ignatius, 2012.

Gutierrez, Gustavo. *A Theology of Liberation: History, Politics, and Salvation*. Translated and edited by Sister Caridad Inda and John Eagleson. Maryknoll, NY: Orbis, 1971. 2nd ed., 1988.

John Paul II. *Man and Woman He Created Them: A Theology of the Body*. Translated and critically edited by Michael Waldstein. New York: Pauline Books & Media, 2006.

Lancellotti, Carlo. "The Dead End of the Left." *Commonweal*, April 16, 2018. https://www.commonwealmagazine.org/dead-end-left.

Lewis, C. S. *The Abolition of Man*. 1943. Reprint, New York: Macmillan, 1978 ed.

Paul VI. *Humanae vitae*. Vatican website (July 25, 1968). http://w2.vatican.va/content/paul-vi/en/encyclicals/documents/hf_p-vi_enc_25071968_humanae-vitae.html.

Ratzinger, Joseph. *Introduction to Christianity*. Translated by J. R. Foster. 1968. Reprint, San Francisco: Ignatius, 2004.

———. "Difficulties Confronting the Faith in Europe Today." Address to Meeting of the Doctrinal Commission of Europe, Laxenburg, May 2, 1989. The English translation appears in *Communio* 38 (2011) 728–37. http://www.vatican.va/roman_curia/congregations/cfaith/incontri/rc_con_cfaith_19890502_laxenburg-ratzinger_en.html.

———. Homily given as Dean of the College of Cardinals, Vatican Basilica, April 18, 2005. http://www.vatican.va/gpII/documents/homily-pro-eligendo-pontifice_20050418_en.html.

———. *Instruction on Certain Aspects of the Theology of Liberation*, The Sacred Congregation for the Doctrine of the Faith, Rome, 1984. https://www.vatican.va/roman_curia/congregations/cfaith/documents/rc_con_cfaith_doc_19840806_theology-liberation_en.html.

———. Homily at the Mass Pro Eligendo Pontifice, 2005. http://www.vatican.va/gpII/documents/homily-pro-eligendo-pontifice_20050418_en.html.

Reich, Wilhelm. *The Sexual Revolution: Toward a Self-Regulating Character Structure*. 1930. Reprint, New York: Farrar Straus & Giroux, 1986.

Sacred Congregation for the Doctrine of the Faith. *Instruction on Certain Aspects of the Theology of Liberation*, August 1984. http://www.vatican.va/roman_curia/congregations/cfaith/documents/rc_con_cfaith_doc_19840806_theology-liberation_en.html.

14

Walter Kaufmann and Modern Manichaeism

GARY FURNELL

In 1969, Walter Kaufmann, a Princeton professor of religion and philosophy, published an essay, *Beyond Black and White: A Plea for Thinking in Color* in response to an ancient idea that seemed to be gaining credibility on American and European university campuses: Manichaeism, the belief that there are two opposing principles, one good and one evil, in operation in the world. Today's manifestations of Manichaeism appear to conform to the observations made by Kaufmann fifty years ago. For this reason alone the Kaufmann essay is well worth considering, quite apart from the additional benefits of its many other merits and occasional, but still enlightening, faults. It is a wide-ranging, provocative analysis that begins with the literature of ancient Greece, looks briefly for any disposition towards dualism in the religions of ancient India, Israel, and Persia, considers Christianity, and then settles to examine the aspects of Manichaeistic thinking that had been transmitted via the universities into the social and political movements of the 1960's counterculture. Kaufmann was ideally placed to make his observations: he was a professor at Princeton University from 1948 until his death in

1980, and a personal friend—and firm critic—of Herbert Marcuse, hero of the hippies and young radicals who became unwitting disciples of Mani, a third-century Persian prophet. What were they seeking to embrace in an updated version of a heresy that was discredited centuries ago? Kaufmann answers: not the truth. In his estimation, that difficult search was beyond them because they lacked the rigor of critical thinking and the vigor necessary to sustain the strain of many hard years of determined study. They were attracted by simplicity, a ready program for activism, and the desire for membership of an exclusive, correct community. Kaufmann ends with a plea for intellectual honesty and humility—and respect for the primary evidence of concrete, lived experience.

IN 1969, WALTER KAUFMANN published an essay, *Beyond Black and White: A Plea for Thinking in Color,* in response to an idea from the third century that seemed to be gaining credibility on American and European university campuses. That idea was Manichaeism, the belief that there are two opposing principles, one good and one evil, operating in the world. Ancient Manichaeism posited two opposing divinities, with the spiritual realm being wholly good and the material world wholly bad. All of life was held to be a struggle between the two irreconcilable principles. Manichaeism mixed Christianity with Zoroastrian and Gnostic ideas.[1] Modern Manichaeism has abandoned the metaphysical content but kept the black-and-white morality, with one side wholly good and the other side wholly evil.

First, some background on Professor Walter Kaufmann. He was born in Germany in 1921. A precocious child, before his teenage years he had declared to his parents that he couldn't believe the Trinitarian doctrine of the Lutheran Church. In his biographical essay *The Faith of a Heretic* he recalls:

> At twelve, I formally left the Protestant Church to become a Jew. Having never heard of Unitarianism, I assumed that the religion for people who believed in God, but not in Christ or the Holy Ghost was Judaism . . . I took my new religion very seriously, explored it with enormous curiosity and growing love, and gradually became more and more orthodox. When I arrived in the United States in 1939, I was planning to become a rabbi. A

---

1. Marais, *History of Philosophy*, 114.

lot of things happened to me that winter, spring, summer; and when the war broke out I had what, but for its contents, few would hesitate to call a mystical experience. In the most intense despair I suddenly saw that I had deceived myself for years: I had believed. At last the God of tradition joined the Holy Ghost and Christ.[2]

Kaufmann pursued an academic career, specializing in social philosophy and religion. He was an acclaimed translator of Nietzsche and Goethe and of Martin Buber, who was a friend. Kaufmann was sceptical about the value of religion.[3] He was also sceptical of much of the posturing of the atheist Existentialists, although he admired some aspects of Jean-Paul Sartre's thought but not his politics. He was alert to intellectual fads, and therein lies his value as an acute observer of the 1960s counterculture.

Kaufmann was ideally placed to make his observations of mid-twentieth-century intellectual fads: he was a professor at Princeton University from 1948 until his death in 1980. He saw the growth, the flowering, and the dissemination of the 1960s counterculture. Also, he was a personal friend—and firm critic—of Herbert Marcuse, hero of the young radicals who became, through Marcuse, as Kaufmann said, unwitting disciples of Mani, a Persian prophet. Why were these idealistic students embracing a variation of a heresy that was discredited centuries ago? Kaufmann answers that there were two key factors: First, they were attracted by simplistic answers delivered in terms of good and bad, liberal or repressive, Left or Right that provided an obvious agenda for activism. Second, through the shared ethical and political positions they could obtain membership of an exclusive community in which there was the glory of belonging to a righteous and vibrant group who had another group of unrighteous, stick-in-the-muds to fight.[4]

In this essay, the focus is on only two features of contemporary culture that derive at least in part from Manichaean thinking. First, the "pre-emptive censorship" of certain views, and second, the absolutizing of a select group of relative values. The unparalleled historical memory of the Church and its breadth of vision—unique qualities highlighted by

---

2. Kaufmann, *Existentialism, Religion, and Death*, 152.
3. Kaufmann, *Existentialism, Religion, and Death*, 157.
4. Kaufmann, *Existentialism, Religion, and Death*, 138.

G. K. Chesterton—could have saved the counterculture from the distorting simplifications of Manichaeism, and could yet save contemporary culture.

Background on Manichaeism

Walter Kaufmann maintains that ancient Manichaeism was informed by Christian ideas. In particular, it was informed by the relative emphasis that Satan receives in the New Testament, and the idea that one's eternal destiny is predicated on belonging to the Children of God, and not the Children of the Devil. Kaufmann notes that Christianity is not dualistic in its metaphysics because there is not a god of evil equal to the god of light. Satan is a creature, not a divinity. Kaufmann summarizes:

> In the third century another Persian prophet, Mani, arose in southern Babylonia and preached what might be called a more Zoroastrian version of Christianity. He was martyred at the instigation of the Magian priests but was survived by the doctrine that still bears his name, Manichaeanism. For a while its impact on the Roman Empire rivalled that of Christianity, and Augustine came under its spell. Eventually the Church condemned the Manichaean heresy, and as a religion it died. The details of this form of Gnosticism are now known only to a few historians of religion; yet Manichaeism is far from dead, *if we use the name inclusively to label that view in which history is a contest between the forces of light and darkness, and men are divided into two camps, with all right on one side.*[5] [Kaufmann's italics.]

Kaufmann writes, "The Manichaean heresy will not die because it invites men to see themselves as the children of light and their foes as the forces of darkness. This dualism was not invented by Mani: 'the children of light' are encountered earlier in the New Testament and in the Dead Sea Scrolls, and the moral dualism can be traced back at least as far as Zarathustra."[6]

It is only with some difficulty that the Church was able to remove the traces of Manichaeism. Kaufmann notes, "The virus of Mani has taken a fearful toll in Christianity, but in our time the churches are going

---

5. Kaufmann, *Existentialism, Religion, and Death*, 127.
6. Kaufmann, *Existentialism, Religion, and Death*, 129.

far toward ridding themselves of this disease—or the plague is leaving the sinking ship of Christianity to smite our ideologues."[7]

Left and Right

Ideologues plagued by Manichaeism have carried it far from its original religious basis into many of the West's secular institutions. Modern Manichaeism first influenced politics, later colleges and universities, and then it influenced the social movements adopted by activist students and academics. Kaufmann says that in the early years of the twentieth century, the political Right highlighted the Manichaean opposition between itself—standing for stability and prosperity—and the chaos of violent communism. The political and moral dualism was Right (perceived as good) versus Left (portrayed as bad). But the outrages of the Nazis and the fascists, and later McCarthyism and racial segregation in the United States, the actions of the French in Algeria and the Americans in Vietnam, and the Western European powers' mismanagement of their colonies was seen to rob the Right of intellectual and moral respectability. The Left then rose to greater prominence, despite plenty of evidence from the Soviet Union, the trapped Iron Curtain nations, and communist China that it was not the party of humanity. Almost immediately, Kaufmann notes, the Left adopted the Manichaean opposites that had been used by the Right in its fight against communism. Only now it was Left—liberating; Right—repressive. Kaufmann records:

> When the New Left appeared, the dreadful silence, apathy, and despair of the McCarthy period gave way to a new ferment in the intellectual community. Students and young faculty formed the vanguard, and the fusion of intellectual and moral concerns roused premature hopes. But almost at birth the New Left succumbed to the virus of Mani.
>
> Why? However unfortunate it is that the New Left swallowed the basic scheme of the Old Right, merely reversing the value signs, the case is anything but exceptional. When the tables are turned, the tables themselves are not subjected to critical scrutiny.[8]

---

7. Kaufmann, *Existentialism, Religion, and Death*, 130.
8. Kaufmann, *Existentialism, Religion, and Death*, 130.

Kaufmann provides his summary of this simplifying morality as it found expression in the 1960s:

> Intellectuals did not suppose that all whites were devils or that all nonwhites were beautiful or virtuous. But many did come to see the world divided into two camps: white oppressors who did not shrink from using atoms bombs, napalm, and torture against the oppressed, mostly nonwhite, who were fighting for their freedom. Given this model, one could readily cut through the complexities of Latin American politics and the Palestinian situation. One need hardly wonder at the popularity of a world view that makes so many crucial and exasperating problems so simple, that makes it easy to choose sides, and that provides the assurance that, having done that, one is wholly in the right and in the company of the vast majority of struggling humanity.[9]

Already, the tendency to make relative values into absolute values is obvious. Kaufmann continues:

> Anyone grounded in Greek tragedy and philosophy, in history or literature, must respond to such simplicity with a conditioned reflex of mistrust. And the more he knows about the issues, the more will suspicion give way to stunned surprise that anyone who claims to be devoted to the life of the intellect should actually believe such a Manichaean view.[10]

Despite the intellectual difficulties inherent in Manichaeism, there were three key cultural conditions that aided the spread of Manichaean-influenced perspectives through so many colleges and universities. One was the situation of young people born in the years after World War II. This generation did not have a direct experience of war. Their fathers had fought in the Pacific, North Africa, and Europe; their mothers had worked in the munitions factories; they were patriotic and hard-working, generally respectful of government and active in the "little platoons" that build society: churches, service clubs, etc. In addition, they grew up in the Great Depression, so they did not take their opportunities for granted. Their children, in contrast, were born into relative peace and a burgeoning prosperity. Associated with this prosperity, there was a bellicose triumphalism about American culture, despite the deprivations of Afro-Americans, and this triumphalism was hostile to anyone who

---

9. Kaufmann, *Existentialism, Religion, and Death*, 132.
10. Kaufmann, *Existentialism, Religion, and Death*, 132.

criticized American values. Kaufmann says this about the generation born in these conditions:

> Nazism and Pearl Harbor happened before their time. The student radicals were born under the aegis of Hiroshima and Nagasaki, their childhood was dominated by the cold war and, if they were Americans, by McCarthyism, and their adolescence by the civil rights struggle. It is all too understandable that democracy seemed much sicker to them than it does to their parents who lived through World War II.[11]

The American social commentator George L. Marlin observed that many among these privileged children became the impatient and imprudent "Me generation":

> These "me generation" kids, estimated to be about 10 to 15 percent of America's college population in the sixties, were alienated from the mainstream because they were different; they were special, superior and enlightened. Hence the old rules of civility and patience did not apply to them; they had to be gratified now. Self-fulfilment had to be immediate. The problems that perplexed man through the ages had to be solved immediately...
>
> The most radical became student activists—members of "the movement" or the "New Left." Starting with the 1964 campus free speech movement through the student anti-war riots of the 1968 Chicago Democratic Convention and culminating in Nixon's Vietnam policies, this student revolution was driven by emotions and slogans, not reasoning or scholarship.[12]

Another factor that aided the prominence of student radicals was the sheer number of students. These privileged young people were baby boomers. When World War II started, there were about 1.3 million Americans studying in colleges and universities. By 1968, the number of students had grown to 6.9 million.[13] This astonishing increase reflected not only the population growth, but also the ambitions and prosperity of ordinary people. The postwar population boom made an influential mass movement among students and academics possible.

A further aspect of modern culture that encouraged many to follow this Manichaean view was the accelerating pace of life and the mind-boggling challenges that confronted society. Kaufmann observed:

11. Kaufmann, *Existentialism, Religion, and Death*, 130.
12. Martin, *Narcissist Nation*, 6–8.
13. Martin, *Narcissist Nation*, 6–8.

> Even when the world was less complex, many people found peace of mind in simplistic world views. Now that the world situation and the societies into which youth finds itself thrown are of a truly frightening complexity, the hunger for Manichaeism is greater than ever. As social and international problems become more involved and unmanageable, the prospect of finding security in a world view that reduces everything to black and white becomes more attractive.[14]

Attendant to this quickening pace of life was the expectation among the young activists that social change should proceed with something of the breathless pace of technological change. Their experience of rapid and obvious change was very different to the experience of previous generations. Kaufmann makes this observation about their expectations:

> Many of the students have very little patience. Their experience of time differs from ours. Even if we fly far more often than our students, we can also remember taking two weeks to cross the Atlantic in a boat, and longer than that to hitch-hike across the United States. Our sense of time was molded by experiences like that, and we are prone to feel that the conditions of the blacks in America has changed a great deal in the last two decades. But our students know that we landed men on the moon less than ten years after Kennedy proclaimed this as a goal, and the speeds reached by the rockets rushing toward the moon have a place in the experience of youth, while we still think in pre-rocket terms.[15]

Despite these factors favourable to the influence of Manichaeism among large numbers of students, Kaufmann asks:

> But isn't Manichaeism too simple to be intellectually respectable? It would certainly be of inestimable advantage if a philosopher could be found who, without spoiling the simplicity of the ancient scheme, had brought it up to date with suitable references to Marx and Freud, adding enough jargon and obscurity to make everything seem very academic and profound. It is easy to imagine the joy of the European students when they discovered such a philosopher . . .[16]

---

14. Kaufman. *Existentialism, Religion, and Death*, 134
15. Kaufmann, *Existentialism, Religion, and Death*, 151.
16. Kaufmann, *Existentialism, Religion, and Death*, 134.

Enter Herbert Marcuse

It is in this context that the voice of Herbert Marcuse—Kaufmann's "immensely likable" friend at the University of California—was heard, and Marcuse's voice seemed to have the urgency of a call to battle.[17] Many hundreds of thousands of (mostly young) people responded, ready to fight the good fight as defined by Marcuse and his colleagues of the New Left. Kaufmann was especially alarmed by the essay "Repressive Tolerance" that Marcuse had contributed to a 1965 compilation called "A Critique of Pure Tolerance." Kaufmann explained why he chose this piece as his focus for his criticism of Marcuse: "This essay of thirty-odd pages is fascinating because it would be hard to find a more Manichaean tract by a philosopher of any standing; and that is the secret of Marcuse's popularity."[18]

In *Repressive Tolerance*, Marcuse advocated that *only* the views of the progressive Left should be tolerated lest those views opposed to the progressive agenda should gain traction and influence both public opinion and policy formulation. Kaufmann warned against Marcuse's Manichaeism and offered this critical analysis:

> Marcuse's basic error is his assumption that all right is on the Left, all wrong on the Right. The moment we cease to see the world in black and white, the instant we see it in color in its inexhaustible variety, we find a multitude of groups and some hate, some aggression, some stupidity, some lack of information, and some errors wherever there are sizable groups of human beings—but fused in ever different proportions with love and humanity, intelligence and information, and even some truth.
>
> There is something highly artificial not only about "the Right" and "the Left" but also about the other pairs of opposite in Marcuse's essay: they all smell of Mani.[19]

English historian Christopher Dawson would agree with Kaufmann's impatience with the inadequacy of terms like the Left and the Right. Dawson noted that if a tall building is on fire, whether you jump from a window on the right or a window on the left makes no difference when you hit the pavement.[20] Chesterton thought that using Left and Right as

---

17. Kaufmann, *Existentialism, Religion, and Death*, 138.
18. Kaufmann, *Existentialism, Religion, and Death*, 136.
19. Kaufmann, *Existentialism, Religion, and Death*, 140, 141.
20. Dawson, *Christianity and European Culture*, 247.

opposing political terms disguised the fact that bullying governments from the Left or Right both had the same effect of crushing crucial freedoms such as freedom of speech, freedom of religion, freedom of association, and the freedom of the family. Perhaps a more accurate and helpful presentation of the various political systems would be to plot governments on a spectrum from intrusive, bullying, big governments through to federalist governments based on the principle of subsidiarity. Governments and institutions that have been influenced by Manichaeism are likely to be among those governments that are bullying and intrusive, and restrictive of the rights of those who oppose their agenda.

Kaufmann highlights the totalitarian ideas that Marcuse promotes as he justifies pre-emptive measures against those who oppose the Left's "progressive" agenda: "He [Marcuse] advocates 'the withdrawal of toleration of speech and assembly from groups and movements which promote aggressive policies, armament, chauvinism, discrimination on the grounds of race and religion, or which oppose the extension of public services, social security, medical care, etc.'"[21]

Marcuse's Manichaeism leads him to justify deliberate and targeted intolerance in public affairs, says Kaufmann. "When Marcuse advocates 'intolerance against movements for the Right,' making it quite clear he means 'censorship and even pre-censorship,' he advocates political intolerance."[22] That is, intolerance of views that are opposed to the Left's activist agenda.

Kaufmann rejects this type of selective intolerance of some views while other views must remain unchallenged. He rejects it because it is simplistic, hence anti-intellectual; it does not honor the complexity that humanity experiences.

> Vigorous criticism of theories and proposals should not be confounded with intolerance, nor need it be Manichaean. Only rigorous exercise of our intellect and examination of the evidence can show us what is tenable and what is not; and the result may well be that more than one view is defensible. It does not follow that all views are equally tenable. Those who find no fault with any view do not show tolerance but only that in some ways they resemble vegetables.[23]

---

21. Kaufmann, *Existentialism, Religion, and Death*, 136.
22. Kaufmann, *Existentialism, Religion, and Death*, 136.
23. Kaufmann, *Existentialism, Religion, and Death*, 140.

Chesterton may have pointed out that despite Kaufmann's desire to move beyond black and white, no writer put pen to paper unless they believed their philosophy was right and its opposite was wrong, and that includes Kaufmann. It seems we can't altogether escape dualistic notions. Indeed, structured rational thought reflects the law of non-contradiction which recognizes that a statement cannot be both true and false at the same time.

Pre-emptive Censorship and Absolutizing the Relative

Where modern Manichaeism has become a pervasive influence, we cannot expect that the voices of conservatism, of traditional values or of the Church, for example, will be given equal airtime or admitted the same level of legitimacy to the so-called progressive voices, the voices of the Left. The sort of intolerance identified by Kaufmann fifty years ago is at work. The voices of progressive liberalism have privileges that can—should, according to Manichaeistic thinking—be denied to the voices that question or oppose them. It is lamentable, but no surprise, that the secular and "progressive" Australia Council, for example, in 2016 withdrew the modest amount of funding they gave to the conservative journal *Quadrant* while increasing the already substantial funding they gave to left-leaning journals, some of which published very little fiction or poetry, had a much smaller circulation, and published less often than *Quadrant*.[24] It is a form of pre-emptive censorship; the withdrawal of support from the unacceptable. In the 2017 US presidential election campaign, Hillary Clinton's condemnation of those who oppose unrestricted immigration, gay rights, and feminism as "deplorables" revealed her Manichaeistic-type thinking and attitude. In Australian debates about domestic violence, too many feminists are displaying their Manichaeism when they derogate men—not some perverse men but masculinity itself—as violent and oppressive while presenting women as blameless victims.

Attendant to Manichaeism is a tendency to absolutize the relative—the very definition of worldliness—to use the phraseology of Søren Kierkegaard.[25] In the simplifying dualism of modern Manichaeism, progressive values are absolutely good and right, and opposing values

24. Windschuttle, "The Australia Council's Revenge."
25. Kierkegaard, *The Sickness unto Death*, 72, 73.

are absolutely bad and wrong. One can see these dualistic opposites at work—taking this absolute form—in the more radical demands of contemporary environmental activists. For instance, we hear them proclaim: No Coal Seam Gas. No Whaling. No Nuclear Power. No Forestry in Native Forests. Do the activists mean that these activities must be banned forever, no matter what the circumstances? Many of them mean exactly that. This seems to be an environmental variation of Manichaeism that says: Untouched Nature is Absolutely Good; Disruptive Human Industry is Absolutely Bad. And so there is the unstinting demand that we absolutize particular and relative values.

Equality was, of course, one of the ideals that the counterculture demanded: equality between black and white, between male and female, between rich and poor. But equality, while a valid spiritual aspiration (the spiritual is the only aspect of man's being under which all men can be considered equal) can never be an absolute political and social aspiration because it ignores the many organic, social, and attitudinal differences among people. This did not stop and does not stop the well-meaning but naive academic and student activists. Emotion was and remains their primary driver rather than wide and varied evidence allied to careful thinking. This indifference to spiritual equality—and the consequent focus on societal equality—is a reflection of an exclusive focus on the realm of the immanent and temporal. It is demand for the realization here and now of an ideal that can only be achieved in eternity, and even then it is a work of God and not man. Kierkegaard noted, "Equalization . . . is the false anticipation of the eternal life, which people have done away with as a 'beyond' and want to realize here *in abstracto*."[26]

In his masterpiece on sociality, *Works of Love*, Kierkegaard saw that the attempt by political revolutionaries and earnest social reformers to impose this secular vision of ideal equality will always be frustrated, and its proponents always agitated and agitating, because the realm of the temporal is defined by the passing of time which is "the very medium of differentiation." Attempts to impose equality by force of law, for example, are vain attempts to arrest time and establish a timeless, ideal condition of equality. Kierkegaard says:

> To bring about likeness among men, to apportion the conditions of temporal existence equally, if possible, to all men, this is a task which pre-eminently occupies the secular world . . . This

26. Hannay, *Kierkegaard*, 276.

well-meaning worldliness is piously—if one may say so—convinced that there must be one temporal condition, one earthly distinction—which one discovers with the aid of calculations and surveys or some other preferred device—in which there is equality. If this condition were to become one and the same for all men, then this likeness would have been achieved. On the one hand, this cannot be accomplished and, on the other, the likeness of everyone's sharing the same temporal distinction is by no means Christian equality . . . And perfect achievement of earthly likeness is an impossibility.[27]

Trying to impose a simple stillness on differentiating and complex reality creates chaos; it invites contentions and schisms; it legislates what turn out to be grosser inequities; and it engenders polarities—the very opposite to the social harmony it seeks to establish. This is obvious today when the secular insistence on an equalizing plurality in philosophy, culture, and religion is, in fact, one of the factors that are splintering society and unearthing tensions and resentments that may otherwise have remained dormant. It results when there is a concerted attempt to make relative values into absolute values.

Chesterton and the Church

The Church could have helped correct Manichaeism in the sixties, as it can correct contemporary forms of Manichaeism. After all, the Church examined the ideas of Manichaeism over 1,500 years ago and found them wanting. G. K. Chesterton championed the unrivalled intellectual expertise and experience of the Church as an aid to humanity as it sought to negotiate the difficulties of life and prosper as individuals and in society. Chesterton wrote:

> There is no other case of one intelligent institution that has been thinking about thinking for two thousand years. Its experience naturally covers nearly all experiences, and especially nearly all errors. The result is a map in which all the blind alleys and bad roads are clearly marked, all the ways that have been shown to be worthless by the best of all evidence; the evidence of those who have gone down them . . . . By this means, it does prevent men from wasting their time or losing their lives upon paths that have been found futile or disastrous again and again in

27. Kierkegaard, *Works of Love*, 83.

the past, but which might otherwise trap travelers again and again in the future . . . . The Catholic Church is the only thing which saves a man from the degrading slavery of being a child of his age. I have compared it with the New Religions; but this is exactly where it differs from the New Religions. The New Religions are in many ways suited to the new conditions. When those conditions shall have changed in only a century or so, the points upon which alone they insist at present will have become almost pointless. If the faith has all the freshness of a new religion, it has all the richness of an old religion; it has especially all the reserves of an old religion. So far as that is concerned, its antiquity is alone a great advantage, and especially a great advantage for purposes of renovation and youth. It is only by the analogy of animal bodies that we suppose that old things must be stiff. It is a mere metaphor from bones and arteries. In an intellectual sense old things are flexible. Above all, they have various and many alternatives to offer. There is a sort of rotation of crops in religious history; and old fields can lie fallow for a while and then be worked again. But when the new religion or any such notion has sown its one crop of wild oats, which the wind generally blows away, it is barren. A thing as old as the Catholic Church has an accumulated armoury and treasury to choose from; it can pick and choose among the centuries and brings one age to the rescue of another. It can call on the old world to redress the balance of the new.[28]

Chesterton noted that one of the roles of the Church is to emphasize the importance of its capacious truths so that man's sight is not restricted by his own contrivances and he consequently leaves disregarded matters that are necessary for his own welfare. He continues:

Now there is no other corporate mind in the world that is thus on the watch to prevent minds from going wrong. The policeman comes too late, when he tries to prevent men from going wrong. The doctor comes too late, for he only comes to lock up the madman, not to advise a sane man on how to not go mad. And all other sects and schools are inadequate for the purpose. This is not because each of them may not contain a truth, but precisely because each of them does contain a truth; and is content to contain a truth. None of the others really pretends to contain the truth. None of the others, that is, really pretends to be looking out in all directions at once. The Church is not

28. Chesterton, *Why I am a Catholic*.

merely armed against the heresies of the past or even of the present, but equally against those of the future, that may be the exact opposite of those of the present.[29]

It is this lack of a wide vision that is the primary problem of any heresy, including Manichaeism. The truth they see is a partial truth, but they emphasize this partial truth and this leads to a distortion of many other truths. Chesterton continues, "The heretic (who is also the fanatic) is not a man who loves the truth too much; no man can love the truth too much. The heretic is a man who loves his truth more than truth itself. He prefers the half-truth that he has found to the whole truth which humanity has found."[30]

Most new ideas are variations of discredited old ideas. But with a perspective limited to contemporary conditions and scornful of the value of tradition, the modern Manchaeists find themselves hailing as fresh and vibrant an idea that is not only stale but rotten. This reveals another benefit of attending to Church teaching: because of the participation in the deep explorations of other people from other times, we allow past thinkers to sometimes amaze us—and offend us—by saying that what we think is right, is wrong—because they've confronted the idea before and thought it through.

The time and effort we lose as we explore their thought is rewarded as we avoid previously explored dead ends and harmful ways. Manichaeism is one of those harmful ways: it leads to a loss of freedom, it promotes relative values as absolute values, and it leads to ordinary people being denigrated as deplorable.

The American theologian Jeffrey Bloechel provides this assessment of the current mania for political and social activism. He says, "It is not impossible that the most lasting effect of the so-called "death of God" will prove to be a diminished capacity to care for one another, unnoticed as we attempt to exorcise our sense of desolation by giving ourselves up to the politics of revolt."[31]

---

29. Chesterton, *Why I am a Catholic*.
30. Chesterton, *On Reading*.
31. Schmiedel and Matarazzao, Jr., *Dynamics of Difference*, 93.

Bibliography

Chesterton, G. K. *On Reading*. https://thepocketscroll.wordpress.com/classic-christianity/why-classic-christianity/gk-chesterton-on-reading.

———. *Why I Am a Catholic*. https://www.chesterton.org/why-i-am-a-catholic.

Dawson, Christopher. *Christianity and European Culture: Selections from the Work of Christopher Dawson*. Edited by Gerald J. Russello. Washington, DC: Catholic University of America Press, 1998.

Hannay, Alastair. *Kierkegaard*. London: Routledge & Kegan Paul, 1982.

Kaufmann, Walter. *Existentialism, Religion, and Death: Thirteen Essays*. New York: New American Library, 1976.

Kierkegaard, Søren. *The Sickness unto Death: A Christian Psychological Exposition of Edification and Awakening*. London: Penguin, 2008.

———. *Works of Love*. Translated by Howard and Edna Hong. Foreword by George Pattison. New York: Harper Perennial, 2009.

Marais, Julian. *History of Philosophy*. Translated from the Spanish by Stanley Appelbaum and Clarence C. Strowbridge. New York: Dover, 1967.

Martin, George L. *Narcissist Nation: Confessions of a Blue-State Conservative*. South Bend, IN: St. Augustine's Press, 2010. Quoted in *Australian Annals* 129.2 (2018) 6–8.

Schmiedel, Ulrich, and James M. Matarazzao Jr., eds. *Dynamics of Difference: Christianity and Alterity. A Festschrift for Werner G. Jeanrond*. London: Bloomsbury, 2015.

Windschuttle, Keith. "The Australian Council's Revenge." https://quadrant.org.au/opinion/qed/2016/05/australia-councils-revenge.

15

Germain Grisez, Ultimate Ends, and the Magisterium

Revising Revisionist Narratives[1]

Reginald Mary Chua OP

In the lead-up to the promulgation of *Humanae vitae*, the Catholic moral theologians on Paul VI's commission on birth control were already sharply divided over the ethics of contraception. In the decades following, ethicists within and without the Church would engage in wide-ranging debates over the value of human goods such as life, marriage, and the pursuit of truth. Germain Grisez (1929–2018) participated in and made landmark contributions to all of these debates. In this paper I identify and evaluate one aspect of his contribution: his critique of ethical instrumentalism. Grisez's views on this score have received much attention vis-à-vis the engagements of his colleagues (the so-called New Natural Lawyers) with positions

---

1. This paper benefited from conversations with Fr. David Willis, OP, who drew my attention to a number of the key texts analyzed in this chapter.

such as utilitarianism and proportionalism. This paper focuses on ways in which Grisez's anti-instrumentalism functions as a potentially wider critique of the mainstream Catholic theological tradition, insofar as it critiques (standard readings of) Thomas Aquinas's moral theology. I argue that Grisez's critique of instrumentalism stands as a challenge deserving of further attention from Catholic moral theologians.

Introduction

IN THE AFTERMATH OF *Humanae vitae*, Catholic moral theologians soon became identified as either "traditionalist" or "revisionist" depending on their reception (or non-reception) of its teachings on contraception.[2] In the intervening decades, a disparate range of scholarly narratives has arisen describing the trajectory of the postconciliar traditionalism–revisionism divide.[3] Some have focused on the fact that traditionalists accept absolute moral truths, in opposition to revisionists' rejection of moral norms capable of holding in every possible situation.[4] Increasingly, however, scholars have identified a more fundamental difference as lying in differing attitudes toward the magisterium. These scholars would agree with John O'Malley's claim that the issuance of *Humanae vitae* in 1968 "occasioned a first postconciliar wrestling with the [Second Vatican] Council's principal unfinished business," one having "everything to do with authority."[5] According to this narrative, the defining characteristic of traditionalists consists in their being prepared to defer to the magisterium as a source of knowledge more authoritative than any other, in opposition to revisionists' rejection of the magisterium as an ultimate source of moral knowledge. This view is helpfully articulated by Lawler and Salzman: "Traditionalists hold that the magisterium is the only authority

---

2. For the most well-known discussion of reception and non-reception, see Congar, "Reception as an Ecclesiological Reality," 43–68. For some historical remarks about the origins of the terms "revisionist" and "traditionalist," see Melchin, "Revisionists."

3. For a helpful overview, see McCarthy, *The Catholic Tradition*, 299–368.

4. Witness, e.g., Eagan, *Restoration and Renewal*, 288: "The main difference between the two groups [traditionalists and revisionists] is their approach to moral norms. More specifically, whether such moral rules are in fact absolute, that is, always-evil acts permitting no exceptions; or whether exceptions are possible."

5. O'Malley, "Vatican II Revisited," 3.

to judge on such development [of moral norms] . . . . Revisionists, on the other hand, while acknowledging, respecting, and appreciating the role of the magisterium to speak on particular questions, do not acknowledge it as the ultimate determinant of moral truth regardless of contrary discernment of the sources of moral knowledge."[6]

Without entering into all the details of Lawler and Salzman's view, what is noteworthy for present purposes is their alignment of the traditionalism–revisionism divide with two clearly distinct sets of attitudes toward magisterial authority in postconciliar moral theology. It is this alignment, which has not been explicitly addressed in the literature, that I seek to interrogate in this chapter. I do so by way of an illustrative case study of a key element in the thought of one the most prominent "traditionalist" figures in narratives of postconciliar moral theology: Germain Grisez. Perhaps most well known for his role as co-author of the so-called "minority report" of Paul VI's Papal Commission on contraception,[7] Grisez has been cited as a determining influence on Paul VI's conservative conclusions regarding contraception and sexual ethics,[8] and has attained a scholarly reputation for being (in the words of Charles Curran) "the most significant figure" opposing revisionist trends in postconciliar American moral theology.[9] Surprisingly, however, many scholars have neglected the fact that Grisez explicitly departed from at least some magisterial teachings in other aspects of his moral theology.[10] My goal in this chapter is to investigate the most prominent instance in which Grisez

---

6. Lawler and Salzman, *Catholic Theological Ethics*, 82.

7. While Grisez and Ford are credited as co-authors of the minority report, by Grisez's account Ford was the full author of the final report. See Grisez, "Paul VI's Birth Control Commission."

8. For an analysis of *Humanae vitae* in light of the so-called "minority report," see Smith, *Humanae vitae*. For a discussion of Grisez's part in the commission, see Norris, "The Papal Commission on Birth Control." For a revisionist account of the composition of *Humanae vitae* according to which Paul VI was "persuaded" by the minority report, see Tentler, "Drifting toward irrelevance?" For a contrary account (crediting Karol Wojtyła as the primary source for the sexual ethics of *Humanae vitae*), see Barberi and Selling, "The Origin of *Humanae vitae*." Of note is Grisez's recent release in 2012 of documents pertaining to the Papal Commission; an analysis of these documents (and Grisez's role in their composition) remains to be undertaken.

9. Curran, *Catholic Moral Theology*, 97.

10. Some critics have asserted that some elements of Grisez's New Natural Law theory implicitly contradict magisterial teaching on issues such as capital punishment and abortion. These assertions are not of my concern here, since I am speaking of an *explicit,* rather than implicit, rejection of magisterial teaching.

does so, namely, his account of the ultimate end of human beings. I argue that Grisez's account of ultimate end reveals an independence from magisterial teaching which is inadequately captured by either "traditionalism" or "revisionism." This analysis is of historical interest, since Grisez is typically regarded as strongly aligned to the magisterium in all respects, and hence an appropriate figurehead for the traditionalist approach to magisterial authority. Grisez's independence from magisterial teaching on the issue of the ultimate end of human beings reveals that this typical portrayal of Grisez requires tempering, a fact that is not generally known. Furthermore, insofar as this aspect of Grisez's moral theology is one that resists categorization in terms of traditionalism or revisionism, the analysis offered in this chapter may also be seen as posing a new challenge to the adequacy of traditionalism and revisionism as conceptual categories for narrating postconciliar moral theology.

In order to make this case, I begin, firstly, with a discussion of the sources of Grisez's alleged traditionalism. Secondly, I turn to Grisez's account of ultimate end vis-à-vis magisterial teaching, before proceeding, thirdly, to a discussion of the philosophical motivations for Grisez's position. Fourth and finally, I consider Grisez's views on the authority of magisterial teaching and the way in which this view ultimately relates to Grisez's account of ultimate end.

Grisez's Traditionalism

Grisez has come to be a figurehead of traditionalist moral theology for a number of reasons, most of which are unsurprisingly tied to Grisez's involvement in formulating and defending *Humanae vitae*'s teaching on contraception. However, while Grisez has on numerous occasions appealed to the binding and authoritative status of *Humanae vitae*, he has never asserted that the encyclical involves an infallible exercise of magisterial authority. Rather, Grisez's position involves the following twofold claim: First, *Humanae vitae*, while not containing any *ex cathedra* solemn definitions, nevertheless contains moral claims about contraception which have been endorsed by a past consensus of the Church, a consensus which itself constitutes an infallible exercise of the magisterium.[11] Second, even if there is no teaching on contraception involving the

---

11. Ford and Grisez, "Contraception," 259–60. See also Grisez, "Infallibility and Specific Moral Norms."

infallible exercise of magisterial authority, it would remain that neither personal experience nor philosophical reasoning are capable of providing sufficient reasons for rejecting teachings of the non-infallible sort such as those contained in *Humanae vitae*.[12]

This second of Grisez's points is noteworthy, as it stands in direct opposition to revisionist accounts of moral theological knowledge (such as that articulated by Lawler and Salzman above). As Grisez puts it, "Because no systematic moral theory can settle any issue with complete certainty by experience and purely rational analysis, experience and reason not illumined by faith cannot undercut the moral certitude of Catholics in accepting the teaching of the bishops and pope. There will be no cogent reason not to accept their teaching except by some clearer claim of faith itself."[13] For now, what is important to note is that Grisez's claims about the superiority of magisterial teaching over experience and reason (as sources of moral knowledge) provide strong evidence for the legitimacy of Salzman and Lawler's categorization of Grisez's work as traditionalist (indeed, "the best known traditionalist attempt to revise neoscholastic natural law").[14] After all, as we have seen, the distinction between traditionalism and revisionism is grounded precisely on the claim that traditionalists privilege magisterial teaching over alternative potential sources of knowledge like experience and reason (which is exactly what Grisez affirms above).

In this chapter I will argue that, ultimately, this apparently straightforward evaluation of Grisez's attitude to the magisterium as "traditionalist" is not entirely satisfactory. I will do so by consideration of an aspect of Grisez's thought which at first glance seems to strongly reflect his broader traditionalist account of magisterial authority, namely, his account of the ultimate end of human beings. Grisez's account of ultimate end stands in opposition to the view predominant in the Catholic tradition (endorsed

---

12. Grisez, *The Way of the Lord Jesus* (hereafter *WLJ*), I.35.S.

13. Grisez, *WLJ*, I.35.S.

14. Salzman and Lawler, *The Sexual Person*, 58. Elsewhere, Salzman and Lawler call Grisez the representative of "a well-known *traditionalist school* of Catholic moral theology" (Salzman and Lawler, "Truly Human Sexual Acts," 664, emphasis in original) and describe his work as a defence of "traditionalist sexual anthropology" (Salzman and Lawler, "Theology, Science, and Sexual Anthropology," 52–53). As it happens, Grisez thinks that personal experience and philosophical reasoning do not *in fact* conflict with the claims of the magisterium on contraception; rather, they support it. For more on Grisez's elaboration of the evidence for traditionalist sexual anthropology via personal experience and philosophy, see Grisez, *Contraception and the Natural Law*.

by Augustine, Aquinas, and others) according to which God alone is the ultimate end of human beings. By contrast, over the course of several decades Grisez has developed an original account of the ultimate end of human beings as consisting not in God alone, but in the kingdom of God. Critically, Grisez's overt reasons for adopting such a divergent position consist chiefly in appeals to magisterial authority. For instance, Grisez says his own account defends a claim which amounts to a "truth of faith"[15] and holds that he would not pit his own view of ultimate end against that of Augustine and Aquinas if it were not for Vatican II which "compels" us to believe his own position.[16] These appeals to magisterial authority appear to support the assessment of Grisez as traditionalist: after all, any such appeal to magisterial teaching as "compelling" is intelligible only against the backdrop of the traditionalist position that magisterial teaching provides authoritative guidance for moral beliefs. I will argue, however, that this straightforward assessment of Grisez's position concerning ultimate end is misleading in a number of ways, and in fact conceals a more complex and nuanced attitude toward magisterial teaching. To make the case for this reading of Grisez, I need to establish that Grisez's position stands in tension (in part or in whole) with magisterial teaching; that Grisez recognizes this to be the case; and that Grisez's account of the authoritative nature of magisterial teaching nonetheless contains elements which support Grisez's adoption of a position that stands in tension with magisterial teaching. The tasks of establishing these claims will occupy the remainder of this chapter.

Magisterium and Ultimate End

Grisez explicitly frames his understanding of the ultimate end of human beings in opposition to the theological views of Thomas Aquinas, according to whom God alone is the ultimate end of human beings. Aquinas

---

15. "I hold it to be a truth of faith that human beings' true ultimate end is the kingdom of God, not God alone" (Grisez, "The True Ultimate End," 24).

16. Grisez, *WLJ* I (draft), 7.P. My assumption for the purposes of this chapter is that my citations from the draft of *WLJ* are of positions which do not contradict any of his later work and hence accurately reflect Grisez's considered views. As Grisez himself has stated in a later assessment of the draft of *WLJ*, "[P]assages in it that are even implicitly inconsistent with the published book do not express Grisez's considered views"; however, "passages in it that are entirely consistent with his later publications yet never repeated elsewhere can rightly be used to round out accounts of his thought" (Grisez, "First draft").

holds that the attainment of this end consists in an intellectual vision of God, i.e. the beatific vision. As Aquinas puts it, "[O]ur natural desire to know cannot be at rest in us until we know the first cause by its essence, not in any way. But the first cause is God … Therefore, the final end of an intellectual creature is to see God essentially."[17]

This view of the nature of the ultimate end and its attainment is drawn substantially from Augustine, whose articulation of the claim that God alone is our ultimate end is effectively contained in his well-known claim at the beginning of the *Confessions*: "You have made us for yourself and our heart is restless until it rests in you."[18] What Grisez takes Aquinas and Augustine to hold in common is the claim that "God constituted us so that we naturally tend toward as close a union with him as possible," and that because of this, "our heart cannot rest unless we are united to God by the beatific vision."[19] For ease, I will refer to this Thomistic-Augustinian understanding of the ultimate end of human beings as the *God-alone view*. By contrast, Grisez argues that the ultimate end of human beings is "integral communal fulfillment" which is "realized" in the kingdom of God.[20] As Grisez puts it:

> Strictly speaking, God alone is not the ultimate end toward which we should direct our lives. That end is integral communal fulfillment in God's kingdom, which will be a marvelous communion of divine Persons, human persons, and other created persons. Every human member of the kingdom will be richly fulfilled not only in attaining God by the beatific vision but in respect to all the fundamental human goods.… Integral communal fulfillment—the ultimate end for all created persons—will therefore be realized in the kingdom as a whole.[21]

"Integral communal fulfillment" is a term coined by Grisez; while we will explore Grisez's account in fuller detail below, what is important to note for now is that "integral communal fulfillment" consists in the pursuit of a plurality of goods, inclusive of God but also of other created goods (e.g. human friendship). Grisez's affirmation that the ultimate end consists in integral communal fulfillment thus directly opposes the claim that God

17. Aquinas, *Compendium of Theology*, 104.
18. Augustine of Hippo, *Confessions*, I.1. For Grisez's interpretation of Augustine's key claim in the *Confessions*, see Grisez, "The Restless-Heart Blunder," 1.
19. Grisez, "The Restless-Heart Blunder," 1.
20. Grisez, "The True Ultimate End," 59.
21. Grisez, "The True Ultimate End."

alone is the ultimate end of human beings. Grisez does not take his opposition to the God-alone view lightly. He says: "I would not dare to think such geniuses and saints [as Augustine and Aquinas] mistaken did I not think that the Church herself, especially teaching in Vatican Council II, compels us to think this."[22] Grisez's most prominent appeal to magisterial authority in support of his account of ultimate end is found in a 2008 article, "The True Ultimate End of Human Beings: The Kingdom of God, not God Alone." There, Grisez cites a number of theological sources for his view (including Scripture and the Catechism); however, his appeal to Vatican II draws on a single major passage from *Gaudium et spes* §39. The text quoted is worth reproducing in full, and reads as follows:

> While we are warned that it profits a man nothing if he gain the whole world and lose himself,[23] the expectation of a new earth must not weaken but rather stimulate our concern for cultivating this one. For here grows the body of a new human family, a body which even now is able to give some kind of foreshadowing of the new age.
>
> Hence, while earthly progress must be carefully distinguished from the growth of Christ's kingdom, to the extent that the former can contribute to the better ordering of human society, it is of vital concern to the Kingdom of God.[24]
>
> For after we have obeyed the Lord, and in His Spirit nurtured on earth the values of human dignity, brotherhood and freedom, and indeed all the good fruits of our nature and enterprise, we will find them again, but freed of stain, burnished and transfigured, when Christ hands over to the Father: "a kingdom eternal and universal, a kingdom of truth and life, of holiness and grace, of justice, love and peace."[25] On this earth the kingdom is present in mystery even now; with the Lord's coming, however, it will be consummated.[26]

This passage is notable for its strong claims about the importance of the pursuit of earthly goods in the Christian life: earthly progress "is of vital concern to the kingdom of God"; on this earth "the kingdom is present in

---

22. Grisez, *WLJ* I (draft), 7.P.

23. Vatican Council II, *Gaudium et spes* §39, n. 22: "Cf. Luke 9:25."

24. Vatican Council II, *Gaudium et spes* §39, n. 23: "Cf. Pius XI, *Quadragesimo anno*, *AAS* 23 (1931), 207."

25. Vatican Council II, *Gaudium et spes* §39, n. 24: "Preface of the Feast of Christ the King."

26. Vatican Council II, *Gaudium et spes* §39.

mystery even now." At face value, it is these claims which lend support to Grisez's claim that Vatican II supports a view of our ultimate end as consisting not simply in God alone but in a collective pursuit of creaturely goods along with God. However, as Ezra Sullivan has recently shown,[27] the claim that earthly goods "remain of vital concern" in the final state of beatitude is one that can in fact be reconciled with an understanding of God alone as the ultimate end. After all, the claim does not say why the creaturely goods of the kingdom are of vital concern: it could be because they are ends in themselves and thus share in the status of ultimate end (thus supporting Grisez's reading), but it could also be simply because they themselves are intrinsically ordered toward God as their true ultimate end (thus supporting the traditional God-alone reading).[28] Since the latter reading is not explicitly contradicted by anything in *Gaudium et spes* §39, the passage cannot be said to provide explicit evidence for Grisez's account of ultimate end over against the traditional view.[29]

As Sullivan further notes, it is also difficult to find in this passage even *implicit* support for Grisez's position over the God-alone view, when one considers that the passage cites *Quadragesimo anno*, a document which explicitly affirms that the ultimate end is God alone.[30] To make matters worse for Grisez, a wide swathe of twentieth-century magisterial documents appear to affirm that the ultimate end is God alone, with

27. Sullivan, "Seek First the Kingdom." The analysis offered in this chapter is indebted in numerous ways to Sullivan's study. However, it also differs on a number of important points: in particular, whereas Sullivan seeks to clarify and defend magisterial teaching, I seek to provide a more charitable reading of Grisez's account of ultimate end and of his relationship to the magisterium on his own terms.

28. Elsewhere in *Gaudium et spes* the latter view seems to be indicated: "All, in fact, are destined to the very same end, namely God himself, since they have been created in the likeness of God" (*Gaudium et spes*, §24).

29. It should be noted that Grisez does not in fact claim that this passage provides explicit support for his own view. Indeed, in the following section I will show how Grisez's own philosophical account of basic goods explains why he would agree with Sullivan on this point.

30. "We, in ascending through them [i.e., created goods], as it were by steps, shall attain the final end of all things, that is God, to Himself and to us, the supreme and inexhaustible Good" (Pius XII, *Quadragesimo anno*, §43). Technically, one might argue that this passage does not explicitly rule out the possibility of something other than God as the ultimate end. However, it suffices to note that it does explicitly rule out the possibility of *created goods* as the ultimate end alongside God, which corresponds more or less to Grisez's position. Since Grisez himself regards the God-alone view and his own position as more or less exclusive alternatives, he would regard this passage as providing explicit evidence for the God-alone view.

some explicitly affirming the view in no uncertain terms, as for instance Pius XI's claim in *Divini redemptoris* that man has "a value far surpassing that of the vast inanimate cosmos. God alone is his last end, in this life and the next."[31] While this claim of *Divini redemptoris* is not an infallible exercise of the magisterium, it is worth noting that the teaching is based upon teachings of Vatican I, specifically, the solemnly defined teaching that God can be known "by the light of natural human reason" as "the principle and end of all things."[32] Philip Donnelly has persuasively argued that this claim of Vatican I implicitly teaches that God alone is the ultimate end of human beings:

> If . . . it is a formally *explicitly* revealed truth that man can with certainty know God as the end of all things, then, of necessity, it is a formally *implicitly* revealed truth that God is the end of all things. God, who is infinite truth, could not reveal the active potency to know with certainty something that is not true; hence, in testifying by His revelation to the active potency to know with certainty a definite object, God must guarantee the truth of the object that can be known. Therefore, since God is the end of all things without exception, He must be the *finis simpliciter ultimus*.[33]

Indeed, Donnelly even says elsewhere that God's status as the unique ultimate end of all creatures is a teaching concerning which "there can be no doubt that all Catholic theologians, no matter what terminology or method of exposition they follow, must and do hold"[34] and is among "the facts concerning which all Catholics are unanimously agreed."[35] The descriptive elements of Donnelly's claims are overly strong (Grisez's explicit rejection of this teaching shows as much), but Donnelly's claims do at least reveal the extent to which the traditional God-alone teaching on the ultimate end is deeply tied to magisterial teaching (and has been widely acknowledged as such).

---

31. Pius XI, *Divini redemptoris*, §27. For discussion of this text and a range of other magisterial documents, see Sullivan, "Seek First the Kingdom," 967–70.

32. "*Eadem sancta mater Ecclesia tenet ac docet Deum, rerum omnium principium et finem, naturali humanae rationis lumine e rebus creatis certo cognosci posse*" (Conc. Vat., sess. III, cap. 2), cited in Donnelly, "The Doctrine of the Vatican Council," 18.

33. Donnelly, "The Doctrine of the Vatican Council," 18–19.

34. Donnelly, "Saint Thomas," 56.

35. Donnelly, "The Doctrine of the Vatican Council," 30.

Grisez's appeal to Vatican II as the source of his position on the ultimate end of human beings thus appears to be problematic, not only because of a lack of implicit or explicit support for his view in the documents of Vatican II, but because Vatican II if anything implicitly teaches the very opposite of his view, insofar as Vatican II is rightly read as upholding the preceding magisterial teachings of the Church.

At this juncture, two questions arise. First, why does Grisez's reading of Vatican II diverge so dramatically from the preceding magisterial tradition which would typically inform one's reading of a magisterial text like Vatican II? Second, what does Grisez *take himself to be doing* in offering such a divergent position? I will deal with each question in turn.

Grisez on Philosophical Anthropology and Ultimate End

In what follows, I suggest that Grisez's citation of *Gaudium et spes* §39 as evidence against the God-alone account of ultimate end is intelligible only in light of his broader philosophical anthropology. Some remarks (however brief) on some of Grisez's key anthropological claims in this regard will help us to understand the philosophical motivations behind Grisez's account of ultimate end, and make plausible the suggestion that Grisez's reading of Vatican II is driven by these philosophical motivations.

Before proceeding, it will be helpful to note some ongoing debates in Grisez scholarship which pose difficulties for an analysis of Grisez's ethics and anthropology. First, scholars continue to debate the accuracy of many of Grisez's exegetical claims concerning Aquinas's account of ethics and the ultimate end of human beings.[36] Those who regard Grisez's interpretation of Aquinas as faulty on a given issue will thus have reason to question the accuracy of Grisez's own characterization of his own substantive philosophical positions, at least vis-à-vis their agreement (or conflict) with the positions of Aquinas and magisterial teaching.[37]

---

36. Here, I am speaking primarily of those aspects of Grisez's philosophical anthropology which are of salience to his account of ultimate end; for more of the underpinnings of Grisez's philosophical anthropology, see Grisez, "Sketch of a Future Metaphysics," 310–40.

37. Most pertinent for present purposes is Grisez's claim that Aquinas takes the ultimate end to be a state which rules out the possibility of human beings having desires or even actions other than something explicitly oriented toward contemplation of God, a reading which has been contested in recent times (see Jensen, *Sin*, 15–40; Dahm, "Distinguishing Desire," 97–114). If Dahm and Jensen are correct, Aquinas's views are in fact much closer to Grisez's own view of the ultimate end as attainable

Second, scholars remain divided over the proper interpretation of a number of Grisez's fundamental philosophical claims, which themselves play a determinative role in analyzing Grisez's philosophical anthropology and ethics. For instance, Grisez's claims about the human person are inseparable from his well-known claim that there are "four orders" of irreducible philosophical discourse; the implications of this latter claim remain open to multiple interpretations, and lead to substantially different accounts of the nature of the human person and human action.[38]

With these caveats in mind, it is worth beginning with one of the most well-known claims underlying Grisez's anthropology, namely, his "basic goods" theory of ethics. Grisez's theory of basic goods is premised on the claim that there exist disparate "fundamental goods of human beings," which include "life, including health and bodily integrity; skillful work and play; knowledge and aesthetic experience; harmony with God; harmony among human beings; harmony among a person's own judgments, choices, feelings, and behavior; and marriage, including parenthood."[39] Grisez calls these goods fundamental because they are not simply valued on the basis of subjective desire, but are grounded in "self-evident principles of practical reasoning that direct actions toward them."[40] Grisez's account of basic goods leads him to affirm that human fulfillment involves the holistic pursuit of a multiplicity of goods: "Each of the fundamental human goods is only one element of human well-being and flourishing, and each realization of any of those elements in or by a freely chosen human action is only one part of an individual's or community's overall fulfillment."[41]

While it is difficult to draw any strict logical link between Grisez's account of basic goods and his theological account of the ultimate end,[42]

---

without eliminating a multiplicity of desires and actions. Other aspects of Grisez's exegesis of Aquinas which scholars have challenged include Grisez's claim that Aquinas affirms the incommensurability of basic goods (see Long, "Fundamental Errors,") that the basic goods are non-moral in nature (see Coyle, "Natural Law and Goodness," 105–31), and that Aquinas accepts something like the Humean "is–ought" distinction (see Veatch, "Natural Law and the Is–Ought Question.")

38. For recent discussion see Girgis, "Subjectivity without Subjectivism"; Tollefsen, "Aquinas's Four Orders."

39. Grisez, "The True Ultimate End," 54.

40. Grisez, "The True Ultimate End," 54.

41. Grisez, "The True Ultimate End," 56.

42. Properly understood, the multiplicity of fundamental or basic human goods does not of itself entail that the ultimate end of human beings consists in a multiplicity

what is important to note for present purposes is that they are closely connected. Thus, when speaking of the heavenly ultimate end of human beings, Grisez strongly emphasizes the multiplicity of goods in the ultimate end in holistic terms that strongly parallel his holistic philosophical account of the basic goods. For instance, Grisez affirms that "human actions done in this life are destined to be an important constituent part of eternal life," and that human actions ought not be treated as "mere means" to attaining eternal life.[43]

It may be helpful to clarify Grisez's view by reference to a criticism that has been levelled at Grisez's "many-parted" account of the ultimate end. According to the criticism, such an account of the ultimate end does not have any real unity, since without a means–ends ordering of created goods to God, created goods lose any meaningful connection to God, and the various goods lose any kind of coherence or unity.[44] By contrast, Grisez rejects the claim that means–ends ordering provides the only way for created goods and God to be unified. Grisez says, for instance, that "while the created goods that pertain to fulfillment in the kingdom are and always will remain distinct from their Creator, those goods will not be things apart from God, and it seems to me reasonable to suppose that blessed creatures' joy in created goods will somehow be *within*, although distinct from, their joyful intimacy with the divine Persons."[45] Whatever it is for joy in created goods to be "within" joy in the divine Persons, Grisez clearly intends to distance himself from any means–ends characterization of the relationship between created goods and the divine good.[46]

---

of goods. This is because Grisez's account of the fundamental human goods does not contain anything that prevents them *as such* from being subordinated to one another as means to ends (for a clarification of this and other points on the ontology of basic goods, see Grisez, Boyle, and Finnis, "Practical Principles"; George, *In Defense of Natural Law*, 32–82.

43. Grisez, *WLJ*, I.34.A. Another place in which Grisez describes means as lacking in importance is in a discussion elsewhere of Aquinas's account of the ultimate end. After raising the issue, Grisez criticizes the Thomistic approach by noting that it "implies a sharp contrast between the ultimate end (heaven) and the means to it (life in this world)" and that, by contrast, his approach "removes the sharp contrast between life in this world and heaven. Thus, it avoids a debilitating either/or—either life in this world is important for itself or heaven alone is important" (Grisez, *Fulfillment in Christ*, 22–23). Grisez implies that both options are problematic, but a further implication is that if earthly life is indeed treated as a means, it loses all importance of its own.

44. For this critique, see Jensen, *Sin*, 43–44.

45. Grisez, "The True Ultimate End," 61.

46. Indeed, by juxtaposing "mere means" against created goods which can (in

This characterization of the relationship between created goods and the ultimate end once again bears strong marks of Grisez's philosophical account of basic goods, according to which basic goods are "reasons for acting which need no further reason."[47] For Grisez, the pursuit of created goods in the spiritual life echoes the rational pursuit of basic goods insofar as both are best characterized in ways that are wholly independent of means–ends instrumentality.

A second connection between Grisez's account of ultimate end and his philosophical anthropology concerns Grisez's critique of Aquinas's claim that the ultimate end must by nature completely satisfy all human desires.[48] Grisez identifies this Thomistic claim in passages from the *Summa theologiae* such as the following: "Since everything desires its own perfection, one desires as an ultimate end that which one desires as a good that is perfect and will fulfill one . . . . It is therefore necessary that the ultimate end so fulfill the human person's desire that nothing apart from it is left to be desired."[49] The notion of ultimate end as "perfect satisfaction of desire" suggested in this passage is one that Grisez regards as highly problematic. For Grisez, it is in fact metaphysically impossible for human beings to be in a state in which all desire is completely satisfied, because a necessary condition of free human choice is that one can conceive of future unrealized possibilities, and seek to attain them: "[H]uman persons are unlike natural entities; it is not human nature as a given, but possible human fulfillment which must provide the intelligible norms for free choices . . . . Human existence is more than conforming to a built-in pattern, as monkeys do when they eat bananas and otherwise do what comes naturally . . . unless human persons have possibilities which are not yet defined, there is no room for them to unfold themselves through intelligent creativity and freedom."[50]

Grisez holds that the capacity for free choice is integral to human nature, and that consequently the ultimate end of human beings will consist (at least in part) in a life of free, intelligent creativity; as a result,

some sense) constitute "integral parts" of the ultimate end, Grisez seems to imply that to treating a good as having some intrinsic value or high significance, is already to treat it in some sense a part of the ultimate good one loves.

47. Grisez, Boyle, and Finnis, "Practical Principles," 103.

48. It is worth noting that this interpretation of Aquinas has been challenged in recent scholarship. See especially Dahm, "Distinguishing Desire," 97–114.

49. Aquinas, *Summa theologiae*, I–II.1.5 co.

50. Grisez, *WLJ*, I.4.F.

he cannot admit any account of the ultimate end which excludes "possibilities which are not yet defined." Aquinas's view, however, appears to exclude such possibilities, since possibilities for action entail the possibility of unrealized desires to attain the goals of these unrealized actions, a possibility which conflicts with Aquinas's claim that the ultimate end leaves nothing to be desired. Implicit in Grisez's critique of Aquinas, then, is the claim that any account of ultimate end which rules out future possibilities for action thereby excludes freedom of will. This claim underlies Grisez's own alternative account, according to which the ultimate end is not a state of perfect fulfillment (in the sense of leaving no future possibilities to be desired), but is nevertheless a state of what Grisez calls "the richest possible fulfillment for a human person." Here is how Grisez describes that state:

> [H]uman persons as human do have a natural "desire" for rich fulfillment . . . their capacities are naturally inclined toward the basic human goods—friendship with God, knowledge of truth and aesthetic experience, and so on. But no single instantiation of any of those goods—not even friendship with God—can utterly fulfill anyone. Everyone has far more desires and wishes than he or she can ever satisfy . . . The richest possible fulfillment for a human person therefore is not something definite; it is open-ended and indeterminate.[51]

The account of fulfillment articulated in this passage has radical implications for Grisez's account of ultimate end, since it involves nothing less than a complete redefinition of the very meaning of "ultimate end." Whereas Aquinas understands the ultimate end in terms of "perfect fulfillment" (or complete satisfaction of desire), Grisez redefines the ultimate end in terms of an ongoing, dynamic, "open-ended and indeterminate" pursuit of fulfillment.

I suggest that the two foregoing aspects of Grisez's account of ultimate end (his claim that basic goods and created goods are to be characterized independently of instrumental or means–ends valuation, and his claim that the ultimate end requires not perfect fulfillment but rather an open-ended pursuit of fulfillment) shed important light upon Grisez's claim that *Gaudium et spes* §39 supports his "integral communal fulfillment" account of the ultimate end. Although in the preceding section it was suggested that *GS* §39 does not explicitly or even implicitly support

---

51. Grisez, "Natural Law, God, Religion," 28–29.

Grisez's claim that the ultimate end includes greated goods as well as God, our present discussion permits us to make an important modification to this claim: if one accepts Grisez's philosophical claims about the nature of instrumental goods and the nature of ultimate end, GS §39 can be seen as implicitly supporting Grisez's account of integral communal fulfillment. After all, GS §39 does arguably provide support for the claim that created goods have intrinsic or non-instrumental value (they are "of vital concern to the kingdom of God"), and it also affirms the freedom characteristic of beatitude ("after we have obeyed the Lord, and in His Spirit nurtured on earth the values of human dignity, brotherhood and freedom ... we will find them again"). Given Grisez's claims to the effect that intrinsic value requires treating a good as part of (rather than a means to) the ultimate end, and that freedom is incompatible with perfect fulfillment, it possible to see how these aspects of GS §39 lend what one might call "conditional support" to Grisez's view: *If* one accepts Grisez's underlying philosophical anthropology, *then* GS §39 can be seen as supporting that position over and against the dominant Aquinas–Augustine position.

Revisiting Grisez on Magisterium and Hermeneutics

What we have seen is that, despite the conflicts between Grisez's account of ultimate end and that endorsed by the magisterium, there is a *prima facie* case for interpreting at least GS §39 as providing support for Grisez's position if one reads it in light of Grisez's distinctive philosophical anthropology. Since the purpose of this chapter is not to evaluate the merits of Grisez's philosophical anthropology but rather the nature of his relationship to magisterial teaching, the question I wish to address in the space remaining is that of the implications which follow from the divergence between Grisez's philosophically informed reading of Vatican II on ultimate end, and Grisez's claims about magisterial tradition preceding Vatican II.

There seem to be two possible judgments to draw: either Grisez knowingly affirmed a reading of Vatican II which brought him into a significant conflict with preceding magisterial teaching (call this the *rupture* view), or else he developed his reading in ignorance of the conflict between his position and that of the magisterium (call this the *ignorance* view). Neither the rupture nor the ignorance view is easily reconciled with Grisez's wider corpus. For instance, the rupture view would appear to contradict the hermeneutical principles affirmed by Grisez (mentioned in the foregoing section of this chapter) regarding the authority of magisterial teaching, according to which magisterial teaching has priority over philosophical reason in determining the view one ultimately adopts. After all, Grisez affirms that "One should believe what Catholics formerly held with faith . . . there can be no reason consistent with faith for calling into question anything which Catholics as a whole held with faith in earlier times."[52] Even noninfallible teachings, according to Grisez, demand a very high degree of credence: "what the teachers of the Church propose noninfallibly *very likely* is divine truth, whose acceptance is necessary for the salvation of those to whom it is proposed. Therefore, such teachings must not be brushed aside as 'noninfallible, and so possibly mistaken.'"[53] It is difficult to see, in light of these claims, how Grisez could justify reading GS §39 in light of his philosophical anthropology rather than in light of the preceding magisterial witness.

On the other hand, it is even more difficult to read Grisez according to the ignorance view: i.e., as simply affirming *out of ignorance* a position on ultimate end which is in fact at odds with magisterial teaching. This interpretation appears to find support in the fact that Grisez's 2008 article makes no mention of magisterial teachings affirming the traditional view of the ultimate end.[54] Grisez's statements elsewhere, however, suggest otherwise. For instance, in a 2005 presentation rejecting the God-alone view of ultimate end, Grisez says:

> Provoked by the preceding arguments and annoyed by my bold and unsparing presentation, many are likely to take offense. Their reaction might be: "How dare he attack a doctrine held not only by St. Augustine and St. Thomas but by most other Church Fathers and Doctors, and taken for granted in many Church documents? Why should faithful Catholics believe him against great saints with brilliant minds? Isn't his lack of diffidence and circumspection evidence of presumptuous pride and

---

52. Grisez, *WLJ* II.1.H. Furthermore, Grisez goes to some lengths to distinguish genuine development of doctrine from the assumptions presupposed by a hermeneutic of rupture. As Grisez puts it in one place: "Catholic teaching plainly develops, and there is no reason to exclude moral doctrine from the process . . . . Simply to contradict what was previously taught, however, would in no sense be to develop it" (*WLJ* I.36.G, 1–2).

53. Grisez, *WLJ* I.35.F, emphasis added.

54. This reading of Grisez appears to be taken by Sullivan, "Seek First the Kingdom."

insensitivity? And isn't it irresponsible for anyone even to call into question—much less reject as at odds with Catholic faith—a perennial doctrine that is tantamount to faith?"[55]

What is important to note is that, in this passage, Grisez acknowledges a *prima facie* case for the traditional view not simply in the Augustinian-Thomistic philosophical tradition, but also in "many" Church documents which make it a "perennial doctrine that is tantamount to faith." In light of Grisez's close engagement elsewhere with the teachings of Vatican I, it is likely that Grisez had in mind the apparently implicit teachings of Vatican I and subsequent documents.[56] It is difficult, then, to suppose that Grisez's account of the ultimate end was developed in ignorance of the preceding witness of magisterial teaching against his position.

What, then, is to be made of Grisez's position vis-à-vis the magisterium? Are we to attribute inconsistency to Grisez, in that he affirmed a position regarding the priority of magisterial teaching over philosophical teaching but failed to abide by it in the case of magisterial teaching on the ultimate end of human beings?

I propose a third way of reading Grisez beyond the rupture and ignorance views, one which does justice to Grisez's various positions without rendering them internally inconsistent. We might call this third reading the *reform* view, according to which magisterial teaching does in fact provide room "from within," as it were, for certain carefully circumscribed forms of dissent. In particular, Grisez makes room for the possibility of magisterial teaching standing in what we might call *partial conflict* with other magisterial teachings. While talk of partial conflict may seem suspiciously close to the discourse of the rupture view, what I am calling the reform view hinges upon a distinction between (to use Grisez's terms) *truths of faith* and *theological explanations*. Grisez explains the distinction as follows:

---

55. Grisez, "The Restless-Heart Blunder," 16. It may be argued that, in this passage, Grisez still understates the case against his view, since the claim that God alone is not just "taken for granted" in Church documents but *implicitly and explicitly taught by* those documents. What is important is Grisez's acknowledgment that the God-alone view is "tantamount to faith" and is widely regarded as such.

56. See Grisiz, *WLJ* I (draft), I.4.G, which extensively cites Vatican I and also approvingly cites the two aforementioned articles by Donnelly. Since Grisez regards the Augustinian–Thomistic position as false, it seems fair to conclude that Grisez does not regard it as a teaching which has been infallibly taught by the magisterium. Grisez's assessment of Vatican I's teaching on ultimate end would thus diverge from those offered in Donnelly, "Vatican Council," and Sullivan, "Seek First the Kingdom."

> To clarify the truths of faith and draw out their implications, theological reflection often joins them with other propositions which seem true. Reflection of this kind naturally leads to commonly accepted positions, which are handed on in the Church as a theological tradition. If not taught infallibly by the Church, such positions can be called *theological explanations*. Examples include the theory of the sacraments as signs, the theology of the condition of humankind's first parents insofar as it goes beyond what faith teaches in attributing perfections to them, and the explanation by analogy with human spiritual acts of the processions of the Word and the Spirit.[57]

Whereas the former cannot be rejected by a Catholic under any conditions, the latter can be (under limited and circumscribed conditions). Indeed, as Grisez goes on to say, "One should not overvalue any theological explanation. Inasmuch as they depend in part on propositions which are not divinely guaranteed, theological explanations should not be accepted with faith."[58] Grisez's distinction permits a corresponding distinction between two kinds of conflict in magisterial teaching: if a given proposition is magisterially enshrined as a truth of faith, but its opposite is subsequently enshrined also as a truth of faith, we have a case of what we might call *absolute conflict*. Grisez makes no room for such conflicts (as evidenced in his aforementioned, unqualified affirmation that "one should believe what Catholics formerly held with faith").[59] However, if a given proposition is magisterially endorsed, not as a truth of faith, but simply as a theological explanation, then any endorsement of its opposite (whether at the level of theological explanation or as a truth of faith) will no longer be a case of absolute conflict, but what we might call *partial conflict*. Grisez's openness to partial conflicts in magisterial teaching is what allows him to be explicitly amenable to the possibility of rejecting magisterial teachings which simply involve theological explanations "handed on in the Church." Indeed, Grisez holds that such magisterial teachings have often been mistaken in the history of the Church: "Theological reflection is carried on not only by professional theologians, but by all thoughtful believers, including popes and other bishops as they preach and teach, and so the Church's teaching authority sometimes develops (or accepts and uses) theological explanations. But

---

57. Grisez, *WLJ* II.1.H.
58. Grisez, *WLJ* II.1.H.
59. Grisez, *WLJ* II.1.H.

even such theological explanations as these could be mistaken, as has happened repeatedly, leading to doctrinal conflicts which divided some bishops from others."[60]

We are now in a position to articulate the reform view of Grisez's understanding of ultimate end in relation to magisterial thought, tying together in the process several threads which have been woven over the course of this chapter. On this understanding of absolute versus partial conflict, Grisez's rejection of the Augustinian–Thomistic account of ultimate end "taken for granted in many church documents"[61] can be seen as an affirmation of a merely partial conflict in magisterial teaching. Specifically, it is a conflict between what Grisez regards as a theological explanation (the Augustinian–Thomistic account of ultimate end) affirmed in pre-Vatican II teaching, and on the other hand, what Grisez regards as a truth of faith affirmed in the conciliar teachings of Vatican II itself (the claim of *Gaudium et spes* §39 that the kingdom of God is the ultimate end of human beings). Grisez's reading of *Gaudium et spes*, without doubt, presupposes the hermeneutical key of Grisez's original philosophical anthropology. This reveals a qualified willingness on Grisez's part to subject magisterial teaching to philosophical critique. As we have seen, the qualifications are manifold: one cannot subject truths of faith (or even teachings likely to be truths of faith, even if not known as truths of faith) to any analogous critique (as per the rupture view, and objections to *Humanae vitae*). Similarly, one cannot reject theological explanations simply on the basis of philosophical critique if the former but not the latter are supported by magisterial teaching (hence Grisez's rejection of contemporary revisionist epistemologies, and his aforementioned endorsement of the traditional view that there is "no cogent reason not to accept [the magisterium's] teaching except by some clearer claim of faith itself").[62] Nevertheless, Grisez's account of ultimate end, placed in context, reveals that these qualifications still leave room for philosophical hermeneutics to play a decisive role in rejecting some at least some magisterial teachings. This role is one which in many respects remains subservient to magisterial teaching; nevertheless, it is one that highlights the inevitable philosophical foundations underlying both sides of the

---

60. Grisez, *WLJ* II.1.H.
61. Grisez, "Restless-Heart Blunder," 16.
62. Grisez, *WLJ*, I.35.S.

apparent conflict in magisterial teaching, as well as the very terms in which the conflict is framed.

Conclusion

While much more remains to be said about Grisez's nuanced account of ultimate end and its standing vis-à-vis magisterial teaching, it seems safe to conclude from the foregoing discussion that Grisez's account of magisterial teaching involves hermeneutic complexities that ultimately give a decisive role to philosophical reason, even while remaining firmly within the bounds of a strong obedience to magisterial teaching. Since these hermeneutic complexities legitimize the possibility of rejecting some forms of magisterial teaching on principled grounds (a possibility actively pursued by Grisez), his account of ultimate end must be regarded as remaining neither in straightforward agreement with magisterial teaching nor in straightforward opposition to it. It is this result which ultimately creates difficulties for popular narratives of postconciliar moral theology such as that put forward by Lawler and Salzman. Insofar as such narratives rely upon the emergence of clearly delineated pro- and anti-magisterial attitudes ("traditionalism" and "revisionism") in the wake of *Humanae vitae*, they fail to accommodate the variety of positions in-between. Grisez, I have argued, is ultimately located in-between: his approach to magisterial teaching makes no room for the sort of purely philosophical dissent from magisterial teaching envisaged by revisionists like Salzman and Lawler, but it nevertheless allows for readings of the very content of magisterial teaching which are starkly revisionist in their own right, as evidenced by the philosophically driven hermeneutic choices underlying his affirmation of *Gaudium et spes* over and against an understanding of the ultimate end of human beings magisterially attested to by Vatican I and a large swathe of the Christian magisterial tradition. Whether Grisez's nuanced account of the relationship between philosophy and magisterial teaching proves ultimately to be an unstable *via media* between traditionalism and revisionism—or alternatively a promising avenue for bridging the divides which remain in moral theology—will be an important question for future work in Catholic theological methodology.

Bibliography

Aquinas, Thomas. *Compendium of Theology*. Translated by Richard J. Regan. Oxford: Oxford University Press, 2009.

———. *Summa theologiae*. Translated by Laurence Shapcote. New York: Benziger, 1948.

Augustine of Hippo. *The Confessions of St. Augustine*. Translated by John K. Ryan. Garden City, NY: Doubleday, 1960.

Barberi, Michael J., and Joseph A. Selling. "The Origin of *Humanae vitae* and the Impasse in Fundamental Theological Ethics." *Louvain Studies* 4 (2013) 364–89. https://doi.org/10.2143/LS.37.4.3047125.

Congar, Yves. "Reception as an Ecclesiological Reality." *Concilium* 77 (1972) 43–68.

Coyle, Sean. "Natural Law and Goodness in Thomistic Ethics." *Canadian Journal of Law & Jurisprudence* 30 (2017) 77–96. https://doi.org/10.1017/cjlj.2017.4.

Curran, Charles E. *Catholic Moral Theology in the United States: A History*. Washington, DC: Georgetown University Press, 2008.

Dahm, Brandon. "Distinguishing Desire and Parts of Happiness." *American Catholic Philosophical Quarterly* 89 (2015) 97–114. https://doi.org/10.5840/acpq2014111841.

Donnelly, Philip J. "The Doctrine of the Vatican Council on the End of Creation." *Theological Studies* 4 (1943) 3–33.

———. "Saint Thomas and the Ultimate Purpose of Creation." *Theological Studies* 2 (1941) 53–83.

Eagan, Joseph F. *Restoration and Renewal: The Church in the Third Millennium*. Kansas City, MO: Sheed & Ward, 1995.

Ford, John C., and Germain Grisez. "Contraception and the Infallibility of the Ordinary Magisterium." *Theological Studies* 39 (1978) 258–312.

George, Robert P. *In Defense of Natural Law*. New York: Oxford University Press, 1999.

Girgis, Sherif. "Subjectivity without Subjectivism: Revisiting the Is/Ought Gap." In *Subjectivity: Ancient and Modern*, edited by R. J. Snell and Steven F. McGuire, 63–88. London: Lexington, 2016.

Grisez, Germain G. *Contraception and the Natural Law*. Milwaukee: Bruce, 1964.

———. "First Draft of *The Way of the Lord Jesus: Christian Moral Principles*." http://www.twotlj.org/CMP-1stDft.html.

———. *Fulfillment in Christ: A Summary of Christian Moral Principles*. New ed. Notre Dame: University of Notre Dame Press, 1991.

———. "Infallibility and Specific Moral Norms: A Review Discussion." *The Thomist* 49 (1985) 248–87. https://doi.org/10.1353/tho.1985.0031.

———. "Natural Law, God, Religion, and Human Fulfillment." *American Journal of Jurisprudence* 46 (2001) 3–36. https://doi.org/10.1093/ajj/46.1.3.

———. "Paul VI's Birth Control Commission," 2012. http://www.twotlj.org/BCCommission.html.

———. "The Restless-Heart Blunder." Unpublished manuscript, 2005. http://www.twotlj.org/OW-RestlessHeartBlunder.pdf.

———. "Sketch of a Future Metaphysics." *New Scholasticism* 38 (1964) 310–40. https://doi.org/10.5840/newscholas196438320.

———. "The True Ultimate End of Human Beings: The Kingdom, not God Alone." *Theological Studies* 69 (2008) 38–61.

―――. *The Way of Our Lord Jesus: A Summary of Catholic Moral Theology.* Vol. 1, *First Principles.* Draft, 1980. http://www.twotlj.org/CMP-1stDft.html.

―――. *The Way of the Lord Jesus: Christian Moral Principles.* Vol. 1. Quincy, IL: Franciscan, 1983.

―――. *The Way of The Lord Jesus: Living a Christian Life.* Vol. 2. Quincy, IL: Franciscan, 1993.

Grisez, Germain G., Joseph Boyle, and John Finnis. "Practical Principles, Moral Truth, and Ultimate Ends." *American Journal of Jurisprudence* (1987) 99–151.

Jensen, Steven J. *Sin: A Thomistic Psychology.* Washington, DC: Catholic University of America Press, 2018. https://doi.org/10.2307/j.ctv14h4ms.

Lawler, Michael G., and Todd A. Salzman. *Catholic Theological Ethics: Ancient Questions, Contemporary Responses.* Lanham, MD: University Press of America, 2016.

Long, Steven A. "Fundamental Errors of the New Natural Law Theory." *National Catholic Bioethics Quarterly* 13 (2013) 105–31.

McCarthy, Timothy G. *The Catholic Tradition: The Church in the Twentieth Century.* 2nd ed. 1998. Reprint, Eugene, OR: Wipf & Stock, 2012.

Melchin, Kenneth R. "Revisionists, Deontologists, and the Structure of Moral Understanding." *Theological Studies* 51 (1990) 389–416. https://doi.org/10.1177/004056399005100302.

Norris, Charles W. "The Papal Commission on Birth Control—Revisited." *Linacre Quarterly* 80 (2013) 8–16. https://doi.org/10.1179/0024363912Z.0000000009.

O'Malley, John. "Vatican II Revisited as Reconciliation: The Francis Factor." In *The Legacy of Vatican II*, edited by Andrea Vicini and Massimo Faggioli, 6–16. New York: Paulist, 2015.

Pius XI. *Quadragesimo anno.* Encyclical Letter. 1931.

Pius XI. *Divini redemptoris.* Encyclical Letter. 1937.

Salzman, Todd A., and Michael G. Lawler. *The Sexual Person: Toward a Renewed Catholic Anthropology.* Washington, DC: Georgetown University Press, 2008.

―――. "Theology, Science, and Sexual Anthropology: An Investigation." *Louvain Studies* 35 (2011) 69–97.

―――. "Truly Human Sexual Acts: A Response to Patrick Lee and Robert George." *Theological Studies* 69 (2008) 663–80. https://doi.org/10.1177/004056390806900309.

Smith, Janet E. *Humanae vitae: A Generation Later.* Washington, DC: Catholic University of America Press, 1991. https://doi.org/10.2307/j.ctt284xt0.

Sullivan, Ezra. "Seek First the Kingdom: A Reply to Germain Grisez's Account of Man's Ultimate End." *Nova et vetera* 8 (2010) 959–95.

Tentler, Leslie Woodcock. "Drifting Toward Irrelevance? The Laity, Sexual Ethics, and the Future of the Church." *American Catholic Studies* 118.2 (2007) 1–20.

Tollefsen, Christopher. "Aquinas's Four Orders, Normativity, and Human Nature." *Journal of Value Inquiry* 52 (2018) 243–56. https://doi.org/10.1007/s10790-018-9657-6.

Vatican Council II. *Gaudium et spes.* Pastoral Constitution on the Church in the Modern World. December 7, 1965. In *Vatican II: The Conciliar and Post Conciliar Documents*, edited by A. Flannery. Collegeville, MN: Liturgical, 1980.

Veatch, Henry. "Natural Law and the Is–Ought Question." *The Catholic Lawyer* 26 (1981) 251–65.

Vicini, Andrea, and Massimo Faggioli, eds. *The Legacy of Vatican II.* New York: Paulist, 2015.

16

The Law of Adam and Eve

Judith Butler Matters, and so Does the Fall and Jesus[1]

DANIEL R. PATTERSON

We cannot understand the present without understanding the past, but sometimes connections between the past and present are hastily assumed or formed. One possible result is that the moral theologian misses an opportunity for fruitful discourse with secular theorists. Take, for example, the influential gender (and queer) theorist, Judith Butler, whose theory is often regarded as the fruit of the sexual revolution because of its decisive theorized letting lose of conceptions of sexuality and gender from traditional conceptions of the body. This paper argues that Butler's thought does not represent fruit that is typically identifiable with the sexual revolution, because her principal concern is not autonomy and individuality, but the hypocritical administration of the "law." This is patently a Christian concern that opens

---

1. This is a revised version of a paper presented at the University of Notre Dame, Perth, at the conference "1968: Five Decades On" run by the Dawson Society. I appreciate the discussion and feedback from the participants for helping refine this article. I am especially thankful for Marcia Patterson, Michael Morelli, Jake Rollinson, and Rory Shiner for their careful and insightful suggestions.

up avenues for productive dialogue. In this paper I will take up Butler's question "What speaks when 'I' speak to you?" and her "ontology of vulnerability" to interrogate Christian thinking about gender and sexuality. The moral theologian is provoked to reflect upon "the law of Adam and Eve" and the doctrine of the fall as theological equivalents to Butler's offerings, by which some are justified, and others condemned. The "law of Adam and Eve" is not the remedy to the social malaise that is often construed as the result of the sexual revolution. Rather, the new Adam and his bride—Jesus Christ and the Church—are paradigmatic for learning how to embrace the body.

Introduction

THE QUESTION UTTERED BY the nations in Psalm 115 has redemptive significance because it brings into sharp relief the futility and danger of worshipping created things which merely appear as life-giving. The question "Where is their god?" recalled by the psalmist in verse 2 was initially posed by the nations to mock, insult, or cause doubt in Israel's mind. The writer, however, takes their question at face value for its penetrating critique of Israel's worship.[2] The nations' question is shown to be worthy of careful reflection because it places the onus on the reader to consider whether the god who is worshipped is created and seen or uncreated and unseen.

An important methodological consideration for this essay is, like the psalmist's, not to blithely dismiss the outsiders' question simply because it is an outsider's question. This is a problem that besets much conservative theological discussion of the body. In contrast, the psalmist demonstrates humble attentiveness in the face of the question despite the question's faulty premise that a god not seen is impotent and thus not able to secure life and blessing. In fact, it is precisely because of this faulty premise that the psalmist takes up the question: the psalmist brings the worshipping community into critical dialogue with itself in order to root out created and seen gods that offer the false promise of life and blessing.

---

2. The nations' question "Where is their God?" is usually posed by the nations to highlight the perceived impotence of Israel's God in their time of need. See Pss 42:3, 10 and 79:10. In Mic 7:10 the question is posed retrospectively by the prophet as the charge and evidence that vindicates their eventual destruction by God.

While the psalmist contends with his contemporary outsider's question, this essay takes up the questioning of another "outsider," the critical gender theorist and feminist philosopher Judith Butler, who I read as critiquing the valorization of the *ideal images* of Adam and Eve in Christian thinking as a means to embodied life and blessing. Butler does not explicitly address the biblical characters of Adam and Eve in her corpus, but in *Gender Trouble* she uses language that has strong Edenic parallels. This reinforces my reading of Butler's gender theory as a re-creation myth. That is to say, Butler does not offer her own creation myth, but she engages the Christian creation narrative, taking aim at the Western civilization pillars which structure natural and normal accounts of gender and embodiment: the images of Adam and Eve. What is striking about this outsider's critique of Christianity's foundation is that Butler reveals a question of theological and ethical importance that is difficult to ignore. If the images of Adam and Eve order the conception of good bodies but we cannot be that body because we are unable live in Eden, what are the ethical implications of using Adam and Eve as a measure to identify and discipline some bodies but not others for not measuring up to naturalized and normalized standards of gender and embodiment?[3]

According to Butler's thinking, which will be explored in more detail shortly, the prelapsarian figures of Adam and Eve must be conceived as constructions that operate as a paternal law guaranteeing existential failure.[4] When one realizes that one cannot meet the law or standard imposed by these images, this person must work their body to conform to the images' demands, which for Butler, is a body-work that is symptomatic of a slave morality. So, Butler contends, if "every identification, precisely because it has a phantasm as its ideal, is bound to fail,"[5] then the identification of man and woman not only find their respective ideals in the phantasmic creatures of Adam and Eve, but they are also enslaved to these images in their quest to become them.[6] In light of this reading

---

3. The argument put forward in this essay can also be used to think though notions of normal and natural sexuality.

4. Butler, *Gender Trouble*, 77.

5. Butler, *Gender Trouble*, 75.

6. Butler, *Gender Trouble*, 72. "Heteronormativity" might be the term that is most synonymous with what I call *the law of Adam and Eve*. The term "heteronormativity" does not name a view of gender that comprises male and female, but refers increasingly to a hegemonic notion of gender, wherein a view of so-called normal gender, comprising a binary frame, serves to privilege those who fall within it. The characteristic theme of heteronormativity is hegemony, which results in the unjust distribution

of Butler's analysis, I suggest an apt title for this paternal law that guarantees failure and induces slave morality is the *law of Adam and Eve*.

In response to Butler's thinking as described here, it is my contention that conforming to the images of Adam or Eve does not bring life but is a form of self-construction that is symptomatic of slave morality. It is a kind of works-based righteousness. This is because scripture does not frame Adam and Eve as humanity's end, but as humanity's beginning. With these critical points in view, this essay examines the subtle installation of Adam and Eve in Christian thinking as a law that one must obey for life, which actually redirects attention away from one's need for a savior, Jesus Christ, the one true way to life, who for good reason is referred to in scripture as the second Adam.

I begin this essay by reflecting on Butler's critique of Michel Foucault's notion of the constructed body. Butler's critique provokes Christian thinking about the way Adam and Eve are used in theology, ethics, and everyday life, for which Jesus's utilization of Adam and Eve in Matt 19:1–12 is instructive. Then, establishing Adam and Eve as both a perfect vision and a law, I show that as a vision they are unattainable, and as a law they are condemnatory. I conclude by taking up the Apostle Paul's inquiry into one's body of death in Rom 7:24–25 and 1 Cor 15:45–48 to argue that one overcomes one's body of death not by turning to the Adam that comes from the earth, but by turning to the Adam who comes from heaven.

Ironically, though not surprisingly given God's use of the nations throughout redemptive history, Butler's understanding of the constitution of human reality in *this* moment is perceptive. While Butler's voice is often deployed to provide what postlapsarian humanity's desirous ears want to hear, we see in this moment that her voice has redemptive significance—a voice from the outside that asks, "Which body do you turn to for life?"

Foucault and Butler: Confronting the Paradoxical Body

According to the thought of Michel Foucault, the ethos of the 1960s sexual revolution cannot be characterized by the mantra "free love." His broad critique of liberationist sexuality, which emerges in his first volume of

---

of grief. See Allen and Mendez, "Hegemonic Heteronormativity," 70–86; Gorringe, *Karl Barth*.

The History of Sexuality, is predicated on the view that the body, and one's use of it, is not free, but always bound up as a nexus of juridical power relations that are both productive and regulatory.[7] Such a view undermines the revolution's utopic vision of freedom by insisting that embodied life or death in life is entirely determined by the *agon*. In other words, the body is a site of political contestation.[8] For Foucault, the body is a constructed reality, meaning there can be no concept of sexual freedom that has not considered the ubiquitous forces that perpetually conspire to construct the body. There is no life or love apart from the disciplined body.[9] From Foucault's perspective, the sexual revolution was the latest moment in the body's history in which the body was subject to discipline, re-narration, or inscription. In that moment, the body assumed another shape, not because it had been freed from the terms that structured the sexual conservatism of the postwar era to be whatever one wanted it to be, but because it was subject to yet another set of social relations.

In the concluding remarks of her published doctoral dissertation *Subjects of Desire: Hegelian Reflections in Twentieth-Century France*, Butler notes the need for a "history of bodies" to be written to locate the "'truth' about desire."[10] At this early stage of her published corpus, Butler is moving towards thinking about bodies as the site where "history encodes itself," thereby linking history, the body, and desire.[11] She poses questions that anticipate her future work: "How, for instance, are we to understand the body as the inscribed surface of gender relations? . . . [H]ow do various bodies signify social positions and even social histories? . . . How do we conceive of the body as a concrete scene of cultural struggle?"[12] Butler is angling towards re-integrating the psyche into accounts of the body or thinking about the body "as a more internally complicated notion," which Foucault explicitly rejects in *History of Sexuality: Vol. I* and *Discipline and Punish: The Birth of the Prison*.[13] In this essay, I am not concerned with Butler's theorizing of the psyche for thinking about the body,[14] but I

7. Foucault, *The History of Sexuality*, 92–95.
8. Foucault, *The History of Sexuality*, 141–43.
9. Foucault, *The History of Sexuality*, 143–45. See also Foucault, *Discipline and Punish*.
10. Butler, *Subjects of Desire*.
11. Butler, *Subjects of Desire*.
12. Butler, *Subjects of Desire*, 237.
13. Foucault, *History of Sexuality*, 112–13.
14. There is no space in this paper to explore this theme. Suffice to say that Butler is

want to focus more on her appeal to and critique of Foucault's politicized body in order to invoke Christian reflection on how only some forms of embodiments are deemed good, to the exclusion of other less normative and naturalized bodies.

In a little-known article called "Foucault and the Paradox of Bodily Inscriptions," Butler engages with Foucault's assertion that the body is constructed by virtue of inscription. Butler questions "whether there is in fact a body which is external to its construction."[15] Thinking of the body as a surface of inscribed cultural meaning suggests to Butler that Foucault "assume[s] a materiality to the body prior to its signification and form."[16] Here, Butler notes that in Foucault's thinking the body exists before it is given meaning, which renders his conception of the body as existing outside of history and therefore beyond contestation. The internal dissonance in Foucault's thinking leads Butler to conclude that his idea of the constructed body as "inscription" installs the very claim he seeks to refute: "a pre-discursive ontology of the body and its drives."[17]

To say that the body is culturally constructed is, for Butler, a paradox. What is "the body" that it can be constructed? When one claims "the body is constructed," is it not apparent that "The body would not be constructed, strictly considered, but would be the occasion, the site, or the condition of a process of construction only externally related to the body that is its object."[18] Butler presses this point of distinction because she observes the tacit installation of juridical frames that foreclose what can be considered good, which in turn justifies the condemnation and discipline of some bodies and the valorization of others.[19] It is this ethical concern that drives Butler's critique of Foucault's "constructed body." The oppressive juridical frames that must be identified and treated include the law of the natural (material) body and the law of the normal

---

seeking to reinstall the psyche in notions of embodiment for agency amidst ubiquitous power operations on the body. Butler, "Foucault and the Paradox," 605–6.

15. Butler, "Foucault and the Paradox," 602.

16. Butler, "Foucault and the Paradox," 604.

17. Butler, "Foucault and the Paradox." Also, in *Discipline and Punish*, Foucault states: "It would be wrong to say that the soul is an illusion, or an ideological effect. On the contrary, it exists, it has a reality, it is produced permanently around, on, within the body by the functioning of a power that is exercised on those who are punished," 29.

18. Butler, "Foucault and the Paradox," 601.

19. In her more recent work, this notion is framed as the unequal distribution of violence, grief, or precarity. See Butler, *Frames of War* and *Precarious Life*.

(cultural) body. Life and death in life are unequally distributed when either the unpoliticized material body or sedimented cultural ideas about the body demarcate utterly what is good or right bodily existence.

The problem underlying the law of nature is that it inadvertently assumes materiality as the presupposition of the body. Where the body exists before being inscribed with meaning, its meaning is irreducibly concerned with function, which renders bio-logic as the essential ground that confers intelligibility on the body before it is taken up into discourse; that is, history. Butler states, "By maintaining a body prior to its cultural inscription, Foucault appears to assume a materiality to the body prior to its signification and form."[20] This notion of body that is essentially material is problematic for Butler because the meaning conferred on the body is assumed to be essentially true, not mythical, and therefore beyond contestation. The material body conceals its own cultural signification and by doing so assumes an essential biological structure that functions as a transcendent and binding law that has authority by appealing to itself as natural.

The ethical ramifications are immediate because not all bodies are automatically justified by bio-logic. Some bodies do not properly image the law of nature—desirously or functionally—and thereby incur the labels transgressor and unnatural. People labelled as such are subject to discipline to make them conform to the law's demands, whether through legal, medical, physical, emotional, or spiritual means. In addition to this, the law of the natural body troubles Butler because it necessarily functions transcendentally, always imposing itself on a culture's desires and attempts to think differently about the body. This undermines and hampers attempts to construct the body in other ways that better account for the diversity of embodied experience.[21]

The second problematic, tacit law of the body in Foucault's thinking concerns the productive power of culture. If the body is circumscribed completely by a given context, then the body is hopelessly bound to the terms of that context. Whereas the totalizing law of nature is grounded in bio-logic, the law determining what is a normal body is grounded in socio-logic: a culture's thinking that sediments over time. For Butler, this law is problematic for the same reason as the law of nature. Whatever society understands as normal embodied experience becomes a given

20. Butler, "Foucault and the Paradox," 604.
21. Butler, "Foucault and the Paradox," 607.

standard against which transgressive and abnormal bodies are identified, measured, and disciplined, ostensibly for their own good—hence Butler's characterization of the law as "paternal."[22] Furthermore, there is no possibility of reconstruction because what is inscribed universally is an inescapable "single drama."[23]

In sum, Foucault laid the groundwork for Butler to comprehend the flaws of modern liberal identity politics, but Butler understands that more work was required. She desires a body that is irreducibly material, yet indistinguishable from history and culture, and as a consequence, she rejects construction as inscription because it fails to overcome, or at least contend with, the paradox of materiality *and* culture. Butler's mature gender theory in *Gender Trouble*, *Bodies that Matter*, and *Undoing Gender* attempts to challenge the totalizing claims of nature and culture on the body without ultimately doing away with either.[24] Therefore, Butler's gender theory is not principally caught up in the 1960s vision of freeing love or unshackling desire, but undermining fictitious laws and idealized images that justify some bodies as good—as natural or normal—while condemning others as transgressive—as unnatural and abnormal—and in need of being made natural or normal in order to be good.

Thus, to listen to Butler's voice requires one to hear the words she penned in *Gender Trouble*, that one "ought to be careful not to idealize certain expressions of gender that, in turn, produce forms of hierarchy and exclusion."[25] Having already expressed a desire to consider questions from the outside, I suggest that Christian engagement with the body and notions of gender heed Butler's warning by assessing whether one's use of Adam and Eve functions as an idealized expression of gender, which, by posing as a theologically justified law of natural or normal gender, produces unjust forms of hierarchy and exclusion.

---

22. Butler, *Gender Trouble*, 77.

23. Butler, "Foucault and the Paradox," 604.

24. This paradox is specifically addressed in Butler, "Contingent Foundations."

25. Butler, *Gender Trouble*, viii. While this quotation is specifically referencing feminist thought, Butler extends the scope of her critique in the next sentence to "regimes of truth."

Adam and Eve: A Vision of Life and a Law that Condemns

The discussion about divorce between Jesus and the Pharisees in Matt 19:1–12 provides a surprising bounty of theological resources for thinking about the relationship between the bodies that populated Eden and those that exist in the era following the fall. Jesus recalls Adam and Eve on two occasions in the discussion, the second more subtly, to explore what it means to live now as men and women in light of the memory of Eden.

Firstly, Jesus presents Adam and Eve as a positive vision of life to refute the Pharisees' appalling suggestive interpretation of the divorce law in Deut 24:1–4. When they ask Jesus whether it is lawful for a man to divorce his wife for any and every reason, Jesus does not reference the law to correct them.[26] Instead, he draws on the images of Adam and Eve in Gen 2:23–24 as a positive vision to illustrate that marriage is not a mere legal standing, but the result of a divine operation of making a man and a woman one flesh. Jesus reveals his desire for postlapsarian marriage in Matt 19:6 when he states, "So they are no longer two, but one flesh. Therefore what God has joined together, let no one separate." Here Jesus draws on the prelapsarian account of Adam and Eve to instruct the Pharisees about God's desire for man and woman in marriage.

But Jesus also uses Adam and Eve in Matthew 19 to instruct the Pharisees in a legal sense. The issue Jesus seeks to navigate in this second instance is a form of thinking that has sedimented over time and resulted in the unjust distribution of grief towards women: it has become normal—made good by being justified by the law—for men to divorce their wives so long as they give a certificate of divorce.[27] The problem Jesus encounters and the reason for his subsequent appeal to Adam and Eve is not immediately evident. One might expect Jesus to revert to restating or explaining the point of the divorce law in scripture to critique the Pharisees' (mis)reading of it. However, the problem is that the Pharisees have undermined the law, and restating the law would merely call upon the very terms used to justify the normalization of divorce and the ill-treatment of women: "Why then did Moses command us to give a certificate of dismissal and to divorce her?"[28] If the law is unable to function within

---

26. Matt 19:3.
27. Matt 19:7.
28. Matt 19:7.

its designed purpose, then Jesus formulates another perfect standard to carry out the necessary critical function.[29]

So Jesus again presents Adam and Eve to the Pharisees, this time not as a perfect image or vision by which they ought to imagine a godly marriage, but as a perfect standard or law, which illuminates the Pharisees' fallen creatureliness and their unjust use of the law to justify sinful behavior. Adam and Eve illustrate the point to which the very presence of the divorce law testified: their fallen state from God's ordained order in Eden. This means that the Pharisees could pervert the law to justify a man's self-absorbed desires and ill-treatment of women, but they could not deny their physical and spiritual dislocation from Eden. This is why, in verse 8, Jesus states: "It was because you were so hard-hearted that Moses allowed you to divorce your wives, but from the beginning it was not so." According to Jesus, the appropriate way to understand the particular law in Deuteronomy 24 is to read it against the backdrop of the beginning that is no longer.

In sum, by appealing to the man in Eden who loved his wife as God ordained, the divorce law is revealed as God's attempt to mitigate the consequences of hardhearted men against women in the postlapsarian era. Jesus invokes Adam and Eve as a positive vision to frame how fallen men and women ought to live in marital relationships. But Jesus also uses God's prelapsarian creatures in a legal sense to frame humanity in this age as fallen. While Adam and Eve constitute the paradigm of what God desires of his creatures, they also operate as a perfect law against which one learns of his or her inability to be the man or woman God ordained in the beginning.

Jesus's interactions with the Pharisees on the topic of divorce in Matthew 19 is instructive for Christian thinking about the body, insofar as his integration of the fall into his reasoning is a model by which prelapsarian Adam and Eve can "apply" to the way we think about embodied life now. As a perfect vision *and* perfect law, Adam and Eve function in different ways for Jesus. This is a difference that is not readily evident in current Christian thinking about the body and issues of gender and sexuality. By applying Jesus's paradoxical use of Adam and Eve to our own thinking about the body, then, Butler's questioning of gender is shown to have more in common with a conservative theological paradigm of the body than one might think.

---

29. See the Apostle Paul's discussion of Torah in the Rom 3:19–20.

Adam and Eve: A Law that Condemns All

The dual use of Adam and Eve by Jesus reveals that a foundational aspect of theological anthropology is that a body is circumscribed by its historical context. Whether Jesus is referring to the very good existences of Adam and Eve in the beginning or the troubled lives of the men and women who no longer live in Eden, what it means to live as a person embodied cannot be loosened from the terms that structure the moment in which it exists. Thus, the body does not exist outside of the moment that supplies the terms of its existence, which means that the body is subject to change when the terms that structure that moment are altered. When humanity was in Eden, the body reflected that "very good" moment, but when humanity was subjected to the consequences of the fall, the body became subject to a new set of terms—death—which characterized that moment. This is why the Apostle Paul can utter the words "There is no one who is righteous, not even one."[30] Then, there is the body that will be resurrected on Christ's return. This body will be glorified, utterly circumscribed by the terms of the new creation. Human existence is not characterized by one embodied experience but is a complex dynamic that is indexed to the moment in which one lives.

The implication of this for theological anthropology, and the Christian ethics that are cultivated thereby, is that embodiment ought not to be conceived in the singular registers of Edenic perfection, postlapsarian groaning, or final glorification. That is, the terms that characterize embodiment in this moment are not singular but multiple. One's embodiment and its limitations and possibilities ought to be conceived in relation to Eden, the fall, and the person, work, and rule of Jesus Christ. Embodiment is circumscribed by this moment, but also transcends this moment by taking part in history as a part of God's creation and potential re-creation.

This means that Butler's critique of Foucault's use of the word "inscription" to describe how a body comes to be is noteworthy. The Christian, along with Butler, must reject Foucault's assertion that bodies are inscribed with meaning because there has never been a body, even those of Adam and Eve, that existed in history as a blank canvas that was later inscribed with value, purpose, or meaning. When God spoke in the beginning, man and woman came into existence and continued to exist as

---

30. Rom 3:10.

such until new terms characterized the context and their bodies.[31] These new terms appear precisely at the point of the fall.[32]

The point of Matthew 19, then, is that the terms which narrate human existence have changed since the beginning, hence the need for the Law (Torah). The Pharisees' thinking and justification of it testify to this change. Jesus's own words in Matt 19:8 explain this very point: "you were so hard-hearted . . . but from the beginning it was not so." This exemplifies *par excellence* the impact of what it means for human existence to be no longer in Eden. The event of Adam and Eve's rejection of God by eating the fruit they were commanded not to eat distorted the first human existence into an irretrievable and unattainable originary image. The reason Jesus could appeal to the beginning to expose the Pharisees' fallen human existence is because Adam and Eve in the beginning function as a binding universal law over all of humanity in every time and place. Humanity no longer lives in Eden but looks back at Eden as a bygone era—a memory that teaches humanity how far it has fallen.

But note that the second appeal to the beginning is not an attempt by Jesus to redirect human sight to that which brings life. The intention of Jesus's appeal to Adam and Eve as a law is to illustrate precisely the opposite: that humanity, of which the Pharisees were a part, stands condemned and in need of saving. Jesus holds out the perfect images of Adam and Eve as a perfect standard that makes those who gaze upon that memory conscious of their dislocated state, aware of their (self) justification, knowledgeable of their sinful actions, sensitized to their hard-heartedness towards God and others, and thus open to their need for God's grace and mercy. Adam and Eve in the beginning function like a universal law that teaches humanity, in its entirety, that it has been dislocated from Eden and now exists in a fallen embodied state out of which it needs to be saved. Like *Torah*, the law of Adam and Eve calls attention to people's limitation before the law, their guilt, and thus their need for a savior.

While cognizant of this theological concept with regard to *Torah* as most clearly explained by the Apostle Paul in Rom 3:19–20, Christian thinking about the body has yet to fully integrate the law of Adam and Eve, a line of thinking that the outsider's questioning of gender anticipates and prompts. Butler's scant reflections on scripture, particularly the Old

---

31. Gen 1:27–8; 2:7, 22.

32. Gen 2:17; 3:6–7.

Testament, prove surprisingly prescient for this purpose. Butler's outsider voice penetrates to the inside of theological anthropology and its consequences for ethics as she identifies the tragedy of the originary scene, which I read to include Adam and Eve: "If the Symbolic guarantees the failure of the tasks it commands, perhaps its purposes, like those of the Old Testament God, are altogether unteleological—not the accomplishment of some goal, but obedience and suffering to enforce the subject's sense of limitation before the law."[33] If the "Symbolic," which is the ideal of Adam and Eve, guarantees humanity's failure to be what God desires of them, then their purpose is to induce obedience and suffering for the ultimate purpose of knowing one's inability to fulfill the law. If this is the end of the drama, then Butler is right to observe that there is no greater goal in view. In this reading, the story of Adam and Eve is the ultimate tragedy, a beginning that ends in catastrophic failure for them and all of humanity. As such, wherever and whenever one conjures the images of prelapsarian Adam and Eve to establish a regime of justified embodiment, one can hope for no greater goal or end for the body. For if Adam and Eve are our hope, they are a false hope, because their images are an unattainable reality, condemning all to their fallen embodied state.[34]

Butler, however, is not a theologian. She is a conscientious and observant theorist of existing forms of sociality. In the passage cited above, she is not reflecting upon scripture, but a version of Christianity that has established the beginning as the end, as though the beginning could be the end, or at least the present, as though the fall is the end of the drama. She is observing Christianity that presents itself as a true tragedy: the impact of the fall on humanity is certain and sealed, as it were, by the angel whom God placed at the entrance to Eden barring humanity's return to eat from the tree of life, not to mention the incurred punishment of death for disobeying God.[35] And then the crucial dilemma of the tragic drama becomes apparent. While one can only exist in the present, one is forced by virtue of one's need for life to dwell *on* the past—without dwelling *in* the past—on the bodies of Adam or Eve in Eden, to fix one's gaze on a body not one's own, a body for which one desperately yearns but cannot

---

33. Butler, *Gender Trouble*, 77.

34. For a rigorous outworking of this argument into an ethic that justifies postlapsarian existence as that which is to be embraced as good, see Rees, *The Romance of Innocent Sexuality*. Rees narrates Augustine's Christianity as a tragedy by reading it through a Butlerian lens.

35. Gen 3:23–24 and 2:16–17, respectively.

have. In this moment, Adam and Eve are revealed as humanity's end, the source of life, a redemptive hope. But where this is the case, one is caught up as an actor in the most tragic drama of all: as a slave to morality, itself an actor in the cosmic drama—the divinized messianic images of Adam and Eve.

The ethical thrust of Butler's gender theory derives from this moment. The reason she encourages her readers "to be careful not to idealize certain expressions of gender" is because such ideals do not operate to condemn all—in contradistinction to what the Christian tragedy teaches—but only some.[36] Even though *all* of humanity stands outside of Eden, unable to attain the originary perfection, Adam and Eve are invoked in a moment of naive hypocrisy to justify some as good and others as transgressive. Some find the means to adjudge themselves as justified by the law of Adam and Eve despite their place in the tragedy. Those who are "justified" in the sight of the law of Adam and Eve assume the right and role of regulating and prosecuting the demands of the law of Adam and Eve.

When Butler expresses concern for the production of "forms of hierarchy and exclusion" by virtue of idealizing certain gender expressions, one could interpret Butler as pointing out the hypocritical use of the law that is enacted by the self-righteous to condemn only some in their bodies. While Butler is surely targeting the unjust administration of the law of Adam and Eve, her goal is more radical because it is foundational: Butler seeks to undo the fundamentally unjust law of gender—Adam and Eve. In other words, the only thing more unjust than the unjust administration of a law is the unjust administration of an unjust law.

While we can agree with Butler in her critique of Foucault that there is no body outside of history, and that the body is subject to the conditions in which it exists, we cannot follow Butler much further theologically, despite her critical observation of the Christian obsession that leads to a fixation on the lost past and descent into slave morality for life. The reason one must abandon Butler at this point is because she seeks to install a foundational law by which *all* bodies are justified. That is, Butler's gender theory is not an eschatological theory, as some suggest, but is in fact a protological theory, or a (re-)creation account.[37] Her intent is expressed in her subsequent engagement with the tragedy as a circumscribing

---

36. Butler, *Gender Trouble*, viii. This theme is taken up in detail in her more recent books. See *Frames of War* and *Precarious Lives*.

37. For example, Coakley, "The Eschatological Body."

law: "This structure of religious tragedy in Lacanian theory effectively undermines any strategy of cultural politics to configure an alternative imaginary for the play of desires."[38] In this passage, Butler is targeting the thought of Jacques Lacan, but it is Butler's concern to control the body-narrating foundational structure that is my concern. The hopeless fixation on the images of Adam and Eve is not only confronting for the Christian thinker who takes pride in looking forward to Jesus Christ for one's final redemption despite one's inevitable present groaning,[39] but is also confronting for Butler, albeit for a different reason. The images of Adam and Eve represent the law that must be undone because it forecloses what is—and therefore who can be considered—a good embodiment. These protological bodies, from Butler's perspective, represent the two laws of gender that have already been exposed in Foucault's thought; namely, the laws of the natural body and the normal body. Adam and Eve represent what is incontestably natural and normal, which for Butler is an utterly socio-logical feature. It is a culturally sedimented view of what is a good gendered body. So when Butler is said to be "undoing gender," she must not be interpreted as seeking to refuse or negate bodies or matter. Rather, she is pressing the point that bodies are made to matter by society. This means that Butler is seeking to show where (constructed) ideal bodies are operating as a law and being used by some as instruments to oppress others. Her thinking, theologically speaking, is not concerned with doing away with Adam and Eve *per se*, but rather the incontestable nature of Adam and Eve as an essential law which serves to rule some in as good while ruling some out as needing to become good, thereby justifying exclusion and treatment to serve that end.

This course of thinking, however, is troubling for the reason that it undermines the basic Christian confession that in the beginning God created the world. If the law of Adam and Eve is able to be perpetually reconstituted with our own (fallen) experiences of embodiment, then scripture's protological claim that man and woman were created by God's word is nonsense. Theologically speaking, Butler's desire to "configure an alternative imaginary" with respect to Adam and Eve is reminiscent of Adam and Eve's own desire to (re)configure themselves according to their own desires rather than God's expressed desire *as* creation. What the Apostle Paul observes as a curse in Romans 1—to be handed over to

---

38. Butler, *Gender Trouble*, 77.

39. Rom 8:18–25.

one's desires—is the reason and grounds for Butler's reframing of God's creation.[40] To render God's creation of Adam and Eve subject to society's desire is to reconstitute God's originary creation with the fallen condition.

Conclusion

With respect to Jesus's use of Adam and Eve in the beginning, discarding Adam and Eve as God created them is not an option for the Christian thinker when considering what God desires for humanity now. This places us in a difficult situation because while Jesus holds up Adam and Eve as God's ordained order, they cannot bring life, but reveal humanity's death in life. The Christian, compelled by the outsider's questioning, must navigate this ethical paradox that Adam and Eve manifest as a vision of life that operates as a law that condemns not just some but all of humanity in their bodies.

The law of Adam and Eve reveals that each human exists as a body of death in need of life. The Apostle Paul in Rom 7:24 gives out an anguished cry: "Wretched man that I am! Who will rescue me from this body of death?" Butler's concern for justice is valid in that only some find their selves condemned by a law of Adam and Eve, but at the same time, the way forward is not to undermine the law to set those free from its violent accusation. If Jesus's words that one does not dwell in the beginning are true, then the law of Adam and Eve condemns all, not just some, and if this is the case then every person ought to be invited to utter with the apostle: "Who will rescue me from this body of death?"

This harrowing question is not a rhetorical flourish that requires no explicit response. This essay has demonstrated how seductive the bodies of Adam and Eve are for thinking about where life might be found when we learn that bodies are characterized by death. Indeed, even the most theologically informed person might, on hearing Paul's question, look to Adam and Eve for life, inviting or demanding a form of slave morality that desires to approximate the ideal images of Adam or Eve to be rescued from death to life. But which Adam ought one turn to for life? The first Adam who is from the dust of the earth and through whom, sin and death comes, or the last Adam who came from heaven and is a life-giving spirit?[41] In the next verse, Paul is emphatic. He does not turn

---

40. See Rom 1:24, 26.
41. 1 Cor 15:45–49.

to the static and lifeless images of Adam and Eve for salvation, but to the living creator and re-creator: "Thanks be to God through Jesus Christ our Lord!"[42] The reason is given shortly thereafter: "If the Spirit of him who raised Jesus from the dead dwells in you, he who raised Christ from the dead will give life to your mortal bodies also through his Spirit that dwells in you."[43]

In a moment when individuals and society are wallowing with glee in their death-ridden bodies, even justifying such death-filled lives with their civil laws and policies, it makes no theological sense for the Christian to offer up the images of Adam and Eve as a means to life. Adam and Eve had no power to save humanity from the 1960s utopic sexual revolution. We ought to see that the perfect images of Adam and Eve still lack the power to save, this time from the current dystopic gender revolution. However beautiful the prelapsarian vision of Adam and Eve is, their bodies denote only what one can never be. However terrible the postlapsarian vision of Adam and Eve is, their bodies ought not to become justifications for nihilistic valorizations of the dead body. Rather, following the Apostle Paul, the Church ought to become known for witnessing to the already resurrected body of Jesus Christ and the embodied life that one has already found in him.

Bibliography

Allen, Samuel. H., and Shawn N. Mendez. "Hegemonic Heteronormativity: Toward a New Era of Queer Family Theory." *Journal of Family Theory and Review* 10.2 (2018) 70–86.

Butler, Judith. *Bodies That Matter: On the Discursive Limits of "Sex."* 1993. Reprint, Abingdon, UK: Routledge, 2011.

———. "Contingent Foundations: Feminism and the Question of 'Postmodernism.'" In *Feminists Theorize the Political*, edited by Judith Butler and Joan W. Scott, 3–21. New York: Routledge, 1992.

———. "Foucault and the Paradox of Bodily Inscriptions." *Journal of Philosophy* 86.11 (1989) 601–7.

———. *Frames of War: When Is Life Grievable?* 2009. Reprint, Radical Thinkers. London: Verso, 2016.

———. *Gender Trouble: Feminism and the Subversion of Identity.* 2nd ed. New York: Routledge, 2007 reprint of anniversary edition.

———. *Precarious Life: The Powers of Mourning and Violence.* London: Verso, 2006.

---

42. Rom 7:25a.
43. Rom 8:11.

———. *Subjects of Desire: Hegelian Reflections in Twentieth-Century France.* 2nd ed. New York: Columbia University Press, 2012 reprint.
———. *Undoing Gender.* New York: Routledge, 2004.
Coakley, S. "The Eschatological Body: Gender, Transformation, and God." *Modern Theology* 16 (2000) 61–67.
Foucault, Michel. *Discipline and Punish: The Birth of the Prison.* Translated by Alan Sheridan. 2nd ed. New York: Vintage, 1995.
———. *The History of Sexuality: An Introduction.* Translated by Robert Hurley. New York: Vintage, 1990.
Gorringe, Timothy. *Karl Barth: Against Hegemony.* Christian Theology in Context. Oxford: Oxford University Press, 1999.
Rees, Geoffrey. *The Romance of Innocent Sexuality.* Eugene, OR: Cascade Books, 2012.

www.ingramcontent.com/pod-product-compliance
Lightning Source LLC
Chambersburg PA
CBHW050619300426
44112CB00012B/1575